Robert Slater

THE BIOGRAPHY

RABIN

20 years after

KIP - Kotarim International Publishing, Ltd.

KIP – Kotarim International Publishing, Ltd.
Edited by: Daniella Maor
Proofreading by: Anna Mowszowski
Layout and Typesetting by: Bat-Chen Nachmani
Cover Design by: Laura Gryncwajg

KIP – Kotarim International Publishing LTD
Publisher: Moshe Alon
www.kotarim.com
kip@smile.net.il

ISBN 978-965-7589-13-7
Printed in Israel 2015

ACKNOWLEDGMENTS – FROM THE PUBLISHER

We are very grateful to Elinor Slater
for her help and encouragement.

We would like to extend a special thank you to
the Rabin Family and all those at The Yitzhak Rabin Center
for their continued support during this project.

We would also like to thank
Kety Katav & Daniel Wechsberg, El-Or Ltd.,
Yehuda Bakshy, Prof. Amnon Rubinstein,
Stef Wertheimer, Raphy Weiner, and Alon Raz.

Table of Contents

FOREWORD

Since I began writing book-length personality profiles in the 1970s, I have sought the cooperation of those who were the focus of these books. Most of the time the person agreed to cooperate with my book project whether it was Jack Welch, the former chairman of General Electric; George Soros, the hedge fund billionaire; Donald Trump, the real estate mogul and TV star; or Bill Gates, the founder of Microsoft. By the time I turned to each of these people I was an established author with a string of book credits to my name. But in the early part of 1976, just after Robson Books in London commissioned me to write a biography of Yitzhak Rabin, I had no books to my credit; all that I could point to by way of a writing career were two stints as a reporter for United Press International (one in Trenton, New Jersey; the other in Jerusalem) and a few months as a reporter in the Time-Life bureau in Jerusalem.

And so, when I approached Rabin to ask him to cooperate in my planned biography of him, I was not at all confident that he would agree. The most direct way to ask for his cooperation would be to buttonhole him at some ceremony or speech, introduce myself, tell him about the project, and hope for an instant yes. But it is simply not acceptable to go around buttonholing prime ministers. So I approached the only person I knew in Rabin's office and more importantly who knew me, and that was his spokesman Dan Pattir. He approached Rabin with my request, and to my shock the answer came back, "The Prime Minister is willing to talk with you about your book." I was ecstatic, for I knew that getting approval to see the prime minister meant that he would give the green light as well to my seeing members of his family, friends, army buddies, and political comrades, all of whom could tell their favorite anecdotes about Rabin.

In the years since my first Rabin biography, published in 1977, I have sometimes wondered why Rabin agreed to cooperate. The one plausible theory I could muster was that because there had been no biography on his life and career until then, he wanted one written. It was only in January 2014, when I interviewed Dan Pattir for this newly-updated version of the book, that I learned that my theory was largely correct. What I did not know was that Rabin through Dan Pattir had put out feelers to some journalist friends in the United States to recommend a biographer with whom Rabin could cooperate. When I came along with my request for cooperation, Rabin had not nailed down a biographer. Dan Pattir pushed Rabin hard to choose me and the prime minister did. I only learned all this 38 years later.

Rabin and I met four times during his first prime ministership in the 1970s; meetings that were crucial to my understanding of his career and his personality. He took a great deal of time from his busy schedule to talk about the past.

Because he was prime minister, I never knew whether an aide would rush in to one of our meetings, telling the prime minister he was needed at once, ending my interview with him on the spot; or whether he would call a halt to our series of interviews, again claiming the press of business. Yet, he never did. Why did Rabin agree to cooperate with my biography of him? I believe that he felt there was some value in setting forth his entire career to an author, a career that began with his birth in 1922 and that wound up with him as prime minister of his country in 1974. He had never recounted his entire career. This was his chance.

Still, getting to see him each time was often nerve-racking. Postponements seemed inevitable. Happily, they came only rarely. Once Rabin postponed one of our scheduled interviews and I only found out the reason later: he had undertaken a secret mission to Morocco to meet with King Hassan. From 1976 when I began the first book and when I joined the reporting staff of the *Time Magazine* Jerusalem bureau, I also met with Rabin periodically for *Time Magazine*, conducting interviews with him once or twice a year. Indeed, closely monitoring his political career was part of my political beat at *Time*.

The first time I interviewed Rabin for the book came on August 2, 1976. I prepared for the interview meticulously. I carefully decided which questions I wanted to ask that first time: I debated whether to ask only about his early days and leave for later interviews, questions about the rest of his career and life. But I worried that this might be the only interview I might be granted. And so I prepared questions that dealt partly with his early days and partly with the later years. I made sure to have questions ready for the most controversial incident in his career: his so-called collapse of May 23-24, 1967 when as chief of staff of the Israel Defense Forces, preparing the nation for a possible war, he literally ceased functioning. What had caused this collapse? Was it nicotine poisoning, the story that he put out to explain his exhaustion and mental paralysis? Was it something else? How did others around him react to the incident?

Until we met, nine years after that incident, he had said nothing publicly, nothing to a journalist or author about what had happened to him and how others in his midst reacted to his collapse. I wanted to be the first person to whom he would talk about the incident, knowing that I was going to publish his comments in my book. But I certainly worried that he might keep silent on the subject just as he had for the past nine years. He might have thought that sitting prime ministers should not be talking about a bout of mental illness that could mar his current and future political career. At that first interview, I brought up the incident and, to my shock and joy, Rabin spoke at length about it and when I checked with Dan Pattir, who sat in on the meeting, he confirmed that these were Rabin's first public words on the subject.

Preparing questions for that first interview was easy compared to the dress code dilemma I faced: should I wear a coat and tie for the interview? It seemed the right thing to do even in Israel, where the dress code was quite casual. I had already come across the story of Rabin's distaste for ties and I assumed that, even though he was prime minister and from time to time wore a tie, I would display a certain understanding of him by not putting on a tie. Wrong! I showed up without a tie and to my astonishment, there he was, in coat and tie. For the second meeting I thought I would learn from the past experience and so I wore a tie. Wrong again. This time he did not wear a tie. My most memorable encounter with Rabin came during the eight days I travelled with him, in my capacity as a journalist for *Time Magazine*, on his plane in October 1993 to China. The most vivid impression of Rabin during the trip was his finding great amusement at the Chinese officials who could not understand how tiny Israel – compared to the giant China – had managed to develop one of the most powerful armed forces in the world, including one of the mightiest air forces.

Working on a biography of a prime minister while he was still in office, and at the same time covering him for a major publication, gave me plenty to do: between the years 1974 to 1977, I spent writing the original book. As I completed the manuscript in the spring of 1977, I was in for a major shock as fear gripped me that the whole project might go down the drain. The premise of the book project was that Rabin would go on to win a victory when elections were held in May, and that he would serve as prime minister for another few years at least. Without him being prime minister, a biography of him might have made little sense. There then came the stunning announcement from Rabin in early April, that he was resigning as prime minister immediately because of the scandal surrounding a bank account he and his wife held illegally in Washington, D.C. Fearing that my publisher, Robson Books, would kill the project upon hearing of the resignation, I called Jeremy Robson, the publisher and editor, the next day to ask him what he planned to do about the project. It turned out that Jeremy had not yet heard the news of Rabin's resignation. I held my breath to see what his reaction would be. He said he thought Rabin's resignation would help the sales of the book and he would of course continue with the project. I was giddily relieved.

When Rabin was elected prime minister a second time in 1992, my then-publisher Robson Books asked me to update the original version, which I did. St. Martin's Press published the book in the United States.

At no point in my book-writing career was I busier than in early November 1995, right after the Rabin assassination. Because I was the only one who had written a biography of Rabin up to that point, the international media sought me out to analyze what his death meant and what kind of person he had been. At the same time, I made a substantial contribution to the award-winning *Time Magazine* cover story on Rabin's assassination and that same week, Harper Collins asked me to write a new version of the book that would include a chapter on the assassination. My new publisher told me that, so eager was it to publish the new version, that it was "crashing" the book, meaning that employees at Harper Collins worked over Thanksgiving weekend. That third version appeared in January 1996.

In the book I write a good deal about Rabin's shyness, so unusual for a politician. With Rabin, it was not hard to explain his being an extreme introvert. He was fundamentally a military man, not a glad-hander like his colleagues Shimon Peres or Yigal Allon. From the time Rabin left the IDF in 1968 and moved to Washington, D.C. to become Israel's ambassador to the USA, he developed better social skills. But he never quite perfected an outgoing political style. I recall vividly attending a reception where he appeared soon after one of our interviews in 1976. The reception was in honor of Arthur Miller, who was also in attendance, just after a theater troupe had put on his play, *All My Sons*. I always assumed – until that evening – that so many guests would have wanted to chat with the prime minister, that such people would constantly surround him. At one point I looked over at him and he was standing alone off in a corner. I wandered over to say hello, asking him what he thought of the play. I don't remember his answer – but I was shocked that he retained such great shyness even as prime minister.

For this fourth iteration, I have added this new "Foreword"; I have also added a new chapter at the end of the book, assessing Rabin's legacy 18 years after his death, based upon interviews I have conducted with some of the same people I spoke to for previous versions of the book.

I wish to acknowledge several key people who contributed much to my research: first, the late Leah Rabin, the prime minister's wife, who met with me four times during my research. I was also fortunate to meet a number of times with Rabin's sister Rachel Rabin Jacoby, at her home at Kibbutz Manara in northern Israel. She shed much light on her and her brother's childhood. I spoke to several hundred people who knew Rabin at various stages of his life, and I owe special thanks to Rabin's aides from his first prime ministership: Dan Pattir, his press adviser; Amos Eiran, his director-general; and Yehuda Avner, his adviser on Jewish affairs, as well as to several aides from his more recent prime ministership: Eitan Haber, the chief of Rabin's bureau;

Shimon Sheves, who served for part of Rabin's tenure as director-general of the prime minister's office; Gad Ben-Ari, Oded Ben-Ami, Nachman Shai and Aliza Goren, who served as his press advisers at various times.

I also wish to thank Deborah Baker for easing matters considerably for me, by helping to translate scores of Hebrew-language newspaper articles; as well as Jean Max, the office manager at the Time-Life Jerusalem Bureau for many years, who rendered important editorial assistance throughout my research. Thanks also to David Rubinger, the late Michael Elkins, the late Jamil Hamad, Ron Ben-Yishai, and Haim Baram. These colleagues often helped to clarify various issues regarding Rabin and Israel.

My family has contributed enormous support and I thank them all, my wife Elinor, our children, Miriam, Shimi, Adam, Tal, and Rachel, and our grandchildren: Edo, Maya, Shai and Maya; Matan, Ben and Ori. I also wish to thank Roslyn and the late Judd Winick, as well as Bea and the late Jack Slater; Judith Resnik and Dennis Curtis, Michael and Bobbi Winick, Ruth and Rashi Fein, Joel and Bernice Breslau and Melvin and Bernice Slater.

Friends who have supported and inspired me in my book writing are: Naomi Ragen, Herb Krosney, Marcus Eliason, Allen Alter and Mel Laytner and I thank them for just being there.

I thank those to whom I turned for interviews for this new version of the book: Itamar Rabinovich, Yossi Beilin, Dan Pattir, Shimon Sheves, Eitan Haber, Uzi Baram, Amos Eiran, Dalia Rabin, and Rachel Rabin Jacoby.

For this new edition, I owe much to Moshe Alon, the publisher and editor of Kotarim International Publishing, and his assistant Anna Mowszowski for their support and work they put into this book. It was Moshe's idea to bring out this new version and I am greatly in his debt. The Yitzhak Rabin Center headed by Rabin's daughter Dalia helped to get this book relaunched and I wish to thank Dalia Rabin and Naomi Rapoport head of the Library and Archives, at the Yitzhak Rabin Center in Tel Aviv.

PREFACE[1]

Yitzhak Rabin, the prime minister of Israel, had just told the former Mayor of Tel Aviv, Shlomo 'Chich' Lahat that this was one of the happiest days of his life. These were emotional words for the normally taciturn, stoical Rabin. It was 9:35 pm, Saturday, 4 November 1995 and the prime minister was standing on the stage at a peace rally in Tel Aviv, attended by more than 100,000 of his supporters.

Rabin had good reason to cheer as for much of his life he had been a soldier, a commander, and a man whose main purpose had been to fight wars and prevent future ones. A brigade commander in the 1948 War of Independence, chief of staff in 1964, Israel's ambassador to Washington, D.C. from 1968 to 1973, prime minister for the first time between

---

1. The author put together the narrative of the behind-the-scenes of the Rabin assassination based on conversations with many people who knew of those events on a firsthand basis. The author also used Israeli newspaper accounts to round out what Rabin associates told him.

the years 1974 to 1977 and for the second time from 1992 to this very day of November 4th.

His efforts over the previous three years to resolve the Arab-Israeli conflict had produced two Israeli-Palestinian agreements and an Israeli-Jordanian peace treaty; hence Rabin's reasons for cheer this evening.

But Israel had grown increasingly divided over the peace process leading to the creation of a Palestinian state and the end of Israel's presence in the West Bank and the Gaza Strip, peace seemed to be purchased at such a heavy price, with so many Israelis being killed in terror attacks. Some Israelis called Yitzhak Rabin a traitor, a murderer. Others calmly discussed the pros and cons of killing him. Steadfast in his belief that in time the peace accords would, like a giant tidal wave, wash away dissent, Rabin refused to hide or to take any special precautions in public, he felt increasingly self-confident; he believed the peace process was irreversible and that he and Yasser Arafat, the leader of the Palestine Liberation Organization (PLO), if left to work out the details, would produce a peace with which Israelis could live. Rabin knew the depth of opposition to him and his peace policies, but he had begun to feel in the last few weeks that the chaos and the turmoil that had beset the country over his peace efforts might soon settle down. "Even with a majority of one, I will continue the peace process," he told friends privately.

Looking into the sea of smiling faces and the huge colorful peace placards at Tel Aviv's main Malchei Yisrael, or Kings of Israel Square, the 73-year-old Rabin felt a new kind of self-confidence: Here was proof, despite the disappointing polls showing the peace process in disrepute, that he and his peace policies had strong backing. In this buoyant mood, a relaxed, contented Rabin swung an arm in friendship around the waist of foreign minister Shimon Peres, long-time rival, but now a co-recipient of the Nobel Peace Prize. He joined the crowd singing "Shir La-Shalom" (The Song for Peace), holding a paper with the lyrics.

Just over an hour earlier, he had spoken briefly to the crowd: "I was a military man for 27 years. I waged war as long as there was no chance for peace. I believe there is now a chance for peace, a great chance, and we must take advantage of it for those standing here and for those who are not, and they are many. I have always believed that the majority of the people want peace and are ready to take a chance for peace."

It was 9:36 pm and Rabin, tucking the leaflet with the song lyrics into his breast pocket, began saying his farewells. Never in love with huge crowds, he wanted to leave the rally a half-hour earlier, when the speeches were over, but became caught up in the intoxicating enthusiasm of the evening and remained for the entertainment. He looked around for his wife, Leah. A few minutes earlier, she had plunged into the crowds and now, approaching her husband, she said in an excited tone, "You cannot believe how many supporters you have out there."

Shimon Peres departed the stage first and headed toward his car, parked near Rabin's. A minute later, Rabin walked off the stage to his car.

For a large segment of the population, Yitzhak Rabin was the man who was selling the country out to the Arabs. Most of his rivals among the Israeli rightwing respected Rabin the soldier, the statesman, while despising his peace policies. A tiny fringe of right-wing religious extremists, however, went further.

At protest rallies, they portrayed Rabin on posters with a red-checkered *keffiyeh* on his head, a subtle insinuation that he was demonically colluding with the Arabs. A month before the peace rally at a protest rally, someone held up a placard with Rabin wearing German SS uniform, suggesting that the prime minister was no better than the Nazis. At these rallies some shouted *"Rabin boged"*, *"Rabin rotzyach"*; Rabin is a traitor, and Rabin is a murderer. Two months before the November peace rally, a rabbi placed a curse on Rabin, calling upon "the 'angels of destruction' to kill him." The curse was due to expire in early November. The leader of Zo Artzeinu, a group of right-wing extremists, said his group held Rabin's government responsible "for its crimes against security and Judaism." A Jewish extremist militia calling itself Ayal, the Jewish Fighters Organization, appeared on Israel Television five weeks before the peace rally, woolen masks over their faces, guns in their hands, promising to kill Jews if it would help destroy the peace process.

The Tel Aviv peace rally had been designed to marginalize these right-wing extremists by providing concrete proof that Israel's peace camp comprised a vocal majority of the country. Yet the tensions and threats the country had experienced were on some minds at the peace rally: a journalist approached one of Rabin's guards and asked if the prime minister was wearing a flak jacket. The guard laughed, and then said: "If he were wearing one, do you think I would tell you?" The same journalist put the same question to Leah Rabin who broke into laughter as well: "A flak jacket? Really? What are we, Africa here? This is Israel." A military man told the same journalist not to worry, that there were sharpshooters all around ready to fire: "Do you think we'd take a chance with the prime minister's life?"

Yigal Amir planned to attend the peace rally as well. He was 25 years old, a third-year law student at Bar Ilan University in Ramat Gan, near Tel Aviv. One of eight children, Amir grew up in an Orthodox Jewish family. His demeanor was usually quiet, but he became emotional when talking about Arabs. He fell into the company of the Ayal extremists and joined in a number of street protests. Once, soldiers carried him against his will from the scene of a protest.

To one friend, Amir confessed that he felt compelled to do something to stop the peace process. Amir had no criminal record and had a license to carry a 22-calibre pistol, which he calmly loaded at his home in Herzliya, a coastal town north of Tel Aviv, just before leaving for the rally by bus. He thought to himself: *Perhaps this time I'll get close enough to Rabin.* He had been stalking the prime minister for most of the past year, but was never able to penetrate the protective screen around him. Amir had also monitored the prime minister as Rabin walked in and out of his apartment in the Tel Aviv suburb of Ramat Aviv. Watching from across the street, Amir hoped for a chance to fire a rifle at him.

Amir arrived at the peace rally at 8:10 pm, just the time Rabin was speaking to the throng. Though police, soldiers and guard dogs mixed with the crowds, the armed Amir walked around the cavernous square undetected. Near the stage, he walked down the 20 steps to the garage where Rabin's new, heavily fortified Cadillac was parked. When asked who he was, coolly, casually, Amir responded that he was the driver for one of the politicians.

At 9:40 pm, prime minister Rabin descended the same 20 steps that Yigal Amir had some time before. To Rabin's right was his wife Leah, behind them a security guard and walking directly behind them was Aliza Goren, the prime minister's spokesperson. She planned to walk Rabin to his car and then say good-bye. A crowd of several hundred people had gathered to watch the dignitaries descend the stairs. There were many police and soldiers as well. Moments before, Shimon Peres had stopped to shake hands with the crowd. A guard whispered to Aliza Goren that he was frightened because some of the crowd had pulled on Peres' hand and wouldn't let go.

Rabin seemed in a hurry to get to the car, he did not stop to shake hands. The rear door of the Cadillac was already open, the engine drowning out the crowd sounds. From behind the steps, a figure appeared, running toward the prime minister, taking out a pistol, which had been lodged in his belt. Rabin was about to enter the rear seat of the car. To the guards who saw the thin, dark-haired man dressed in black trousers and shirt race towards Rabin, Yigal Amir was apparently just another person who wanted to shake the prime minister's hand. Instead, when he was within a few feet from Rabin, Amir aimed his pistol at point-blank range.

He fired three shots. Two of the three hollow-point bullets smashed into Rabin: one bullet ruptured his spleen and the second severed the major arteries in his chest, shattering his spinal cord and drenching the leaflet with the song lyrics, still in his breast pocket, in blood. The third shot grazed one of the guards. As Amir pulled the trigger, he said: "It's nothing, nothing. I'm joking. It's not real. It's not real." It was, however, very real. Rabin clutched his stomach and fell forward. Menachem Damti, the prime minister's driver, who had been waiting near the car to help Leah Rabin into it, heard the shots and rushed to the driver's seat.

The wounded guard, believing that the attack might not be over, fell on top of Rabin. The guard saw a huge amount of blood on his body and believed that it came from his own wound, not thinking that it might be Rabin's. To the guard it was not clear if the prime minister had been hit as well. "Listen to me," he shouted, "and to me only! We're going to get up now and get into the car and leave." Rabin did not respond, but somehow the guard managed to pull him up and throw him into the car. "Move!" the guard shouted to Damti, slamming the door shut. The car raced away.

The crowd started screaming and falling to the floor. It was natural to assume that if three bullets had been fired, there might be more to come. The entire incident took no more than a few seconds, and even those who were nearby could not tell precisely what had happened. Aliza Goren never even saw the assassin, never saw Rabin fall. He was simply not there, when she looked at where he had been standing; though she did see the gun and the smoke and fire from the shots. She felt as if she was watching a movie, it was all too unimaginable. She understood that someone had tried to shoot the prime minister, but she convinced herself that he had not been hit.

Meanwhile, another security guard grabbed Leah Rabin and helped her into a car directly behind her husband's. "What happened?" she asked as the car took off. "There were shots from a toy pistol," the guard said. "It wasn't real, it wasn't real. Someone shot in the air to frighten him, to create an atmosphere of chaos and fear."

When Leah's car reached the General Security Services headquarters, located just minutes away from the Tel Aviv square, she asked: "Where is he? If it wasn't real, where is Yitzhak?" "We don't know," the guards insisted. "We'll tell you when we do." Leah was escorted to a room and left there alone. She made one phone call to her daughter Dalia. "They've shot Dad," she said sadly.

As Rabin's car sped to the hospital, word that something untoward had happened spread throughout the crowd at the rally. Most were too far from the prime minister's car to have heard the shots, let alone witness the shooting itself. The question on everyone's lips was: "What happened?"

"Shots were fired," said one person. "They were fired near the prime minister, but he wasn't hurt," said another. A third had heard that the prime minister was hit, but not seriously. A fourth said: "The prime minister was hit, and he was in bad condition."

Shimon Peres had been in his car ahead of Rabin's when he heard the shots. "Stop!" he told his driver, "I want to get out." Peres' security guard yelled, "No!" He wanted the driver to pull away. "I'm not listening to you," the guard told the foreign minister, "I am ordering the driver to drive away."

As the car moved off, the guard asked Peres if he wanted to go to his home in Jerusalem. "No," said Peres, "I want to go to Yitzhak."

Concerned that the shots might have been part of some organized conspiracy against other members of the government, the guard took Peres to the same building where Leah Rabin had been taken, the General Security Services headquarters. The guard went inside to find out more details about the shooting. For the next 40 minutes, Peres remained in the car. At times, a guard would come back to report a few more details to him, and Peres could only reply, "I want to see Yitzhak."

After rushing off in the direction of Ichilov Hospital, a few minutes' drive from the rally, driver Menachem Damti shouted back to Rabin: "Are you hurt? Are you hurt?"

"I think so," Rabin answered, "but it's not bad, it doesn't hurt so much." But then the prime minister began to breathe with difficulty and the guard, though wounded himself and losing strength, gave Rabin mouth-to-mouth resuscitation. Damti kept asking the guard where they should go. All roads were blocked and it was difficult to work out how to get to the closest hospital. To make sure they were heading the right way, Damti stopped and picked up a policeman who climbed in the front seat and began giving directions.

Within seconds of the shooting, a swarm of police and soldiers grabbed the gunman, Yigal Amir, and took his weapon from him. They thrust him against the wall of the adjacent shopping center and formed a human wall around him. People in the crowd turned to Rabin's spokesperson Aliza Goren, hoping to learn what had happened. But she did not know. She did know that it was imperative that she get away from the crowds so she could use her mobile phone with some privacy. When she broke away, the only phone number she could remember was that of Danny Yatom, the prime minister's military attaché. She reached him at home.

"They shot him," she shouted into the phone. "Shot who?" the usually reserved army man asked. "They shot Yitzhak."

"It's not true."

"Danny," said Aliza, "they shot him. I don't know if he's

hurt or not, he just left. Try to find out if he's hurt and if he is, tell me where he went."

Yatom's first call, before he sought to determine whether Rabin was hurt, was to the Israel Defense Forces headquarters. The army needed to know that the prime minister might be injured. Yatom then called Rabin's car and got back to Aliza, "He's hurt and on the way to Ichilov." Aliza and two aides ran to the hospital.

Rabin's car arrived at Ichilov Hospital at 9:45 pm. Sirens were blaring. The car door was opened and the prime minister was immediately placed on a stretcher. His chest was drenched in blood, his eyes were closed. He was unconscious, with no blood pressure and no pulse.

Bodyguards ran into the hospital in front of the stretcher, yelling: "Clear the room. Rabin has been hit." Dr. Motti Gutman, a senior surgeon at Ichilov Hospital, was on duty in the trauma unit. He was quickly located and told that an emergency case had just arrived with a devastating injury. He was shocked to find that the seriously wounded man was the prime minister. Used to such cases he remained calm, but just knowing that Yitzhak Rabin's life was in his hands put all sorts of extra pressure on the physician.

At 9:55 pm, Rabin was wheeled into the operating room. Eitan Haber, the director of Rabin's bureau who was like a son to the prime minister, was just arriving at a small reception in Tel Aviv given by Ido Disenchik, a senior Israeli journalist in honor of the outgoing Israeli ambassador to Paris, Avi Pazner. The prime minister and his wife were due at the party after the rally. Haber asked a security guard outside the front door of Disenchik's home whether the Rabins had arrived and was surprised to find out they had not yet left the rally. Haber joined the other guests at the reception, among whom was Dr. Gabi Barbash, head of the Ichilov Hospital. Called to a phone, Barbash listened briefly, then, ashen-faced, walked over to Haber: "Yitzhak has been shot. I think it's critical." Haber raced downstairs and asked the guard what they were saying over his earpiece. The guard said he could not make out what was happening.

Haber raced through red lights to reach Ichilov. While driving, he had the presence of mind to call American ambassador Martin Indyk to tell him that Rabin had been shot. Reaching the hospital, Haber heard someone yell cheerfully: "Terrific, Rabin is dead." Once inside the building, Haber kept opening doors and looking into darkened rooms, trying to find someone who could tell him about Rabin's condition. At one stage he came upon the operating room where the doctors were operating on Rabin himself.

Israel Television's news anchorman Haim Yavin was at home at 10 pm, 20 minutes after the shooting, when he got a phone call about the shooting from his colleagues at the television studio in Jerusalem. He was at the studio 15 minutes later. Yavin's steady, reassuring television presence has led him to be compared to the American anchorman, Walter Cronkite. Yet even he was unsettled. Never before had he been forced to anchor an assassination attempt on a prime minister. What if Rabin was seriously hurt? What if he should die? Yavin asked himself if he could keep his cool on the air during such awful circumstances for the nation. He knew that he would have to try. Yavin could not imagine that Rabin was seriously hurt, but, as word filtered in to the studio, he began to understand that this would be one of the most difficult assignments he had ever undertaken.

Israel Television had no rules about what was to be said over the air in the event that a prime minister was shot. An event of this magnitude had never happened before. Nor had it been thought possible. And therefore no one had thought it necessary to list some dos and don'ts about what, when, and how to tell the nation that its prime minister was dying or dead.

Yavin went on the air at 10:20 pm. Comparisons to the television coverage of the Kennedy assassination were inevitable, but Yavin believed, even as he was going on the air live, that the two events were not entirely similar. After all, Lincoln had been killed before Kennedy. But for Israel, this marked the first time that a political leader had been gunned down while in office. For the next half hour or so, Yavin quietly explained to the anxious nation that Rabin was in the hospital, that doctors were working on him, and that there was still no news on how serious his wounds were.

Uri Dromi, the director of the Government Press Office, heard the news, like so many other Israelis, when his mind was on things other than the rally. He was at Jerusalem's Cinemateque restaurant having coffee with his wife and friends. His relationship with Rabin had been special, close. In November 1966, then-chief-of-staff Rabin, visiting the Hazerim Air Base near Beersheba, placed wings on 19-year-old Dromi's uniform, signifying that Dromi was the outstanding graduate of the flying school. Dromi was awed. Rabin warned him: "I might prick you," Dromi replied: "I don't mind."

At 10 pm, Dromi's mobile phone rang. A colleague was reporting to him from the rally: "It was a great rally but there was some commotion and sirens at the end. I don't know what happened." Dromi sensed trouble and called army headquarters but got no answer. Then a BBC reporter called him and mentioned that Rabin had been shot. Dromi could not let himself break down even after hearing this shocking news. He went over to into "disaster syndrome," as he described it, and tried to keep his mind focused on the long night of dealing with the press that would be his main job. He planned to drive to the hospital in Tel Aviv at once to help with the handling of journalists there.

When Aliza Goren arrived at Ichilov, it was around 10:20 pm. The first person she recognized was the prime minister's driver, Menachem Damti, whose hand was covered in blood. "What happened?" she asked with desperation in her voice.

Goren refused to believe what he was saying: "Are you a doctor? How can you say that?"

Just then, Leah Rabin arrived at the hospital. She still had no information about her husband's condition other than he had been shot. Somber, head bowed, Leah presented a jolting contrast to the person who had been happily mixing with the crowds at the rally a few hours earlier. Leah said nothing, just looked at Damti. He repeated to her what he had just told Aliza Goren.

"Oy, oy," Leah said, shaking her head back and forth, her face betraying the deep worry she felt. Aliza tried to calm her. "Let's wait until the doctor says something."

Leah then saw the others who had gathered inside the hospital: Eitan Haber; Shevach Weiss, the Knesset spokesperson; Jean Friedman, the organizer of the rally; Tel Aviv's mayor Roni Milo; Danny Yatom; Ephraim Sneh, the health minister; the director of the Mossad. Members of the immediate family were there as well: the Rabin children,

Yuval, 40, and Dalia, 45, with her husband Avi, and Rabin's two older grandchildren. Leah said nothing, just stared into their faces. She could tell without asking that her husband was in very bad shape. A few people tried to comfort her, to say that perhaps it would be all right. But she could tell from their faces how serious the situation was.

Meanwhile, the doctors began dealing with the stricken prime minister. Their first thought was to get a pulse. Gutman and his team inserted a tracheal tube and began to ventilate Rabin; they then inserted a chest drain and started to administer drugs and the first of 22 pints of blood. Rabin's pulse was restored but remained weak. A doctor left the operating room to talk to the family. "We've stabilized the situation. He's got a pulse of 90, but the situation is very serious."

Aliza Goren thought to herself: *It's bad. He doesn't sound optimistic at all.*

The main effort in the operating room was directed at trying to stop the massive bleeding from the damage to the prime minister's lungs, spleen, and tissues surrounding the heart and spinal column. Every few moments or so, it seemed to the family and friends gathered with Leah, the doctors emerged to provide another report on what was happening inside the operating room:

"We've removed the spleen."

"We've opened his stomach."

"We've opened the chest."

"He's bleeding internally."

Eitan Haber approached Dr. Gabi Barbash with a plea: "Look me in the eye and forget all the controversies and fights between the hospitals. Tell me if there is some doctor in Israel or abroad whom I can bring here." "If my father were here," Barbash replied, "I would put him in the hands of the doctors who are here."

Meanwhile, Leah Rabin had a question for Aliza Goren: "Where's Shimon?" It dawned on her that Peres was not at the hospital and it struck her as curious. Goren had no ready answer. Finally, foreign minister Peres arrived. He had persuaded his guard to bring him to the hospital. By this time, many ministers and Knesset members had come over from the rally. A hospital spokesperson cornered Goren to tell her that journalists outside the building were clamoring for any bit of information on Rabin's condition. "What should I tell them?" she was asked. "Mind your own business." Aliza snapped. "I don't want any information released without consulting us first."

It was a few minutes after 11 pm. The doctors operating on Rabin, tears in their eyes, looked at one another and simply stopped their work. The prime minister was dead. Had he been a 20-year-old man, Dr. Gutman thought, perhaps he might have survived, but probably not. Dr. Barbash approached Haber. "That's it. He's dead." Haber asked Barbash to go and tell the family, and Barbash went down the hall into the small room where the Rabin family and a few friends had gathered. His face revealing the tragic news he was about to convey, Barbash said simply: "I'm sorry the prime minister is no longer with us." Members of the family screamed. In a broken voice, Leah said to Roni Milo: "It's too bad they didn't shoot me, instead of Yitzhak."

Haber sat down at a small desk and began composing the official death announcement in the name of the Government of Israel. Haber showed the statement to Peres, now the acting prime minister, and told him he was going to read it to the journalists outside the hospital.

Back at the television studio, Haim Yavin listened as his producer whispered the message through his electronic earpiece: "He's dead, but don't say anything on air yet." The producer had learned the awful news from a source at the hospital. In fact, Rabin had been clinically dead from the moment he arrived at the hospital, but that had not prevented a supreme effort to try to revive him.

Thoughts raced through Yavin's head. How could he muster the inner strength to tell the nation that Yitzhak Rabin, Israel's prime minister, was actually dead, felled by an assassin's bullet? He felt hesitant and nervous and embarrassed all at once. Something told him to wait a few minutes. He told himself he needed to be 100 percent sure. He asked the producer to find a second source at the hospital. For the time being, Yavin had to continue his commentary, pretending that he still had no solid information about the prime minister.

Meanwhile, British Sky Television broke the news a few minutes after 11 pm and Yavin quickly realized that quoting Sky would be a good way of preparing the country for the tragic news. He quoted the British network but added that there was no official confirmation.

At 11:15 pm, Yavin was in the middle of an interview with an organizer of the rally. Suddenly there was a voice whispering into his earpiece: "You can announce it. He's dead. We have it from a second source now." And so, Yavin interrupted his interview and said with great gravity that prime minister Rabin had died of the wounds suffered in the attack. Yavin held back the tears. He had a job to do. Off camera, he would cry, but not now.

Eitan Haber would have preferred to wait a while before making the official death announcement, if only because he knew that Rachel Rabin Jacoby, Rabin's sister was at that very moment travelling to Tel Aviv from Manara, her Kibbutz in northern Israel. Haber did not want her to hear the news over the radio, but he had no choice. He had to tell the nation.

For three years, Haber had written all of the prime minister's speeches and had decided who saw Rabin and who did not. He had been with Rabin every moment since the elections in June 1992. And now it was over. Haber walked into the night and the bright television lights and waited for the shouting and scrambling of the journalists to cease; but the noise and the jostling continued; so he too shouted, screaming to the country and the world that the prime minister was dead, that he had been felled by an assassin's bullet.

"Rabin is dead," someone shouted in the crowd of journalists. "Rabin is dead." The word filtered back to the edges of the crowd, numbering some 1,000 by now, and then the tears and wailing began. Cabinet ministers went into shock. Shimon Peres's driver began weeping. A group of teenagers wearing Peace Now T-shirts lit candles for the prime minister.

Leah Rabin wanted to see her husband. The doctors told her it would not be easy for her to view the body, but she insisted. She wanted to say farewell. The doctors agreed. She was accompanied by her daughter Dalia and son-in-law Avi, as well as Peres, Goren, Yatom, and Sneh. They walked into the room where the body lay and Leah approached her fallen husband first. The prime minister's body was covered to his shoulders with a white sheet. His lips were swollen and his forehead was very red from the hemorrhaging.

Leah kissed him on the forehead and then she spoke to him. Sneh took the prime minister's head in his hands and hugged him for a long time, crying deep sobs. Next was Peres: He gave Rabin a long kiss on the forehead. Goren did not touch the prime minister. She simply stared at him, still unable to believe what had transpired. And then she cried, thinking to herself: *A few hours ago he was the happiest man in the world.*

CHAPTER ONE

ENCOUNTER IN THE OLD CITY

Yitzhak Rabin's parents were born in Russia and grew up under the uncertain and frequently violent tsarist rule of the late nineteenth century. Life for the Jewish population of Russia during that time was particularly harsh, punctuated by officially sanctioned pogroms. Confined to one region called the Pale of Settlement, the Jews preserved their way of life, but had to endure both persecution and extreme poverty. Many of them decided to seek refuge in other countries, America being the most popular destination, Palestine one of the least.

Nehemiah Robichov was born in 1886 in Sidrovitch, a poor hamlet near Kiev, numbering no more than a handful of Jews. Already impoverished, the family's plight was immeasurably worsened by the death of Nehemiah's father when the boy was quite small, leaving his mother to bring up the children alone striving to make ends meet. By the time he was ten years old, Nehemiah had found work in a local flourmill. Some time later, he left his home, job, and family, and settled in a larger town, also near Kiev, and again found work in a flourmill. His family heard from him occasionally, but the connection was tenuous. When he left for the United States at the age of eighteen, he severed all ties with his family in Russia.

During those teenage years, Nehemiah acquired enough of a taste for socialism to make the Kiev police aware of his presence. Although he was not politically active, he somehow aroused the suspicions of the authorities, which were on the point of arresting him when he left Russia. He arrived in New York in 1904 completely alone, knowing no one; without knowing a word of English. He found employment in a New York City bakery, but New York was to be no more than a transit stop. After moving on to St. Louis, and there as well working for a short time in a bakery, he then travelled on to Chicago, where he spent most of the thirteen years he lived in the United States. Now in his early twenties, he became part of a circle of Jewish intellectuals, bachelors like himself, who propounded socialist and Zionist ideas and lived for the day when they could translate their dreams into reality in the Yishuv – the tiny Jewish community in Palestine. The young men formed a close-knit group, holding heated political debates, practicing their English on one another, and wondering whether they would survive on their meager incomes.

Young Robichov found work in a factory as a tailor. Although his life was hard, Nehemiah was greatly impressed with America and its values, and in later years he never tired of talking about the qualities he had found there. It is hardly a coincidence that his son Yitzhak also fell under the spell of America. "I was brought up on my father's stories about the United States," says Rabin[2], "He always used to say it was the country in which he had learned the meaning of freedom and where he had gotten the taste for education, and where organizations existed to fight for workers' rights." By the outbreak of World War One, Nehemiah Robichov had become a confirmed Zionist. Being a keen candidate for the Jewish Legion, he was then recruited by two leaders of Palestine Jewry, David Ben-Gurion and Yitzhak Ben-Zvi, to assist the Allied efforts to oust Turkey from Palestine. But when the young tailor went to the recruiting center, he was disqualified from service because of an ailment in his legs. Longing to get to Palestine, he was determined to try again, this time under a different name. Calling himself Nehemiah Rabin, he walked into another recruiting center offering to serve in the Jewish Legion and was accepted. The new recruit left Chicago for Palestine in 1917. Prolonged by stopovers in Canada, England, and Egypt the journey lasted months.

Rabin's mother Rosa Cohen was born in the town of Mogilev (in present-day Belarus) in 1890, the daughter of Rabbi Yitzhak Cohen, a devoutly religious man who totally opposed Zionism, believing that Jews should try not to force the fulfillment of their destiny, but await the Messiah's coming. Rosa's family moved to Bialystok and then in 1896 after her mother died, to Gomel, neighboring Rabbi Cohen's brother, Mordechai Ben Hillel Hacohen, who, in contrast to Rosa's father, was a staunch Zionist and not at all religious. Both brothers had large families, Rabbi Cohen with eight children, Mordechai with seven. A year after the move,

2. Rabin in conversation with author, August 2, 1976

Mordechai took his entire family to Palestine. It was partly fear that his sons would be jailed by the authorities as well as the pogroms of the 1870s and 1880s that had left a terrifying impression on the Russian Jews that led Mordechai Ben Hillel Hacohen to leave for Palestine.

Yitzhak Cohen would let nothing stand in the way of his religion and showed the same determination when it came to the education of his children, sending his sons to a Yeshiva in spite of the Russian regime. Rosa was quite content to go to the local Christian Gymnasium, but Rabbi Cohen baulked at the idea that his daughter would violate the Jewish Sabbath by attending Saturday classes. Already showing some determination of her own at this young age, Rosa would sleep at friends' houses on Friday nights to prevent her father from finding out the truth, and on Saturdays attended the Christian school as usual. In order to pay the school fees, she gave private lessons. Like her uncle, she had no interest in the religious rituals of Judaism, but like her father, she disapproved of Zionism.

More than anyone else in the family, Rabbi Cohen symbolized the old order. At home he often sang haunting Hasidic melodies, reminders of the past to which he clung with much tenacity. But the old order was changing and the change was taking place all around him. When he was away from home, the children would debate the country's ills and the troubles of the Jews in particular.

Although many of her friends had thought about leaving Russia, and some had already left for America or Palestine, Rosa preferred to stay. At that time, her father managed some of the forest estates belonging to the Tsar's brother-in-law outside St. Petersburg. She would seek out the laborers on the estates – the "wild people" as her father called them – to tell them about the coming revolution.

At the outbreak of the Bolshevik Revolution, she held a job in a military enterprise – a brick factory in the suburbs of St. Petersburg. Her only reason for working there was to bring in some money which she would then share among her fellow workers so that they would not go hungry. In September 1917, she enrolled in the Polytechnic Institute for Women, where she took up chemistry but did not complete her studies. Rosa was dismayed to discover that the long-awaited revolution actually made life worse for Russian Jews. She was ordered to join the Communist Party but refused. Because of her uncooperative attitude, she was moved to an out-of-the-way factory in southern Russia, where the workers soon demonstrated their support for her by going on strike. The government's response was to cut off the factory's supply of raw materials. Rosa moved to Kiev, and began to think about leaving her homeland. Hounded by Bolshevik secret police, and with no prospect but more misery, she decided sometime in 1919 to emigrate. She found a job as a medical aide on the Red Cross train from Kiev to Odessa. She had no desire to go to Palestine, although she had relatives in Jerusalem; instead she planned to join some friends in Sweden. Upon arriving in Odessa, she found that the only ship sailing from that port in the near future was the *Russland*, which was bound for Palestine.

Desperate to leave Russia, Rosa decided to take the opportunity. She believed her stay in Palestine would be only temporary, just a brief visit to her family there. On the *Russland*, she met some Jewish pioneers, mostly men who were bound for the Lake Kinneret (Sea of Galilee) region to build a settlement and farm the land, and whose idealism and energy appealed to her. After a two-day visit with her Uncle Mordechai and his family in Jerusalem (whom she liked to refer to as the "extreme Zionists"), she rejoined the pioneers she had met on the boat.

Although only 28, Rosa looked much older. Her face was lined and her hair had begun to turn grey. She was tall, and had a long neck, and some of the settlers thought she had an aristocratic air to her. But with characteristic toughness, she plunged into the grueling work during that first winter on the shores of the Sea of Galilee. One of the main jobs of the Kinneret pioneers was to plant Eucalyptus trees in the swamps, a task that gave her both a taste of the hardship of pioneer life, as well as an attack of malaria.

The doctor advised her to go at once to a more healthy part of the country. It was nearly Passover, and she decided the time had come to pay a longer visit to her uncle. Rosa had spent only a few months with the Kinneret settlers but her stay had left a deep impression on her. As she joined her relatives in April 1920, she began to examine her preconceived attitude and rigid prejudice against settling in Palestine. She had been disappointed to find that the country was not as developed or populated as she had imagined, but she was impressed with the Jews she met. One of these was Rachel Yanait, who was particularly active in women's agricultural training. Watching her at work, Rosa began to identify with the aims and aspirations of the Yishuv. She did not have to wait very long before her questions and doubts about Zionism were resolved.

The Palestine that Nehemiah Rabin and Rosa Cohen came to was on the verge of extraordinary political ambiguity and confusion. Until the 1920s, Jews and Arabs had lived and worked side by side for years in the Holy Land, both Semitic peoples, neither interested in forcing the other out of the area. The Jewish community in Palestine had been until then quite small. Even in 1881, when pogroms became rife in Russia, the Yishuv numbered only 25,000; the Holy Land seemed to offer not much more than refuge from persecution. Although living conditions were tough, in 1914 nearly 100,000 Jews were living in the Yishuv and after the Balfour Declaration in 1917, Jews began to settle in much larger numbers. The swelling Jewish population found itself confronted by rapidly developing Arab nationalism, creating for the first time in the region a genuine Jewish-Arab political conflict. A further complication during the post-war years was the presence of the British, who in 1920 were given responsibility for Palestine by the League of Nations.

If the Jews of the Yishuv did not expect the British to embrace their cause wholly, at least the Balfour Declaration with its sweeping talk of favoring "the establishment in Palestine of a national home for the Jewish people," seemed to be an encouragement to them to stay on in the region and increase their numbers through immigration. But in the years to come, the Yishuv found that British policy steadily veered away from the goals of the Balfour Declaration, and instead sought to hinder further Jewish immigration into Palestine.

Nehemiah Rabin had volunteered for the Jewish Legion as part of a plan to settle in Palestine but had, by his own admission, some misgivings about staying. In later years he often joked to his children that the night on which he gave the most serious consideration to his future, his hair turned white. In the end, he chose to stay in Palestine because he could not imagine himself, an ardent Zionist, returning to live in the Diaspora after actually setting foot in Eretz Yisrael. In New York, Nehemiah had become friendly with Yitzhak Ben-Zvi, later to become the second President of Israel. Just after the war both men were stationed at Sarafand, a military base near Tel Aviv, and from time to time they would travel together to Jerusalem, where some friends of Ben-Zvi were making arrangements for the Jews' protection in the Holy City. Among them were Rachel Yanait, whom Ben-Zvi later married, and Zvi Nadav. Ben-Zvi felt that Nehemiah's experience as a gunsmith in the Legion could be valuable and suggested that he should join them. The three began to organize the training of others in the use of arms, and became part of the new defense committee set up by Ze'ev Jabotinsky, another of the Jewish Legion's founders. Nehemiah was chosen to represent the Legion solders on Jabotinsky's committee. He was also put in charge of the arms storehouse and given the task of ensuring that weapons were clean.

On Saturdays the committee members would go out into the fields between the outlying Jerusalem districts of Bet HaKerem and Rehavia to practice throwing hand grenades. Oddly, Arabs and British watched while they trained.

As the Jewish holiday of Passover neared in April 1920, tensions between Jews and Arabs intensified. Disturbances began on April 4. On that cool, sunny day, Jews, Christians and Muslims were getting ready for the start of their respective religious festivals. The holy sites of all three religions are situated within the confines of the crowded, walled Old City of Jerusalem, with its ancient cobblestones, open-air markets, and tiny alleyways.

As the Arabs paraded towards the Dome of the Rock, a British military band preceded them. From a nearby balcony, the British military governor and his entourage watched the procession. Also watching but from rooftops outside the Old City, were members of the Jewish defense committee. At the Dome of the Rock, an Arab nationalist leader agitated the crowd against the Jews, rousing the Arabs to sudden uncontrolled violence. With placards, with daggers drawn, shouting, "We shall drink Jewish blood," they swept towards the Jewish Quarter of the Old City, where two thousand Jews lived and worked. At the main entrance to the Old City, the Jaffa Gate, Jews confronted Arabs in battle, and when the fighting was over, six Jews, four Arabs, and a British soldier lay dead. Two hundred and eleven Jews and twenty one Arabs were wounded. Inside the Jewish Quarter elderly Jews were locked in a house, which was then set on fire. Some women nearby were raped. Stores were looted and burned. Arab policemen, to whom the British had assigned responsibility for maintaining order in the Old City, fled in fear or openly joined the Arab rioters.

When fears about the possibility of Arab riots in Jerusalem had first arisen, the British, anxious to keep Jewish soldiers away from the area of conflict, had ordered Nehemiah and his Jewish Legion colleagues to Jericho, twenty-five miles northeast of Jerusalem. But, hearing that the Jews of Jerusalem were in danger, they had hurriedly returned to the Holy City. Nehemiah went to Jabotinsky's house to see what the other members of the defense committee were doing. He discovered that some had watched the riots from a distance, powerless to help because the British had sealed off the Old City when the trouble began. Others, gathered at Jabotinsky's house, had been embroiled in organizational disputes which seemed somewhat irrelevant at that moment, with the shouting of the Arab mobs nearby drowning their words. A curfew had been imposed on the Old City. The Passover holiday was barely twenty-four hours old.

The next morning Nehemiah persuaded the committee to let him and some colleagues reconnoiter the Jaffa Gate in order to see how to best help the Jews inside the Old City. When they found that the British had barred Jews from entering the Old City, they broke into Hadassah Hospital and took clothes used by cleaning men. Disguised in these uniforms, they managed to enter the Old City unchallenged.

The riots resolved all Rosa Cohen's doubts about Zionism. Accustomed as she was to persecution in Russia, this new violence in Palestine appalled her, and her sympathy towards the settlers aroused. Dressed as a nurse, she had no difficulty in getting past the guards at the Old City gates. As she crossed a courtyard near Jews Street inside the Jewish Quarter, Nehemiah, who was continuing his efforts to help the Old City Jews, caught sight of her nurse's uniform, and called out to her, demanding to know what she was doing there. Rosa retorted that it was none of his business, and the two began to argue. Then, before he realized what was happening, she seized his gun and began to struggle with him. Locked in combat, the two were still screaming at each other in Yiddish when a group of British soldiers came upon them, separated the pair and managed to calm them down. Realizing that they were there on the same mission, they decided to work together. Thus began the romance of Nehemiah Rabin and Rosa Cohen.

By the second and third nights of the riots, the defense committee had started moving Jews from the mixed Jewish-

Arab districts to the new part of the city. Nehemiah was held for three days at the Migdal David prison and fined £5 for illegal possession of arms. His release from prison coincided with his demobilization from the Jewish Legion. He began working on the special labor force organized by the British to install new telephone lines in Palestine. Rosa went to Haifa where she found work as an accountant in the Hiram construction firm. She met Nehemiah again in Haifa in 1921 and in that year they got married.

The exact date of the wedding is unknown because both frowned upon celebrating anniversaries and their own birthdays, though later, as far as their children's birthdays were concerned they did relent. Rosa Cohen, as she preferred to be called even after her marriage, became involved in defense and labor, the two interests which would occupy her time almost wholly for the next two decades. She volunteered to make the rounds of the various homeowners in Haifa to subscribe to the Defense Fund, and collected the impressive sum of £750. On the labor front, she fought against the policy excluding Jewish workers from the Haifa port.

Rosa became pregnant in 1921 but continued working into the ninth month of her pregnancy. In February of that following year, while walking to work, a dog bit her on the leg. With the birth of her first baby imminent, Rosa felt she must have the best possible medical care. A warm relationship had developed between her and Mordechai Ben Hillel Hacohen's family in Jerusalem, and she knew that they would welcome her. When she arrived at their huge, two-story house on Ethiopia Street, she came under the care of her cousin, 26-year-old Hannah Hacohen who immediately took her to the nearby Shaare Zedek Hospital. A few days later, on March 1, 1922, Rosa gave birth to a baby boy whom she and Nehemiah named Yitzhak after the boy's maternal grandfather.

Rosa was eager to return to Haifa, but Hannah insisted that she stayed on with them for another month to recuperate. The Hacohen's house, built by an Arab for his harem in the previous century, had twenty rooms and was always full of overnight guests and lodgers, so the additional presence of a mother and her newborn baby was nothing out of the ordinary. Through his banking connections, Mordechai Ben Hillel Hacohen knew a number of important statesmen, and it was not unusual to find him dining at home with such eminent people as Baron de Rothschild and Winston Churchill.

By the spring of 1922, the Rabins were reunited in Haifa. Nehemiah had begun to work for the Electric Corporation, and Rosa resumed her work on behalf of Haifa's defense. In early 1923, she became the first commander of the Haifa Hagana, the embryonic underground defense unit established to protect the Jewish community of the city against Arab attacks. Running the city's defenses and taking care of an infant hardly seemed compatible, but she managed to do both.

In 1923, the Rabin family moved to Tel Aviv and lived at first in an apartment on Chlenov Street, not far from Jaffa.

Nehemiah became one of the first workers in Pinhas Rotenberg's Palestine Electric Corporation, one of the main pillars of the Yishuv economy. Quiet and easy-going, Nehemiah remained a diligent worker with the company for thirty years. His daily routine predictable and uncomplicated was in sharp contrast to his wife's hectic life. Rosa, with her strong will and boundless energy, was not only the more colorful among the two parents, but also the more dominant in her children's lives, despite the fact she was scarcely at home.

Forever preoccupied with the welfare of Jewish workers, she inspired her children and filled them with awe. Significantly, Rabin remembered her against the background of the workers movement of those years: she had her own position, her own principles, and she was ready to fight for anything that seemed a worthy cause to her. She was a very austere, extreme person, who stuck to what she believed in; there were no compromises with her. Rachel, Rabin's younger sister (born on February 1, 1925), remembers, too, that "she had an ability to organize and a very authoritarian personality."[3]

Others remembered Rosa for that strong personality. In 1923, Rosa Cohen had been an accountant for the Solel Boneh building contractors. In later years, Golda Meir recalled to Yitzhak Rabin that she had once been a cashier at Solel Boneh. Rabin replied that his mother had been a cashier in the same institution. "No," Golda corrected Rabin, "I was the cashier your mother was the accountant."[4]

Often Rosa would pin small pieces of paper to her dress, notes to herself reminding her of tasks that she had to do, whether taking medicine to someone or attending a meeting. "When we were out in the street with mother, shopping or on our way to visit people," Rabin recalled, "we would never get to our destination on time. We were always being held up because on the way she would meet someone who took

---

3. Rachel Rabin in conversation with author, August 14, 1976

4. Yitzhak Rabin, *The Rabin Memoirs* (English version), Weidenfeld and Nicolson, 1979, p. 3

the opportunity to ask her something or to talk things over with her."[5] "We couldn't walk ten minutes without someone stopping us and talking with her. I used to pull at her dress and she would buy me ice cream to keep me quiet."[6]

Rosa was sickly, an aspect of her life that haunted the young Yitzhak. She suffered from a heart problem. "I was dogged by the fear that it would bring her to her grave," Rabin wrote in his 1979 *Memoirs*, "whenever she had a heart attack, I would run as fast as I could to call the doctor, terrified that I would return to find her dead. Rachel and I lived in the shadow of this dread throughout our childhood, and we were very careful not to upset her."[7]

Rosa always had time for other people's problems. She rarely had time, however, to sit through meals in her own house and was always dashing off to some important meeting or to somebody who needed her personal attention. These commitments kept her away from home for most of the day. In addition to the work she had been doing in Haifa, she took on a variety of causes when she moved to Tel Aviv, eventually gaining a seat on the Tel Aviv City Council, which strengthened her position in the struggle for workers' rights. One of her toughest battles was waged over the right of Tel Aviv workers to their own schools.

The working-class people of the Yishuv felt the general schools were not providing the right kind of education for their children, who needed to know how to settle the land, how to work it and make a living off it, not simply how to read and

---

5. Yitzhak Rabin, *My Father's House*, p. 25

6. Rachel Rabin in conversation with author, August 14, 1976

7. Yitzhak Rabin, *The Rabin Memoirs* (English version), p. 4

write. Since the general schools were controlled by the same conservative political elements that ran the Municipality, the workers had no chance of making changes in the curriculum. The only alternative was to establish their own schools, but even getting approval for this was difficult. Eventually, in 1924 the Tel Aviv workers' organizations established the first workers' school, known as Beit HaChinuch leYaldei Ovdim (House of Education for Children of Workers). It was located in the center of the city on Tschernichovsky Street, next to Gan Meir, a good-sized park where students could grow vegetables and flowers.

During the first few years, the school was housed in two long uninsulated huts which, when it rained, would be surrounded by a huge pool of water. "It was hot in the summer and wet in the winter," Rabin would later write, "but we loved it, we loved the special atmosphere that pervaded it. We loved to study in the hut, that is to say, on those days when it was possible to study, for if the flooding rose beyond a certain level, the students would have to adjourn to the dining room."[8] She enrolled her son at the age of six in the autumn of 1928, and the boy spent the next seven years there, graduating at the age of thirteen in 1935.

The aim of the school was to produce workers for the Yishuv, not intellectuals nor merchants, but men and women who, when they finished their education, would go to the new kibbutzim, which were being established around the country. As *kibbutzniks*, farmers who would settle the land and at the same time establish a Jewish presence in as many parts of the country as possible. They would be fulfilling

---

8. Yitzhak Rabin, 'I Was One of the 'Sons of Yoreh', *Haaretz*, November 19, 1965

the goals of both the labor movement and of Zionism. The school not only supplied the fundamentals of education, but also furnished the children with an ideology, a direction, and a model for future experiences. The whole approach and philosophy of the school thrilled Rosa.

As many of the parents worked all day, the school provided midday meals for the children and remained open until 4 pm, much later than the regular schools. This fit in very well with Rosa and Nehemiah's busy lifestyle. The longer school hours served the purposes of Beit HaChinuch equally well, for the children were kept there for the better part of each day, six days a week, enabling the teachers to have the maximum influence on them.

With his parents away from home most of the time, the school clearly dominated Yitzhak's childhood and he remembered his years at the school with a warmth and enthusiasm that he rarely exhibited otherwise. Unwilling to go home right away after school, the students gathered outside the school's entrance, sat down in the sand, and talked. Even on their day off, Saturday, teachers and students frequently met and took long walks together, exploring the countryside. These nature hikes forged a link between the children and the land. They certainly gave Rabin a familiarity with his surroundings that later in life proved invaluable.

In his first few years at Beit HaChinuch, Yitzhak displayed little aptitude for formal studies. However, he was keenly interested in sports, especially soccer, and he enjoyed tending the school garden and looking after the school's donkey, Dionio, which was made his special responsibility. The other students helped Yitzhak build a special wooden stable. "Every morning when it rained," recalls Rabin, "I would rush to the stable to see how the donkey was, if it was well, or if it had drowned in the rain."[9] This sense of responsibility, developed by Beit HaChinuch at such an early age, was to stay with him and become ingrained in his character. "Today I am certain," he said, "that during those childhood years, they weren't the most comfortable, but they were very beautiful. I developed the feeling of responsibility towards a job, and my love of landscape and the earth, and a feeling for comradeship."[10]

Eliezer Smoli, one of the school's ten teachers, was one of the major influences on the boy, although their first encounter was hardly auspicious. The subject of their meeting was Yitzhak's record at school, which by his own acknowledgment had hardly been impressive. Smoli took up the matter with the boy, only to be told that Yitzhak had no intention of making any more effort; he was quite content to go along at his own speed. However, what Smoli could not accomplish, Rosa Cohen could; with a sudden outburst that affected the child so much, he made a new attempt to learn to read and write, and finally succeeded.

With Smoli for his teacher, Yitzhak began to discover that learning could be fun: "He succeeded in implanting in me a feeling for landscape, for nature, for farm life, and for society. He did this not with words or lectures, but rather by means of excursions, exciting experiences and stories."[11]

Not surprisingly, Beit HaChinuch was one of Rosa Cohen's favorite public projects, and she became the school's so-called unofficial patron; not only caring for the

9. Ibid

10. Ibid

11. Rabin, *My Father's House*, p. 39

pupils, she also looked after the school's needs and cared for the welfare of the teachers. In much the same way she had helped hungry workers in Russia, she gave her wages to make sure the children at Beit HaChinuch had enough food. In addition, she managed to persuade her Uncle Mordechai – no easy matter – to give the school a £3,000 loan so it could move into more modern buildings.

Mordechai Ben Hillel Hacohen was convinced that the school was designed to turn the children into communists. As he was fond of Yitzhak and hoped the boy would think of him as a stand-in for his grandfathers, when Rosa invited him to see the school for himself before deciding on the loan, he accepted. His first impressions of the school led him to think he had been right in believing it to be a communist institution: children dressed in blue shirts and a flag hanging from each classroom wall. However, after testing the children on their knowledge of Jewish subjects, he seemed satisfied that they were being taught properly, and happily agreed to the loan.

During the years of his childhood, Yizhak Rabin was something of an enigma to teachers and fellow pupils alike, a mixture of introversion and self-confidence. Because he was so quiet, few people really knew him. Some mistook his shyness for rudeness. Some found it the outward reflection of genuine modesty. Others felt it was a cloak for a sensitive mind. He rarely spoke in class or outside it, for that matter. He walked to and from Beit HaChinuch every day with his classmate Ada Tamir, but he seldom talked to her. He showed great tenderness and devotion to his sister Rachel, but some of the girls at Beit HaChinuch were afraid of him. "He was shy," one remembered, "and his way of trying to conceal it was to hit us." He was not at ease in the company of girls in those days as Rabin freely admitted: "I am an introverted man from many points of view. Everyone likes a certain amount of privacy. Some people are more expressive and some are less. It seems to me that I belong to the second type."

Although shy and introverted, he was also self-confident and there was a streak of stubbornness in him. With his parents away from the house all day, he quickly learned to fend for himself. He could not run home to his parents. Once, when he was about six, he was on his way home with friends when some Arab youngsters began to throw stones at them. Yitzhak and his companions grabbed some stones of their own, and a fight ensued which eventually ended in a draw. When he was seven years old, a new outbreak of Arab riots was directed against the Yishuv, during which some five hundred Jews were wounded. The boy was bewildered and filled with a sense of uncertainty which stuck in his mind. Much later he wrote: "I lived through such riots as a small boy alone in an empty house, with parents seldom there. I didn't know what was going on."[12]

Every summer until he was fourteen years old, the boy would spend a few weeks visiting the homes of his great-uncle Mordechai and of his cousin Hannah. By the end of the 1920s, the Hacohen family comprised some of the most important figures of the Yishuv, and has remained one of the leading families in the country. Since the founding of the State of Israel, members of the family have been in the forefront of the country's leadership: Yigael Yadin became Israel's second chief of staff, a world-famous archaeologist

---

12. Ibid., p. 48

and a major force in Israeli politics; David Hacohen served for a while during the 1950s as chairman of the prestigious Committee for Foreign Affairs and Defense of the Knesset, Israel's parliament; Uzi Narkiss was the commander of the Central Front during the Six-Day War of 1967 and helped to conquer and reunite Jerusalem.

Mordechai Ben Hillel Hacohen's house was near that of Hannah, who was married to Arthur Ruppin, for many years the director of the Settlement Department of the Yishuv. Even though it was summer and holiday time, Uncle Mordechai tried to improve the drifting minds of the youngsters. Once he asked Yitzhak to help him sort out the books in his library, more to give him some appreciation of the written word, than because he really needed his assistance. The exercise gave the boy a chance to browse through some of the great works of Jewish and general literature.

Rabin's childhood gave little indication of his later deep involvement in military life. Unlike the Israeli boy of today, who might be inclined to emulate such military leaders as Moshe Dayan or Rabin himself, the young Yitzhak had no indigenous military heroes to admire. The British were the only soldiers in Palestine in those days, and a youngster of the Yishuv was hardly likely to idolize them.

When Yitzhak was six or seven he started to read a little bit about what was going on. "Therefore, my attitude towards the British was that they were outsiders. I looked at them with suspicion. Later on my feelings towards them grew to dislike." In any case, he had been brought up to believe that farming was a far more worthy pursuit than soldiering. "I can't recall being very much impressed by any political leader during my schooldays," he said, "the hero then was the farmer, the guardian, the kind of person who had achieved something that was considered to be symbolic of pioneering in those days. They were not people who had won political prestige, but people who had conquered and achieved."[13] He seemed destined for a career in agriculture, and would have thought it absurd, if the idea of becoming a military figure had been suggested to him then.

13. Rabin in conversation with author, August 2, 1976

CHAPTER TWO

"HAVE YOU EVER THROWN
A HAND GRENADE?"

The Rabins' household was simple. In 1931, the family moved from Shadal Street to a two-roomed apartment on HaMagid Street, closer to the pulse of Tel Aviv life. This was to remain the Rabin home long after Rosa's death in 1937. The apartment contained only the minimum furniture necessary for the simplest existence: beds, a few chairs and a table, nothing decorative. It was highly functional, and at night became a hive of activity as Nehemiah and Rosa took turns holding their defense committee and labor association meetings there.

When Nehemiah was host to the Metal Workers Committee, the shouting could be heard up and down the tiny street and the neighbors would complain; defense committee meetings were much quieter, in the interests of preserving secrecy. To make room for the meetings, and, almost as frequently, for the overnight guests, the children would be moved from bed to bed, sometimes even sleeping at neighbors' or friends' houses.

Aware that the children required more attention than she was able to give, Rosa had persuaded a neighboring family on Shadal Street to move with them to the same apartment block on HaMagid Street, where the two families shared a large kitchen on the same floor. Most days when the two Rabin youngsters returned home from school, they were looked after by the neighbors, for whom they felt a good deal of affection. Much later Rabin was to say: "I didn't like it [i.e. the arrangements at home], but I did understand it. In a way, it created a kind of astrosphere in which each one of us had his own life, had his own circle in which he was alone even though there was a feeling of family unity."[14]

That sense of family unity was strongest on Friday evenings, the only time during the week all four sat down together for Shabbat dinner. During the rest of the week, Nehemiah made breakfast for himself and the children as Rosa was usually out of the house early. For their main meal, in the middle of the day, the children ate at Beit HaChinuch. The evening meal was prepared hastily, since time was always short and Rosa was so busy. The hectic pace of their lives obviously made a lasting impression on the boy. Talking about his relationship with his own children, he implied with a sense of regret and alluded to those prolonged periods when he was left on his own: "Whenever I was home, I always tried to the best of my ability – not always with success – not to think about work, and to free myself for the children,

---

14. Rabin in conversation with author, August 2, 1976

so that to some extent they wouldn't have the feeling that I experienced during my childhood."[15]

The household had a definite routine – so much so that Rabin remembers it as being run "like a military camp." They all shared the chores. Nehemiah usually did the washing in the afternoons, standing outside the house, tossing clothes about in a wooden washtub. If the children needed money for something, they knew where the purse with change was kept, but as a rule they did not go to it, aware that the funds were meant for more important things than satisfying their whims. They didn't seem to mind. Oddly, although the Rabins lived an extremely simple life, the children grew up believing that they were not poor. "It was considered shameful to speak about money," Rabin recalled. Ironically, the Rabins employed a maid for a certain period, a most un-socialist addition to the household. Despite her presence, the children had to continue helping with the chores.

The unmaterialistic Rabins were true socialists in another respect: Their home was largely free of religion, though a strong sense of Jewishness filled the house. When the family lived on Shadal Street in the 1920s, they were directly opposite the Sephardic Synagogue, which Rabin still vividly recalled in his later years, together with its spiritual leader, Rabbi Uziel, who was also a neighbor of the Rabins. A leading figure of the religious community in Tel Aviv, Rabbi Uziel eventually became Chief Rabbi of the Yishuv. Though Yitzhak was not religious, the sight and atmosphere of the synagogue had an effect on him and left him with a profound belief in Judaism as a positive force. This was all the more

---

15. Rabin, *My Father's House*, p. 58

remarkable in view of his father's intense dislike of religious ceremonies even, to the point of later refusing to light the traditional candle on the anniversary of Rosa's death. Although free of religion, the Rabin household inculcated enduring values in the young boy, the most prominent among them humility.

In physical appearance, Yitzhak took after his father with his strong build, high forehead, wavy black hair and penetrating eyes. From Nehemiah the young boy also took his quiet, serious manner, and his deep voice. Rosa, whom Rachel favored, left her imprint on the boy in other ways. Because of her long absences from home, she had little influence on Yitzhak on a day-to-day basis, but she served as a model of the ideal public servant and he deeply admired her. Both parents had a major influence on the direction of the boy's life; it was from them that he learned socialism and came to prize socialist ideals. Also, growing up in a household that was forever concerned, however little was actually said, with problems of defense, he absorbed early on the vital importance defense was to the Yishuv, and the absolute necessity for each member of the community to devote a large amount of his or her time to it. Rosa was a member of the supreme command of the secret defense organization, the Hagana, during the 1930s. Guns were brought into the house and stored away and Nehemiah was at times mobilized and away from home for weeks on end. Nehemiah and Rosa tried to keep this part of their lives separate, and to insulate the children from the growing Jewish-Arab tension, but it was not always possible. One day, a woman who was looking after Rachel picked up a gun that she had found in the flat. It went off, narrowly missing the little girl.

When Yitzhak finished his studies at Beit HaChinuch at the age of thirteen, his parents faced the same dilemma which had confronted them when he was six: how to avoid the general schools of Tel Aviv? Rosa decided that she herself would establish a two-year agriculture-oriented school, somewhere in the country, so that working-class youngsters like her son could continue their studies in an appropriate environment. It would be a kind of extension to Beit HaChinuch. Rosa wanted her children to carry on what she had started in those first days in Palestine with the Kinneret group, and hoped that Yitzhak and Rachel would decide to settle in the same region. The school she founded was in Kibbutz Givat HaShlosha (in its original place of settlement west to Petach Tikva) outside Tel Aviv.

The tiny Yishuv (which had numbered 60,000 in 1919) grew to 600,000 in the 1930s. The British had given the community permission to establish a Va'ad Leumi (National Council) also stipulating that an appropriate Jewish agency should work with them in implementing the pledge of the Balfour Declaration of a Jewish national home, and the World Zionist Organization was recognized as such. The Arabs looked askance at the Declaration, believing it to be an infringement of their own rights in Palestine, and that at best it ought merely to entitle the Jews to a limited Jewish minority in the Holy Land. During the 1920s, there had been an increase in Jewish-Arab tension in Palestine over the question of the Jewish right to immigration, resulting in a rise in Arab violence. The British tended to put the blame on the Yishuv for encouraging immigration and therefore provoking the Arabs. Arab-sponsored riots in 1929 had led to a tougher British attitude towards Jewish immigration.

The Yishuv responded by encouraging young Jews to establish settlements in the remote and hazardous parts of Palestine, asserting by this act that the country was big enough for Jews and Arabs to live together, no matter how many Jews arrived from abroad. Between 1936 and 1939, fifty three 'Stockade and Tower' settlements were built, so-called due to their fortifications and their thirty-six-foot high towers, topped by searchlights, which ringed the settlements.

In April 1936, the Arabs again began to riot. For three years the violence continued, as Arabs killed Jews on the streets and conducted raids against the outlying Jewish settlements. The British did little to stop them. What kept them at bay was the 25,000-strong force of the Hagana, the underground self-defense organization of the Yishuv. The heaviest fighting between Jews and Arabs tailed off by1937, but there were sporadic outbursts of shooting until 1939. During the three years of rioting, an estimated 2,200 Arabs, 450 Jews and 140 British were killed. The Yishuv, ably defended by the Hagana, emerged strengthened, notwithstanding the loss of life. Not only had not a single Jewish settlement been abandoned, but owing to the 'Stockade and Tower' operation, strategic settlements had been established near the borders of Lebanon, Syria, and Transjordan. The Hagana, too, still technically illegal, had grown stronger and more self-confident in these last years, though it continued to be under-trained and poorly equipped.

If the Arabs could not defeat the Jews on the battlefield, they did win political points by once again provoking the British into more severe action against Jewish immigration. In July 1937, the six-member Peel Commission, appointed by the British to improve Jewish-Arab relations in Palestine, issued a 404-page report after spending six months conducting hearings and touring the Holy Land. It concluded that the British Mandate was impractical and should be replaced by separate Jewish and Arab States. The Jews should be given the coastal plain, the Jezreel Valley, and Galilee (altogether 2,000 square miles) and the Arabs, the rest of Palestine; Jerusalem would become an international enclave linked to the coast by a corridor. The Jews grudgingly accepted the plan, dismayed at the small amount of territory conceded to them, but recognized that they would at least have some control over immigration into that area. The Arabs were contemptuous of the plan and immediately stepped up terrorist activity, whereupon the British outlawed the Arab Higher Command and ordered the arrest of the Mufti, who, however, managed to escape.

In 1938, the British placed Palestine under military administration, but this did little to restore peace. A year later, in May 1939, seeking a compromise, the British announced a White Paper which would allow 15,000 Jews to immigrate annually to Palestine over the next five years, after which further Jewish immigration would be stopped altogether. Jewish land purchase was to be cut back drastically. To the Yishuv leadership, the White Paper was nothing less than the renunciation of the Balfour Declaration.

The turmoil of the late 1930s in Palestine touched Rabin personally. Upon enrolling at Givat HaShlosha School in 1935, he had his first encounter with military life: Hagana training sessions began when a youngster was thirteen years old; they took place for several hours every day at the school. Rabin was taught how to use a pistol and how to stand guard.

Like most Jewish youngsters in the Yishuv, the boy joined one of the youth movements after his Beit HaChinuch days, choosing one that was labor-oriented. It was known as HaNoar HaOved (Working Youth), and met in HaBayit HaAdom (the Red House), on the Tel Aviv beach. There in the afternoons, the youngster discussed a variety of subjects, including the Bible, literature, music, economics, and social problems. Rabin found such talks boring but he was fascinated by social problems and economics. He spoke very little, preferring to listen.

Occasionally there was rivalry between the different youth clubs. At the festival of Hanukkah, for instance, Rabin and his fellow members collected candles and paraded through the streets of Tel Aviv, singing holiday songs and carrying their flag, a blue-and-white banner with two red strips attached to it, the symbol of the socialist cause. The right-wing Betar youth movement, which had engaged in fistfights with them on previous occasions, attacked them and a battle broke out between the two groups.

During his two years at Givat HaShlosha, Rabin became more assertive, more interested in his studies and in October 1937, he began his studies at the Kadoorie Agricultural High School for boys, located near Kfar Tabor in the Lower Galilee. By choosing the two-year course the school offered, rather than the four-year academic high school education available in Tel Aviv, which enabled a youngster with ambitions to go on to university, he was setting himself toward a career on a kibbutz. Getting into the school posed quite a challenge for the boy: although only in its fourth year in 1937, there were already some 150 boys competing for the thirty places available. Though Beit HaChinuch had given him a strong foundation in certain fields, it had not given him much of an academic grounding in English or mathematics for instance. He had indeed made much progress at Givat

HaShlosha, where the principal had commended him as "a good student in the important subjects, industrious in his work, and well-behaved," but still he failed the entrance examination to Kadoorie. Several months later, the school authorities permitted a second attempt and this time the boy was determined to pass. He worked between ten and twelve hours a day at his studies, and when he took the exam again, he passed with flying colors and found that the preparation had given him a taste for learning.

Conditions in the three-story, white-stone school building were primitive: all twenty-five boys in Rabin's class lived in one large room on the second floor. The building was rarely heated; even in winter the boys took ice-cold showers at the end of each day.

He had hardly begun there when the sad news came that his mother had died. Rosa's death in November 1937 caused widespread grief within the Yishuv. Some one thousand people attended her burial. In honor of its founder, the Givat HaShlosha School decided to change its name to the Rosa Cohen School. Natan Fiat, the principal of Kadoorie, wrote to Rabin in Tel Aviv on November 16 to express his sorrow at Rosa's death: "Your mother was one of the great women in Israel whose names are associated with the lofty idealism of the nation... May you find comfort in studying for the profession you have chosen, for your own good and for the good of the public which your mother loved so much and to which she gave so much of her time in her short life."

Although most subjects fell easily within his grasp, Rabin found English particularly difficult. His report card shows that he did best in zoology, chemistry, botany, poultry breeding, and beekeeping. He had a good record in physics and agronomy as well. Both his teachers and classmates expected him to become an outstanding scientist one day, and perhaps take up research at the prestigious Weizmann Institute in Rehovot, one of the major scientific institutions of the Yishuv. At graduation he won the top prize: the Walker Prize for Scholarship. However, although he had earned the most points for his work, the school directors felt that another boy was equally bright, and the two of them should share the prize. The boys agreed, but the donors of the prize, the British Authorities, insisted that the school should give it to Rabin. In the event, neither boy collected the seven and a half British pounds' worth of farm equipment that went with the prize.

Some of Rabin's happiest moments at Kadoorie were spent on the soccer field as captain of the school team. He adored the game, and would go to matches on Saturdays with his father when they were together in Tel Aviv. He was intolerant of those on his own school team who did not play well, and was not slow to make his disapproval obvious.

When he began at Kadoorie, Rabin had absolutely no ambition to become a full-time soldier. He thought only about farming and moving onto a kibbutz: "My purpose in life was to serve my country and I believed that the best way to do it was to prepare myself to be a farmer."[16] At Kadoorie however, his military training intensified and it was during this time that he began to sense that he would probably become personally involved in the Arab-Jewish struggle. Kadoorie was in the peculiar position of being run under British auspices but unable to take advantage of the protection of the British army because the school was so isolated. In fact, the British took little interest in the

16. ABC News documentary, "Rabin: Action Biography," April 15, 1975

defense of the school, and the students realized that it was fundamentally their own responsibility.

Yigal Allon, then a sergeant in the Hagana for the Lower Galilee region and a future Israeli political leader, was responsible for training the Kadoorie youngsters. But even before Allon could begin training the boys in earnest, the school had been organized informally so that the students were prepared in the event of an attack. The top class was responsible for the weapons, which consisted entirely of rifles. Rabin's class dealt with all the other tasks, including message-carrying and supplies. At night the boys took turns doing guard duty. Tensions ran high, the training and guard duties interfered with the boys' work and the school was more like a fortress than a place of study. Towards the end of 1937, the school came under attack, though the students soon realized that the Arab assault was more in the nature of sabre-rattling than an actual attempt to overrun it, with the Arabs simply firing rounds at the school building.

In the summer of 1938, the riots worsened and the British decided to close the school down three weeks before the end of Rabin's first year. In the autumn, he gladly answered a summons from Allon to join him at Kibbutz Ginosar, where Rabin remained for the next six months. As soon as he arrived, he joined the other youngsters being given a ten-day training course nearby at Migdal, where they learnt to use revolvers, rifles, and hand grenades. Allon took a liking to Rabin, recognizing that he had qualities which could be put to military use. Allon remembers: "He had a sort of analytical approach to problems. He would never say he understood something before he really did understand all that it involved. Once he said that he understood, you knew that he did." As his first commander, Allon justifiably takes credit for discovering Rabin's soldiering abilities.

Following the six months at Ginosar, Rabin spent another similar period of Hagana duty at Ramat David in northern Palestine. He returned to Kadoorie during October 1939, and graduated from the school on August 20, 1940. Fiat wrote to Nehemiah Rabin, asking him to attend the graduation so that he could discuss the boy's future, and suggested that instead of becoming a farmer, as most of his students did, the boy should study water engineering at the University of California. Fiat was certain that Yitzhak would be accepted because of his academic record; he would probably not even need to take an entrance examination, though he would have to improve his English. The idea appealed to Rabin who realized that water would be a major preoccupation of the Yishuv in the years to come. His father made the necessary application to the university, and Rabin awaited the reply at Kibbutz Ramat Yohanan, near Haifa, where he joined a group which planned to establish a settlement somewhere in the region. It was while he was waiting that another offer came up that he felt he had to accept.

Sooner or later, the events of World War Two were bound to impinge on the boy. After the publication of the White Paper in 1939, it had been extremely difficult for the Jews of the Yishuv to swallow their differences with the British and fight side by side with them against a common enemy, but David Ben-Gurion (who had become chairman of the Jewish Agency in 1935 and as such was the Yishuv's leader) issued a directive: "We shall fight the war as if there were no White Paper, and we shall fight the White Paper as if there were no war."

In the spring of 1941, members of the Hagana High Command felt that the Yishuv's chances of defending itself against a possible Nazi invasion were lessened by the Zionist leadership's decision to permit so many Palestinian Jews to serve abroad in the British army. In the event of the Nazis overrunning Palestine, the Jewish settlements would be at the mercy of the Axis Powers and the local Arabs. The Hagana comprised dedicated but relatively untrained men, recruited from the ranks of the workers on a part-time basis; what was needed was an independent, well-equipped mobile, and permanently mobilized task force subject, of course, to the Hagana's authority. This special task force was formed in May 1941 by Yitzhak Sadeh, a Russian-born Hagana veteran and was recruited in total secrecy. The Palmach (as it was called from the acronym for "Shock Companies") came into existence at a time when the morale of the Yishuv plummeted to a new low. An undercurrent of resentment had been building among those who wished to see more dynamic action and leadership. The Hagana itself was coming in for a great deal of criticism from the Yishuv, who tended to see its members as draft dodgers, and the organization as failing in its primary objectives.

At first the Palmach attracted young idealists; but they lacked the necessary soldiering talents. The new fighting force required the best possible recruits and it needed them in a hurry. Appeals were made to the pioneering youth movements and to the collective settlements, where idealism already flourished and where the best potential for future soldiers existed. Very quickly the Palmachniks grew into an elitist band which enjoyed an almost legendary reputation; it was, after all, the very first institution of the Yishuv to be controlled and run by a generation actually born in the country. In contrast with the under-trained Hagana recruits, the Palmach force comprised six companies of soldiers who had the benefit of full-time commando-style training. By 1947, the Palmach constituted some 3,100 soldiers, including 1,000 reservists, both men and women, and fully half of its members had spent three years of full-time training as compared with the fifty days that were all many of the Hagana soldiers had been given.

At about the same time the Palmach was being formed, the military situation of the Allies worsened and the British began to plan an offensive into Syria and Lebanon in an attempt to stave off a German attempt to take over the entire Middle East. For such an offensive, the British needed a special force that could cross Palestine's northern frontier easily, whose members knew the terrain and the necessary languages, and who could be relied upon to carry out sabotage missions. The Palmach fit the bill perfectly. The situation was urgent, and an alliance of sorts was struck: The British agreed to allow the Palmach autonomy outside the framework of the British army, even to the extent of respecting its clandestine nature and not demanding the real names or addresses of those Palmach members participating in action; in return, the Palmach gained experience in playing a direct role in the security of the country. The most experienced of the Palmach – Companies A and B, one hundred men in all – were recruited for the operation.

One day, the kibbutz secretary at Ramat Yohanan approached Rabin and asked if he was willing to volunteer for a special unit. He agreed, and was told to await further instructions. Six weeks passed before a company commander by the name of Moshe Dayan came to the kibbutz and asked him some questions:

"Do you know how to fire a rifle?"

"Yes,"

"Have you ever thrown a hand grenade?" Dayan asked him.

"Yes", said Rabin again, wondering where this was leading.

"Do you know how to operate a machine-gun?"

This time the boy answered somewhat reluctantly, "No..."

"Can you drive?"

"No."

"Can you ride a motorcycle?"

"No."

"Alright," said Dayan, "you'll do."[17]

The Allied invasion took place in June 1941; a week before the invasion began, Palmach teams went into action, some scouting the northern border, some crossing into Syria and Lebanon. Rabin, recruited into Company B, was told to report to Kibbutz Hanita, which skirts the Lebanese border inside Palestine. By coincidence, on the day that his orders arrived, he had invited his father to Ramat Yohanan. Telling him only that he had to go off, but hoped to be back the next day, Rabin disappeared. Nehemiah waited a day or so for his son to return and then went back to Tel Aviv to await further news. Three weeks later, looking tired but happy, Yitzhak visited his father in Tel Aviv and explained where he had been.

Allon, in charge of Company A, had taken his force across the northeastern border of Palestine. Moshe Dayan had led Company B, in which Rabin was serving, along the Mediterranean coast, across the northern border near Rosh Hanikra. Rabin belonged to one of several groups within the

---

17. Ibid

company, which were to infiltrate Lebanon and destroy the telephone communications between the cities of Tyre and Sidon along the Mediterranean coast. He and two colleagues crossed the border, twenty-five kilometers (15 miles) from their starting point, at night, and then marched another ten kilometers (six miles) inside Lebanese territory to the village of Binai-elJubal. Being the youngest (he was nineteen); Rabin was chosen to climb the telephone poles, pliers in hand, and cut the lines. Before all three returned to base, under the cover of darkness and dressed as civilians, they were in danger not only from the Lebanese but also from the Allied forces that had not been notified of their arrival.

The assignment was the most dangerous that the young man had yet been given but he found the experience stimulating. "No one forced me to do it," he said, "it was on a voluntary basis. I enjoyed it. I must admit that my part was very simple in that invasion: a lot of walking, no fighting, though you had to get up a telephone pole, that wasn't easy."[18] The Lebanese raid provided the Palmach with valuable experience. The strike force learned how to set up proper commands, how to acquire much-needed intelligence, and how to use its men properly; perhaps most importantly, the experience gave the Palmach a necessary boost to its self-confidence and enhanced its reputation among those in the Hagana command, who openly wondered whether the force was really essential.

After the raid, when Rabin was reunited with his father and sister, he said little about the operation, but when, upon his return to the kibbutz, he was invited to address several hundred kibbutz members in the dining-hall, he accepted.

18. Rabin in conversation with author, August 2, 1976

Dressed in shorts, an open-necked shirt, and sandals, Rabin gave a lengthy description of the operation, demonstrating genuine ability to analyze military events precisely and lucidly. His audience was fascinated and convinced that here was someone with a bright military future. With the success of the Lebanese raids, Yitzhak Sadeh pressed the Hagana to give the Palmach its own training camps, and, reluctantly, the High Command permitted the establishment of two such bases. One was in a eucalyptus grove in Kibbutz Ginosar; the other, to which Rabin went, was in the heart of a forest near Kibbutz Beit Oren, near Haifa. Conditions were austere: The Hagana provided no tents for the men, who slept under trees on straw mats. Eventually, disturbed at the cost of maintaining separate training camps with funds so short, and now with Syria and Lebanon under Allied control, the Yishuv leadership, never very enthusiastic about the Palmach anyway, ordered them to be disbanded. The Palmachniks reluctantly obeyed orders, but continued to remain partially mobilized.

In the autumn of 1941, Allon commanded the first training course for Palmach section commanders at Kibbutz Alonim in the Western Galilee. The Lebanese raid had boosted Rabin's reputation and he was one of sixty who had been selected to train there. Almost imperceptibly, the youngster who had aimed to settle on a kibbutz and had been educated for that kind of life had become a soldier.

Early in 1942, Allied fortunes in the Middle East again worsened, and there seemed a real danger that the Germans would overrun Palestine. Once more the British turned to the Palmach, to enlist their aid in harrying action against the enemy if things went badly. This time, the British offered to finance and train three hundred members of the Palmach as saboteurs and scouts. The Palmach agreed. A full-scale course covering sabotage and demolition was organized in a camp in a forest, near Kibbutz Mishmar HaEmek in northern Palestine. There Rabin and his fellow trainees studied topography, tracking, and map reading. The battalion was now considered a tactical unit, the main principle of the Palmach training being: active defense, seizing the initiative and launching pre-emptive attacks at any hour of the day or night. However, when the British sensed victory in the Middle East early in 1943, after El Alamein, they decided to end their shaky alliance with the Palmach, disbanded the camp at Mishmar HaEmek, and confiscated the Hagana arms that had been used in the joint effort there.

Once again the Palmach – an expensive luxury for the Hagana – seemed destined for dissolution. But Yitzhak Tabenkin, a veteran leader of the kibbutz movement, saved the day by proposing that the Palmachniks become part-time farmers on the kibbutzim, earning their own living, in return for which they would be given bed, board, and cover for their secret military work. For fourteen days a month the Palmach men would work as farmers, and for the other sixteen they would be free to pursue their military activities, using the kibbutzim as bases. Since the recruits anyway came largely from the settlements, and since at the time kibbutzim could not afford to be without their workers for long – as well as the presence of young Palmach soldiers providing extra defense – both the Palmach and the kibbutzim benefited.

Some Palmachniks were hostile to the idea, embittered by implications that their services were not considered worth the Yishuv leadership's direct support. A number of them enlisted in the British army rather than join the kibbutzim but the majority, including Rabin, remained in the Palmach.

Like the rest, Rabin spent most his time on military affairs, but whenever he could he helped out, trying to involve himself as much as possible in the life of the kibbutz, the life for which he had been educated.

In 1943, he became a platoon commander at Kfar Giladi, a kibbutz founded thirty years earlier and located in the Hula Valley close to the Lebanese border. There, he was involved in directing the movement of illegal Jewish immigrants from Syria and Iraq via Kfar Giladi to safer points further south.

Although Rabin and his platoon engaged in no military encounters during this period, he took the opportunity to train his men in the modern tactics he had studied in his command course. Until then, the men had been used to fighting like partisans, moving around on foot with packs on their backs without the advantage of transport. Rabin taught them how to conduct lightning attacks using a car or a jeep, instituted night journeys over long distances, and toughened up his men by allowing them as few breaks as possible.

Training in the Palmach was all the more challenging because it had to be done without arousing the suspicions of the British, whose attitude towards the strike force was ambiguous at best and more often downright hostile. When the Kfar Giladi platoon went on a Spring march near the Dead Sea, it was in the guise of a sporting club. On the way, the food the men had brought with them turned rotten, and they had to use their wits to survive in the hot desert. During the maneuvers they launched a simulated attack on a tiny oasis, using live ammunition. As the men moved towards their target, a young soldier, excited and disoriented, lobbed a hand grenade in his commander's direction. Rabin yelled a warning to the soldier beside him as the grenade fell about a foot away from them. Fortunately the sand absorbed the explosion and they escaped without injury.

The final difficult and dangerous mission was the organization of a secret truck convoy, which had to get past the British at the southern tip of the Dead Sea in order to pick up waiting supplies. The maneuvers had been the first in which full-scale live-ammunition exercises had been carried out at platoon strength, and all those who participated remarked about the calmness under stress and the quick thinking of the 21-year-old platoon commander.

It took a certain amount of personal discipline to remain in the Palmach during the War years. The pressures on members of the strike force to join the British army were heavy. Rabin believed that the Palmach should remain independent of the British army but informally linked to it in case fighting broke out in Palestine.

Rabin kept up the spirits of his men, sometimes by doing the unexpected, sometimes by demonstrating his own loyalty to the cause. By this time he had gained a reputation as a quiet but forceful and exemplary leader; however on one occasion Rabin uncharacteristically appeared to defy standing, Hagana and Palmach orders. Members of both the Hagana and the Palmach were under strict orders not to carry weapons openly for fear that the British would stop them, exposing the underground organization. Obtaining enough weapons and ammunition was, however, a constant problem. In the autumn of 1943, Rabin's platoon was impatiently awaiting a three-inch mortar it had requested from the Hagana Command. One day, as the platoon was going through a training exercise, Rabin surprised his men by suddenly riding off on his motorcycle in the direction of a Hagana training-ground near Kibbutz Ein Hashofet, apparently to visit friends there. As he approached, he noticed a three-inch mortar very much like the one his platoon had requested. He picked it up and returned with it to his men. Impatient for the platoon to gain experience of certain kinds of weapons, Rabin perhaps overlooked the fact that he was jeopardizing the whole organization by being so overt. Members of his platoon recall that the Hagana was furious, but no one could remember Rabin being brought to account for his action. Riding back to the platoon's base, then at Kibbutz Tel Yosef, twenty-five kilometers (15.5 miles) from the training ground, Rabin was most likely thinking grimly to himself how difficult it was to train under the con, but his men were amused as well as impressed at the thought of their young commander riding a motorcycle through the streets of Afula with a live mortar inside his satchel bag.

Despite his handsome appearance, Rabin had no great reputation as a ladies' man. He led a busy life and found little time for such amusements. Then, in 1944, he met a young high school girl from Tel Aviv named Leah Schlossberg – a dark-haired fifteen-year-old, born in Koenigsberg, Germany on April 8, 1928, who had immigrated in 1933 with her parents and sister. Their first meeting occurred in an ice-cream store on Tel Aviv's Allenby Street. Eyeing her future husband, Leah thought of the description of King David: "Chestnut hair and beautiful eyes!" No words were exchanged then. They bumped into one another several more times; eventually they sought out one another. Leah asked friends who this attractive man was and she learned his name was Yitzhak Rabin. "Something about him; his appearance, his walk had captured my heart. He seemed different. Then one day we came face to face and I asked him: 'Your name is Yitzhak?' He answered: 'Yes.' 'And I'm Leah.'"[19] Members of the Palmach were already romantic figures in the eyes of high school girls, but certain aspects of Rabin's character also attracted Leah. "He had great serenity," she remembered. "He was terribly shy. He struck me immediately as being extremely intelligent, seeming to make very critical and severe judgments of people. There was a tremendous sense of dedication to what he was doing, but he loved it. There was no question about it."[20]

When she graduated from high school in 1945, Leah joined the Palmach and was stationed at Kibbutz Ein Harod, where she went through the usual military training for new recruits.

Although the Palmach was not active in military missions during the war, membership in itself was a dangerous thing. It was, after all, an underground organization the very existence of which had been tolerated by the British only in the early days of the war. Rabin had to be especially careful since, as a commander in possession of information about the size of various Palmach units, their locations, weapons, and members, he would be of great interest to the British; whose clutches he narrowly escaped.

In the late summer of 1944, he and his platoon had been training at Kibbutz Tel Yosef, living over the kibbutz cowshed. As platoon commander, Rabin had his own room which also doubled as the platoon headquarters. Next door to

---

19. Leah Rabin, *All the Time His Wife* (Kol Hazman Ishto), Idanim, 1988, p. 41

20. Leah Rabin in conversation with author, August 8, 1976

him, sharing a room, were Yehuda Tagar, Yochai Ben-Nun, and Amos Horev, his three squad commanders. One day, a Palmach commander named Yitzhak Tavori from Kibbutz Afikim, visited Rabin to talk about a course he was preparing for Rabin's platoon. As he sat on Rabin's bed, Tavori gazed at the young commander's pistol lying on the table. Then, before the stunned Rabin could prevent him, he picked it up, aimed it at his own head, and pulled the trigger. The bullet penetrated his brain, killing him instantly. Rabin called to the other officers to come quickly, and he, Tagar, and Natan Gorali, the kibbutz's liaison man with the British, began to consult about what should be done.

The problem was not just how to explain to the British police the presence of an illegal gun; if the British searched Rabin's room they were bound to find evidence of the Palmach. It was therefore agreed that they should pretend it was Tagar's room, and that Tagar would take whatever punishment the British decided upon for illegal possession of arms. The three also decided that Tagar should make the thirty-minute drive to British police headquarters and report the incident, thus giving the others time to remove all obvious traces of their activity from the room. In the event, the police did not come to the scene of the suicide for several days, and the incident passed off without serious consequences for the Palmach.

Meanwhile, Zionist leaders both in Palestine and in the Diaspora were pressing the case for Jewish statehood in the Holy Land. Rabin, a simple platoon commander, was not involved in the political struggle. He was in any case cut off from the outside world most of the time. Like most other young men of his day, he thought the idea of a Jewish State a far-off dream, not a practical goal that might be realized in the foreseeable future. "I don't believe that in the last half of the 1930s or the early part of the 1940s I thought in specific terms how we would become a Jewish independent state," he recalled. "I believe I thought in more practical terms of what could be done to advance the cause, by being stronger, by increasing the Jewish population, by founding more settlements, but I was not thinking then in political terms, how to bring about a Jewish State."[21]

In the early 1940s, when he was attached to settlements belonging to the leftist HaKibbutz HaMe'uchad movement, Rabin had certain reservations about the partition plan proposed by the Peel Commission. Gradually, he moved into the political camp of David Ben-Gurion, who felt that a Jewish state should be set up as quickly as possible. As statehood appeared increasingly imperative, it became more and more crucial for the Palmach to adopt the proper military strategy and tactics, in order to function as a national liberation army.

The Palmach prided itself on adjusting to the military situation it faced, rather than relying on conventional military wisdom, taught by specialists unfamiliar with the Middle East. Practically all the young Palmach commanders fell under the unorthodox but powerful tutelage of Yitzhak Sadeh, the leading theorist of the Palmach, who advocated the use of surprise tactics and unconventional methods.

The strongest military influence on Rabin in the 1940s was, he feels, his immediate commanders. Indeed, they were bound to be influential if only because the training camps located on remote kibbutzim were so isolated, Rabin rarely

---

21. Rabin in conversation with author, August 2, 1976

left his kibbutz; even the long marches that took him away from the region were infrequent. Thus he, like the others, heard and saw little of the outside world. Information about what was happening outside Palestine arrived slowly, if at all. The only military theorists with whom the Palmach came into contact on a regular basis were the local commanders. Later, Rabin devoured books about World War Two, but he was more interested in the various resistance movements than in the conventional armies of the European powers.

In the four years since he had become a member of the Palmach, Rabin had acquired a reputation as one of the leading thinkers of the strike force. Other commanders, even his seniors, often sought his advice or opinion. He was not only a willing and persevering soldier; he had a special understanding of the unique role of the Palmach.

If this burgeoning Jewish commando force was going to ignore most established military doctrine, it could only do so by replacing it with new theories and practice, and for that it needed men of special intelligence, men like Rabin who could work out a practical solution for everyday problems, who could take into account the major restraints imposed on the men – the relative paucity of manpower, the lack of weapons – and overcome them by capitalizing on their one advantage: familiarity with the terrain.

Rabin won the admiration of more senior commanders not so much for bravery in the field of battle – although he frequently demonstrated cool-headedness under fire – but rather for the painstaking way in which he examined military problems and for the originality of his thinking. When military theory was being fashioned not by some unseen hierarchy, but by the rank-and-file soldiers themselves, everyone had his own ideas about what methods to use. Advice came from many quarters, but Rabin, by nature quiet, shy, serious, and thorough, took the time to look at problems in depth. Before he committed himself to an idea, he examined it for flaws from every possible angle. "You knew," said one of his squad commanders at Kfar Giladi in 1943, "that you were in the presence of a man who took full responsibility for his decisions and who made decisions in the full consciousness of what he was doing."

Rabin's self-confidence stemmed from his uncanny foresight and from his own thoroughness. He particularly enjoyed military tactics, in which he excelled. His superiors, both Yitzhak Sadeh and Yigal Allon, whom he greatly respected, had drilled into him that he must avoid slavishly following the military doctrines of others. Copying their tactics meant copying their mistakes too, and this the tiny Palmach force, with the heavy constraints already imposed on it, could not afford. If any models were to be employed, the French and Yugoslav partisans would serve to show how thorough familiarity with native terrain could be exploited. Inventiveness was much more valuable than knowledge of historical precedent. Rabin understood this completely.

With the end of World War Two, the half-million Jews of the Yishuv were determined to help the Jewish refugees from Europe find a secure, permanent home in Palestine. The British, however, remained adamant in their refusal to allow immigration beyond the limited number set down in the 1939 White Paper. As the refugees crowded together in displaced persons camps throughout Europe, desperate to reach Palestine, hopes rose in the summer of 1945 that the seemingly pro-Zionist Labor Government newly come to power might open up the gates to them, but by the Summer's end, it had become painfully clear that the British Government's policy had not changed at all. The British not only refused to let Jews enter Palestine, they wanted to evict so-called illegal immigrants who had successfully reached the country. More than any other action of the British, this incensed the Yishuv leadership.

When the Hagana learned that the British planned to return a group of 203 immigrants who had entered the country on foot from Syria and were being kept in the Atlit Detention Camp eight miles south of Haifa, it set about rescuing them. It was the first major, open military confrontation between the Yishuv's military forces and the British. All previous anti-British actions, on behalf of the Hagana, had been small and carried out under cover of night; this time the attack was undertaken in broad daylight, with a far more daring objective than the hit-and-run raids of the past.

The Hagana selected the Palmach First Battalion for the task, which had responsibility for the northern region of Palestine. Commanding it was Nahum Sarig; his deputy was Rabin. In the weeks before the operation, Rabin helped to collect weapons from Palmach units from a dozen nearby kibbutzim and bring them to the staging area at Kibbutz Beit Oren, near Atlit. Some Hagana men infiltrated the detention camp under the guise of teachers. They passed the word to Jewish policemen working there to jam the rifles of the Arab policemen inside the camp, ahead of the attack on October 10, 1945.

The 250-man attacking force comprised three units: one, led by Rabin, was to break into the camp, capture the police quarters, and prevent the police from interfering with the rescue; a second, led by Sarig, was to take the refugees to trucks waiting along the main Haifa-Tel Aviv road (from there they would be driven to Kibbutz Yagur); a third, remaining outside the camp, was to set up roadblocks and to take on the British at the nearby army base if they gave any trouble.

Rabin's men met with little resistance from the policemen and managed to disarm them without a shot being fired. After thirty minutes – the time allotted for the refugees to be safely escorted from the camp – Rabin signaled his men to begin the long march to Kibbutz Yagur. Feeling that the operation had gone well, he offered his unit the choice of marching to Yagur or running two kilometers to catch the trucks heading for Yagur with the refugees. The unit elected to race for the trucks, but, as they neared the main road, they came upon a dismal sight: Suitcases, which the refugees had not been able to bring themselves to leave behind in the camp, lay strewn along the wayside, leaving a well-marked trail for any RAF spotter planes overhead to follow. Even worse, the youngsters and the weak among the refugees were slowing up the entire evacuation.

Rabin and Sarig held an urgent consultation, realizing that the present plan would have to be scrapped, for the refugees would never manage to reach the trucks before the British arrived. They decided to split up the refugees between them: Sarig would take the hundred strongest to the trucks and then on to Yagur, while Rabin would accompany the weaker ones on foot to Beit Oren, a nearer kibbutz. With luck, Rabin's group would soon be reinforced by the unit that had been keeping the British army base under surveillance.

Since the new plan required Rabin's refugees to make the tough climb up Mount Carmel, he immediately ordered his group to abandon its belongings. The ascent still proved agonizingly slow; to speed the march up, the soldiers carried the younger children. The youngster on Rabin's shoulders, unnerved by the whole experience, urinated on the commander, who, sweating from the grueling march, barely noticed. At one point, a British patrol came upon the refugees. When the Palmach force confronted it, shooting broke out and one British policeman was killed. It was the only casualty of the entire operation. Sarig and his refugees arroved safely at Kibbutz Yagur just before dawn, but having been slowed down, Rabin's group failed to reach Beit Oren before daylight. Spotting British forces near the kibbutz, Rabin told his refugees to hide in the forest. The Palmach force prepared for a battle with the British, but nothing happened.

The refugees' only hope of escaping the attention of the British was to steal into the kibbutz. Rabin placed thirty of his soldiers at the front of the group and thirty in the rear, and using an entrance unknown to the British, he led his charges into the settlement. The British failed to realize what was happening until it was too late. With the kibbutz under siege, and fearing the British might stage an attack, another deception became necessary: The Hagana organized buses from Haifa bringing no fewer than fifteen thousand Jews to Beit Oren, where they casually walked into the kibbutz and mingled with the refugees, making it impossible for the British to distinguish those who had been rescued from Atlit. Unable to cope with the situation, the British left, and the refugees were safe.

Word of the Atlit success and Rabin's role in it filtered back to Kibbutz Ein Harod, where Leah was stationed. "The next day," she recalled proudly, "the man who ran the kibbutz's defense came up to me and shook my hand. I felt so happy because they recognized that Yitzhak and I belonged together." [22] Characteristically, Rabin played down his role in the operation. "The planning and execution weren't bad," was all he would say.

Between 1945 and 1947 only 71,000 Jewish immigrants reached Palestine; immigrant ships found it increasingly impossible to break the British blockade. On May 14, 1946, the British detained 1,760 men, women, and children, including three hundred orphans, who were passengers on the Hagana ship *Max Nordau*, after it was caught nearing the Palestinian shore. The Hagana ordered the Palmach to respond in massive terms. Railways, bridges, and police stations became prime targets. Rabin's First Battalion was again active. When Sarig ordered Rabin to storm the British Police Mobile Forces station at Jenin in June 1946, the young deputy commander felt reconnaissance work inside the station was vital. He disguised himself as an electrician, and went by motorcycle to the station. There, he easily gained admittance by pretending to have come to make a routine check; once inside he moved around freely, and left as soon as he had all the information he required.

Elated at his success, Rabin drove his motorcycle at breakneck speed to Haifa where Sarig and Allon, the overall Palmach commander, awaited him. In his haste, he failed to notice the truck in front of him quickly enough, and crashed. He was thrown some distance and knocked unconscious. His next recollection was of waking up in the Rothschild Hospital in Haifa. His left leg had been broken in two places, and he was wearing a large cast. Still in possession of his soldierly instincts, he made sure that one of the Hagana operatives in the hospital transmitted the information he had obtained at

22. Leah Rabin in conversation with author, August 8, 1976

Jenin to his commanders. Command of the Jenin operation was given to someone else, but the mission was abandoned. After a brief time in hospital, Rabin went home to Tel Aviv to convalesce with his father in their flat on Hamagid Street.

On June 18, the Palmach decided to carry out a coordinated series of attacks on eleven bridges around the country in an attempt to deal a major blow to the British. In the attacks ten of the bridges were destroyed or severely damaged. The incident predictably angered the British and provoked a widespread search for Hagana and Palmach leaders. On June 29, 100,000 British soldiers and 1,500 police surrounded numerous Jewish settlements and virtually laid siege to them. Curfews were imposed on major cities with Jewish populations. Twenty-seven settlements were searched for arms and three thousand Jews were taken to detention camps at Atlit, Rafiah, and Latrun. Most Hagana leaders had been forewarned of the British plan and had gone into hiding; relatively few arms were discovered.

On 'Black Saturday', as that day became called, Rabin, his father, and a friend were arrested. They were taken to the British unit's headquarters in a school on Balfour Street, where the British informed Rabin that he and his father were on their wanted list. He and Nehemiah were conveyed to Latrun in an armored car, not the most comfortable means of transport for someone with a broken leg. There, they were fingerprinted and kept for several days, before being taken to Rafiah at the southern tip of the Gaza Strip for more permanent detention.

Life was hardly comfortable. The prisoners were crowded together into a few large huts. They were given thing stretches and blankets, but little else. Things improved when the men were distributed among some twenty huts, where they were allowed newspapers and could listen to the radio, but had few other comforts. Nehemiah's dignified conduct under this regime served as a model for his son: "Our being together in the same prison camp was a great comfort," Rabin recalled. "In everything he did and in the way he behaved he had only one purpose: to lighten my load, in case things were getting me down."[23]

Nehemiah was released after three weeks, but Rabin was detained for six months. The thought of escaping rarely crossed his mind. The Hagana and Palmach had already instructed the men that they were to avoid attempts to break out on their own and instead wait for forces from the outside to free them. Indeed, during his stay at Rafiah, Rabin received word that the Palmach might attempt a rescue. At the same time, rumors began to circulate that the British planned to move Jewish prisoners to East Africa. According to the rescue plan, which Rabin subsequently learned about, Palmach men were to attack by sea and evacuate the prisoners. "We would have had to go a few kilometers on sand," he recalled. "I was scared to death that because of my leg they wouldn't risk taking me along. I walked about all day long to make sure that my leg would not fail me." For two weeks, he carried out the most intensive kind of physiotherapy to strengthen his leg. The rescue mission was eventually abandoned, but Rabin's leg improved dramatically.

When a Jewish Agency representative Dr. Chaim Sheba tried to obtain Rabin's release, the head of British intelligence

23. Rabin, *My Father's House*, p. 55

replied, "He'll remain in detention even if he breaks both legs." The most that Sheba could do for him was to have him sent to the Gaza military hospital for treatment. The period of imprisonment gave Rabin time to think about his future, which looked bleak. "I found my leg misshapen and lifeless... I remained depressed, seeing myself as a semi-cripple for life and convinced that my leg would never again function properly.[24]

Because of his injured leg, he felt his days as a soldier had come to an end and used his spare time to study algebra, realizing it would be necessary if he were to resume his formal studies and reapply to study water engineering at the University of California. Rabin was released after a six-month long detention.

It was not easy to decide to give up the only life he had known since leaving Kadoorie six years earlier, and he could not make any decision without reference to his commanding officers. He went to see Israel Galili, then the commander of the Hagana forces, and Yigal Allon, the commander of the Palmach. The meeting proved decisive for his future: "You are free to do whatever you want," Galili told him and then went on: "The World War is over, but our war has only just started." It was a subtle but clear-cut command. Rabin weighed his options briefly and resolved to remain in the Palmach. With the battle for the Yishuv's survival imminent, he had no wish to be ten thousand miles away in California quietly engaged in studies.

---

24. Yitzhak Rabin, *The Rabin Memoirs* (English version), p.13,

CHAPTER THREE

"THE HELL WITH IT –
TURN THE RADIO OFF"

The violent activities of the Jewish resistance movement increased during the winter of 1946-47, leaving the Mandatory Government with only two alternatives: to continue the frustrating struggle against an embittered and increasingly stubborn foe, or to get out and turn the entire problem over to the United Nations. Hoping to salvage the situation at the last minute, Foreign Secretary Ernest Bevin proposed in that winter that 96,000 Jewish immigrants be permitted to enter Palestine over the next two years; that a new trusteeship under the UN be formed; that a constituent assembly would be called in four years, to prepare a constitution for an independent Palestine; and to come into force only after Jewish and Arab consent was given. But both Jews and Arabs turned the idea down. Hence, on February 18, 1947, Bevin announced that Britain would submit the Palestine problem to the UN General Assembly. He did not say whether the British Government would abide by the UN's decision, but the meaning of Bevin's action seemed clear: Britain was paving the way for its departure from Palestine.

After his release from the detention camp in the winter of 1946-47, Rabin was approached to take on a surprising new assignment. Yigal Allon, the commander of the Palmach, was considering whom to appoint as head of the strike force's Second Battalion, whose main task was to guard the water pipeline, which ran through eleven new settlements in the southern part of the country. The logical choice should have been someone experienced and senior; instead, Allon decided on Rabin, now twenty-five years old.

In his new job, Rabin joined in the endless debates about whether to use the traditional British military doctrine or the unconventional, untested homegrown methods of the Palmach. He held no brief for the British way, as he clearly demonstrated in the summer of 1947 when he gave Haim Laskov, the British-trained veteran of the Hagana and at that time a security officer for the Palestine Electric Corporation, a tour of the defenses of the Negev settlements under his command. Stopping at one of the concrete security towers ringing the settlements, Laskov berated Rabin for relying on these 'death traps', and argued that these watch towers would simply be targets for enemy armor, artillery and aircraft fire. An advocate of the Japanese bunker and slit trenches (foxholes) used regularly in the British army, Laskov noted that these were being employed only sparingly at the settlements. Rabin was convinced that the settlements would have to deal with only lightly armed Arab bands; the towers, with the advantage they offered of long-range observation, seemed preferable to foxholes. When regular Arab forces eventually did storm these settlements during the War of Independence, these turned out to be useless, and only those settlements which gave greater emphasis to slit trenches were able to defend themselves successfully.

When the United Nations finally issued their decision on November 29, 1947, Rabin felt the same bittersweet emotion that others in the Yishuv were experiencing, knowing that a fierce struggle lay ahead for the Jewish community in Palestine. At that time, he was assigned to staff headquarters in Tel Aviv, where he had the task of ensuring that the needs of the Palmach units around the country were met, often visiting commanders.in the field for on-the-spot assessments. On February 1, 1948, the Jewish Agency and the Va'ad Leumi called a general mobilization, and the Palmach called up men from the reserves. Though the fighting was intensive between December 1947 and the following spring, the war did not become truly conventional until May, when the British left and the regular forces of the neighboring Arab nations attacked the Yishuv.

In the early part of 1948, the Jews found it increasingly difficult to get supplies through to the 100,000 Jewish residents of Jerusalem (one-sixth of the Yishuv, of whom two thousand lived in the crowded Jewish Quarter of the Old City). Normally, thirty truckloads of supplies drove daily along the Tel Aviv-Jerusalem route, but the Arabs stepped up their attacks during this period. They realized the deep significance Jerusalem held for the Yishuv and believed that an Arab victory over the Jews there would inflict a deathblow to the entire Yishuv. Their attacks on the convoys carrying supplies to Jerusalem occurred for the most part in the beautiful, mountainous area between the ancient Roman fort of Castel and Sha'ar Hagai. Between these two points the road runs through a narrow, deep, wooded ravine. Arab snipers hidden high above the road were easily able to pick off drivers and vehicles without the risk of being spotted and hit by return fire. On March 24, hundreds of Arabs attacked one of the convoys. When the shooting was over, seventeen Jews were dead and fourteen armored cars destroyed. In the coming week, two more convoys bound for Jerusalem were ambushed and by the end of March efforts to send supply convoys through to the city had come to a standstill; Jerusalem was, in effect, under siege.

The Jews, however, were determined to open the road regardless of the cost. At the end of March, David Ben-Gurion ordered the Hagana command to bring up a force of fifteen hundred men to break open the way to Jerusalem. Operation Nachshon, as it was called, was a success. In early April, the Hagana captured the Arab strongpoint on Mount Castel, commanding the Tel Aviv-Jerusalem road, and opened up the route again for supplies. Meanwhile Rabin was mopping up Arab resistance in the villages near the road and making sure that no village was left intact enough to be used as a base of operations by the Arabs. Nachshon's success brought demands from Hagana units around the country that the men borrowed for that operation should now be returned to help in the battles taking place elsewhere. Responsibility for guaranteeing the safety of the road fell once again on the Palmach, which had had the same task before Nachshon.

To do the job, a new brigade was organized, the second to be formed from among the Palmach units. The Harel Brigade, as it was called, comprised two battalions; one was ordered to secure the eastern end of the road, the other, the western end. Its commander was Yitzhak Rabin.

The Hagana command had to make a difficult decision: whether to order Rabin's brigade to attack the Arabs in the villages near the road before letting the convoys through or whether to try to guard the convoys as closely as possible without undertaking separate operations against the Arabs. Common sense dictated the strategy of the separate attacks, but time was of the essence: the Jews of Jerusalem desperately needed supplies. Rabin would have preferred to attack the Arab villages first and let the convoys wait until the road was as safe as possible, but his counsel did not prevail.

Between April 15 and 20, 1948, the five days during which the Harel Brigade was guarding the Jerusalem Corridor, three major convoys arrived safely to Jerusalem and Rabin's men captured three Arab villages. Each convoy consisted of between 250 and 300 supply trucks carrying food and (secretly) arms and ammunition and extended for 16 kilometers (ten miles) as they travelled the narrow, winding road. Fortunately, the gentlemanly British officers were reluctant to search the women soldiers travelling in the vehicles, but whatever arms they found while frisking the men were confiscated. However, though the road was temporarily made safer for the convoys, the operation was carried out at considerable cost in human life, and ended before it could have a decisive effect, much to Rabin's regret.

The fighting during this brief period, as Rabin acknowledged later, was among the toughest he experienced in his whole military career. It was "the most difficult part of the War of Independence for me, a war fought by those who believed and who were far more confident than could be expected – a war with really empty hands."[25] Exhausted

---

25. Rabin in a speech in Tel Aviv, June 1, 1973

from continuous fighting, with little ammunition, the Jewish forces went into battle under the worst possible conditions. As the fighting went on and more and more of Rabin's men were killed or wounded, the survivors grew angry, despondent, bitter; they turned on each other, and they turned to Rabin for reinforcements, for some sign of hope. He could give them neither. Oddly, his pleas for more help found some in the Hagana command openly skeptical that things could be as bad as he described them. Seemingly without justification, he acquired something of a reputation. "He was not the only one to exaggerate the seriousness of a situation in order to get more equipment from the general staff and more reinforcements," Yigael Yadin, then the Hagana's chief of operations, remembered, "but he certainly succeeded in painting a situation in bleak terms."[26] Rabin's frustration was real and stemmed from his inability to muster more troops and, more importantly, from not being permitted to finish what he and his men had begun, for he had learned much to his anger, that his brigade was to be diverted from the Corridor to Jerusalem itself.

Operation Jebussi was being planned and the Harel Brigade was to join the Jerusalem-based Etzioni Brigade. He and his men were to go into the city on the next convoy. Rabin wrote much later that the decision to move the brigade was a serious mistake, for it meant that the Jerusalem Corridor, left undefended, would fall once again under Arab control.[27]

---

26. Yigael Yadin in conversation with author, June 17, 1976

27. Yitzhak Rabin, 'Harel in the Jerusalem Campaign.' Zarubavel Gilad and Matti Megged ed., Sefer Ha-Palmach, Tel Aviv: HaKibbutz HaMeuchad, 1953, p. 908.

David Shaltiel, the Hagana commander in Jerusalem, summoned the Harel Brigade to the city after a series of events had dramatically escalated the situation there. On April 13, a convoy of doctors from the Hadassah Hospital and professors from the Hebrew University had been ambushed at Sheikh Jarrah, a section in east Jerusalem. Seventy-eight Jewish doctors, nurses, students, patients, faculty members, and Haganah fighters were killed. The British had done nothing. Five days later, Arab forces had taken over the Augusta Victoria Hospital on Mount Scopus, a vital strategic point because it overlooked the city. In addition, there were increasing reports of an imminent British evacuation of strategic positions inside Jerusalem well before the May 15 deadline. Though reinforcement for the Jewish forces fighting in the city had been promised within ten days, Shaltiel felt the situation was urgent and asked the Hagana command for eight more companies at once.

Riding in Rabin's bumper-to-bumper convoy on April 20 were David Ben-Gurion and Yitzhak Sadeh, who was to command the impending Operation Jebussi. The 350-truck convoy, stretching for sixteen miles, was the largest ever to make the journey to Jerusalem. It carried loads of flour, rice, sugar, margarine, and matzo for the Passover festival. The vehicles at the head of the convoy arrived safely in Jerusalem, but thousands of Arabs hidden in the hills at Sha'ar-Hagai had planned a mile long ambush. They opened up with a barrage of gunfire, which damaged the first few vehicles to enter the ravine, and these blocked the way for those behind. Some of the drivers tried to make their way between the damaged vehicles but this only added to the confusion. The Arabs were well dug in. Efforts to dislodge them failed, but the return fire from the convoy was enough to hold them off.

Rabin realized that reinforcements were vital if the convoy was to be saved, and managed to get through the blockade to Ma'ale HaChamisha, a kibbutz not far from Jerusalem. There he organized help, which set out in the evening in armored cars and on foot, and freed the convoy. All but six of the vehicles were able to get out of the ambush; but twenty Jewish soldiers were killed. Rabin, Ben-Gurion and Sadeh arrived safely in Jerusalem. However, the Arabs were again in control of the Jerusalem road and Jerusalem was under siege once more.

Commanders like Yitzhak Sadeh were continually urging more aggressive action on the part of the Jewish forces within Jerusalem before the British left on May 15, on the assumption that Arab resistance would be weaker before the date. They were eager to battle with the Arabs, believing that well-managed offensives could turn the tide in the Jews' favor. Sadeh told Rabin that if only they could press home their attack now, "Jerusalem will be in Jewish hands forty-eight hours after the British leave." He envisaged a simple mopping-up operation, but he failed to take into account the Arabs own growing determination and eager anticipation of the British departure.

Rabin thought that for the Jewish forces to achieve the maximum impact against the Arabs, it was far better to cut off their supplies than to risk a head-on confrontation. Jewish control of the Ramallah-Jerusalem Road would eliminate Ramallah as a source of supply for the Arabs, an argument he made forcefully to David Shaltiel; but to no avail. In Shaltiel's opinion, the plight of the beleaguered Jews in the Old City demanded that attention be focused on the city itself rather than on its surroundings. Since the British were likely to be in Jerusalem until May 15 at least, Rabin felt it made better sense to concentrate on the suburbs, as the British still held the key strategic points inside the city and occupation of those was essential to the control of Jerusalem. However, Shaltiel felt that the British presence, although a nuisance, was not so great an obstacle as to warrant further delay.

Operation Jebussi's plan was to cut off the Arabs' sources of supply while Jewish forces swept over the northern and southern fringes of the city, driving out the enemy and blocking their much-needed access routes. It was partly what Rabin had been advocating, though he had wanted Jewish forces to operate outside the city rather than from within. Had Jebussi succeeded, Jewish troops would have gained some of the most strategic points of the city: in the north, Nebi Samuel (the highest of the Judean hills), the Arab quarter of Sheikh Jarrah, and the Mount of Olives (both in the eastern part of the city), while other Hagana forces took control of the Arab quarters of Katamon, the German Colony, Talpiot, and Silwan (all in the south), thus virtually encircling the city.

From its very outset, Operation Jebussi met setbacks. Nebi Samuel was the first reversal, when the Jewish troops lost the vital element of surprise. An earlier raid against nearby Beit Iksa had succeeded, but the Arabs were alerted to the fact that a bigger attack was imminent and wisely dug in at Nebi Samuel, waiting for the Jews to make their move. When the battle was over, forty Jews lay dead and the vital strategic point they had hoped to conquer was still in Arab hands.

Sadeh and Rabin could do nothing but hope for better luck in the battle for Sheikh Jarrah, where a Jewish victory would effectively sever the Arab road link between the Old City and

Ramallah. Ironically, though the attack was successful, the British proved to be the most serious problem: since Sheikh Jarrah was on their evacuation route, they insisted the Jewish forces withdraw from the section, promising not to turn it over to the Arabs after the Jews had left. Rabins men refused and the British countered with artillery and heavy tank fire. Rabin's troops were forced to depart from Sheikh Jarrah but only temporarily. The British kept their word and permitted the Jewish soldiers to reoccupy the areas as soon as they themselves had left Jerusalem.

In the battle for Katamon, which eventually fell, casualties were high and conditions were made worse by the shortage of ammunition. At times, Rabin's men had to stop fighting altogether and await the arrival of the plane flying in shells from Tel Aviv. Ten Hagana men died and another eighty were wounded in this battle, which also left eighty Arabs dead. With the fall of Katamon, Arab resistance in the southern part of Jerusalem began to crumble, but it was only a partial victory, since Jewish forces were in control of only one of the three points they needed to conquer in order to turn the tide.

Once again summoning his troops elsewhere, Rabin experienced the same frustrations he experienced in the Jerusalem campaign. Operation Maccabi was a series of attacks aimed at reopening the road to Jerusalem, which, regardless all efforts, numerous strikes, and a high number of casualties, remained in Arab hands. During this operation, however, Rabin also experienced serious difficulties in his personal relations with the men under his command, making the entire enterprise unpleasant and unhappy for the young brigade commander.

One reason for the considerable strain in relations was the unusually high number of casualties suffered by his Harel Brigade, which had embittered the troops. Harel's two battalions had lost 220 men, with another 617 wounded and 220 suffering from severe fatigue between April and June 1948. In other words, roughly half of the 1,500-man brigade could be counted a casualty of one sort or another, a statistic for which Rabin, as the brigade commander, had to take responsibility. The casualty figures were on the men's minds and Rabin was a prime target for their anger. They were used to commanders who could mix easily with them, who could show their feelings with an affectionate slap on the back or a friendly word, whereas Rabin's aloofness and serious manner placed a constraint on his relationship with his soldiers.

Rabin had many problems in particular with one battalion commander, Joseph Tabenkin, an outspoken ambitious man whose nature clashed with the subtle, cautious, and introspective Rabin. The two men argued continuously over battle tactics, and because they were in senior positions, their antagonism set the tone for relations between Rabin and the other men.

In Operation Maccabi, the main target for the Harel Brigade was Beit Mahsir, a large Arab village that had been serving as a base of operations against Jewish convoys. Tabenkin thought the timing of the attack was wrong and made his opposition known to Rabin. He felt that the brigade was not ready to tackle such an important assignment as Beit Mahsir, but Rabin was adamant in his refusal to put off the attack.

The attack began on May 12 and took three days to complete. Rabin had hoped that it would take only one day, and believed Tabenkin had deliberately slowed up the operation to give his men time to rest. In fact, according to Uzi Narkiss, who commanded the force that took the village on the third day, things went considerably easier than he had expected. He blamed fog for the delay on the first day and the men's unwillingness to fight in daylight for the delay on the second.[28]

Once Beit Mahsir had been taken, control of the road to Jerusalem was once more in Jewish hands but extended only to Sha'ar Hagai. Pushing beyond it to the southeast, the Hagana repaired the road where possible, until it maintained supremacy all the way to Kibbutz Hulda, near Latrun. As both the Harel and Givati Brigade (which joined the Harel Brigade for Operation Maccabi) had to be removed from the Jerusalem Corridor to deal with the full-scale invasion of regular Arab armies, Latrun, situated above the Tel Aviv-Jerusalem road, was left for the Arabs to take without opposition and the road to Jerusalem was again blocked.

David Ben-Gurion stood before the National Council in the small, shabby Tel Aviv Museum at 4 pm on May 14, 1948 and proclaimed the creation of the State of Israel. With Jerusalem under siege, Tel Aviv was selected as the site of the proclamation; but Jerusalem was chosen as the capital of the new State. Dr. Chaim Weizmann was chosen president and David BenGurion prime minister.

While the Jews of Tel Aviv rejoiced in the streets, waving flags, dancing, and singing, Rabin and his men were trying to recuperate from the battle over Beit Mahsir, sixty miles east of Tel Aviv. When the announcement of statehood had

---

28. Uzi Narkiss in conversation with author, October 21, 1974.

come over the radio, an exhausted soldier trying to sleep had yelled for it to be turned off. Rabin himself was so tired that he gave no thought to the significance of the broadcast: "I was so preoccupied with the battle problems that it took me hours to realize what a change had taken place. But I always remember that tired soldier who said, 'The hell with it, turn the radio off.'"[29]

At midnight, eight hours after the State was proclaimed, the British High Commissioner sailed from Haifa, and the Mandate came to an end. That same evening the regular armies of seven Arab States – Syria, Iraq, Trans-Jordan, Egypt, Saudi Arabia, the Yemen, and Lebanon – invaded Palestine, determined to crush the Jews before they had time to put the new State on a firm footing. Eleven days later on May 26, the Provisional Government of Israel approved the creation of the Israel Defense Forces (IDF), which were to be the one and only armed force of the new country.

As independence was declared, the plight of the two thousand Jews in the Old City of Jerusalem became even more desperate; except for a few Hagana soldiers and some arms that were smuggled into the quarter in trucks containing food and medical supplies during December and January 1947, the Arabs had kept practically all Jewish traffic out of the Old City, with the full knowledge of the British. The 20,000 well-armed Arabs in the city (there were altogether 65,000 Arabs living in Jerusalem) hoped that the Jews of the Old City, half-starved and cut off from the Jews in the New City, would simply leave; but the Hagana could not surrender such precious territory without a fight. The option

29. ABC News documentary, April 15, 1975

of a hasty evacuation was rejected and the decision made to defend the Quarter.

Arab attacks after May 14 against the Jews both inside and outside the Old City were stepped up. David Shaltiel decided to mount an operation on May 18 to break through the gates of the Old City and reach the besieged Jewish Quarter. He asked Rabin if he was prepared to send his troops in to help with the rescue. The question posed a serious dilemma for Rabin, since he had not been instructed to take part in the Old City attack by the general headquarters of the Hagana. Rabin sent his operations officer, Etiel Amichai, to talk to Shaltiel and after some discussion it was agreed to call Rabin into the deliberations.

According to Shaltiel's plan, Harel units under Rabin would try to enter the Jewish Quarter through the Zion Gate, the closest to the Jewish Quarter, and provide a diversion to draw the Arabs away from the Jaffa Gate, where units of the Etzioni Brigade would try to break through. Rabin agreed to the plan, but with great reluctance.[30] For one thing, he could not understand why the main attack had to come at the Jaffa Gate, when the Zion Gate was much closer to the Jewish Quarter. For another, he was surprised to find that Shaltiel planned to use troops in the Jaffa Gate attack who were much less experienced than his own. He suggested instead that they combine their forces for one major assault on the Rockefeller Museum, at the northwest corner of the Old City outside the wall. The museum overlooked the only access road to the Old City, and whoever controlled the building could effectively keep enemy reinforcements from reaching the Old City. Shaltiel was not persuaded and the two men

---

30. Rabin in conversation with author, August 31, 1976

exchanged harsh words before Rabin agreed to participate in the attack.

In the event, an administrative breakdown caused the Etzioni Brigade units to arrive late for their planned attack on the Jaffa Gate, and the soldiers alighted from armored cars in full view of the Arabs, who successfully held them off. Ironically, the Jaffa Gate attack served to distract the Arabs from Rabin's forces, who, meeting little resistance, captured Mount Zion outside the Zion Gate. The next night, May 19, they broke through the Zion Gate, bringing the besieged Jews much-needed supplies and ammunition. But their small force could not possibly hold out against the Arabs in a daylight attack, so they were forced to retreat towards Mount Zion under cover of darkness. Yigael Yadin asserted that the plan failed to secure the approval of the Hagana command "and that created chaos."[31] About ten days later, plans were laid for another attack through the Zion Gate in the south and the New Gate in the north; by then the Jews of the Old City were nearly starving and desperately low on ammunition. However, on the morning of the planned attack, on May 28, representatives of the Jews in the Old City began discussing surrender terms with the Arabs. Among the bewildered soldiers watching from Mount Zion four hundred yards away, as the Jews walked to Arab headquarters carrying a white flag, was Rabin. As part of the surrender terms, 290 Jews between the ages of four and 70 were taken prisoner and another 1200 were allowed to pass through the lines to the New City.

The failure of the Jews to relieve the Old City in May 1948 left a legacy of bitterness, especially among those

---

31. Yigael Yadin in conversation with author, June 17, 1976

who felt that the troops under Rabin should have stayed on and fought during the May 19 attack, instead of retreating. Some even criticized Rabin personally, but he justified the withdrawal on the grounds that if the force had remained, it would not have been able to succeed.[32]

The crucial part of the war occurred between May 15 and June 10 as Arab gains brought about mounting Jewish anxiety about their very survival. While the Jews searched about desperately for money and arms, the Arabs made the most of their advantage: The Egyptians brought their troops within twelve kilometers (7.4 miles) of Rehovot; the Jordanians gained control of the Arab towns of Ramla and Lydda (today Lod, where Israel's only international airport was situated); Syria had put a bridgehead across the Jordan River in the Upper Galilee; the Jewish Quarter in Jerusalem's Old City had fallen; and Israeli attempts to capture the key towns of Latrun and Jenin had been staved off. Heavy casualties, shortages of arms, and a dwindling supply of manpower placed the Jews in a precarious position.

However, the factors that eventually proved decisive were the Hagana being generally better trained and more highly motivated than the Arabs; many of the Arab attacks against Jewish settlements were repulsed and Jewish forces liberated both the Upper and Lower Galilee, including the port of Haifa. By early June, the war was at a stalemate, paving the way for a one-month cease-fire, which took effect on June 10.

On June 22, Rabin had come to headquarters for a meeting, but arrived early in order to visit Leah, who was working

---

32. Yitzhak Rabin in conversation with author, August 31, 1976

there. As he approached the building, he saw the *Altalena* ship and two landing crafts nearing the shore. Following Ben-Gurion's ban on separate armed groups within, the new state, the right-wing organization the Irgun had agreed on June 1 to dissolve itself. But on June 11, its ship *Altalena* set sail from southern France with a cargo of 5,000 rifles, 250 light machine guns, a number of anti-tank weapons, and some nine hundred men aboard. The Provisional Government of Israel ordered the Irgun to surrender the ship and its arms, fearing it would use the arms to stage a coup against Ben-Gurion's new government. If it did not surrender, the ship would be taken by force.

On June 21, the *Altalena* reached the shore of Kfar Vitkin, unloading some weapons and most of the men. Refusing to cave in, the ship anchored off and headed south to Tel Aviv, where units of the Tel Aviv Brigade had begun to deploy themselves along the beaches. As the ship approached, the soldiers decided to disperse, abandoning their weapons and creating a total breakdown of order. Allon, the Palmach's commander, was summoned by Hagana headquarters to take command of the situation but was there only for a short time leaving Rabin, who had known nothing of the background to the *Altalena* affair, effectively in charge.

Rabin had only forty men under his command, most of whom had been wounded at the front and were convalescing at headquarters, acting as military policemen in the meantime. Rabin began to organize them for battle, unthinkable though it was that they should take up arms against fellow Jews. Many of the former Irgun men, now enlisted in the Defense Forces, left their units as the *Altalena* again refused to surrender. The Irgunists and Rabin's men exchanged fire, both sides using machine guns, hand grenades, and rifles.

Rabin picked up the phone and spoke to Moshe Kelman, the commander of the third Palmach battalion, telling him to bring his unit to headquarters immediately. The fighting lasted ten hours. Eventually, the ship was set on fire by a field gun from the shore, the passengers and crew helped to safety by Rabin's units. Fourteen Irgunists died in the battle; Rabin lost one of his men and several were wounded. The army took control of the boat and the day after, Rabin began to prepare a Palmach unit nicknamed the Desert Beasts for a raid on the Irgun headquarters on King George Street in Tel Aviv.

On September 20, 1948 the government gave the Irgunists twenty-four hours to agree to obey all the laws of the infant state: to have all its members liable for enlistment serve in the Israel Defense Forces, not in separate units. The Irgun surrendered its arms and complied.

The *Altalena* affair had been the most serious test the new state had had to confront, but Rabin never had any doubt about the correctness of the government's action in taking up arms against fellow Jews. To him, the principle of statehood was at stake, and the Irgun was challenging that principle. The *Altalena* had been a threat to the legal government and that could not be tolerated.[33]

In July 1948, Tabenkin replaced Rabin as commander of the Harel Brigade. Yigal Allon made Rabin his operations officer for Operation Dani, an offensive that lasted from July 9 to 19, 1948, aimed at capturing territory east of Tel Aviv and relieving the Jewish population in Jerusalem. With the advent of Operation Dani, Rabin took on the first of a series

---

33. Ibid

of planning posts, which would occupy him for the rest of the war. The Arabs were too close to Tel Aviv, necessitating an operation against Ramla and Lydda. Successful as the operation was, in the process, Rabin had a close scrape with death. He and Allon had decided to move their command headquarters to a more advanced position so they would have a better idea of how the fighting was progressing. Allon was behind the wheel of an open Ford convertible, and had decided to take a short cut through a field, as the car approached the front line just south of Ramla. Suddenly, the car was jolted by the explosion of a land mine underneath the front wheels and the two men were thrown out. The mine ripped through the car, completely destroying the vehicle, but neither man was badly hurt. Rabin received a minor foot injury.

Rabin had never actually proposed marriage to Leah, but neither doubted that they would marry each other.[34] The ceremony took place on August 23, 1948 at Beit Shalom (House of Peace) in Tel Aviv, and was obviously an ordeal for the 26-year-old officer. He had been shy about his relationship with Leah up to the very day of the wedding; he told Allon and others whom he invited that the wedding was to start thirty minutes later than was actually the case, in the hope that the ceremony would be over by the time they got there. However, the rabbi was thirty minutes late, so Rabin's subterfuge failed and all the guests had arrived by the time the ceremony began. Yitzhak appeared in uniform as did his comrades in arms. After the wedding the newly-weds moved into Leah's parents' flat on Rothschild Boulevard in Tel Aviv,

---

34. Rabin in conversation with author, August 31, 1976

their home for the next two and a half years. It was a choice dictated both by concern for Leah's ageing parents and by the Rabin's lack of finances.

Rabin had no time to get used to his new marital state. The war was far from over, and within a day of the ceremony Yeroham Cohen, then an intelligence officer for the newly created Southern Command, was pounding on his door. Allon was waiting for Rabin to join them at the nearby Workers Restaurant, where he asked Rabin to serve as deputy commander of the Southern Front in the role of chief operations officer. The second cease-fire, which began on July 21, 1948, was still in effect. Planning for Southern Front operations was to begin right away, since everyone expected the war to resume in the autumn. During that summer, the IDF created military ranks, and Rabin, upon his appointment to the Southern Front, became a lieutenant-colonel, the third highest rank in the new army.

The cease-fire along the Southern Front remained intact until the autumn, but it slowly gave way to renewed fighting between Israeli and Egyptian forces. On October 6, the Israeli high command ordered an all-out attack on the Negev in an attempt to drive the Egyptians out once and for all. It began nine days later and lasted a week. By October 22 Operation Ten Plagues (better known as Operation Yoav[35]), resulted in the Israeli forces opening the main road to the Negev and capturing Beersheba, as well as the coastal strip between Ashdod and Kibbutz Yad Mordechai. But although the Egyptian army had been pushed further south, away from the populated areas of the new Jewish State, they remained in the Negev, inside Israeli territory.

---

35. The editor

Ten Plagues ended in a formal truce between the Israeli and Egyptian troops, however fighting persisted as both sides sought to improve their positions. Egyptian soldiers at the Fallujah crossroads, southeast of the Mediterranean port of Ashdod, refused to surrender to the Israelis in early November, despite being surrounded and short of food. Only after the Egyptian high command had acknowledged that it could offer no reinforcements did Egypt surrender. Though Allon conducted the negotiations, Rabin had a chance to talk to a young Egyptian liaison officer named Gamel Abdul Nasser. Nasser asked whether the insignia Allon and his men were wearing – a sword between two ears of corn – was that of the Palmach. When told it was, Nasser smiled ruefully and said, "That being so, everything is clear to me." He was intensely interested to know how the Israelis had managed to force the British to leave. Rabin explained what military measures were used, and Nasser smiled appreciatively. "You know," he said with a wry grin, "we are fighting the wrong enemy at the wrong place at the wrong time. Our main enemy is the British, and our main problem is how to gain real independence. We should be fighting the colonial power rather than you."[36]

In November, after much bitter argument, Palmach headquarters was finally disbanded. Oddly enough, a separate Palmach command under Yigal Allon had existed even after the formation of the Israel Defense Forces in May 1948. The three Palmach brigades had been placed under the control of the IDF's general headquarters in the spring of that year, but they still maintained their distinctive character. The

---

36. Yeroham Cohen in conversation with author, October 7, 1974

Palmach command had only administrative responsibilities, however, since the general headquarters directed strategy and tactics were at the discretion of the local brigade and front commanders. It hence became increasingly inefficient for this independent Palmach structure to continue.

As the dissolution of the Palmach was being implemented, the Israeli forces in the south prepared themselves for more fighting. The Egyptian army was still not broken and remained unwilling to negotiate an armistice with the Jewish State. The Israeli goal was to control the entire Negev, but the main Egyptian forces were entrenched in two spots there: along the Mediterranean coast between Rafiah and Gaza and, further inland, between the villages of El Auja and Bir Asluj (south of Beersheba). Throughout December, the IDF tried to drive the Egyptians from these places in Operation Horev.

In early December, the Israeli command decided to concentrate its attack on Auja, since the Egyptians there presented a greater threat to the central Negev than they did along the coastal strip. The only road that was feasible was an ancient Roman one but it seemed unlikely that it could transport heavy trucks and tanks. While others debated whether to risk taking the road, Allon sent Rabin, who believed it would be possible to use the route if some repairs were made to it. He was right, and for that decision he won widespread praise. Ten days later, on December 27, Israeli forces captured Auja and were thus positioned for a further advance into the Sinai and an attack on the rest of the Egyptian army.

Acting without orders from the high command in Tel Aviv, Israeli forces under Allon and Rabin thrust further south on December 27 into the region of Abu Ageila and El Arish, part of Egyptian territory inside the Sinai, increasing the fear of the outside powers – particularly the US and Britain – that Israel intended to remain in the Sinai. But Allon and Rabin felt the Israelis would be missing a golden opportunity to inflict serious damage to the Egyptian forces and, in the process, to force them to talk about making peace with the Jewish State on a serious basis.

On December 29, Abu Ageila fell to the Israelis. That morning, exhilarated at their success, Rabin, Allon and Cohen drove into the village, established a headquarters' tent, and began planning an attack on El Arish, further south along the Mediterranean coast. By midday, they were in a convoy on its way to El Arish, but three miles outside the Arab town the Israelis received orders from Yadin, the IDF's chief of operations in Tel Aviv, to halt the drive.

Allon sent for a Piper Cub in order to fly immediately to Tel Aviv to protest personally to Ben-Gurion. He ordered Nahum Sarig, the commander of the Negev Brigade who was about to lead the drive into El Arish, to march on the town the next morning unless he had heard to the contrary. Rabin and Cohen drove to Beersheba to wait in the Southern Front communications van for word from Allon, who finally phoned at 2 am. He had bad news: The brigade was to go no further. Rabin was furious. He was sure that an Israeli victory was imminent. Gloomily, he and Cohen drove through the night until they reached Abu Ageila, where they passed word to Sarig to make no further approach toward El Arish.

During the next week, Allon struggled to convince Ben-Gurion that Israeli forces should finish the task of defeating the Egyptians at El Arish. The Prime Minister resisted all pleas. He himself had come under strong pressure from Britain and the US to withdraw Israeli troops from Egyptian soil. Furthermore, he feared that Israeli military activity in the Sinai would interfere with international efforts to bring the Arabs and Israelis together at a peace conference. He dismissed Allon's and Rabin's contention that leaving the Egyptians in full strength and unchallenged so close to the centers of population in Israel might trigger another war in the near future.

Armistice negotiations between Israel and Egypt began on January 13, 1949 at the Hotel of Roses on the Island of Rhodes. Rabin attended the talks as a member of the Israeli delegation, representing the Southern Front. The senior Hagana commanders had wanted Allon to go, but he refused, still angry that the military campaign against Egypt had ended so abruptly. He would have liked Israel to take the Gaza Strip, the southern half of the Negev, and the Hebron Mountains before negotiations got underway. The country would then have been in better position to keep the Egyptians at bay and to make another assault on Jerusalem, this time from the rear. However, Ben-Gurion would not entertain such thoughts. Allon could have sent any of three men working under him: Rabin, Amos Horev, or Zarubavel Arbel, chief of intelligence for the Southern Front. He was not eager to send Arbel since he wanted him to work on Operation Uvda (the campaign to capture Eilat, the northern port on the Gulf of Aqaba, and the southern Negev from the Jordanians). Rabin too, wanted to stay and participate in the Negev campaign and he suggested that Horev go in his place, but Ya'acov Dori, the chief of staff of the IDF, insisted that if Allon wasn't going, then Rabin must: As operations officer he was the most knowledgeable about force deployments and terrain. Allon persuaded Rabin that it was indeed important for him to attend. "See to it," he told Rabin, "that no agreement is reached which is less than peace. And don't agree to anything which gives us less than Gaza."[37]

Rabin had a personal reason for not wanting to participate in the talks. He was unsure how to tie a necktie, as were many other Israelis who normally shunned them in the warm climate of the Middle East, and at Rhodes he would have to wear a tie to all meetings! However, before he left, Yeroham Cohen made up a tie and loosened it sufficiently so it could be slipped over the head. But that was not the end of the story. When the Israelis and Egyptians were about to sit down for a negotiating session one day in the hotel, Rabin was missing. As he was the representative of the Southern Front, the others felt they could not begin without him. Yigael Yadin, the leader of the delegation, found him in his room looking most dejected. It transpired that a valet had spotted the made-up tie and decided it needed ironing. Without reference to Rabin, he had taken it away, pressed it, and returned it unmade. Rabin was at a loss, and had decided to miss the session. Yadin tied it for him and the two men moved downstairs to carry on with the business of making peace.[38]

Rabin's presence at the talks was particularly helpful to Yadin, who felt relieved that an officer from the Southern Front was on hand to give advice and support. The two men developed a good relationship that was cemented partly by the secret planning they were engaged in for the forthcoming Operation Uvda. Rabin, reflecting the generally gloomy mood in the Southern Command, felt ambivalent about the

---

37. Yigal Allon in conversation with author, May 18, 1976

38. Yigael Yadin in conversation with author, June 17, 1976

negotiations. He participated in them, offered advice to the best of his ability, but wondered like Allon did, why the talks were taking place before the Israelis had thoroughly beaten the Egyptians on the battlefield.

When he was not involved in the talks, he took part in some of the sports provided in the hotel. He learned how to play billiards and mastered the game well enough to beat most of his challengers. He played table tennis, too usually, partnered with Yadin. The game room at the hotel could be said to have played a crucial part in the negotiations for it was there that Israeli and Egyptian officers mingled during the recesses, and though at first both sides were cool, friendlier relations did develop. Rabin learned as much about the real aims and aspirations of the enemy in that room as he did at the negotiating table. What he found out both pleased and disturbed him. He was glad to hear the Egyptians say that peace was inevitable and that the Rhodes talks were an important part of the process of achieving it; but less pleasing was the Egyptian view that it might not be possible to attain true peace as quickly as the Israelis had hoped, that it might even take years. Rabin remembered: "Their mood was optimistic, even euphoric, but not for the immediate future. They said: 'It is impossible now to make peace, but once we establish a relationship, etc. etc., then we hope that it will be possible.'" Rabin deduced that the Egyptians meant they could not make peace until certain military objectives had been achieved, for the Egyptian people would not accept peace on those terms.

Though hopeful about the prospects for peace, Rabin was also realistic. He knew there was still work to be done on the battlefield and he disliked the direction the Rhodes talks were taking. On February 10, two weeks before the agreement was finally signed, he wrote to Allon that he felt that the Israelis were giving too much away at the peace table. Except for Yadin and Rabin, the other members of the Israeli delegation were prepared to accept, more or less, Egyptian demands, which Rabin thought would erode many of the gains made on the Southern Front. "In my opinion," Rabin wrote to his commander, "any concession now is too early. We have had a long breathing space and we can endure a war of nerves better than the Egyptians."

The Egyptians were demanding that Israeli forces vacate the Gaza Strip fringes and make the entire Negev a neutral zone, and that they withdraw from Beersheba, the key town in the southern Negev. Yadin returned to Israel for consultations, carrying Rabin's letter to Allon with him. Rabin was confident that Yadin would not return to Rhodes unless he got a clear decision on standing firm with the Egyptians. "Except for the two of us," Rabin wrote to Allon, referring to Yadin and himself, "all the members of the delegation are ready for additional compromises... simply to achieve an agreement with the Egyptians. It is possible that, after coming here as a senior member of the military delegation, I will be forced to put my signature to something I cannot agree to." He asked Allon to consider replacing him with Horev or Arbel: "I have had enough of diplomacy and politics."

Arriving in Israel, Yadin bore the news that Rabin could not be a party to the agreement under present circumstances. He asked Allon not to try to persuade him to sign the agreement; Allon retorted that if he were Rabin, he would not sign the document either. The front commander answered Rabin's letter, sending his reply back with Yadin the next day, February 15. "Naturally," he wrote, "the talks are not only influenced by the military situation. The political element is the determining factor... Our mood here is not optimistic. I'm afraid that the blow we inflicted on the Egyptians has not been exploited sufficiently in the negotiations, and it seems to me that the enemy is growing stronger... I know that it is not in your power to greatly influence the decision. But my situation is thus... The atmosphere is poisoned and they [Ben-Gurion and Moshe Sharett, the foreign minister] can't bear advice contrary to their views, which, of course, are slanted by political connections and quite a bit of outside pressure." Allon added that he would try to make his feelings known to Ben-Gurion, although he saw no hope of persuading the prime minister to share his own and Rabin's view of the negotiations at Rhodes.

"I understand your fear that at the end you will be forced to sign a document of compromise, but Yadin has promised me that it will not be so. Nevertheless, if the decision is taken out of our hands, you will act of course, according to your conscience. My suggestion about sending Zarubavel [Arbel] or Amos [Horev] in your place has been refused, so carry on trying to influence the talks... I hope that we shall see each other soon... Shalom from all the friends who are simply longing for your return and are cheered in the meantime by the story that's going the rounds about you and your tie."

Rabin was furious at what the Israelis were about to sign. "Why should Egypt get a slice of Palestine?" he asked Walter Eytan, one of the delegation's leaders, a few hours before the signatures were about to be affixed to the document. Eytan told him: "An armistice with Egypt is worth the Gaza area. And besides, this is only a temporary military armistice. When we have full-scale peace talks, then we can press for better boundaries." Rabin was not convinced. He felt that by leaving Egypt in control of the Gaza Strip and Jordan in control of the Hebron Mountain region south of Jerusalem, the likelihood of another round of war was greatly increased. He consulted Allon, who could offer him no comfort: "We have to obey orders, but since the absence of your signature is not going to reduce the legality of the document, if you have finished your job and have drawn the best possible map, you might as well come home."[39]

On the night before the signing, the Israelis and Egyptians celebrated with a festive banquet, which Rabin attended, though he did not intend to sign the next day. Both sides were in good humor. At one point, colonel Rahmani, an Egyptian officer, asked why the Israelis had not struck harder in Gaza during Operation Horev. Rabin explained that the Gaza thrust was simply an Israeli feint to distract the Egyptians from the real assault farther inland. "You should have attacked Gaza," Rahmani told him, "it would have caused us quite a setback."

That same night, Rabin flew home on a UN plane. He carried with him an unusual item: a carton of butter. It was a present for Leah's mother who missed this precious commodity more than anything else during Israel's wartime austerity. Allon congratulated him on his work in Rhodes and on his integrity in refusing to sign the armistice accord. "This agreement," he told Rabin, "will not bring peace. If Egypt really wanted peace, they would have negotiated for it immediately without this armistice. The cease-fire will eventually bring a new war with Egypt." Rabin agreed.

The armistice agreement was signed on February 24, 1949 and with it came the hope that the Arab-Israeli conflict

---

39. Yigal Allon in conversation with author, May 18, 1976

might be on its way to a peaceful resolution. But, since nobody believed that it would happen quickly, each side had tried to get the most out of the peace talks. Israel, for its part, had fought off Egyptian efforts to force an Israeli withdrawal from the entire southern Negev. Egypt managed to retain its hold over the Gaza Strip. It was agreed that the Jewish State would keep Beersheba, but that everything west of a line running between that city and Eilat would be an area of restricted military movement for the Israelis, and everything to the east of the line would be an area of restricted military movement for the Egyptians. In effect, this gave Israel the freedom of the operation it desired to act against the Jordanians, without violating the armistice accord with Egypt. Plans for Operation Uvda were already underway and the Israelis, in pressing the Egyptians to agree to this territorial division, knew exactly how they intended to deploy their troops in the Negev region. On March 6, 1949 the Israelis began the operation against the Jordanians, and six days later raised the Israeli flag over Eilat, 155 miles south of Beersheba, the final phase of the War of Independence. As part of the operation, the southern Negev had been conquered and the western shores of the Dead Sea, Ein Gedi, Masada, and the Judean wilderness secured.

CHAPTER FOUR

CHIEF OF STAFF

The tiny Jewish state had achieved its independence in a bloody, 17 month-long war that had claimed 6000 Jewish lives, slightly more than one per cent of the entire Yishuv population. Soldiers, exhausted from the long battle, thankfully donned civilian clothes again, wondering how long it would take to make the new State of Israel truly secure. Most accepted the painful reality that it would be a long time. After all, hostile neighbors who, despite defeat, were still not ready to live in peace with the Jews bordered Israel to the North, East, and South. Even after Egypt (in February 1949), Lebanon (in March 1949), Jordan (in April 1949), and Syria (in July 1949) had signed armistice agreements with Israel, they remained bent on its destruction, using every kind of intimidation short of all-out war: An economic blockade was imposed; diplomatic and trade relations were withheld; transit to and from Israel through the Suez Canal and Arab countries was forbidden; and a campaign of terrorism began.

With the War of Independence over, the Israelis turned to the task of gathering in all those Jews who wanted to immigrate. By virtue of a law passed in the Knesset in July 1950 known as the Law of Return, every Jew automatically had the right to immigrate to Israel and become an Israeli citizen. With that, Jewish immigrants poured into the new country. In 1949 alone, nearly 250,000 came and by the end of 1951, Israel's population had increased to 1.5 million, more than double the figure at the time of the War of Independence.

The end of the war had marked a major turning point in Rabin's life. Had he wished, he might have entered civilian life and tried to acquire the university degree in water engineering that he had hoped for at the close of his high-school days. But by temperament he had become a military man, fired by the need to provide security for the new nation. The wretched fighting conditions he had experienced, particularly during the battles for the Jerusalem road in 1948, had left him determined to do what he could to make sure Jewish soldiers were better equipped to fight the next war, if there should be one. "I had sworn," he said, "that if I lived to see the end of the war and continued in military life, I would do everything in my power to see to it that we should never fight under such conditions again."[40]

At 27 years old, with his whole life in front of him, continuing in the Israel Defense Forces was no easy matter for a veteran of the Palmach like Rabin. Although disbanded in November 1948, the organization officers retained a strong sense of allegiance to it. Ben-Gurion, who could not

40. Raphael Bashan, *Maariv*, June 13, 1967, Rabin is quoted in the article

tolerate this seemingly misplaced loyalty, embarked upon a campaign to root them out of senior army positions. Yigal Allon, for example, the commander of the Southern Front, discovered while abroad that he had been relieved of his post. Proud of the Palmach's record, Rabin found his loyalty divided. He agreed with Ben-Gurion that it was right and necessary to disband the Palmach, but strong ties of friendship and brotherhood bound him to his wartime colleagues in the strike force. It pained him that Ben-Gurion had shunted the Palmach aside, when without it a real catastrophe would probably have befallen the Jews. "We won the War of Independence," Rabin remarked sorrowfully of those days, "but we lost it within the army."[41]

In June 1949, Rabin was appointed commander of the Negev Brigade. In the autumn of that year, he was faced with the most serious test of his loyalty in the clash between the IDF and the Palmach. The Palmach had called its third national conference for October 14 at the Tel Aviv Exhibition Stadium. IDF officers who were Palmach veterans were placed in an awkward position, since Ben-Gurion had issued orders banning uniformed officers from attending. Rabin, now the most senior-ranking Palmach veteran still in uniform, was in a dilemma. He did not want to disappoint his Palmach colleagues by not appearing, but there had been rumors that the prime minister would dismiss any officer who did attend, and Rabin did not want to jeopardize his career. Realizing that it was particularly important to keep Rabin, as the most senior officer, away, Ben-Gurion devised

---

41. Yitzhak Rabin in conversation with author, August 31, 1976

a plan that would give him an excuse not to attend the conference. The prime minister asked Rabin to meet him on the evening of the conference, in order to go over some military matter. Rabin could scarcely refuse, or at least so Ben-Gurion thought. The two men began talking at 4:30 pm in the prime minister's home in Tel Aviv. The conference was due to start four hours later. Among the subjects they discussed was the conference: Rabin told the prime minister that he was wrong to put the men of the Palmach in such a dilemma. Ben-Gurion replied simply that there was no room in the army for separate organizations. But the question of Rabin's own attendance at the conference did not arise. At 7 pm, Ben-Gurion suggested that they break for a meal and continue talking afterwards. Looking at his watch, Rabin replied that he had to go somewhere. He quickly made his excuses, and left. The prime minister made no comment but he must have known where Rabin was going. Dashing home to change out of uniform into a white shirt, Rabin, still out of breath, told Leah about his meeting with the prime minister, and then ran off to the reunion, arriving late.

This act of defiance on Rabin's part might be construed as courageous or foolish, but it certainly demonstrated his integrity and the strength of his convictions. "I saw in Ben-Gurion's order," he said later, "a demand to dissociate myself from my friends, with whom I had fought and passed through the seven circles of hell, both before and during the war."[42]

As it turned out, the premier did not dismiss for attending the conference, but two days later he was

---

42. Interview with Yitzhak Rabin, *Yediot Aharonot*, February 1, 1974

reprimanded for breach of discipline. Though he escaped punishment at the time, Rabin was to pay for it with the delaying of his promotion to chief of staff. Rabin did not gain that top post until January 1, 1964, fifteen years after the incident. Some believed he might have been given the appointment as early as 1953, after Mordechai Maklef and before Moshe Dayan, had he not defied Ben-Gurion that evening. In late 1952, Maklef had wanted to appoint Rabin deputy chief of staff, but Ben-Gurion vetoed the idea, citing the conference incident. Also in 1960, the incident was still very much in Ben-Gurion's mind. Shortly after he appointed Zvi Zur as chief of staff, he summoned Rabin, then deputy chief of staff, and told him that part of the reason he had been passed over for the top post was his disobeying of orders in 1949.

Yet, five years later in 1965, a more relenting Ben-Gurion brushed the entire episode off as trivial. "Do you remember objecting that I had put you into a dilemma by asking you not to attend that conference after the war?" the former premier asked Rabin when they met at an occasion in Tel Aviv. Slightly embarrassed that the subject had been raised, Rabin was silent. "And then I said: 'If that is the way you feel, you must go,'" Ben-Gurion added with a twinkle in his eye. Now Rabin felt constrained to reply: "I am glad that's the way you remember it. But if what you say is correct, why was I reprimanded?" Ben-Gurion replied tersely, "That was all wrong."[43]

Though he did not lose his job over the affair, Rabin was still not clear about what kind of future he would have in

---

43. Leah Rabin, who was present on both occasions, recounted to the author the exchanges between Rabin and Ben-Gurion in 1960 and 1965.

the army. The post of commander of the Negev Brigade kept him active, but the post scarcely satisfied his instincts for leadership. In the autumn of 1949, the brigade was demobilized, effectively leaving Rabin with nothing to do. He learned that Haim Laskov, the veteran British-trained Hagana officer, had begun to organize a battalion commanders' course and expressed interest in joining it as a course instructor. Laskov had been given the job of retraining and reorganizing the IDF after the war, a task that required great ingenuity and resourcefulness, as the army was little more than a mélange of military philosophies and styles. It lacked organization and structure and it was beset by conflicts, between those who had been trained by the British and those who had served in the Palmach. What was needed was a meeting place to sort out the differences and impose some kind of unifying system. Laskov was delighted to recruit Rabin, but only on condition that the young man was not politically active; he did not want to find that he was subverting the training course by giving undue emphasis to Palmach doctrines. Urging Rabin to improve his understanding of English so that he could read the manuals, Laskov accepted him as an instructor. At about the same time that he began working on the course, Rabin was promoted to colonel, a rank the IDF introduced in early 1950.

Three one-month courses were arranged at the outset, with a gap of about one month in between, to give Laskov and his staff time to review and change the course material. Laskov had recruited, among others, six men from the Palmach (including Rabin), three former British army officers, and an air force man. Rabin joined the group as the second course was getting underway.

It was indeed a testing ground for ideas and opinions on terminology, tactics and strategy, staff procedures, operational planning techniques, and standing operational orders for war. Now that the pressure of war was over, officers could formulate the knowledge they had acquired, learn from each other's experience, and perfect or discard techniques. Rabin, whose reputation as an able military planner was now established, took over as head of the course when Laskov left.

The Rabins' first child had been born on March 19, 1950, a daughter named Dalia. In the autumn of 1952, the Rabin family moved out of Leah's father's apartment in Tel Aviv to the nearby suburb of Tzahala, a favorite area for army officers. It was to be their home for the next 20 years off and on. The house, three-and-a-half rooms in size and simply furnished, marked the first time that Yitzhak and Leah had their own home. All the men in the neighborhood wore uniform; in front of each house was a car with military license plates. Life slowly became normal. They made friends with whom they spent evenings playing scrabble, Rabin even found time for jobs around the house and gardening. Five years later, on June 18, 1955, his son Yuval was born.

The IDF's failure to cope with Arab infiltration, together with the self-evident truth that the army simply could not afford to rest on its laurels, were strong incentives to continue the painstaking job of organizing the army efficiently. Rabin's job was to prepare contingency plans for every possible military situation. As far as he was concerned, the Israelis had to meet aggression with aggression in every instance, and this entailed careful planning and checking of every detail in every operation. During visits to units stationed near the frontier, Rabin would constantly be asking all kinds of operational questions, testing the men's readiness for battle, basing his interrogation on his own detailed knowledge of both sides of the border. He believed a steadfast policy in this matter to be vital, and determined that the soldiers under his command should be adequately prepared for battle.

In early 1956, Rabin was appointed Commander of the Northern Front. So that he would be closer to his work, (command headquarters were in Nazareth) the Rabins moved to Haifa[44] In 1957, Aharon Doron was serving under him as commander of the Golani Brigade and recalled Rabin being "mainly interested in the operational side of whatever we were doing. It's not that he neglected logistics, but he didn't want to be involved in such matters. For instance, he wouldn't inspect units for dust or untidiness. He loathed having to bother with the question of whether a soldier's rifle was clean or not. He believed that was someone else's job, not his."[45]

Oded Messer had also learned this lesson on his very first day as Rabin's deputy in the autumn of 1957, when the Northern Command had planned a small operation to destroy a building along its northern flank near the border. Rabin asked Messer to check on the planning of the operation. When he reported back that everything had been duly checked, Rabin asked him who from northern headquarters was overseeing the operation when it took place. Messer replied that because it was small, a brigade commander would be present; surely there was no need for anyone from headquarters to be there. Rabin told him: "You never know. Such small operations, in

---

44. Slater, Robert. *Rabin of Israel: Warrior of Peace.* New York: Harper Collins, 1996, p. 108

45. Aharon Doron in conversation with author, May 2, 1976

the general atmosphere of our relations with the Syrians, can very easily develop into a big incident. So my principle in the Northern Command is to have someone on the spot that is able to take the fullest responsibility. Even if the operation is so small that a platoon commander could easily lead it, I insist that either myself, or you, or the chief operations officer be present."

His zeal was demonstrated on several occasions. One day in September 1957, Messer had taken a group of fifteen men on a reconnaissance mission along the Syrian frontier. A Syrian force had taken control of a key hill in the area near Tel Azaziat, high up in the eastern Galilee, and when Messer's party approached the spot, shooting began. It was 9 am. Withdrawal became the wisest course after several of the Israelis had been wounded, but they had difficulty in disengaging because of their advanced position. Against their small arms the Syrians had mortars and other heavier weapons. Fortunately, because of what Messer jokingly called Rabin's pedantry, the force had radio liaison with the command's headquarters in Nazareth. When Rabin heard that several men had been wounded, he rushed to the scene. Though it was clear that the men had to extricate themselves as soon as possible, they also had to impress upon the Syrians that they were not going to yield an inch without putting up a good fight. Rabin promised the men tanks, and instead of an immediate retreat, the men hung on grimly until the armored vehicles arrived two hours later. While the tanks went into action, the wounded were taken to safety. Although the Syrians held onto the hill, the Israelis made their point: now the enemy understood that they could not attack with impunity. The size of the territory was of no consequence, it was the principle of not yielding that mattered.

At the end of 1957, changes were about to be made in the army's high command and Rabin was obviously a candidate for one of the important posts. Moshe Dayan called in Rabin, Meir Amit, and Zvi Zur, all senior officers, and told them that he was going to relinquish the post of chief of staff and that he had recommended to Ben-Gurion that Amit take over the position, with Zur as his deputy. In addition, he had proposed to the premier that both he (Dayan) and Rabin should go on study courses on behalf of the army. The strategy was not lost on Rabin, who bitterly resented being bypassed again for the chief of staff post. He agreed to the study course, but asked that it be abroad. Dayan refused the request; he himself was going to study at the Hebrew University in Jerusalem and he thought Rabin should go there, too. Rabin refused to go on a course at all. In the end, Ben-Gurion chose Haim Laskov as Dayan's successor as chief of staff, Zur became Laskov's deputy, Amit became head of the Central Command, and Rabin remained commander of the Northern Front.

During the summer of 1958, the Rabins left Haifa and returned to their home in Tzahala. Leah started teaching English, a move that did not please her husband, who argued that her investment of time and effort was not worth the small compensation. Leah stood her ground, continuing to work for two years before admitting to Yitzhak that he had been right. Remaining at home after that, Leah felt pleased that she could offer their children the kind of home that Yitzhak had missed because of Rosa Cohen's prolonged absences from home. "I felt," she wrote, "though he never said it, that it was important for Yitzhak to know that I was home with the children and that enabled him to throw himself body and soul into whatever he was doing... I sensed that if anything compensated for his own childhood, and for the immense effort invested in what he did, it was the security of knowing that I was at home on a full-time job."[46]

In early 1959, after three years as commander of the Northern Front, Rabin concluded that he was going no further in the army; that his chances of becoming chief of staff were slender and that he might as well consider returning to civilian life. Instead of picking up his earlier ambition, to become a water engineer, he considered business administration. He had been administering a major organization, the IDF, for years now. The skills he had acquired would surely stand him in good stead in the business world. He approached Laskov with a request to study at the Harvard School of Business in Boston, Massachusetts. Laskov agreed, and Rabin promptly applied for a two-year course. He was to leave for the United States in the summer of 1959 and begin his studies that autumn, but his plans were overtaken by events.

In April 1959, a decoy and mobilization practice of reservists was arranged, and as usual in exercises of this nature, code names were broadcasted over the radio, signaling men to go to their bases immediately. Unfortunately, the public had not been warned that the mobilization was only a practice run and a great many thought the call-up was real and that Israel was about to go to war again. In the wake of this error, a shake-up in the top command occurred. Chaim Herzog replaced Yehoshaphat Harkabi, the director of military intelligence. Meir Zorea, director of the general branch, left and Rabin became a prime beneficiary of the changes that occurred. Taking over from Zorea, at the age of

---

46. Leah Rabin, *All the Time His Wife*, p. 101

37, he had finally joined the inner circle of the top command, and from that moment on was considered a likely candidate for the post of chief of staff. Even Ben-Gurion could do little to stop his progress now. Appointing Zvi Zur chief of staff, the prime minister knew that Rabin would be troubled at being passed over, so he summoned the disgruntled Rabin and offered comfort: "You will be the next chief of staff." Though Rabin may have thought the promise somewhat empty, Ben-Gurion repeated it to him several times over the next few years.

One decision, however, which Rabin was able to influence, involved the planning of the new Knesset (Israeli Parliament) on the Givat Ram ridge in Jerusalem. The building, located two kilometers (1.2 miles) from the border, was originally designed with its entrance facing towards the Mar Elias Monastery in the Judean hills to Jerusalem's east. Since the Jordanians had gun emplacements near Mar Elias, Rabin advised that the entrance to the Knesset be situated elsewhere, to ensure that people arriving there could not be cut down by gunfire.

Rabin commanded the respect of those around him, even when there were differences of opinion. "Some say he is unable to make decisions," said Oded Messer, his senior assistant in those days, "but I don't believe this is so. If by decision-making ability they mean the ability to make quick decisions, they are right. He is perhaps slow to make a decision, but when he decides, the decision is based on sound judgment. He sticks to the decision, and uses every means to carry it out."[47] Ruhama Hermon, Rabin's long-time secretary, had vivid memories of army officers making sure

---

47. Oded Messer in conversation with author, May 19, 1976

they had done their homework before meetings with Rabin: "Generals used to tell me that when you came to a meeting with Rabin, you had to know the subject inside out, because he always asked you about it, and he always knew better than you did."[48]

In late 1960, Rabin was again visiting the United States, a country for which he felt a long-standing and deep affection. He was impressed with the American army, its sophisticated weaponry, its size, its obvious preparedness. He was struck by the American atomic deterrent, a weapon, he said, which small countries like Israel should be familiar with, "because every atomic explosion can affect them, even though at first glance these countries seem to be on the fringe of events."[49] Though he admired the electronic gadgetry and equipment at the US Army's disposal, it was the concept of deterrence which intrigued him most. "Just like us," he told *Maariv* on December 9, 1960, "the Americans base their defense on deterrence, that is to say, the ability to wipe out the other side if it tries to destroy you; the ability to destroy combined with the reluctance to go to war." He was also impressed by the general political acceptance of the need to maintain the army's preparedness and to provide the necessities for its organization. Rabin thought that adoption of deterrence might solve some of Israel's military problems. In a speech in December 1962, he said that it was "necessary to use the weapon of deterrence to maintain a normal way of life on the border, in addition to it being vital for the security of Israel's existence. The IDF should try to avoid clashes with the

---

48. Ruhama Hermon in conversation with author, June 24, 1976

49. *Maariv*, January 24, 1961

Syrians as much as possible," he advised, "and adopt a policy of deterrence, which would give the nation the necessary security without the costly involvement of fighting. It is preferable to demonstrate a readiness to use strength," he told his listeners, "rather than to deal the blow."[50]

In October and November 1963, accompanied by Aharon Yariv, deputy director of military intelligence, Rabin visited the US and France. In the United States, he and Yariv put forward the Israeli case for acquiring more tanks. They visited Fort Bliss in Texas, where Israeli units were learning how to use Hawk anti-aircraft missiles, which Rabin found most impressive. In France, Rabin inspected the French 'wonder tank', the AMX 30, in which Israeli defense experts had shown much interest. Rabin thought the French AMX 30 tank very good, but very expensive. Astounding the French by asking to ride in the tank as is it went through its paces, one French general commented that Rabin was so well versed in armor, it seemed as though he must have begun his career as a tank commander.

On December 5, 1963, the government authorized the appointment of Rabin as the seventh chief of staff of the Israel Defense Forces. His appointment to this position, shortly after Ben-Gurion's resignation as prime minister the previous June, seemed hardly a coincidence. Levi Eshkol, who replaced Ben-Gurion as prime minister as well as becoming defense minister, did not have the same suspicious attitude towards the Palmach as the 'Old Man' (David Ben-Gurion's moniker[51]) did. However, there were suggestions

---

50. Rabin's remarks during a speech at a Soldier's House in Netanya are quoted in *Maariv*, December 18, 1962

51. The editor

that the ageing prime minister had given his blessing to the appointment before leaving office.

Rabin's supporters were pleased that someone with strength and wisdom was to replace the retiring chief of staff, Zvi Zur, whom they considered weak and uninspiring. Rabin, now forty-one, radiated confidence, and others responded to this quality in him. He was described in *The Jerusalem Post* on December 16, 1963 as: "Soft-spoken... with a hint of freckles, a quiet but authoritative voice and unhurried movements, all conveying the impression of a man at peace with himself. He is capable of a most un-general-like grin, especially when non-military subjects like hobbies are discussed." In his first Order of the Day on January 1, 1964, he said: "Let us continue to secure the sovereignty of the State in its entirety, to set up the conditions that will enable development to take place, and to build up a fighting force that will deter every enemy."

Now that he had at last attained the position for which he had been training, in effect, for most of his life, it was clear that he would carry out no revolutionary changes in the structure and style of the IDF. He was too conservative by nature for that, and he was too much a part of the military establishment to consider altering the very system that had brought him to this position. He had few anxieties about the task before him. Naturally there were uncertainties about the Arabs, who had been making some bellicose noises of late, reviving fears that they might be preparing for a third round of war. But everything seemed to point to the contrary: Israel's borders had never been so quiet. Gunfire had not been heard along the Egyptian front since 1956, which was remarkable given the level of violence there before the Sinai Campaign. There were always skirmishes along the northern border, but no one seriously thought Syria would take such a drastic step as war. Egypt was always potentially the main threat, if only because it was the most powerful of the Arab nations. As Rabin prepared to take up office, fifty thousand Egyptian soldiers were involved in a war of several years standing in the tiny country of Yemen, thousands of miles away. Nevertheless, the increased flow of arms into Egypt during the early 1960s was an uncomfortable reminder that President Nasser was capable of unleashing a very effective war machine against the Israelis, even though he was already fighting a war in Yemen.

While some were optimistically predicting in the mid-1960s that Egypt posed no real threat to Israel, Rabin took a more realistic and cautious view, warning in an interview in *Yediot Aharonot* on April 15, 1964 that the "principal danger to Israel lies in Egypt's determination to create and obtain weapons that will enable them to hurt us." He was worried by the complacent resignation shown by some of his countrymen, who in their darkest moments became convinced that time was inevitably on the side of the Arabs. He railed against such gloomy thoughts, insisting that Israel could prevail, if only it took the proper measures. Syria had not signed the armistice agreement of 1949 with the intention of coming to peace terms with Israel. But this did not mean they were ready to launch a major war against the Jewish State, at least, not without the support of the Egyptians, though they could make themselves a nuisance to the Israelis. That was precisely what they tried to do during this period. Unsure of their ability to defeat Israel on the battlefield, some Arab states, especially Syria, looked around for other ways to strike. Israel's heavy reliance on water resources seemed a weakness worth exploiting.

In 1964, the Israelis were completing the National Water Carrier, Israel's largest water project, for carrying water from the Jordan River in the north to the arid regions of the south. The Arabs gathered in Cairo from January 13 to 16, 1964 for the first of what became periodic summit conferences. They resolved to allocate 6.25 million pounds sterling to diverting the sources of the Jordan River in Syrian territory, which would thus disrupt the Carrier project. They also decided to establish a unified Arab command. The Israelis made it clear that any attempt by the Arabs to divert the Jordan's sources would be considered an act of war by the Jewish State, thus forcing the Syrians to turn to Egypt for support. But President Nasser would not be a party to the diversion plan, calculating that Egypt was not ready to take Israel on in an all-out war. Syria, nevertheless, went ahead with attempts to sabotage the Carrier, and put additional pressure on Israel by clandestinely supporting terrorist activity on a major scale. The IDF was in a quandary over these attacks: opposed on both moral and practical grounds to a policy of reprisal raids that would result in the killing of Arab civilians, it still knew that it could not tolerate such attacks.

Between 1964 and 1966, the strategic problems facing Israel were sufficiently limited and allowed Rabin to conduct a methodical campaign to build up the armed forces for a battle that seemed, at best, far off. The Syrians' bark, for the moment, appeared more ferocious than their bite. This was due in part to Rabin's cautious but ultimately successful policy of repulsing Syrian attempts to harm Israel, not only with cross frontier tank battles, but also with the Air Force: On November 13, 1964, Rabin ordered an air strike in retaliation for a Syrian raid on two border kibbutzim – Dan and Dafna. It was the first time that Israel's Air Force had been ordered into action in peacetime. Rabin's policy was helped by the fact that the Syrians never seemed to have a government in control long enough to consolidate military action. Throughout 1966, the Syrian problem worsened. Between February and July, there were ninety-three border incidents involving the laying of mines, shootings, and acts of sabotage. Rabin would often visit the Syrian frontier. Not every visit, however, was as eventful or dangerous for him as the one in August 1966 near Lake Kinneret (Sea of Galilee), when, following an Israeli reprisal raid against the Syrians, he toured the frontier where the raid had occurred. Joining him were Ezer Weizman, the new chief of operations, and David Elazar, head of the Northern Command. The three men donned swimming trunks in order to conceal their ranks from the Syrians, who were no doubt watching their movements from the Syrian side of the border. Suddenly, the Syrians spotted an Israeli naval patrol boat that had run aground on the eastern side of the lake, its 10-man crew still aboard. Though technically the boat was in Israeli territory, the Syrians were within shooting distance. The three senior Israeli officers decided to board the boat to try to help refloat it. There were armed Syrians only fifty yards away, but for some inexplicable reason, they held their fire. Eventually, another naval boat towed the grounded one to safety, though not before the Syrians had photographed Rabin and the other two generals trying to free the boat. Israeli forces, after they overran the Golan Heights in 1967, discovered the photographs in Kuneitra. Unaware of the identities of the men in the photo, the Syrians had kept the pictures.

Rabin felt that the Syrian government posed far more of a threat to Israel than the Palestinian guerrillas whom it sponsored. In his efforts to warn the Syrians against further provocations, he got into some minor trouble with his own government. In an interview published on September 11, 1966 in *Bamahane*, the IDF weekly, Rabin said he believed that Israel should react to Syrian acts of aggression by taking steps directly against the perpetrators "and against the regime which supports those acts." A week later, prime minister Eshkol, slightly embarrassed by Rabin's bluntness, told the Cabinet that while Israel would hold Syria responsible for the sabotage incidents across its borders, Rabin's statement in *Bamahane* had been misinterpreted. Israel, he explained, pursued a policy of noninterference in the internal affairs of other governments. He was satisfied that Rabin had not intended to convey any other idea; however, the Cabinet Security Committee decided to reprimand the chief of staff. Rabin took the news calmly: "I deserved it," he said tersely.

In March 1966, Rabin made a good-will trip to the Far East, where he visited six countries during three weeks. The trip gave him a glimpse of a part of the world that he did not know. He visited the Philippines, South Korea, Burma, Thailand, Cambodia, and Japan, where he was fascinated to find a strong sense of tradition despite the technological advancements of a highly industrialized nation. He gave some lectures to military colleges and in his spare time took photographs. What intrigued him most was the way the small Asian countries he visited were forced to adjust to the might of China, a country that would inevitably, Rabin felt, swallow up the rest of Asia. "It will take time," he told those travelling with him, "but this is China's natural living area."

Rabin's relationship with Eshkol was subtle and complex. The two men did their best to appear in harmony at all times, but in private they often clashed. Yet Eshkol relied on Rabin to be his chief adviser on military affairs, and Rabin reciprocated with total loyalty. Originally, Eshkol had wanted his relationship with Rabin to be on a very formal footing, and had asked him to put every order to his soldiers in writing, against his signature, presumably so that Eshkol could have a record of them and pass judgment on them. Rabin eventually persuaded the prime minister that such formality was highly impractical. He found Eshkol's ways difficult in other respects, too. For instance, Eshkol insisted on meeting members of the general staff privately, without the chief of staff's presence. At first Rabin objected strongly, but in the end he yielded to the prime minister on this point, though it remained a bone of contention between the two men.

However, these differences were overshadowed by their unanimity on the vital question of security. Eshkol came to rely totally on Rabin's judgment in the matter of reprisal raids against terrorists. Rabin, in Eshkol's view, had almost infallible judgment. Even the fiasco of the Samoa raid was quickly forgiven and Eshkol defended Rabin publicly. This incident occurred on November 13, 1966. Israeli soldiers in half-tracks and light tanks carried out a reprisal raid against the village of Samoa inside Jordan, which was sheltering Palestinian guerrillas who had been operating on Jordanian territory. The Israelis did their best to avoid inflicting civilian or Jordanian Army casualties, in order not to bring international censure upon themselves. The object was to demolish only those houses used by guerrillas and nothing else. The buildings were cleared before being destroyed, and the operation would have gone off smoothly, but for the unexpected arrival of a Jordanian infantry battalion. The

Israelis fired warning shots, but to no avail; some fifteen Jordanians were killed before the battalion retreated. Rabin became the target of strong criticism within the Cabinet. "I had no way of knowing," he told the ministers, "that the Jordanians would be foolish enough to try and shoot at such a strong opposing force." Rabin was prepared to offer his resignation over the affair, and, as one official who saw him appear before the Cabinet put it, "He came with tears in his eyes." But Eshkol stood by him and he weathered the storm.

Completing his third year in the post, at the end of 1966, Rabin had some important achievements to his credit. He had strengthened both the infantry and the armored corps, improved the managerial systems of the IDF, streamlined the administration, and introduced new techniques, including the use of computers. He had reorganized the support services of Ordnance and Logistics as well, determined to make sure that the errors of the 1956 Sinai Campaign did not recur. In addition, he had established a new Israeli strategy for dealing with the Syrians, and it appeared to be working.

By the early 1960s, it had become customary for Israeli chiefs of staff to serve that long and no more, though the prime minister could, if he chose, ask the army chief to stay on indefinitely. Eshkol could have asked Rabin to step down after three years of service as chief of staff, but in view of the uncertain situation prevailing along the northern frontier, and pleased with Rabin's record, the premier asked him to continue in the post.

On December 25, 1966 the Cabinet confirmed Eshkol's request to extend Rabin's service for another year. The public response was friendly. Newspaper editorials praised him, with *Maariv* calling him "a commander of stable thought, much action and many accomplishments." *The Jerusalem Post*, echoing this, proclaimed Rabin "a cool and determined leader." Rabin himself, as usual, said little about the job. "Difficult," he told one newspaper interviewer, "but interesting." That was all.

CHAPTER FIVE

IF THERE IS WAR, WE WILL WIN

From February 1966, when another coup had brought to power a new government in Syria, the Syrians had been using terrorism against Israel as much to lure the Egyptians into the contest as to harry the Jewish State. Until May 1967, Egyptian president Gamal Abdel Nasser had been able to refuse the Syrian bait, insisting that he would not become involved in a war with Israel "for the sake of one Syrian tractor."

On the eve of the Six-Day War of June 1967, the public mood in Israel was one of self-confidence, a feeling which Rabin as chief of staff encouraged at every turn. "In the eventuality of war," he said simply on March 24, 1967, "the Israel Defense Forces will win." It was a statement he made often, and he firmly believed it. The terrorist incursions, especially from Syria, indeed required the army's constant vigilance, but they did not affect the strategic dominance Israel enjoyed and would continue to enjoy. However terrorism was escalating and could become an uncontrollable problem if it was not dealt with firmly. There was a danger that the Syrians might mistake Israeli constraint for weakness, and another major cause for concern was the growing power of the Arab war machine, built-up over the past few years by vast amounts of arms from the Russians. In mid-May Rabin warned of this.

On the United Nations-patrolled Israel-Egyptian border, however, there had been no trouble for the past decade. Because of this, Israel had pared its defenses down to a few armored brigades, which were training near the southern frontier, but were not permanently stationed there. "As long as there is no political cooperation among the Arab countries," Rabin said in an interview in *Yediot Aharonot* on May 14, 1967, "one need not expect any military cooperation against Israel." Only on the northern frontier, where Israel and Syria were playing a tit-for-tat war of nerves, were there skirmishes. The most serious incident erupted on April 7, 1967, when the Israelis shot down six Syrian planes. The Syrians had already been warned about aiding terrorists in their forays across the border, and when Syrian warplanes appeared in the skies on that April day, the Israelis struck, determined to teach them a lesson. "Today," Rabin said with typical understatement, "they discovered they had made a small error."[52] The destruction of the planes put new pressure on Egypt to join Syria in a renewed all-out war against Israel; the Soviet press was quick to claim that the Israeli air attack heralded the invasion they had been forecasting for months.

---

52. Quoted in Robert J. Donovan (and the staff of the *Los Angeles Times*), *Six Days in June: Israel's Fight for Survival*, New York and Toronto: New American Library, also a Signet Book, 1967, pp. 48-49

Syrian inability to challenge Israel alone, together with Egyptian unwillingness for another round of war, made the Israelis over-confident. Reflecting this mood, Rabin travelled to London early in May for a four-day private visit. Though he engaged in fund-raising activities for Israel, for the most part, he avoided making arrangements to meet British Government leaders. His personal mood was relaxed enough for him to go to see a play. He had no special worries about the near future. But it was the calm before the storm.

Conventional Israeli opinion places the blame for the Six-Day War squarely on the shoulders of President Nasser. But in darker moments, Israelis have wondered whether they may have contributed to the tensions of that period, and thereby helped to bring about the war themselves, in some indirect way. Unpleasant and uncomfortable broodings, they must nevertheless be taken into account, especially since, as Rabin himself pointed out, the Egyptians gained the impression between May 10 and 15 that Israel was planning a major attack against Syria. One event, linked with Rabin at least in the public's mind, has often been cited as the main Israeli contribution to the deterioration in the Middle East at that time. On May 12, a senior Israeli military officer held a background briefing for newsmen, during which he gave the distinct impression that Israel was planning a major military move against Syria, ostensibly to crush the terrorists, but with the ultimate aim of overturning the Syrian regime. It was widely believed at the time that the briefing officer was Rabin himself, a view that has subsequently been discredited.[53] However, the chief of staff himself hinted in an interview in *Lamerhav* in May 1967, that Israel might

---

53. Dr. Benjamin Geist, "The Six-Day War". Jerusalem: doctoral dissertation, Hebrew University, October 1974.

take military steps beyond the kind normally used against terrorists. Syria might be the target, he warned, because its government had supported the terrorists. Whether or not Rabin was the briefing officer on May 12, the briefing itself apparently spurred Nasser into taking action against Israel; indeed, he claimed later, that it was the main factor that led to his decision to move troops into the Sinai three days afterwards.

Rabin had been invited to spend the evening of May 14, the eve of Israel's nineteenth Independence Day, quietly with some friends at the home of Venezuelan industrialist Miles Sherover in Jerusalem. Uzi Narkiss, Rabin's colleague from the Palmach days, and now commander of the Central Front, which included Jerusalem, was there. So were Yigael Yadin, Rabin's former commander from the 1948 war, and Rabin's boyhood companion Mordechai 'Moka' Limon, the commander of the navy during 1951-1954 and now, the Ministry of Defense's representative in Paris. Rabin was light-heartedly recounting stories of his earlier wartime experiences when the telephone rang. It was colonel Rafi Efrat, his adjutant. The message he relayed to Rabin was from Aharon 'Arale' Yariv, the director of military intelligence: The Egyptian army had been ordered into a state of alert, scheduled for the next afternoon. Rabin took the news calmly. "Very interesting," he told Efrat in his deep voice, showing no unusual sign of concern, "we're going to have to keep our eyes open." The prime minister of course had to be briefed on the news, but there seemed as yet no cause for alarm. Returning to the gathering, Rabin rejoined the conversation without mentioning his telephone call.

A military parade had been planned in Jerusalem for the morning of May 15, as part of the Independence Day celebrations, but it had been decided to keep it low-key: Only infantry units were to take part, there were to be no armored vehicles or aircraft. The last thing the Israelis wanted was to provoke the Jordanians, who since 1948 had continued to control the eastern half of the city. The 1949 armistice agreement with Jordan had defined the kind of arms that could be kept in Jerusalem and the Israelis had no intention of breaking the pact. The Israeli leaders began to assemble in the lobby of the King David Hotel at 9 am. Some 18,000 Israelis had gathered at the Hebrew University stadium, a ten-minute drive away. Another 200,000 people were crowding the parade route. By 9:30 am, prime minister Eshkol, Rabin, and their party were due to leave for the parade in a convoy of three cars. When Eshkol arrived, Rabin took him aside and gave him the latest news about the Egyptian state of alert. The two agreed to meet after the parade, by which time Rabin knew that the Egyptians had begun moving troops, totaling more than two divisions into eastern Sinai. The troops were taking up positions in the center of the Sinai, but, curiously, were not being deployed near the permanent, reinforced Egyptian division stationed along the length of the Israeli border. It was decided to declare a state of alert and send reinforcements to the undermanned southern frontier. The general staff was surprised at the Egyptian move but no one felt undue alarm. No one believed that Egypt intended to take on the Israelis in a full-scale war, when 500,000 Egyptian soldiers committed to the struggle in Yemen.

At 5:30 pm, Rabin was back in his office in Tel Aviv, where he heard a brief report and then telephoned General Israel Tal. Thirty minutes later, Tal arrived at Rabin's home in Tzahala. "The Egyptians," Rabin informed him, "have entered the Sinai with a force of 500 tanks." There was no knowing whether the Egyptians intended war, whether it was simply a ploy to extricate themselves from Yemen, or a move to impress the Syrians. Whatever the reason, the IDF had to be prepared; Tal was to put all regular units of the armored corps on alert, but not to mobilize the reserves yet. Within a few hours, over a hundred Israeli tanks were deployed against the Egyptian forces arrayed on the other side of the frontier.

Forgoing a special Independence Day reception given by the mayor of Jerusalem, Teddy Kollek, Eshkol called together Rabin, foreign minister Abba Eban, and Ya'acov Herzog, the director-general of the prime minister's office. Rabin informed them that the army was reinforcing its Negev positions with an armored brigade, as the Sinai borders were virtually bare, and that the general staff feeling was that the reserves need not be called up for the time being, because Egypt was unlikely to start hostilities.

On May 16, Rabin went ahead with a tour of army units, to which he had invited all the former chiefs of staff. "The Egyptians are continuing to concentrate troops in the Sinai," he told them. "Usually, they keep about one division and 250 tanks in that area, but they've supplemented them with another hundred [and another 150 were on the way]. There's no doubt that it's a show of strength, but what will they do next? "[54] Dayan predicted that Egypt would demand the withdrawal of the UN forces from the Sinai and, inevitably getting its way, would then be in a position to seal off the Straits of Tiran at the foot of the Red Sea, the easiest place

54. Quoted in: Michael Bar-Zohar, *Embassies in Crisis*, Englewood Cliffs, New Jersey: Prentice Hall Inc., 1970, p. 29

to blockade Israeli shipping. Rabin, on the other hand, could not accept that the situation would deteriorate so rapidly or so dangerously.[55] However, it did.

Nasser found the presence of the 3,400-man UN Emergency Force in the Sinai uncomfortable, while he was engaging in a show of strength. He demanded the evacuation of the force, but only from the Sinai not from either the Gaza Strip or Sharm El-Sheikh. Even so, the situation was worsening. Rabin suggested to Eshkol that Nasser had been carried away in an excess of megalomania, while Arab propaganda had incited the masses to believe that Israel, in spite of the outcome of the Sinai Campaign, could be defeated. Rabin assured the prime minister that all precautions were being taken; a reserve brigade of tank crews had been mobilized the night before and others would soon be called up. But he was still reluctant to believe that Egypt meant war. "It's a war of nerves," he told the Knesset Security and Foreign Affairs Committee, while acknowledging that his main concern was that Nasser would now try to block the Straits of Tiran. Everything seemed to point that way. The one small ray of hope lay in the fact that Nasser had not demanded that all the UN troops leave. Perhaps he was merely bluffing after all. No one could be sure what Nasser had in mind.

Addressing newspaper editors on May 18, Eshkol and Rabin asked them to stress the falsity of reports that Israel had concentrated its troops along the Syrian frontier, and was preparing for an attack. The least they could hope to do was remove any suspicion in Nasser's mind that Israel was on the brink of launching an attack against Syria. Rabin expressed foreboding about the UN withdrawal. "What are

---

55. Ibid, pp. 27-29

you worried about that for?" asked Hannah Zemer, reporting for the morning newspaper *Davar*. "Let the UN get out of Gaza. It hardly matters." Choosing his words carefully, Rabin replied: "I don't think the UN force will leave Gaza without abandoning Sharm El-Sheikh. Neither do I think that Nasser will take Sharm El-Sheikh without closing the Straits."[56]

The UN secretary-general U Thant responded far too hastily, some thought, to Nasser's demand, by threatening to withdraw the entire UN force, confident that the Egyptians would back down from this ultimatum in order to avoid war. Since Nasser's original demand did not specify whether all or only part of the UN force should leave, or for how long, U Thant came in for some severe criticism for his quick capitulation. Some even suggested that Nasser was only bluffing, but with U Thant's unexpected compliance, he could not lose face by backing off. He insisted that all UN troops must leave, including those in Gaza and Sharm El-Sheikh, and by May 19 the UN force had been removed entirely.

By then there were 70,000 Egyptian soldiers and 600 tanks in the Sinai. Egyptian units had moved into Sharm El-Sheikh. Even more ominously, some of the Egyptian troops fighting in Yemen had been transferred to the Sinai. In order to reassure the nation that things were normal, the Israeli leaders tried to put on a show of confidence; Rabin went to Lod Airport near Tel Aviv twice within a few hours, first to see off the Liberian chief of staff and then Israeli president Zalman Shazar, who was off to Canada. Meanwhile, Eshkol,

---

56. Ibid, p. 46

feeling that Israel was not doing enough to prepare for possible battle, ordered Rabin to mobilize the reserves.

By May 20, Rabin and his staff had refined their strategy in case of war. This time, unlike in 1956, when the aims of the Sinai Campaign were more limited, the objective would be the destruction of the Egyptian army. This necessitated the prior destruction of the Egyptian air force, Rabin thought, and meant that Israeli tanks had to conquer the forward and central parts of the Sinai. Once this was accomplished, Sharm El Sheikh would fall without any special difficulties. Although the 48 American Skyhawks and 50 French Mirages that had been ordered for the air force had not yet arrived – indeed the Skyhawks only reached Israel after the war and the Mirages never came because of the French arms embargo – the Air Force under Ezer Weizman's direction had nevertheless developed into a dynamic force. Its 197 combat aircraft included 72 Mirages, 20 Super Mysteres, 40 Ouragons, 40 subsonic Mysteres, and 25 Vautour light bombers. The next few days were unquestionably among the most difficult in Rabin's life. Like many others, he had been caught off-guard by the swift and dramatic developments since May 15, unwilling to believe that war would come. He certainly believed that Israel had no reason to attack Egypt unless strongly provoked and up until May 23, that had not happened. After the war, in an interview on Israel Radio on June 24, Rabin said that "he could not think of a more serious mistake than to take military action before the other side makes an act of war." The closing of the Straits of Tiran would constitute such a *casus belli*, in his opinion, but until then, the consensus was that Israel should keep its powder dry. To his surprise and dismay, he soon found that virtually everyone in high office had developed the habit of deferring to him, including the prime minister (who was also the defense minister). He became, in effect, the final authority, the key decision maker, a position normally held by the premier. It was unfamiliar territory, and he felt that decisions involving peace and war were too important to be made by only one person. He yearned to share the burden, but subtly, irrevocably, he had been chosen by the others to render the final opinion. The experience wore him out and took its inevitable toll. "For me," he said later in one of the rare instances when he talked about this period, "it was hell."[57]

He was caught in the middle of contradictory pressures. While some were insisting that the nation should take all necessary measures to protect itself against the Egyptian threat, including a daring, pre-emptive strike, others were expressing fears that Israel, by mobilizing, was simply provoking Egypt into a war that no one, including Nasser, really wanted. Above all, he was beset by doubts and anxieties about letting the nation down, about using his skills too little or too late. If war came, Rabin would take it as a sign that he had personally failed somehow, and so he drove himself to explore every avenue in order to prevent this outcome. "He was forever haunted by the feeling that he hadn't done enough," his wife Leah recalled.[58] He was one of only a handful of men who knew the facts, among others: that most of the ground-to-air missiles ordered from the United States had not yet been installed and that of Israel's four submarines, only one was actually available for immediate service. He was only too conscious of how sparse

57. Rabin in conversation with author, August 31, 1976

58. Leah Rabin in conversation with author, August 8, 1976

Israel's defenses were in the Sinai and was preoccupied with thoughts of the damage the Egyptian army could inflict on the Israelis, should they open fire soon after May 15. The burden lay heavily on his shoulders. "I was put in a position where the government was saying: 'What do you want us to do? You have to tell us.' And when I told them what we had to do, they asked what was going to be the price, and I said it was going to be heavy, that it wasn't going to be a picnic, it was going to be a war."[59]

Despite the number of leaders who met, conferred, argued, and gave advice, Rabin realized that the final decision on whether Israel should go to war was his. "I had the feeling, rightly or wrongly, that I had to carry everything on my own. I felt that I had been chosen to be the one who carried the burden, but that I had no right to make the decision, and I was torn between these two feelings."[60]

The personal hell Rabin was going through was evident to his close associates. "Suddenly," his secretary Ruhama Hermon remembers, "he felt he didn't know what to do. He had to decide everything by himself. What would happen to those young boys who were going to fight? Maybe it was the wrong step, and if something terrible happened, it would be his fault."[61]

The pain and tension showed on Rabin's face. Finding he could share the load with no one else, he turned inward; it was difficult to talk even to those with whom he was close. Eshkol noticed the change in him, too. He found the chief of staff increasingly nervous, and mentioned it to his

---

59. Yitzhak Rabin in conversation with author, August 31, 1976

60. Ibid

61. Ruhama Hermon in conversation with author, June 24, 1976

aides. Rabin naturally set the mood for the men around him, and if he was edgy, others took their cue from him. One senior official, who watched as Rabin spoke to newsmen, remembers "his stammering, nervous, incoherent replies. It was almost as if he had lost his nerve, was out of control."[62] He wanted guidance. He had plenty of advice, all of it contradictory, and from people whose judgment he had little reason to trust; what he needed was to talk to someone whom he respected. He turned to David Ben-Gurion, "my teacher," as he liked to call him. Rabin's relationship with Ben-Gurion had generally been good except for the unfortunate incident concerning the Palmach conference in 1949. Rabin phoned the 'Old Man' and they agreed to meet at 7 pm that day, Sunday, May 21, at Ben-Gurion's home in Tel Aviv.[63] The meeting shattered Rabin's morale. "As soon as I opened the door I didn't even have a chance to say hello. Ben-Gurion launched into the attack: 'What's going on? Are you trying to endanger Israel? In 1956 I didn't begin the war until I was sure the skies over Tel Aviv and our other cities were protected by the French air force and here you are, entering into a war in just any old way.'" The decision to mobilize the reserves over which Rabin had a great deal of influence particularly annoyed Ben-Gurion. Egypt, he thought, had only been bluffing in the Sinai, but in view of the Israeli call-up Nasser would probably now be provoked into taking serious military action. "I thought I would be given some encouragement by Ben-Gurion," Rabin said,

---

62. The official, who worked closely with key Government figures during this period, asked not to be identified

63. I have relied heavily on the account of the Rabin-Ben-Gurion meeting furnished by Aryeh Disenchik in *Maariv*, April 14, 1976. Bar-Zohar, op. cit., also discusses the meeting

"but it was just the opposite. The load of responsibility that I carried on my shoulders grew even heavier." He came away from the meeting shaken and shocked, with none of his doubts resolved about the correctness of the decisions he had taken. Instead, the doubts were joined by feelings of guilt. He was now even less sure that the preparations he had made were sufficient, or even that they were not in themselves provocative, and, worst of all, he was less confident than ever that Israel could stand up to such a war.

On May 22, Rabin met foreign minister Abba Eban in Eban's Jerusalem home on Balfour Street. Eban came away from the meeting even gloomier than before. He had asked Rabin how he could help in the military crisis. The chief of staff replied tersely: "Give me time, time, time. We need time." Conscious of how thin the Israeli defenses were in the Sinai at that moment, Rabin was searching for ways to postpone a confrontation with the Egyptians. If his mind had been overburdened, so, too, his body had been overtaxed. He had been working between fifteen and twenty hours a day since the crisis began eight days before. He went home each day, but only to snatch a few hours' sleep. He had increased his cigarette smoking to between 60 and 70 cigarettes per day. He tried to be everywhere at once: as chief of staff, he felt he should be with his troops to make sure that they were adequately prepared for war, if it came; but Eshkol required his presence at high-level meetings, and this proved a physical and psychological drain on his energies.

Nasser's decision to close the Straits of Tiran on May 23 reached Aharon 'Arale' Yariv at 1:30 am. Yariv then phoned Rabin, who in turn placed calls to Eshkol and Eban. At 7:30 am Rabin joined Eshkol and the general staff in the war room in Tel Aviv. Victory was certain, Rabin told them, but the price would be high (after the war, he acknowledged that he had in mind war losses numbering thousands of dead, with tens of thousands wounded.) The night before, Rabin had told his wife that if Nasser closed the Straits of Tiran, it meant war; but now that it had happened, he refrained from advocating the opening of hostilities. Cabinet ministers, continuing to defer to Rabin's judgment, were content not to press for war, as long as the chief of staff did not think it necessary. At 9:30 am Rabin met the Ministerial Committee on Defense. Those who attended described his briefing as very sober. He gave the impression that war could still be avoided; though the Egyptian closure of the Straits of Tiran, cutting off Israel's southern port of Eilat, had been considered by Israel act of war. The Israelis needed to gain time. Rabin proposed that Israel should take the matter to the United Nations Security Council. Eban, however, argued that turning to the Security Council was a sign that Israel had no intention of acting militarily itself, and that it would weaken its position. That morning, the Israelis hoped that the Western powers, particularly the US, Britain, and France, would make it clear to Egypt that blocking the Straits constituted interference Israel's shipping, but such a complaint was not made. The US merely asked Israel for another forty-eight hours in which to come up with some diplomatic action that would persuade Nasser to rescind his decision to close the Straits. The Israelis, with little other choice, agreed. A decision was taken to send Eban to Paris and Washington for further discussions.

What happened to Rabin during that day and its interminable meetings was shrouded in mystery and controversy in the years following the Six-Day War, but undoubtedly something dramatic did befall the chief of staff, an illness that was variously described by various people. Leah Rabin said later that this was the day he "broke."[64] The change in him was obvious to everyone who saw him. "He was on the verge of exhaustion," remembered Leah. "I told him if he didn't rest, I didn't see how he was going to make it."[65]

One of the first to arrive at Rabin's home on the evening of May 23 was Yariv. He sensed that Rabin was tormented by the fear that he had not ordered enough men and arms to the southern frontier, to defend the country against the Egyptians massing there during the past week, and told him that he was wrong to be so worried, that everything was proceeding well. But despite his efforts to cheer Rabin up, Yariv could see that he was scarcely listening. He seemed like a man in a dream, hardly speaking. Discouraged, Yariv went home and had been there only a short while when Leah's sister telephoned. She had just learned of the chief of staff's troubles from Leah and begged Yariv to go back to the Rabins' house. Instead, Yariv went to the airport to meet Haim BarLev, head of the general staff branch from 1964 to 1966; Rabin had summoned him back from a Paris study mission. Yariv later regretted going to the airport rather than to see Rabin again, feeling he might have been able to prevent the events of the next twenty-four hours.

Most of those who saw Rabin during his illness have described it as both physical and psychological. "He had to rest," said close friend Ya'acov Hefetz, who was then

---

64. Leah Rabin, *All the Time His Wife*, p. 112

65. Leah Rabin in conversation with author, August 14, 1976

serving as the chief of staff's financial adviser. "I don't like to use the word collapse, because he didn't collapse. He was physically worn out. He had worked so hard."[66]

Rabin only rarely spoke directly about the illness in public, and though many Israelis knew about it after the war, the precise details were never publicized at that time. The first detailed version to be made public is the now-famous document by Ezer Weizman, which was published in April 1974 at the height of Rabin's first campaign for the prime ministership.[67]

Weizman gave a similar account in his memoirs. It has been suggested that his version should be viewed with a certain amount of skepticism, since he bore a grudge against Rabin for not supporting his candidacy for the position of chief of staff when Rabin retired in December 1967. In addition, Rabin and Weizman had a history of cool relations, although Weizman later acknowledged that he had received everything he wanted from Rabin in the way of equipment for the air force. However, no one, including Rabin, disputed most of the facts, which Weizman presented in his account of Rabin's illness.

Weizman contended that Rabin showed signs of stress even before May 23. "As the suspense built up, and especially as mobilization went ahead and intelligence reports poured in telling of Egyptian forces entering the Sinai, I sensed that the chief of staff was progressively losing his balance. Rabin had altered previous decisions, could not make up his mind," and, Weizman wrote, "such things had the effect of creating

66. Ya'acov Hefetz in conversation with author, August 26, 1976

67. The document appeared for the first time publicly in *Haaretz*, April 22, 1974

insecurity all around him." According to Weizman, Rabin phoned him at 8 pm on the evening of May 23, his voice weak, pleading with him to come round immediately. He found the chief of staff sitting in semi-darkness. Speaking with quiet deliberation, Rabin told him: "I have involved Israel in its greatest war yet. I have involved Israel through the series of mistakes I've made. Since this battle is going to be fought primarily in the air, and as we cannot afford a leader who makes mistakes I want to resign. You take over as chief of staff." [68]

Weizman records that he was shaken by this and took a few moments to answer Rabin. "You know that I want to be chief of staff," Weizman told him, "but not in this way. I won't accept the post. In the present difficult circumstances, the changeover would be a heavy blow to the army's morale. The government is already hesitant about going to war, and your resignation won't help them make up their minds. As for you, Yitzhak, if you resign now, you'll be finished for the rest of your life. Summon up all your strength. I promise to do the best I can to help you get through. You'll be the victorious chief of staff. You'll reach the Suez Canal and the Jordan."

Rabin looked at him uncertainly. "Are you sure?" he asked. Weizman replied firmly, "I'm as sure as I'm sitting here." He advised the chief of staff to get some rest and promised to return in the morning. Meanwhile, he gave instructions that all telephone calls to Rabin be rerouted to him for the time being and contacted an army doctor. When

68. For Weizman's version of the events of May 23-24 1967, I have relied on a conversation I held with him on May 16, 1976, as well as on the Weizman document and *On Eagles' Wings*

the doctor Eliahu Gilon arrived, he and Weizman agreed to describe Rabin's illness as 'nicotine poisoning', a plausible enough diagnosis in view of his heavy smoking. Leah Rabin said the doctor decided her husband needed twenty-four-hours' rest, and gave him an injection to help him sleep. Under the effect of the sedative, Rabin slept most of the time until 3 pm the next day and awoke feeling "one hundred per cent better."[69]

Rabin spoke only in the most general way about that day, without attempting to describe or assess what had happened to him. He cast doubt on Weizman's version but did not discuss it thoroughly. People close to him suggested that it would be in his best interests to reveal the truth; the public was bound to be sympathetic and understanding. But he always rejected the idea. "The truth is," he said on Israel Radio on June 24, 1968, a year after the war, "that I had a certain accident, as a result of which I left my work for about twenty-four hours. The accident was mine and mine alone, and only I carry the responsibility for it. The descriptions that I read are not correct." When asked if he had been suffering from anything more than nicotine poisoning, Rabin gave no reply.

In his 1979 memoirs, Rabin wrote of the incident: "Late that evening, after a day of tension and meeting after meeting in smoke-filled conference rooms, I returned home in a state of mental and physical exhaustion. Even since then, I have repeatedly asked myself, what happened to me that evening? How did I get to such a state? Now, twelve years later, I still lack a definitive answer. There can be no doubt that I was suffering from a combination of tension, exhaustion, and the

---

69. Leah Rabin in conversation with author, August 14, 1976

enormous amounts of cigarette smoke I had inhaled in recent days... The past few days had seemed endless. Meals were taken on the run and only when the occasion arose. I had hardly slept and I was smoking like a steam engine. But it was more than nicotine that brought me down. The heavy sense of guilt that had been dogging me of late became unbearably strong on May 23." He remembered Ben-Gurion's words that he bore the responsibility for what was about to happen. Though he felt that the IDF was properly prepared, he still felt guilt-ridden: "Perhaps I had failed in my duty as the prime minister's chief military adviser? Maybe that was why Israel now found itself in such difficult straits? Never before had I come close to feeling so depressed." He acknowledged that he asked Weizman: "Am I to blame? Should I relinquish my post?" But he emphatically denied ever saying that he offered the chief of staff post to Weizman. "I made him no such offer, nor was I empowered to 'bequeath' the job to him or anyone else. That is not a chief of staff's prerogative."

Formally speaking, Rabin was correct that one chief of staff couldn't appoint his successor. But these had been extraordinary times: It was the eve of war, the Israeli chief of staff had suddenly taken ill and been placed on the sidelines. Weizman, as head of the General Staff branch, was certainly an understandable choice to take over as acting chief of staff on an emergency basis. Rabin admitted that he was considering resigning, and he must have realized that his resignation would perhaps put Weizman in charge of the IDF, at least for the foreseeable future.

Weizman had called a meeting of the general staff for 8:30 am the next morning (May 24). Before going there, he visited Rabin at about 7 am. According to Weizman, Rabin again asked him if he was prepared to take over, but Weizman assured him he had not changed his mind. After calling on Rabin, Weizman stopped at the house of his brother-in-law and Rabin's neighbor Moshe Dayan. They had a brief talk, from which Weizman gained the impression that he had been right to refuse to take over from Rabin: Dayan implied that Weizman would not win the support of his army colleagues for seeming to 'grab' the job of the chief of staff while Rabin was temporarily incapacitated.

At 8:30 am, Weizman met the army's regional commanders and placed the army in battle formation. Rabin later wrote that he felt Weizman had acted "rashly" in calling the general staff together without his knowledge. The air force was put on alert. Around the room there were some bewildered stares, as commanders wondered where the chief of staff was. Weizman had decided that neither the generals nor the public at large would be told about Rabin's state of mind at that time. Only certain staff officers were let in on the secret, and even they were not told the entire story. Weizman ordered the generals not to communicate with Rabin. Some at the meeting already knew the situation and needed no explanation. Ya'acov Hefetz, who was at Rabin's house during his illness, said that the chief of staff switched from cigarettes to chocolates once he became sick. But, he added, nicotine poisoning was not the whole truth. Rabin was physically worn out. Never before had such a responsibility rested on the shoulders of an officer, a military leader. It was a mixture of physical and mental fatigue.

During the late morning of May 24, Weizman visited Eshkol to inform him about the previous hours' events and the orders he had issued in place of Rabin. Eshkol thanked him, telling him that he had done the right thing. Late in the afternoon, Eshkol met Rabin's doctor at military headquarters in Tel Aviv and asked him what Rabin was suffering from. Weizman reported that Dr. Gilon (who refused to talk about the incident) said, in English, "acute anxiety." Whatever Rabin had – whether nicotine poisoning or 'acute anxiety' or some combination of the two – he had recovered enough by mid-afternoon of May 24 to see his brother-in-law, reserve general Avraham Yoffe (who was to command a division in the Six-Day War). He informed his visitor that the doctor had said he was weak from too much smoking. Yoffe tried to boost his spirits by reporting that the soldiers' morale was high, and he urged Rabin to make a pre-emptive strike against Nasser. Rabin closed the brief conversation with the news that he would be back at work the next day.[70]

The following day, Rabin saw Eshkol at the prime minister's office in Tel Aviv and told him he was fit to work. "I had a personal problem," Rabin told Eshkol, "I do consider myself fit for duty now. Yet if you think I should relinquish my post, I shall accept your decision without protest." Eshkol dismissed Rabin's offer to resign with a "No problem" and turned to other matters.

The main problem facing Rabin was how to reestablish his authority, having been away from his post at such a crucial juncture. General Tal felt the whole incident could be shrugged off if handled quickly and honestly. To his regret, Rabin did not follow his counsel. He returned to his duties, but refused to talk about the incident. Tal felt that by not talking about it openly and immediately the episode might not only be misunderstood now, but even exploited by some, later on. The immediate response of many who were told

---

70. Yitzhak Rabin, *The Rabin Memoirs* (English version), p. 64

of Rabin's illness was to interpret it as a sign of Israel's weak leadership. Here was Eshkol's chief military adviser giving way under pressure at a time when the entire nation was looking to the army and the government to take the proper measures against the Egyptian threat. Eshkol's radio address to the nation on May 28, during which he frequently stammered and lost his place and seemed generally unsure of himself, added to the growing national self-doubt and dissatisfaction with the leadership.

Nasser's closure of the Straits of Tiran on May 23 was followed by other actions that gave the distinct impression of a country determined to go to war. "Everything Egypt had was being sent in to the Sinai," Rabin recalled. Towards the end of May, Egypt, Syria, and Jordan made joint defense arrangements; the combined potential Arab strength aided also by Iraq, Kuwait, Saudi Arabia, and Algeria amounted to some 547,000 soldiers, 5,404 tanks, and over 900 aircraft. The Israelis had a fighting force of 275,000, 800 tanks, and nearly 200 aircraft. It was now crucial that Israel determine how much support it could count on from the United States. Unlike 1956, Israel now seemed to be standing alone, without the support of any other country, not even France, which was refusing to supply planes because of the arms embargo they had imposed on June 2. Rabin had no doubts about where the United States stood. He felt sure it would withhold support, but he wanted the American position to be made clear once and for all, so that Israel would know it was on its own. Ya'acov Herzog, the director-general of Eshkol's office, proposed that a cable be sent to foreign minister Abba Eban in Washington asking him to clarify with US officials the extent to which they were willing to implement past pledges. Rabin persuaded Eshkol that Israel needed this clarification, in effect to free its hands, and the prime minister reluctantly agreed. In *Maariv* on June 2, Rabin explained that the cable had not been designed to secure a military pact with the US, but rather "to clarify for ourselves exactly how we stood, and how much we could rely on others. The purpose was to point out to Israel that in fact we had no one to rely on but ourselves, that we were on our own and we alone were responsible for our fate. That helped us to make a decision."[71]

During those latter days in May, when fears were being expressed that the Egyptians might attack at any moment, the unwillingness of the Cabinet to take decisive action cast gloom over the nation. The generals begged the government to march against Egypt, arguing that firm military action was needed, not subtle diplomatic maneuvering. Rabin made frequent trips to the fronts during this period and broadcast messages over the radio, boosting the army's morale and calling upon the soldiers to be patient. "I know the waiting is hard," he told them on May 30, "but I can assure you if war comes it will not be fought on our soil." The army, Rabin liked to say afterwards, was like a "coiled spring,"[72] with many of its commanders itching for battle. On May 31, Rabin was telling the nation over the radio that war was imminent, and the army had to be on its guard. "The transition from peace to a state of war may be precipitous," he warned, "and this fact obliges us to maintain our constant preparedness, to be ready for instant action." He visited the Jerusalem reconnaissance company on an inspection tour, and discovered that the company commander, Major Yossi, was also a Kadoorie graduate. Rabin noted that he was the major's senior by ten

---

71. Ibid

72. Ya'acov Hefetz in conversation with author, August 26, 1976

years. "That's what makes me to my regret chief of staff, instead of commander of a reconnaissance unit," he joked. He told the men: "It's a question of nerves, who will break first. We don't want to fight, but as long as they are on our borders we can't go home."[73]

Rabin's long-time friend Uzi Narkiss, commander of the Central Front, took him on a tour of Jerusalem's front lines. Narkiss was concerned that if the fighting began, Jordan would make a rush for Government House, the one piece of non-Jordanian territory in Jerusalem which could be captured without difficulty. He asked Rabin to approve the moving of Israeli troops into the demilitarized zone, bringing up a bulldozer to dig trenches, both of which would be blatant violations of the 1949 armistice agreement, under the very noses of the UN officers in Government House, which served as UN headquarters. Rabin at first had his doubts about the idea, but he eventually agreed and Narkiss gave the order.

The prospect of Israeli soldiers fighting again in Jerusalem greatly moved Rabin. Lunching at the Jerusalem Brigade Headquarters that day in early June, he encouraged the hundred officers in the room to think of what they might accomplish in the coming days. "I fought here in '48," he said. "I hope if we have to fight here in this war, that you will complete what we were unable to finish."

The government took no decisions as May ended, although the public was demanding action of some kind, blaming the nation's leaders for their indecision and pressing for the appointment of Moshe Dayan, the popular hero of the Sinai Campaign, as 'Israel's Savior'. Rabin, painfully aware of Eshkol's indecisive image, accepted the nation's will and

---

73. Avraham Yoffe in conversation with author, June 14, 1976

supported Dayan's candidacy for the national leadership. He feared, however, that Eshkol would decide to give Dayan command of the Southern Front, thus ousting Rabin's old Palmach colleague, Yeshayahu Gavish, who had an excellent reputation as a field commander, and so Rabin pressed for Dayan's appointment as minister of defense, which, on June 1, he was duly made. A day later, the Israeli leadership secretly planned to launch hostilities, setting the date of Monday, June 5.

The Israelis had gained the time they needed to plan the strategy of the coming war. Right up until the last moments, the plan, approved by the Cabinet, was for a limited offensive to capture Gaza and northern Sinai, which would place Israel in a strong bargaining position for the reopening of the Straits of Tiran and the withdrawal of Egyptian forces from the Peninsula. It was known as the 'minimalist' or 'limited' strategy, and was closely identified with Rabin, as was another concept ingrained in the planning of the IDF: the notion of the 'mailed fist'. Rabin had once explained, before the war: "We use our armor like a mailed fist, thrusting with speed and momentum deep into enemy territory not to take his positions, but to throw him off balance and make his position untenable." Even though this was at the risk of advancing along a wide front, and having few lines of communication, Rabin believed that by using the 'mailed fist' the IDF could overwhelm the main force of the Egyptian army, concentrated along Israel's southern borders, and once this was accomplished, the Egyptians would soon reopen the Straits.

Israel's perilous military situation called for a bold, dramatic strategy, one that would immediately place the enemy on the defensive. "Our overriding concern," said Rabin, "was that no matter who made the first move, our first act must be to strike a crushing blow at the main body of the enemy force. A major achievement on our part was needed within hours, a day, or the first few days, in order for this to have its effect on the fighting spirit of the other side. A victory in the air was needed both to crush the enemy air force quickly and so that our planes would be free to assist ground and sea forces."[74]

The basic military plan for combating the Egyptians had been outlined and developed in 1964. It was a plan that Rabin had helped devise, and one which had become part of the operational thinking of the IDF. However, the new defense minister had reservations: Even if the IDF captured Gaza and northern Sinai, he thought, there was no guarantee that the Egyptians would reopen the Straits. Dayan favored an Israeli sweep into the Sinai with the aim of putting the entire Egyptian army out of action, and occupying the area, which would thus restore the credibility of the IDF. Yeshayahu Gavish's diary stated that Rabin told him shortly after Dayan's appointment to give the 'limited plan' to the minister for approval. Gavish had his own, wider plan, but Rabin told him to stick to the 'limited' one. The Southern Front commander urged Rabin to let him mention his personal plan, and Rabin finally agreed. At the initial meeting between Dayan and Rabin, at which Gavish was present, the new defense minister told Rabin to present the plan. Rabin ordered Gavish to present it. Unsure of what to do, the Southern Front commander asked Rabin: "Which of the two?" Rabin apparently persuaded by now that the

---

74. *Maariv*, June 2, 1972

'limited' plan needed alteration, answered: "The second one" (i.e., Gavish's wider plan, which resembled Dayan's). On the basis of this, orders were then issued that the attack, if and when it came, would be mounted on three axes into the Sinai, in the general direction of Bir Gafgafa, and toward the Mitla Pass.

No matter how effective Israeli air strikes might be, the nation would still be faced with the massed enemy armies on three fronts. Jordan seemed to pose the smallest problem: The general view at military headquarters was that if King Hussein could find a way of keeping his country out of the fighting, he would. Accordingly, the IDF organized the Jordanian front, including Jerusalem, along defensive lines. Even though Rabin had sounded eager to finish the job left incomplete in the Jerusalem fighting in 1948, he was in fact anxious to avoid a clash in the Holy City if possible, because of the heavy price Israel would have to pay in human life. The Syrians were a greater threat, but the Israelis decided to concentrate their attention primarily on the Egyptian front, and only when victory was assured there would they turn to their northern frontier.

The Six-Day War began on the morning of Monday, June 5. Beginning at 7:45 am, wave after wave of Israeli planes swept over nine Egyptian airfields. Every ten minutes two pairs of planes would carry out precision bombing raids: First, the runways were put out of action with delayed-action bombs; then aircraft on, or near, the runways were attacked (supersonic fighters had top priority, then other combat aircraft, and only at the end were transport planes bombed.) Aircraft in the open were attacked with cannons and rockets, bombs were reserved for runways and hangars. Before the pilots went into battle, Rabin told them in a voice choked with emotion: "I have so much to say to you; I cannot find the words. Let me paraphrase Churchill's words: Never in the field of human conflict has the fate of so many depended on the skill and courage of so few. It is you who will decide the destiny of our people and our state."

Three hours after the first planes swept over the unprotected Egyptian fields (the Egyptians thought underground sites too costly), Rabin learned from Air Force Headquarters that the raids had been an enormous success. He telephoned Leah with great satisfaction in his voice. "The Egyptian Air Force is totally destroyed," he told her. In the afternoon, Israeli planes attacked two Jordanian and five Syrian air bases with much the same success. One Iraqi air base was struck, too, but the Israelis discovered that most of the enemy aircraft were at other, more remote airfields. By the end of the first day of the war, Egypt had lost 122 supersonic planes, 75 subsonic fighters, 27 light bombers, 30 TU-16 medium bombers, and 32 transports. Most of the 452 Arab aircrafts destroyed during the entire war were knocked out on the ground. Israel lost only 26 aircraft in the initial two days of the war and 46 throughout the entire six days (all but three to ground fire).

The war was effectively decided during that first day of battle. At the outset, the Israeli leaders portrayed the daring air strikes that opened the war as a defensive reaction to Egyptian aggression. "On the morning of June 5," Rabin told a news conference two days after, "the shelling of settlements started on the border, as did troop movements and the movement of considerable air groups. We had to defend ourselves. Israel is too small a country to take only half measures in its defense."

Once the enemy's air force was out of action, it was time for the ground forces to go into battle. Later that morning, Rabin's calm voice giving the order to move came over the tank officers' receiving sets, and the tanks began rolling in the direction of the Sinai to take on the Egyptian army.

A few hours after Egypt and Israel began fighting, Syria launched an attack, its Migs strafing a number of villages in the Haifa region. On the second day of the war, attacks by three Syrian armored columns were beaten back. The Syrians, however, kept up their fire against the settlements and built up areas near the frontier throughout the war. Although a partner in the defense pact with Egypt, Jordan waited on the sidelines during the first morning of the war. But during the afternoon, apparently basing their decision to join hostilities on reports from Cairo that the Israeli air force had been knocked out of action, the Jordanians launched an air attack and began artillery shelling of Jewish Jerusalem, an Israeli airfield in the north, and the suburbs of Tel Aviv. During the early evening of June 5, artillery shells, fired from Qalqilyah on Jordanian soil, fell on Tzahala and Tel Aviv, eight miles away. A nearby house had taken a hit and shells passing overhead forced Leah and the children to race for a foxhole. "I want to be where my father is," 12-year-old Yuval said quietly. His father, the chief of staff, was in Tel Aviv at general staff headquarters in the underground war room.

Leah and the children returned home. Phoning her husband, Leah asked him if he knew that Tzahala had come under fire. "Yes," he said coolly, adding, "by morning it will be OK." At 1 am on the second morning of the war, Rabin broadcast nationally a summary of the day's events. He described the extent of the Israeli ground penetration into the Sinai that day, revealing that the IDF had captured Rafiah and El Arish, as well as parts of the Gaza Strip. He said little about the Jerusalem fighting, except that Government House, the former UN headquarters, was now in Israeli hands after falling to the Jordanians earlier in the day, and that Israeli troops had captured certain points around the Holy City. Finally he told the nation of the devastating blow struck to the enemy's air force (Some senior army men had pressed Dayan and Rabin to announce the Israeli air victory earlier in the day, in the hope that this would keep King Hussein from entering the war, but they had decided to delay the communiqué.)

Rabin spent most of the early part of the war in the command room in Tel Aviv. Except for a few brief visits to the fronts, he did not leave the command post. Those who worked with him during those days found him quieter than usual, more evasive, and some attributed this to the fact that he was still recovering from his illness, from nearly two weeks earlier. He slept on a folding camp bed in his office, a telephone nearby. He went home twice in the first few days, but only for brief visits. His adjutant, Rafi Efrat, urged him to rest more but he resisted. He was invited to make a tour of the West Bank of the Jordan but refused to go, saying that while the war was still on, he had to be where the decisions were taking place; the West Bank fighting, spasmodic and brief, scarcely required his personal attention. On another occasion he flew by helicopter to a point outside Beersheba, some 80 kilometers (49.7 miles) from Jerusalem. When he landed, he was informed that three seriously wounded soldiers were in danger of losing their lives if they were not evacuated at once. Rabin immediately put his helicopter at their disposal, waiting three hours for it to return and enable him to continue his tour. Later, when the Israelis had taken Jerusalem, he was invited to attend a victory concert there, but with some anger in his voice he explained why he couldn't bring himself to go: "Today, when soldiers are being killed? I have no time for concerts."[75]

By the third day, Rabin was able to tell his countrymen that the Egyptian forces had been totally destroyed and that Jerusalem had been reunited and was in Israeli hands. He concluded with these words: "All these actions were achieved by the Israel Defense Forces, alone and unaided."

From a strategic point of view, the war could not have gone more smoothly: "From the beginning," Rabin told a newsman after the fighting, "to its end, there were no real errors. I mean errors that might have influenced the result of the entire campaign. It is true that small mistakes were made along the way, but it is almost unbelievable that a war of this dimension and pace could be fought with so few errors. It was all due to the excellence of the command at every level."[76]

On the fourth day, Gavish, the Southern Front commander, cabled Rabin: "I am happy to inform you that our forces are sitting on the banks of the Suez Canal. Half of the Suez Peninsula is in our hands."[77] Though the Sinai fighting was tough, it went more smoothly than the Israelis had imagined. "I estimated that the campaign against the Egyptian army

---

75. Yitzhak Rabin in conversation with author, August 31, 1976

76. Quoted in: Abraham Rabinovich, *The Battle of Jerusalem*, Philadelphia: Jewish Publication Society of America, 1972, pp. 66-67.

77. Quoted in: Randolph S. and Winston S. Churchill, *The Six-Day War*, London: Heinemann, 1967, pp. 104-05.

would continue from one to three days, longer than it in fact did," Rabin told *Maariv* on October 4, 1967.

The battle for Jerusalem was more complex. Uzi Narkiss, the Central Front commander, was asking for approval to launch an assault on various places around Jerusalem, including Latrun and the Abdul Aziz Hill, but the military leaders wanted to make sure the fighting on the Sinai front was going well first. The battle for Jerusalem began at about 11 am on the first day of the war. Narkiss wanted to open an attack just before midnight on June 5 focusing on the police school and the Sheikh Jarrah district. In view of the Israeli victory against Egypt in the air, Rabin thought a daylight attack the next day better, because they could then have the advantage of air support, but Narkiss argued that such support was useless, as it was unlikely that the planes could hit their targets with enough precision within the city. Rabin told him: "Discuss both plans with Motta [Mordechai] Gur, and let me know which you consider best. I'll make a decision based on what you decide." Narkiss and Gur (then commander of the paratroop brigade in Jerusalem), agreed to attack at night, and the assault was set for 2:30 am, June 6.

The purpose of the attack was to encircle Jerusalem. Gur's paratroopers hoped to reach Mount Scopus and the Mount of Olives in the eastern part of the city, and from there to move out towards the Jericho road, cutting Jerusalem off from the east. The first target, as the paratroopers set out, was the Jordanian police school compound that had been converted into a fort during the fighting. Beyond it was the major Jordanian fortification on Ammunition Hill, which beyond that lay both Mount Scopus and the Mount of Olives. Battling their way through intense fire from the school,

Israeli troops cut through four fences before reaching the Jordanian trenches on the periphery of the compound. The battle for the trenches was achieved only by fierce hand-to-hand combat. At Ammunition Hill, the next Israeli objective, a system of bunkers and 40 machine gun emplacements had been built. Behind heavy stonewalls, the fighting was even more difficult, but eventually, with the loss of 21 Israelis, the Jordanian position fell.

A scheduled attack on the Augusta Victoria Hospital, located between Mount Scopus and the Mount of Olives, was called off because of heavy Israeli casualties in battles elsewhere in the city. It was, however, taken the next day (June 7), as was the Jericho road, thus closing the ring around Jerusalem. With that, Mordechai Gur ordered his troops to storm the Lions Gate that would begin the conquest of the Old City. Once the Old City had been breached, Israeli soldiers moved quickly through its tiny alleyways to take control of the Temple Mount and the adjacent Western Wall, the holiest site in Judaism. No moment of the conquest of Jerusalem during the Six-Day War was sweeter for the Israelis than this. After a 19-year absence, the Jews had returned and regained the Jewish Quarter, which had beensurrendered to the Arabs in May 1948.

When the Israeli military leadership entered the Old City, it was naturally a very emotive occasion. Dayan at first wanted to make a triumphant entry on his own, but he apparently had second thoughts and asked Rabin and Narkiss to join him. The experience of entering the Old City as the chief of staff of the triumphant Israeli forces moved Rabin to the extent that he later described that day as the "peak of my life."[78] As soldiers raced up to embrace him at the Western Wall, he told them: "It is with affection and pride that the whole nation salutes you today for the decisive victory you have brought us." Thousands were listening to his words over the radio, in addition to those at the Wall. "It was not handed to us on a silver platter. The fighting was savage and hard. Many of our comrades in arms have fallen in action. Their sacrifices shall not have been in vain... The countless generations of Jews murdered, martyred and massacred for the sake of Jerusalem say to you: 'Comfort yet, our people; console the mothers and the fathers whose sacrifices have brought about redemption.'" He reminded his listeners that he had been in the city and fought for it during the War of Independence; his entry into the Old City was therefore "for me perhaps the most important event that has occurred during these fifty-five hours." Years later, speaking on American television, he talked again about the experience: "I think, if there can be something for a human being that can be called the fulfillment of a dream, that is what I felt when I neared the Wall then. To a Jewish boy who was born in Jerusalem, grew up in Palestine, managed to see the creation of a Jewish state, commanded a brigade in '48 and failed to liberate the Wall, who became nineteen years later chief of staff, and then as chief of staff to be able to bring about the liberation of the Wall, who can achieve more than that?"[79]

---

78. Quoted in: *The Jerusalem Post*, October 9, 1967; from a speech by Yitzhak Rabin in Tel Aviv on September 21, 1967.

79. Quoted in: Moshe Ben Shaul, ed., *Generals of Israel*, Tel Aviv: Hadar Publishing House Ltd., 1968, p. 24

Pressure mounted throughout the first few days of the war for Israeli action against the Syrians. Daily artillery exchanges between the Israelis and Syrians continued from June 5 to 9. The Israeli settlers who farmed within range of the Syrian artillery situated on the Golan Heights saw the war as an opportunity for settling old scores. The Northern Front command, headed by David Elazar, was in full accord; Rabin himself, a former commander of the Northern Front, openly sympathized with their wishes. Only Dayan objected, haunted by the Soviet threat, that if Israel attacked Syria, the Russians would enter the war directly. "In the Six-Day War," Rabin said later, "we all had traumas. For Moshe Dayan it was the Russians; for me it was the Arab armies deployed against us."[80] Dayan also felt that an Israeli attack on the Golan Heights would need air support, and he could not guarantee this until the battles for the Sinai and Jerusalem were over.

However, Rabin, supported by Elazar, pressed the matter and by June 7, Dayan was ready to cede a little. He told Rabin that he would approve an Israeli assault against the Syrians, but the IDF were only to occupy Syrian territory up to three kilometers (1.8 miles) from the international boundary, a limitation that effectively meant taking over the Golan Heights ridges, but nothing more. Rabin found the conditions unacceptable and told the defense minister so: "To attack just for the sake of three kilometers (1.8 miles) is to expend effort and to shed blood without gaining anything worthwhile." Displaying little interest in the project, Dayan said: "If you abide by my conditions, fine, if you want more, no." Rabin decided to consult Elazar before making a final

---

80. Interview with Yitzhak Rabin, *Maariv*, October 4, 1967

decision. He promised himself that he would not budge from his opinion, confident that Elazar would agree with him. Elazar concurred wholeheartedly: "I'm not for the plan either. If the limit is three to four kilometers (1.8 to 2.4 miles), get back to Dayan and tell him no. I'm not going to take responsibility for the shedding of blood for nothing. It wouldn't change the basic situation and I don't see any purpose in fighting for it."[81]

The pressure intensified. At a Cabinet meeting on the night of June 8, Rabin presented a plan for attacking the Golan Heights, but told the ministers that whatever the IDF accomplished depended largely upon how much time it had before a cease-fire was imposed. In an unprecedented step, settlers from the farm villages under the Golan Heights were permitted to attend the Cabinet session to present their reasons for wanting the attack. The Cabinet favored Rabin's plan, with the exception of Dayan, so it was put off. It was midnight on the fourth day of the war.

Rabin felt able to sleep at home for the first time since the fighting had started. His wife Leah found him in a 'foul mood' because the war was about to end and Dayan was unwilling to approve an attack on the Golan Heights. When Rabin returned to command headquarters the next morning (Friday), he was greeted by Weizman, who said that Dayan had been looking for him half an hour before; the defense minister had changed his mind and was now in favor of taking the Golan Heights. Dayan had told Elazar to prepare the attack. Dayan and Eshkol had a written agreement dating from the defense minister's appointment, which stipulated that Dayan could not open a new front without Eshkol's

81. Quoted in *Maariv*, June 9, 1967

approval. Dayan contended that he had merely ordered preparations for the Golan attack, and could have called them off at any time in the next few hours if Eshkol, when told of the decision, had opposed it. Explaining why he had made no great effort to contact Rabin before ordering the attack, Dayan claimed later that the chief of staff had gone on record as being in favor of the plan and it had only been he (Dayan) who had opposed it. In effect, he was saying that he considered contacting Rabin unnecessary.

Rabin telephoned Elazar immediately and learned that Dayan had told him to begin the attack at noon and to see to it that it went quickly. "Nonsense," Rabin told the Northern Front commander, "it's going to be a tough fight. Do it carefully. Plan, don't rush; do it as quickly as possible, but don't rush."[82]

Feeling that Dayan had underestimated how long it would take to overcome the Syrians, Rabin rushed to Northern Command headquarters by helicopter to direct the fighting personally. "Don't forget 'Galinka'," Rabin had warned Elazar over the phone before leaving. Both men vividly remembered a friend of theirs from the fifth battalion of the old Harel Brigade, who had been killed at Abu Ageila in the 1956 Sinai Campaign. The chief of staff felt that Dayan had ordered the men to rush into battle at Abu Ageila, without due preparations. He was determined that it shouldn't happen again.

By 7:30 am, Rabin was at the northern command post, helping to redirect the troops who had been pulled back the night before. The air force went into action at 9:40 am and two hours later an armored brigade led the Israeli ground

---

82. ABC News documentary, April 15, 1975

forces into battle. The Syrians, with five infantry and four armored brigades atop the rocky slopes of the Golan Heights, were ready. The Israelis used bulldozers to clear the way for their armored vehicles on the lower slopes, and, aided by the air force, achieved a firm foothold by the end of the day. At some points during the assault, infantry soldiers climbed the Heights on foot and fought hand-to-hand for the Syrian strongholds. On Saturday morning, June 10, the IDF continued the attack, and within a few hours the Syrian defenses collapsed completely. In many cases, so swift was the Israeli victory that retreating Syrian soldiers had no time to destroy weapons, ammunition, or secret documents. Tanks were abandoned with their engines still running and their radios on. Kuneitra, the Syrian administrative capital on the Golan Heights, fell without a fight at 2 pm. When a cease-fire went into effect at 6 pm that day, the IDF controlled the entire Golan Heights up to a line which extended from the western peaks of Mount Hermon, south through Kuneitra, then descending to the Yarmuk River.

Sometime during the fighting on Friday, June 9, Rabin visited the troops on the Golan Heights. As he was touring, soldiers who had been listening to their radios rushed up to ask him if he had heard the news: Nasser had resigned. Rabin's reaction was cautious; he told the men that this was probably a political maneuver and that Nasser would return.

The war was over. Israel had won a victory of startling proportions, "Greater," Rabin said, "than any known in Jewish history." The IDF stood on cease-fire lines which encompassed 70,000 square kilometers of territory, three and a half times the size of pre-war Israel. One million Arab inhabitants of the land captured by the Israelis had come under Israeli occupation. Israeli troops controlled the western bank of the Suez Canal and the western bank of the Jordan River, a pair of seemingly ideal boundaries.

Notwithstanding the losses and casualties suffered, a mood of euphoria set in on the Israeli side, reflected in the widely felt conviction that the Arabs now had no choice but to establish a durable peace. The loss of the precious territory conquered in the war would, so Israelis were persuaded, induce the Arabs to seek negotiations at once.

The Israelis made a distinction between Jerusalem and the other conquered territories. On June 15, 1967, the Cabinet decided to annex East Jerusalem and the surrounding areas: Mount Scopus, the Mount of Olives, Sheikh Jarrah, Sur Baher, Shuafat, and the airport at Atarot (Kalandia). On June 27, the Knesset confirmed the decision: Israel would negotiate with the Arabs for the return of all the occupied territories except Jerusalem. The Holy City, now united under the Israelis' control, was to remain in their hands.

Some thought the Egyptians would be forced to make peace as their army had been so badly defeated. While acknowledging that it would take the Egyptians at least a decade to rebuild their war machine, Rabin thought the chances for real peace no better and no worse than before the war. He was keen to deflate the jubilant mood, for fear that it would give Israelis false illusions, and for the same reason he disliked any glorification of the war. Also the names that had been suggested for it seemed to him ridiculous. "I do not think this war needs a special name," he told the army magazine *Bamahane* on July 5, 1967, "Its extent and results speak for themselves. All the names suggested until now 'The War of Daring', 'The War of Salvation', or 'The War of the Sons of Light', are too pretentious. The simplest, and to my mind, the most apt name is the 'Six-Day War,' reflecting the six days of creation." Even that seemed ostentatious, but the name stuck.

In a magnificent and moving speech at the Mount Scopus campus of Jerusalem's Hebrew University on June 28, 1967, where an honorary doctorate had been conferred upon him for his service to the nation during the war, Rabin said: "The elation of victory has seized the whole nation. Yet among the soldiers themselves a curious phenomenon is to be observed. They cannot rejoice wholeheartedly. Their triumph is marred by grief and shock, and there are some who cannot rejoice at all. The men on the front lines saw with their own eyes not only the glory of victory but also its cost: their comrades fallen beside them, soaked in blood. And I know that the terrible price the enemy paid has also deeply moved many of our men. Is it because neither their teaching nor their experience has ever accustomed the Jewish people to exult in conquest and victory, that they receive them with such mixed feelings?"

It was unquestionably one of the most remarkable speeches Rabin had ever made. At a time when the nation was swept up in the army's stunning victory, he chose to reflect on the suffering that had been inflicted on both sides.

What the people saw of Rabin in those days before, during, and immediately after the Six-Day War, they liked and admired. He had expressed the nature of the Israeli victory to the country and to the world, and he was given a good deal of the credit for the victory. Only one other, Moshe Dayan, cast a longer shadow, and the two men were often compared, with the question constantly being asked: Which one deserved the most credit for the Israeli victory?

Soon after the war, Leah Rabin found her daughter Dalia on her bed crying, "Mother, there is no justice. No justice at school, no justice in the scouts, none anywhere." Her mother asked: Why did she feel this way? "All the children say that Dayan won the war, not Daddy." Leah tried to calm her down: "Dalia, I know there will be many who say that, and others who say differently. Each of them made a massive contribution to this victory, which is so gigantic that there is glory for both of them and a lot of others. Now do me a favor and don't cry. There's no cause. Even if this success has many fathers, whatever happens, your father has a very respectable place in it."[83]

The question of whether Rabin or Dayan deserved the most credit for Israel's triumph was difficult to answer. Rabin did so much to prepare the army for that major test of 1967, that his role can hardly be understated as Dayan's enthusiasts would like it to be. On the other hand, Dayan's dramatic reentry into the government on June 1 proved so decisive in lifting the sagging morale of the army and the public, that his contribution to the victory cannot be minimized. Rabin's admirers argue with much justice, that the military machine Dayan found when he entered the picture had already been readied for battle, and it only needed to be ordered into operation. The war was carried out so efficiently that the senior general staff were less crucial to the day-to-day running of the war, than they were for instance in the Yom Kippur War of October, 1973, in which hard, risky decisions had to be made all the time. Rabin's role was thus reduced during the actual six days of fighting. He made decisions, the timing of certain major offensives, but

83. Leah Rabin, *All the Time His Wife*, p. 117

the key assignments were handed over to subordinates like Haim Bar-Lev, Ezer Weizman, and local field commanders. Rabin seemed content with this arrangement. Some thought it uncharacteristic of him, normally a man who liked to make all the decisions, big or small. But as Dayan took over most of the planning, it seemed natural to Rabin to accept it. Dayan's defenders contend that the defense minister wisely enlarged the strategic plan against Egypt to include a knockout blow to the Egyptian army and the occupation of the Sinai Peninsula, something the original plans lacked. However, a decade after the war, Dayan admitted that Rabin had disobeyed his order to halt the IDF 30 kilometers (18.6 miles) west of the Suez Canal. According to Dayan, Rabin believed such a restraint "would have been bad for Israel."[84]

Dayan tried to stem the rising tide of Rabin's popularity: He rebuked Eban for including Rabin's name in a Security Council speech when the foreign minister was listing the heroes of the war. A week after the war, Dayan made it clear that he felt all credit was due to him and to him alone. "Anyone who says that I came in and found everything ready is just trying to obscure the issue." He did his best to keep Rabin out of the limelight, a fact which made Rabin's position as chief of staff less and less attractive after the war. Ironically, the Israeli public realized little of the tension between the two men and lavished its praise on Rabin rather than on Dayan. Dayan became the darling of the international community, the hero of the foreign media. An Israeli public opinion poll nominated Rabin as the Man of the Year in 1967 with 42.1 percent, followed by Dayan with 27.4 per cent, and Eshkol, third, with 10 per cent. A

---

84. Quoted in *Yediot Aharonot*, November 14, 1976

second Israeli poll at the time, which canvassed opinions as to who had contributed most to the Six-Day War effort, put Rabin on top, with 45.6 percent, and Dayan in second place, with 31.5 percent. The polls were indicative of a point that needs to be stated: the international press had generally underestimated Rabin and his work before and during the war, largely because so much attention was focused on Dayan.

Because he was able to triumph both on the battlefield and in his own personal crisis, Rabin's behavior during the pre-war 'waiting period' seemed largely irrelevant to Israelis. The Six-Day War made Rabin a military hero. His reputation soared at home and abroad. Suddenly he was the triumphant leader of the Israel Defense Forces and no longer just another chief of staff. He came to symbolize the legendary feats of the IDF during those six days in June 1967. No event shaped the image of Yitzhak Rabin in the public's mind as much as the Six-Day War. For the rest of his public career he would be identified with that war: with the frightening moments on its eve, with the glory and triumph of the Israeli army during those six days, and with the spectacular changes in Israel's political map. When people asked themselves in later years whether Yitzhak Rabin would make a worthy prime minister or defense minister, his intimate involvement in the 1967 war was all the credential he required. The Six-Day War, therefore, became Yitzhak Rabin's calling card for political leadership.

CHAPTER SIX

ON TO WASHINGTON

The Six-Day War swept away the nation's self-doubt, and replaced it with a new spirit of self-assurance. However, peace was no nearer. Israel was militarily in a strong position, but little else had changed for the better; the Russians were as great a threat as ever. Rabin argued that Israel's best strategy was to ensure its military supremacy, while at the same time making its peaceful intentions and goodwill clear to the Arabs. To remain the strongest force in the Middle East, Israel had to strengthen its ties with the US. To convince the Arabs that it sought peace, Israel had to show itself flexible on the question of returning Arab territories occupied in the Six-Day War.

Some thought it might be possible to enter into relations with the Arabs without having to give up any occupied lands; Rabin believed this view was unrealistic. "A genuine agreement can only be achieved at a price, and the price is territory. To go to the Egyptians and say: We want peace, but you must agree to our new border being the Suez Canal is a beautiful dream; in reality it's impossible."[85] In his capacity as chief of staff, Rabin spent much of that post-war summer explaining the Israeli 'miracle' to an avid public. The nation had a new hero: Newsmen pursued him; in Ramat Gan, a street was named after him. However, he was preparing to retire from military life. Despite his sudden fame and the glory of the moment, he had a few regrets. He had built up the IDF into a supreme war machine, and seen it perform nearly flawlessly, but the work of the past four years had taken its toll. He found it unbearable to have to make decisions every day that affected the life and death of his men. Few people knew this, for he continued to be a very private man. He was eager, too, to take leave of Moshe Dayan, who saw no room for him in the army over which Dayan as defense minister now presided: Their relationship, already cool, had deteriorated still further after the war.

For years, Rabin had been mulling over the idea of spending an extended period in the United States. From his father he had learned to admire the sense of freedom that prevailed in the US and the raw energy this freedom released. As early as November 1963, when they were visiting Washington, he had confided to Leah his ambition to become Israel's next ambassador to the US when Abe Harman, the current envoy, retired. He realized Israel's links with Europe were becoming tenuous after the 1956 Sinai campaign, and it was clear that the US was emerging in the early 1960s as the Jewish State's main ally.

In a conversation with Eshkol just before the Six-Day War, Rabin had proposed himself as the next Washington envoy.

---

85. Interview with Yitzhak Rabin, June 5, 1968

The prime minister had seemed surprised at the idea, but before a final decision could be made, the May crisis leading up to the Six-Day War intervened. Initially, Eshkol was cool towards the idea, fearing that the presence of a senior military man in Washington during the height of the Vietnam War might damage Israel's image as a non-militaristic nation, but he eventually came round to supporting Rabin.

The public knew little about these developments because all news concerning changes in military personnel was censored for fear of lowering morale among the soldiers. By the time word did get out, Rabin had secured the enthusiastic backing of Eban and had even put pressure on the foreign minister to let him begin the Washington assignment earlier than the scheduled date of March 1968. "I can't stay in the army one day past December 31," he told Eban. "In fact it's going to be hell to stay until then." But there was little Eban could do to bring the date forward.

Rabin's colleagues were saddened at his departure. There was to be only one sour note. Ezer Weizman had long expected that he would replace the outgoing army chief. As the day approached for Rabin to leave, Weizman was eagerly hoping for some words of encouragement and support, but none came. Finally, he decided to take up the matter directly. In a personal confrontation that was marked by Weizrnan's bitterness, Rabin remained non-committal. Weizman left the meeting, slamming the door. Haim Bar-Lev was chosen to succeed Rabin, leaving Weizman furious.

The new ambassador, now age 46, arrived in Washington on February 17, determined to consolidate the prestige Israel had won from the Six-Day War. He had come to the United States to help bring peace to the Middle East, he told newsmen upon his arrival. "If I am not successful in achieving this," he went on, "at least I will try to make Israel strong. In my previous job, my primary mission was to prevent war, and when this became impossible, I had to win the war. We failed in the first mission. We succeeded in the second." One newsman, greeting Rabin at the airport, asked if it was significant that Israel had sent its top soldier to Washington. "In Israel," Rabin replied, "practically everyone is a soldier, and some of us become generals." The Soviet newspaper *Izvestia* greeted Rabin's arrival in the United States with a front-page article, which accused him of being "one of the leaders of Israeli aggression against the Arabs."

On March 6, he presented his credentials to president Lyndon Johnson at the White House. To his sister Rachel he wrote, "I'm speaking to people, giving lectures, etc., and apparently that is to be my way of earning a living here. My English needs improvement but I'm polishing it up."[86]

On March 31, Rabin was invited to the home of Washington journalist Eli Abel to watch the president speak to the nation. At the end of his speech he announced to everyone's surprise that he would not seek re-election. For Rabin, the implication was clear: If Johnson were telling the truth, the ambassador would soon be dealing with a new, unknown Administration. Before that would happen, though, the US was to go through much more painful turmoil. Rabin's most immediate experience of this came in April when Washington erupted in a series of racial disturbances, which turned the streets of the capital into a veritable battlefield. Rabin was shocked, but curious "I watched people looting

---

86. Letter dated February 22, 1968

and policemen just standing by. No one dared do anything."[87]
Although foreigners, the Rabins found it difficult to insulate
themselves from what was happening around them.

Other events during those first six months touched Rabin
personally, too. A meeting had been arranged between the
ambassador and Robert F. Kennedy while Rabin was in New
York City on June 4, the day before the California primary
for the presidential nomination. In view of the senator's
full schedule, Kennedy's aides had suggested just a picture-
taking session with no talks beforehand. Rabin, however,
insisted that the two men talk before the photographers were
allowed in, and Kennedy's staff gave way, but it was all
academic. After winning the primary the next day, Kennedy
was slain by an assassin's bullet.

Events in the United States during much of 1968
depressed and worried Rabin. He began to feel that the US
was fast becoming a second-rate power, whose deterioration
could have far-reaching consequences for the entire world.
The most stunning proof for Rabin of the decline of
American power, was the Johnson Administration's failure
to discover the Soviet plan to invade Czechoslovakia on
August 20, 1968. By an odd chance, Rabin gained firsthand
knowledge of Washington's late awakening to the Russian
move. Rabin had been talking to Johnson's national security
adviser, Walt Rostow, in the White House one day, giving a
detailed briefing to him on the importance of Jerusalem to
Israel, when the White House aide learned that the Soviet
Union had invaded Czechoslovakia and there was nothing
the United States could do. Rabin was a sad witness to the
weakness of a crippled giant.

---

87. Interview with Yitzhak Rabin, *Maariv*, April 13, 1973

Rabin also felt grave concern about America's difficulties arising out of the Vietnam War, which was absorbing the country's resources and diverting its attention not only from its domestic crises but also from the problems of the Middle East. As a military man, he was appalled at the way the United States was pursuing the war. "The first thing that shocked me was the lack of direction. I couldn't make out a goal, let alone any clear-cut idea of how to achieve it."[88] He revealed his feelings about the war to Joseph Alsop, the writer of a nationally syndicated newspaper column, who cited the heavy casualties suffered by the enemy as proof of the effectiveness of the American war effort. Rabin argued that this was nonsense and that a war of attrition was futile: "Head counting won't lead anywhere, that is not the way to wage a war." Alsop was furious at this attack on American policy.[89]

Rabin was an unusual ambassador, very different from the type of diplomat whose flawless command of the language was matched by an unerring sense of protocol. Rabin knew virtually nothing of the world of diplomacy, and what he came to know of it he disliked. As the architect of Israel's stunning victory in the Six-Day War, he had arrived in Washington with an impressive reputation. He was, in the view of his close friend US senator Henry Jackson, "the George Marshall of the Six-Day War, a brilliant strategist and tactician."[90] Few men could talk about their country's

---

88. Ibid

89. Ibid

90. Ibid. Senator Henry Jackson in conversation with author, September 15, 1976

military situation as well as Rabin could about Israel's: His expertise was not lost on either the Administration or Congress. However, there was some nervousness on the part of a few American officials about his being a military man, based on the assumption that a diplomat ought to be a diplomat, and not a general. His inability to speak English fluently was also a handicap when it came to establishing personal contact. He tried to improve his English by taping his speeches and replaying them in order to be word-perfect. Before facing a panel of newsmen on CBS's *Face the Nation* for the first time in 1969, he asked aides to fire questions at him for practice. He issued instructions to his speechwriters to keep the language plain, so that he would sound the same in private conversation as when making a public speech.

To his dismay, a great deal of his time was taken up with an institution he found alien and irrelevant: the Washington cocktail party. He disliked the ritual reception lines, the polite formality, and above all, the formal wear. Maurice Amitai, an aide to US senator Abraham Ribicoff, and later head of the American-Israel Public Affairs Committee in Washington, once teased him about the discomfort he was obviously feeling that evening in his tuxedo: "I guess you came early," he joked, "in order to make the most of the evening."[91] The remark brought a grimace from Rabin. One traditional trait of the diplomat, verbal self-restraint, Rabin could never master. It made for lively conversation, but it soon gave him a reputation for being less than the model diplomat. Once, during a luncheon with a British editor, he patiently explained why he thought Britain didn't matter anymore in geopolitical terms and why only the US was

---

91. Maurice Amitai in conversation with author, September 15, 1976

important. "And he's supposed to be a diplomat?" the editor remarked later.

Rabin was proud of the difference between himself and the traditional type of envoy, and encouraged people to think of him as only a temporary member of the diplomatic corps. A career diplomat would never look bored at banquet tables, as Rabin did. A career diplomat would remain politely non-committal, but not Rabin. His manner was for many a refreshing change, and appealed to a wide variety of acquaintances. Senator Jacob Javits, one of a handful of American Jews in the Senate, found his sense of mission admirable. A ranking member of the Nixon Administration praised him as well-organized, orderly, and systematic.

Despite initial problems, Rabin found the job liberating. Gone were the awesome responsibilities of military life and the barriers, which his rank interposed between him and others. Even his natural shyness proved no great handicap, as he intended to become acquainted with official Washington slowly and carefully. He was extremely interested in the way the American government functioned, particularly in the field of foreign affairs. "For me, it was the best school in which to learn world politics. I wouldn't have learned what I did in ten years at a university."[92] He was most impressed with the intricate mechanism known as 'checks and balances', which prevented any of the three branches of government from becoming too powerful. It provided a stability, which, particularly in 1968, seemed crucial to the American political system.

Rabin's first aim upon arriving in Washington was to capitalize on the military triumph of the Six-Day War and

---

92. Yitzhak Rabin in conversation with author, October 7, 1976

convert it into diplomatic gains for Israel, whose relationship with the United States was far from perfect. Unfortunately, it was a time when America was experiencing a popular movement towards retrenchment.

Traditionally, the Israeli ambassador looked to the strong American Jewish community of six-million as the key source of support for the Jewish State; for that reason Eban and Harman had spent far more time talking to Jewish rather than non-Jewish groups. They had found these audiences friendly, often effusive. Rabin, too, reached out to the American Jewish community, but the initial contact was cool and formal. Language was still a problem; he was a sabra, and that was strange to some American Jews. "Some people," said his close friend Norman Bernstein, a leader of the Washington Jewish community, "would have liked him to be more of a personality, a man who would come and embrace them, put his arm around them and be close and friendly. Basically, that was not in his nature."[93] Another difficulty Rabin had with American Jewry was his view that the US was failing to recognize how dependent on it the rest of the free world had become. The most glaring manifestation of this was the increasingly isolationist attitude within the American society, an attitude that could only hurt Israel. He was appalled to find American Jewish leaders supporting such isolationism. "Yitzhak Rabin has one code of morality," according to Marvin Kalb, the ex-CBS diplomatic correspondent and a close friend of Rabin, "and that is the security of the State of Israel." That code of morality drove him to approach groups, whom no Israeli ambassador had previously considered worth approaching: church bodies;

93. Norman Bernstein in conversation with author, September 17, 1976

military think tanks; members of the American ring-wing, who regardless of their political views held opinions that accorded with his own; also finding considerable support for the Jewish State among Baptists during his trips to the South. He continued to speak to Jewish groups, but less often than his predecessors had, preferring to concentrate on reaching a section of America that he felt had gone untapped for too long.

Although the United States had been the first country to recognize the State of Israel, the relationship between the two nations had been under constant strain in the previous years. This was reflected in the way American presidents treated Israelis, both those who came on occasional visits and those who took up temporary residence in the US. As late as the presidency of John F. Kennedy, prime minister David Ben-Gurion was accorded the privilege of meeting the president only in a New York hotel. The United States reserved White House invitations for its closer friends. Israeli ambassadors were consequently quite often left out in the cold. They were able to maintain a wide-ranging network of official contacts, but never came close to the senior men in the Administration. Talks with the president were rare. American Jewish leaders, such as the Republican Max Fisher of Detroit or the Democrat Abraham Feinberg of New York, were asked to press Israel's case with the president. With the growing warmth of the Kennedy and Johnson Administrations towards Israel, matters improved, but only slightly. Rabin, a diplomat who had no time for conventions that kept him from doing his job effectively, was determined to change the system: "I wanted to be in a position where the Administration and the Congress would turn to me rather than to a middleman."[94] American Jewry, particularly the leaders, rebelled quietly. They didn't mind Rabin's decision to enter into a direct relationship with the government that much, but they did object to being used in emergencies to pressure key officials in the Administration without having some say in discussions.

Rabin's first task was to obtain economic and military assistance from the US; his second, to convince the US that Russian penetration in the Middle East must be deterred; his third, to persuade the Administration to let those involved in the Middle East dispute, resolve their problems without Superpower dictation. His policy was to suggest that Israel's goals converged with American interests in the Middle East, and this simple fact, he thought, would be enough to keep American arms flowing into Israel.

Rabin had troubles with the Johnson Administration from the start. The State Department official responsible for the Middle East was Lucius Battle, a man Rabin described once as "pleasant, cultured, and positive, but very reserved and formal." The ambassador might have made some progress with him, but in October 1968, Battle resigned, and Rabin's relations with the Department took a decided turn for the worse. The problem was Battle's replacement, Parker Hart, a former ambassador to Turkey, who had spent most of his diplomatic career in the Arab world. Rabin's first encounter with Hart in October 1968 was memorable: "I entered his office and thought I must be having a heart attack. I thought the ceiling would collapse on me. On every wall, on every

---

94. Yitzhak Rabin in conversation with author, November 18, 1976

side, covering every centimeter, they were staring at me; Arab rulers, with and without *keffyehs*, with and without moustaches; sheikhs, princes, rulers, presidents. The only agreeable picture in the whole gallery was that of the Turkish president."[95]

Rabin was, not unnaturally, shocked at such insensitivity on the part of the man with whom he would have to deal so closely on vital matters, affecting the Jewish State. Realizing that his main contact in the State Department was an 'Arabist' "in mind and blood" (Rabin's own words), the ambassador was distressed that he now had no one with whom to discuss the delivery of Phantoms. For the remainder of the Johnson period, he worked through the Pentagon almost exclusively, a precarious undertaking for a foreign envoy, but under the circumstances the only practical solution.

Understandably, Rabin looked forward to the inauguration of the Republican Administration of Richard Nixon in January 1969. Nixon had campaigned on the pledge that he would turn the previous era of confrontation into one of negotiation. He saw the necessity for fulfilling his promise in the Middle East where the Russians, having become a Mediterranean power for the first time after 1967, posed a direct threat to American interests. The Arab-Israeli conflict, in which the antagonists were the client states of these two Superpowers, provided ominous possibilities for future confrontation.

The Israeli ambassador's acquaintance with Nixon dated from August 1966. Defeated for the presidency in 1960, Nixon was hoping for another opportunity in the 1968 elections. In search of it, he travelled abroad extensively,

95. Interview with Yitzhak Rabin, *Maariv*, April 13, 1973

gaining experience and meeting foreign heads of state. In Israel, where Nixon seemed something of a political has-been, he was accorded a rather less than royal welcome. During the early part of the visit, Nixon and Rabin were guests at dinner in the Tel Aviv home of the American *chargé d'affaires*, where the conversation centered on Nixon's recent visit to Southeast Asia. Rabin was the only other guest who had any firsthand knowledge of the region, having been there only a few months before. With this in common, the two men got on well; and Rabin offered Nixon a military helicopter for a day of touring round the country. It was an experience that Nixon did not forget: He was the first American in public life to visit the country after the Six-Day War and it was during that trip that he said, "If I were an Israeli, I would never give up the Golan Heights." At a Tel Aviv news conference, Nixon declared that Israel should not withdraw from occupied territories until there is a peace settlement.

The two men met once more for ninety minutes in the Mayflower Hotel in New York in August 1968, shortly before Nixon was named the Republican Party's choice for president at its convention. Rabin had sought the meeting, depressed by what he saw happening in the US and sensing that Nixon, with his professed belief in a strong America and desire to honor American commitments abroad, would signal a change in the country's direction. Nixon assured Rabin that he was confident he could pull America out of its doldrums. Both he and his likely Democratic opponent, senator Hubert Humphrey of Minnesota, wanted some kind of understanding with the Russians; but Nixon did not think it possible to conduct negotiations without being strong. It was an opinion that accorded perfectly with Rabin's own.

Rabin was cautiously optimistic about the new Nixon Administration; the Democrats had shown little favor towards Israel and had provided little political support. In his view, and when it came to the crunch, there was a slight chance that Nixon would be more sympathetic to Israel than his predecessor.

The first few months of the Nixon administration gave glimmerings of hope in this direction. After foreign minister Abba Eban met Nixon in March 1968, Rabin was buoyed up by the results of their talks and believed that Israel could look forward to enjoying strong support from the president. However, in the months ahead, Nixon's maneuvering with the Russians made him less sure, though this did not prevent the two men from continuing their good relationship.

Rabin found that he could adopt a relaxed tone with Nixon. In 1969, the president had invited a number of foreign ambassadors in Washington to a formal dinner at which they were expected to wear in addition to white ties any military decorations they had received. Rabin was slightly taken aback. The Israeli army, shunning formality, had made it a practice not to award military decorations, and hence he had none to wear. During the dinner, Nixon noticed Rabin's apparent modesty and asked him about his medals. "I would have thought a general such as yourself would have plenty of them," he said with a laugh. Rabin replied: "Mr. President, the only award I received after the Six-Day War was an honorary doctorate from the Hebrew University, and it's a little difficult to pin a certificate on my suit."[96]

Diplomatic activity in the Middle East was proceeding in 1969 with the mission of UN emissary Gunnar Jarring, for

---

96. Dan Pattir in conversation with author, August 24, 1976

whom Rabin had little respect. He preferred to see Israel and Egypt use the good offices of the US to work out a peace agreement. The Jarring mission could not bring the sides to talk with one another and so his effort failed.

Meanwhile, Nixon's secretary of state William Rogers, an attorney and a relative novice in foreign affairs, sought Russian support for an American peace proposal. The 'Rogers Plan', called for the return of virtually all the occupied lands to the Arabs, in return for which the Arabs would recognize the State of Israel and agree to secure borders. Unlike Nixon's national security adviser, Henry Kissinger, Rogers knew little about the Middle East but evinced a strong interest in the region. Rabin, despite the fact that he genuinely liked him, was never able to establish a warm relationship with Rogers. Their personalities were in sharp contrast, as were their methods of work. Rabin was serious, straightforward to the point of bluntness, without much humor. Rogers was light hearted, outgoing, casual, and always informal. The ambassador's early difficulties with English gave his presentations a ponderous formality, for which Rogers had little patience. For his part, Rabin regretted that the secretary had so little knowledge of the Middle East. Rogers saw himself less a policymaker than an arbitrator among disputing factions, leaving Rabin feeling helpless after their talks. Discussions between the two men were often lengthy, with Rabin doing most of the talking; Rogers tired quickly of the subjects that passionately interested the ambassador.

When Rogers announced his plan in December 1969, it widened the breach, not only between the two men but, more importantly, between their two countries. It brought US-Israeli relations to their lowest point since president

Eisenhower had forced the Jewish State to withdraw from the Sinai after the 1956 war. Rabin was incensed at the proposal; it seemed to him a major diplomatic affront to Israel. One of the worst aspects of the Rogers Plan in Rabin's eye was the change it reflected in American policy towards the Middle East. Until the plan was announced, the US had never publicly stated what it believed Israel's final boundaries should be. Now, with the Rogers Plan advocating an almost complete return to Israel's pre-1967 frontiers, the Arabs would never agree to anything less; and the US, having taken this public stand, could not bargain for anything more at the peace talks.

To Rabin's dismay, the Americans were tending more and more to limit Israel's bargaining power and to tell Israel what it should do. He knew that it was impossible to expect the US to withdraw from its peacemaking role in the region, but he wanted it to focus in public on principles – which had been the case under Johnson – and not details. He feared that Rogers was laying the groundwork for an American-Soviet settlement, which would be imposed on the parties to the conflict. Israel had long resisted this as ultimately pro-Arab in design.

Rabin had to contend with his government's fears that rejecting the plan might provoke a new postponement of arms deliveries. Rabin argued that Israel had managed to strengthen its relations with the US to a point where it could afford to turn down peace proposals without fear of the consequences, and he strongly advised the Cabinet to reject the Rogers Plan. When the Cabinet decided to accept his advice, it called upon Rabin to draft the wording of its rejection. Rabin delivered a personal reply to the proposal through the Israeli Embassy. The vehicle was a pink sheet communiqué, an idea conceived by Yehuda Avner of the Embassy staff; it was usually distributed by the Embassy to newsmen and Washington officials to explain Israeli policy. It was couched in forthright terms that were, at least to the mind of the secretary when he read it, less than diplomatic. Rogers was stung into stating that diplomats on American soil should know better than to make public any criticism of the US government. From that point on, relations between the two men were beyond repair. In public they remained cordial to one another, but Rabin began to look elsewhere for friends in high places. No Israeli ambassador had ever dealt so consistently with the highest echelons of the American government and even after his relations with Rogers had soured, he was always allowed access to the secretary of state. One of his most important relationships, developed with assistant secretary of state for near eastern affairs, Joseph Sisco, a State Department veteran, who had once been considered pro-Israeli, though by the time Nixon came to power, he had become a strong exponent of the new even-handed American policy towards the Middle East.

A deep friendship developed between the two men. Where Rogers was often impatient with Rabin, Sisco was not. Rabin found in Sisco someone with a sympathetic understanding of the Middle East, as well as a skill and an optimistic view in dealing with the region that he felt were lacking in Rogers. Better than others, Rabin thought, Sisco realized that the Middle East had become a focus of Superpower rivalries, and that far more was at stake in the Arab-Israeli conflict than the survival of the Jewish State or the future of Arab nationalism.[97]

---

97. Joseph Sisco in conversation with author, September 9, 1976

Twice a week, the two men met for lunch, usually at a favorite French restaurant in Georgetown. They spoke constantly over the telephone and often watched National Football League games together. "I enjoyed a personal relationship with him," Sisco said, "as much and probably more than any relationship I've ever had with an ambassador over the years." Sisco admired Rabin's ability to understand the mechanics of international relations beyond the context of the Middle East. He found that Rabin, with his thorough knowledge of military affairs, could make a very convincing argument that a strong Israel boosted American military potential in the Middle East. In addition, he found the ambassador a man of integrity whose word was his bond.[98] Though his relationship with Sisco played an essential part in keeping him in touch with the highest levels of the American Government, to affect the change in American policy towards the Middle East, which Rabin considered necessary, he had to influence the top policymakers and one man in particular: Henry Kissinger.

The two men had first met in 1966, when Rabin invited Kissinger (then an influential behind-the-scenes figure in Vietnam diplomacy) to lecture at the National Security College in Israel. A second meeting occurred in January 1968, just before Rabin took up his Washington appointment. Kissinger had flown in from Moscow and during his stay in Israel had an extended lunch in Tel Aviv with the ambassador-designate. They talked about the role of the Soviet Union in the Middle East, a subject in which both men were particularly interested. Though Kissinger was impressed

---

98. Ibid

with Rabin's grasp of international affairs, the two men had no contact for some time after Rabin arrived in Washington.[99]

As Kissinger, in the early stages of the Nixon Administration, showed little interest in the Middle East, Rabin tended to share the sense of mistrust that some American Jews felt about him, which stemmed from the fear that his very Jewishness would make him over-anxious to prove his impartiality in the Middle East. It was not until the time of the Jordanian crisis in September 1970 that the two men got to know one another better, and it became clear that they had much in common: Both enjoyed thrashing out the complexities of international affairs, both knew that it was impossible to look at the Middle East without taking into account the larger issues of Superpower politics. They enjoyed the intellectual exercise and found one another stimulating. Each in his own way enjoyed the secret, manipulative aspects of diplomacy. In Rabin, Kissinger found a cool-headed, rational Israeli who didn't stray from the main issues with meanderings into ancient history, as had been his experience with Golda Meir who had become Israel's prime minister in 1969. Neither man liked to gossip, at least not to one another. In Kissinger, Rabin found much to admire: "He is a great manipulator of events and people. He has a unique combination of academic knowledge and a pragmatic approach to problems, which is something one doesn't find nowadays."[100]

The American showed sensitivity to Israel, which the ambassador had not met before in Washington. The key of

---

99. In several conversations I had with Rabin's aides from his days as ambassador they described his attitude toward Henry Kissinger

100. Yitzhak Rabin in conversation with author, October 7, 1976

course to Kissinger's thinking and Rabin understood this, was his mistrust of the Russians. "We have to work together," Kissinger told Rabin early in his ambassadorship, "to make it clear to the Arab countries, that there is nothing to be gained through cooperation with the Soviet Union."[101] It was a goal which Rabin shared. Kissinger pressed the envoy to accept the notion – an alien one to most Israelis – that the Jewish State would be better off if the US could develop closer ties with the Arabs. Rabin shrewdly countered that Israel could understand this, but the US would have to offer it some kind of compensation, if an American-Arab axis was to be formed. Kissinger accepted Rabin's argument.

Rabin was a major influence on Kissinger's thinking about the Middle East and managed to persuade him to give serious consideration to the need to provide the Jewish State military and political support. It was due to Rabin, too, that Kissinger eventually rejected the prevalent view in the State Department, about the desirability of the two Superpowers working out a Middle East settlement, the 'imposed peace', which the Israelis feared so much.

Just about every facet of American life fascinated Rabin. He enjoyed travelling around the country and particularly liked the West Coast for its great natural beauty. An amateur photographer, when he could find the time, he would roam the countryside around Washington with his camera. He and his wife had not known such a sense of ease since their days at Camberley in 1952. "I enjoyed my job, I enjoyed being in America. I enjoyed most the contacts I had, even

---

101. Ibid

though there were difficult days and unpleasant meetings, and unpleasant events."[102]

Leah, who was a great social success and made many firm friends in her own right, had charge of their social calendar. A major enterprise, as she made a special point of looking after all the arrangements herself, including the setting of the tables, arranging the flowers and supervising the meals. The Rabins' cook kept her own diary to make sure that no returning guest was served the same dish twice. The one task Leah forswore was the seating arrangement: "To decide people's fate, even for two hours at a dinner party," she once said, "is cruel."

In 1970, Rabin's son Yuval celebrated his Bar Mitzvah in a Washington synagogue. A year later on December 5, Rabin's father Nehemiah died at the age of 85. He had been taken ill in November, but had refused to allow Rachel to send for Rabin, knowing that his son was busy with a visit that prime minister Meir was making to the US. The funeral was delayed until Rabin arrived in Israel, two days after Nehemiah's death.

The Rabins had a wide circle of friends in Washington. Wherever he went, the ambassador tended to attract a crowd, eager to listen to his military experiences, especially those of the Six-Day War. Talking about such things animated him. "I used to listen to him with wonderment," noted Marvin Kalb, who was a frequent guest at Washington cocktail parties. "When he talked strategy and tactics, he sparkled. The effect was to convey total self-confidence."[103] A popular lecturer on military subjects at the Pentagon,

---

102. Ibid

103. Marvin Kalb in conversation with author, September 15, 1976

he inevitably made friends among the upper echelons of the US Army, to whom he was primarily a military man, not a diplomat. While at formal meetings with Pentagon officials, they addressed him as 'Mr. Ambassador,' admiral Thomas Moorer, the chairman of the joint chiefs of staff of the US Armed Forces, once told him: "To me, you're General Rabin, and a general is much more to me than any ambassador, so let's be done with this 'Mr. Ambassador' bit."

Rabin made particular friends among the leaders of the Washington Jewish community, mostly men of means who were interested in Israel's cause. His political friends, too, tended to be strong supporters of Israel, like senators Henry Jackson of Washington, Stuart Symington of Missouri, and Jacob Javits of New York. Jackson liked the ambassador's habit of getting straight to the point. Symington felt relaxed enough with Rabin to ask him the most sensitive questions: When the two men were returning from a trip to the Sinai soon after Rabin had left Washington permanently in 1973, the senator asked him point-blank whether or not Israel had the atomic bomb. Without changing his expression, Rabin gently but firmly switched the subject.

At times, Rabin was surprised how much sympathy for Israel actually existed in Washington. One unlikely person, who became a close friend, was the national newspaper columnist the late Rowland Evans. A frequent critic of Israel, with whom Rabin was always at odds over American support for the Jewish State, Evans held that the US would be better off paying more attention to the Arabs and less to the Israelis, and that the Russians posed no great threat in the Middle East, unless the Americans drove the Arabs into their arms by siding with Israel, rather than acting even-handedly.

He also questioned whether the US needed to invest so much money in Israel. "But I never persuaded Rabin," said the columnist, "and he never persuaded me." Evans described Rabin as "the hardest-working diplomat I've ever seen in Washington."[104] Perhaps the oddest friendship Rabin struck up during his Washington days was with the Russian ambassador, Anatoly Dobrynin. Besides being champions of the Arab cause, the Russians had no diplomatic relations with Israel, having broken them off during the Six-Day War. Yet when Rabin arrived late at the funeral of two American diplomats, murdered by Arab terrorists in Khartoum on March 2 1973, and was unable to find a seat in the VIP section, Dobrynin noticed him, rushed up with a friendly greeting, and ushered him to the VIP stand, where he made room for Rabin next to him.

With Egypt engaging in a low-keyed war of attrition in 1969, it was clear to Rabin that Israel would have to call upon the US to supply more sophisticated weapons to the embattled Jewish State, in particular the American-made Phantom fighter jet. Israel wanted 50 of them. Some progress had been made during Eshkol's visit in January 1968 to President Johnson's Texas ranch, when Johnson had promised that the Israelis would soon get the planes it had requested. Rabin intended to speed up their delivery when he became ambassador, but his efforts were complicated by the fact that some Israeli leaders – notably foreign minister Eban – seemed no longer especially disturbed by the time the Johnson Administration was taking to reach a final decision. The Americans argued that the Israelis already

---

104. Rowland Evens in conversation with author, September 15, 1976

had strategic superiority in the Middle East and did not need such sophisticated weaponry. The decision to finally sell the planes came in October 1968, not coincidentally a few weeks before the American election, when presumably it would most benefit the Democratic presidential nominee, Hubert Humphrey. Johnson made the decision only after the Russians had turned down an American proposal to curtail arms shipments to the Middle East. Johnson was retiring in January, and it would take some time before a new Administration would actually send the arms.

In a dramatic press conference on March 23, 1970, secretary of state Rogers announced that the US had decided to turn down the request of 25 more Phantoms and 100 Skyhawks. To soften the blow, Rogers announced that the US would give Israel a $100 million economic credit.

Meanwhile, Israel was facing increasingly violent Egyptian attacks and some Israeli leaders were advocating air raids deep into Arab territory, to strike at airfields and other military installations. However, fears were expressed about what the United States might think and what the Soviet Union would do. American support was seen as crucial, especially since the deep bombing raids might trigger Russian intervention on the Egyptian side. The Israeli government looked to Rabin for guidance. He told them that the United States understood the argument in favor of the raids, that they might put a stop to the war of attrition, and therefore would not stand in their way. Thus Israel began the raid early in 1970, and during the first three months of the year some twenty such attacks were carried out against Egyptian bases and airfields. One Israeli fear about the raids materialized soon after they began. Nasser won a Soviet commitment to step up Russian participation in the Arab struggle against Israel.

By the end of 1970, 200 Soviet pilots were flying Egyptian aircraft; some 4,000 Soviet instructors were working in various branches of the Egyptian army; and between 12,000 and 15,000 Soviet officers and soldiers were manning 80 SAM missile sites. Some of the blame for this increased Russian involvement fell on Rabin; but he remained adamant that the raids had been essential, even at the risk of Russian intervention. Israel had been at a distinct disadvantage on the ground, with Egyptian troops far outnumbering Israelis near the Canal. Without the raids, Israel might well have faced another full-scale war. In addition, he felt that the raids would serve to bring the US into the region on a much larger scale: as the Soviet presence in the Arab world grew, so too did the American commitment to Israel.

By creating a kind of American-Soviet standoff in the region, the raids contributed to bringing the war of attrition to an end. In August 1970, Israel and Egypt agreed to a cease-fire under American sponsorship. Israel accepted it only after US assurances of more military and economic assistance. The cease-fire brought with it fresh hopes, that serious negotiations for peace would take place and both Meir and Nasser made gestures towards improving the atmosphere. The Israeli prime minister announced that the Jewish State might give up its demand for direct negotiations with the Arabs, to help pave the way for peace talks. Nasser replied that he would recognize the State of Israel, if the Israelis would agree to withdraw from the occupied territories. However, peacemaking efforts were brought to a temporary halt in September by Nasser's death on September 28, 1970, as the diplomats watched to find out what new policies would emerge in Cairo with Nasser's successor, Anwar al-Sadat.

Rabin's determination to play a major role in the policymaking of his country inevitably led to a clash with Abba Eban, the foreign minister. His influence grew when Meir decided early in 1970 that she wanted more personal control over Israeli-American relations. She admired Kissinger's system of receiving direct reports from American ambassadors in such sensitive spots as Moscow and Peking, thus circumventing the State Department, and decided she could circumvent her own Foreign Ministry. Rabin was to report directly to her, and at the same time Eban would get copies of all cables exchanged between the Washington Embassy and the prime minister's office. Eban initially accepted the change, though he was annoyed to find that in fact a number of cables were not sent to him, for his information. Rabin's direct line to Meir prompted reports in the Israeli press of a simmering feud between the ambassador and the foreign minister. Actually, Eban showed no animosity towards Rabin for virtually usurping his own advisory role. His quarrel was with Meir. As for Rabin, the new arrangement gave him greater standing with American Administration officials. It was an obvious measure of Rabin's growing influence on Israeli policy.

The government in Jerusalem tended to attach little importance to Rabin's personal problems with Eban, as the ambassador had so thoroughly proved his worth. The Israeli relations with the US growing closer were reflected in the increasingly large military aid programs shepherded by Rabin through the Administration and Congress. "Rabin," said a senior Embassy official who worked closely with him, "managed to change our status from that of a liability to that of an asset. Israel was now a country which took care of itself, kept the Soviet thrust at bay in an area that the US thought essential, and conducted its affairs reasonably well."

It was the Jordanian crisis of September 1970, which, more than any other diplomatic affair brought Rabin to the attention of the senior members of the Nixon Administration. Rabin had kept an anxious eye on events in Jordan over the previous few years. Wondering whether the moderate King Hussein would be able to keep the radical Palestinian guerrillas at bay; guerillas who claimed to represent the two million Palestinian refugees who had fled when the State of Israel was declared in 1948, and who were now scattered throughout the Middle East. Hussein had long feared that the Palestinians living in Jordan were plotting to overthrow him in order to turn his country into a Palestinian-run state. The crisis began on September 1, when Palestinian guerrillas tried to assassinate King Hussein. Fighting broke out between the Jordanian army and the Palestinian forces. A few days later, on September 6, Palestinian terrorists, hoping to publicize their cause beyond Jordanian borders, hijacked four commercial jets, flew them to Jordan, and defied the king for days, while the passengers were forced to wait in the hot desert until the incident was resolved. Meanwhile, Syria decided to aid the Palestinians, and by September 20 had sent some 250 tanks across the Jordanian border. Hussein appealed to the US for help. A Syrian advance into Amman, the Jordanian capital, could well trigger Israeli intervention, and if that happened, the entire Middle East would probably flare up in a general Israeli-Arab war, creating the possibility that the Russians might enter the fray.

Israel had mobilized its troops and was poised for war should the Syrians get too close to the Jordanian capital. The US Navy's Sixth Fleet, which normally sailed in Mediterranean waters, moved in closer to the eastern shoreline. The Russians were warned that unless the Syrians withdrew from Jordan, the region faced dangerous consequences. The Middle East was on the brink, but unlike the 'Waiting Period' before the Six-Day War, this time the crisis was being played out in secret. Only the diplomats and the generals knew what was going on. The public was kept largely in the dark.

Nixon realized that the US actually needed the State of Israel to keep the crisis from exploding into war. The Russians, like the Syrians, had to be restrained, but the US was scarcely in a position to do this. America was not keen to risk a third world war just to keep Palestinian guerrillas from overrunning a tiny Middle Eastern kingdom. The American deterrent was not much of a weapon in this situation and the president knew it. Israel, however, could not afford to have the Palestinians in power along its eastern border; hence, the Israeli deterrent was credible.

Rabin realized the president's dilemma. Nixon agreed that Israel could not allow the Palestinians to take control of Jordan, but he was determined that if the US was going to rely on Israel to such a degree, and in effect, to exploit the Israeli military presence in the region, then it would do so for a price. On the evening of September 20, and as the Jordanian crisis deepened, both Rabin and Meir, who was at the end of a visit to the US, were present at a fundraising event. During the evening, Rabin received an urgent message from the White House; the president wanted him in Washington immediately for consultations. Within a few hours, an official White House plane had brought Rabin to the president. Prompting the dramatic summons was the American fear that the Syrians might begin to advance towards Amman and the realization that only the Israeli army could keep them at bay. At a top-secret meeting Rabin and Nixon worked out contingency arrangements for the possible battle. The American leader wanted to know that Israel was willing to move into Jordan on its own. Rabin wanted to make sure that an attack by the Jewish State would not weaken it on other fronts. He pressed Nixon to pledge that if Israel attacked Jordan, the US would protect its rear flank at the Suez Canal with the Sixth Fleet. Never before had Israel won such a promise from the United States, the closest thing to a defense pact the two countries could reach.

The defense arrangement was never put into effect: The significance of the White House meeting between Rabin and the president was not lost on the Russians, and when the IDF began massing on the Jordanian border, their presence there made it clear to the Syrians that it was too dangerous to march on Amman. Syrian tanks began withdrawing on September 22. Within five days, Hussein was in Cairo, invited there by Nasser to work out a deal with the Palestinians. In late September, Hussein and Yasser Arafat, the Palestinian guerrilla leader, came to terms. The fighting gradually tapered off and by July 1971, Hussein had eradicated all guerrilla bases in Jordan.

Rabin discovered, in the wake of the Jordanian crisis, that he was welcomed by top-level Washington officials with more warmth than ever. His shrewd assessment of the situation had made a great impression on American policymakers. Some Israeli newspapers suggested that Rabin, with his coolness under pressure and the quality of his mind, had reminded the president of his hero, general George Patton. During a visit to the home of Arthur Goldberg (a former Supreme Court justice and UN ambassador) in Virginia, Rabin joked to friends about his new acceptance: "I know more ways in and out of the White House than the Secret Service."

By the autumn of 1970, the United States had reversed its previous policy and decided that only massive arms shipments to Israel would induce the Jewish State to keep the momentum for peace going. This apparent volte-face was largely due to Rabin, who had always argued that Israel would be much more willing to enter into peace talks with the Arabs if it was militarily strong. The US announced in October 1970 a $545 million arms package for Israel for the following years, including 18 more Phantoms (by then the Jewish State had 74) and 200 tanks, among them the ultramodern M-60s. The Administration justified its change of policy on the grounds that it wanted to restore the arms balance, which appeared to have shifted in favor of the Arabs.

The last two years of Rabin's ambassadorship witnessed a flurry of diplomatic activity as efforts were made by the UN and the US to bring the conflicting parties to the conference table, but little progress was made. Egypt made a series of overtures to the Soviet Union in order to prepare itself for the much-vaunted battle with Israel. The year 1971 was to be president Sadat's 'Year of Decision', but he had to postpone it. A year later, Sadat fell out with the Russians, and expelled 20,000 advisers from Egypt. It was one of several Arab moves that gave a deceptive impression of tranquility in the Middle East.

In appreciation for president Nixon's growing pro-Israel stance, Rabin made no secret of his preference of the president over the Democratic candidate George McGovern in the upcoming 1972 presidential elections. Rabin feared McGovern as an excessive budget-cutter and an isolationist, neither good for Israel. A known quantity, a man of proven deeds, Nixon was the most likely to keep American arms flowing to Israel.

One of the more dramatic examples of Rabin's assertiveness as ambassador occurred when the Israelis on February 21, 1973 shot down a Libyan civilian jet that overflew the Israeli-occupied Sinai desert. It was carrying 113 passengers and crew. In the days preceding the incident, Israel had picked up rumors of an Arab terrorist plan to crash an aircraft into an Israeli target. Thus, news of the approaching Libyan airliner caused great alarm. After signaling the plane to land but getting no response, Israeli jets finally shot it down. Of the 113 aboard, only five survived.

The Israelis insisted that they had had no way of knowing whether there were civilians aboard, and that their main concern had been that the aircraft was heading in the direction of the country's nuclear research center at Dimona. Despite all this, international opinion was very much against the Jewish State. Again Rabin's advice was sought and he said: "To ask advice on how to present the incident is nonsense. It can't be presented well. The best thing is to let it be forgotten. It was the height of stupidity. If Israel had looked for a way to make its position in the world more difficult, it couldn't have found a better one." He demanded that both the chief of staff, David Elazar, and the head of the air force, Benjamin Peled, be dismissed, otherwise Rabin threatened he would resign. The demand seemed odd, at least with regard to Elazar, a long-time friend of Rabin. His ultimatum was ignored in view of the fact that his return was imminent in any case. During her visit to Washington in March, Meir carefully explained to president Nixon why the plane had been shot down and her explanation seemed to have been accepted.

Rabin left Washington in March 1973 with mixed feelings. The prospect of returning to Israel jobless after such exciting, productive years was not inviting. One event during the last weeks of his ambassadorship cheered him. His secretary, Ruhama Hermon, secretly approached many of the American officials and congressmen with whom Rabin had worked in Washington and invited them to a farewell party for him. Sisco paid Rabin the unusual tribute of writing an article about him in the *National Jewish Monthly*. "The overriding feature of our professional relationship," he wrote, "has been frankness. There is a similarity in our approaches to common problems and in our styles of operation. Like myself and unlike the traditional diplomat, Ambassador Rabin is direct and always to the point. Let's face it, at times even blunt. He says what he means and means what he says. This may bother some people, it has never bothered me."

Rabin's final day as ambassador, March 11, 1973, was as busy as usual. The night before he had made a speech in Chicago and only arrived back in Washington at 2 am. Six hours later, he was at his desk drafting farewell notes to the officials with whom he had worked over the previous five years. Later in the morning, he spoke to Israeli consuls who had flown in from different parts of the US to bid him goodbye. He issued no final statement at the airport, but his one brief remark to newsmen as he boarded the plane summed up his feelings well enough: "I was happy to serve here and at the same time I'm happy to return home." Sisco had once told him that when the United States turned to Israel now, it did so with the respect shown to a Super- power. No European country could claim as much, he added. Yet the departing ambassador had created a storm of criticism in the wake of this achievement. Notwithstanding *Newsweek*'s praise for him in December 1972 "as one of the two most effective envoys in Washington" (the other was Soviet Ambassador Anatoly Dobrynin), one journalist wrote: "It is fair to say that no other diplomat in recent years here has been attacked so often for displaying such a noticeable lack of diplomacy."

CHAPTER SEVEN

"BUT YOU ARE MY CANDIDATE!"

Rabin's whole future after he left Washington was a continual source of speculation; some had even expected him to return to Israel as early as 1969. Israel's domestic politics were volatile and unpredictable and his possible role in a future Government was constantly being weighed in Jerusalem. Rabin enjoyed the speculation; it enhanced his reputation in Washington.

In early 1969, he had been mentioned as a possible minister for education, though, ironically, he was not then a member of a political party. Later that year, it was rumored that he might replace Dayan as minister of defense.

In 1970, Pinhas Sapir, the minister of finance and leader of the Labor Party (many called him the party's kingmaker) had told Rabin that he could become prime minister if he returned to Israel quickly and worked hard. But the ambassador had declined, calculating that his chances were slim and his present post was worth too much to yield.[105]

In the spring of 1971, press reports were predicting that Rabin would be recalled to Israel by the end of the year. In early 1972, he was being mentioned in Jerusalem as the next minister for development. Sapir had even gone to Washington to offer him the post, but it was a particularly delicate period in American-Israeli relations and Rabin had asked for a delay of three months before returning to take up the job. He left the meeting with Sapir with the clear impression that the finance minister had made a commitment; Sapir, however, felt under no obligation. Because of Rabin's refusal to take up the assignment immediately, in April 1972, Golda Meir appointed Haim Bar-Lev, a former chief of staff, to the post. The ambassador was astonished at this turn of events, but there was nothing he could do. Two months later, Rabin's name had again cropped up when justice minister Ya'acov Shimshon Shapira resigned unexpectedly. But criticism had been mounting against Meir for appointing too many generals to the Cabinet hence, Rabin was again passed over for someone else.

In January 1973, Rabin, now 50 years old, announced for the first time publicly at a dinner at the Waldorf-Astoria in New York that he would be a candidate for the Knesset when elections were held the following October. "I am returning." he said, "ready and willing to fit into political life in Israel. But I don't know how it will be done." In February, he had another meeting in Washington with Sapir, but this time the two men had little to talk about. Rabin had hoped Sapir would agree that the previous year's offer of

---

105. Arye Avneri, *Sapir*. Tel Aviv: Peleg Publishers, 1976, pp. 316-18

a Cabinet post still stood, but the Labor Party's share of Cabinet portfolios in Meir's Government coalition had been met with Bar-Lev's recent appointment. Sapir had advised him to act as a spokesman on behalf of the Labor Party during the election campaign; he would not only win votes for the party, but it would be a way of drawing the public's attention to him. The idea appealed to him, not least since it was the one way he could remain in public life.

For the first time in 32 years, Rabin found himself out of public service. Not having the responsibilities attendant upon a senior military officer or a diplomat, he had time to meet people he had never talked with before. The experience convinced him that politics was the right place for him. He hoped for a seat in the Knesset and a Cabinet post, even if only a junior one, in the new Government Meir would form after her reelection (which was a near certainty) in the autumn of that year: "I had no illusion in those days that any of the existing ministers was a candidate for replacement, and therefore I knew it would be a long, hard, uphill road to a key post in the Cabinet. But I was ready to travel it. I accepted the fact that I was a newcomer to politics."[106]

He considered himself a natural candidate for inclusion in the Labor list, though he had not actually joined the party until 1971. "Whether or not I reach a high position in political life," he said, "my place is in this camp. I was raised in a proletarian home and I was educated in the values of the Labor Movement. There can be no cause and surely no career which would bring me to change places."[107] Party

---

106. Yitzhak Rabin in conversation with author, October 7, 1976

107. Interview with Yitzhak Rabin, *Maariv*, August 10, 1973

leaders assured him that he would be given a safe seat on the Labor list of candidates for the Knesset when it was drawn up in the autumn. He would campaign, therefore, both as a strong candidate for the Knesset and as a possible Cabinet minister. Party officials in charge of conducting the election were delighted with his decision. "He was a new man, with a great legend," said Dov Tzamir, the Labor Party's information director and eventually, Rabin's chief lieutenant during his campaign for the prime ministership. "We were convinced that a man like Rabin could put some excitement into the campaign. There was no doubt that he would be greeted enthusiastically."[108] Tzamir was right. By July, the Labor Party had realized that Rabin was a valuable political asset.

There was talk within the Labor Party that Rabin was an up-and-coming man who might one day be a suitable replacement for Golda Meir. When the possibility was mentioned to Rabin, he rejected it out of hand, addressing himself to the more practical consideration of whether he would win even a junior seat in the next Cabinet. He was cheered in August to read that a public opinion poll on whether he deserved a Cabinet post gave him a 61 percent rating.

Israel's electoral system is based on the list system of proportional representation, with each party presenting to the voters a list of candidates for the 120 seats in the Knesset. The voter therefore chooses an entire party list, instead of particular candidates; each party is represented in the Knesset according to the proportion of votes its list receives. On September 24, 1973, the Labor party chose its

108. Dov Tzamir in conversation with author, June 20, 1976

list of candidates for the Knesset: Rabin was twentieth on the list, a very safe placing. All during August and September, he canvassed for votes, sometimes speaking as many as nine times a day. He talked to audiences about the subjects he knew most about: the Arab-Israeli conflict, American-Israeli relations, and the country's defense. Although the border with Egypt had been quiet since the cease-fire of the previous August, some members of the government were disturbed that too little was being done diplomatically to preserve the peace. Rabin, however, was confident about Israel's position.

The Yom Kippur War, which began on October 6, took the whole country by surprise. There had been signs of the impending Egyptian and Syrian attacks: The Arabs had moved men and armor into battle position in the days leading up to the war, but Israeli intelligence made a grave error of judgment in assuming that the might of the IDF was sufficient to prevent the Arabs from declaring war. The war caught Rabin in the midst of a busy campaign schedule. He had completed a week of speechmaking around the country on Friday afternoon, October 5, and planned to spend a day at home with his family.

Yom Kippur would begin at sunset on Friday evening. His son Yuval was in the third month of his compulsory service in the navy and had come home for the holiday, but at 2 pm on Friday, he was suddenly summoned back to his base. That was Rabin's first indication that things had taken an abnormal turn. His son-in-law, Avraham Ben-Artzi, was also at the Rabins' home that day. An officer in the armored corps unit directed by Dan Shomron (the commander of the Entebbe rescue mission of July 1976), Ben-Artzi was to have had an operation on his knee on Sunday, October 7 and so was not called up. But when he heard that Yuval had been ordered back to the navy, he contacted his unit in the Sinai and shortly afterwards decided to journey south to join his battalion. His sudden return increased Rabin's suspicions but he could do nothing except wait for news.

At 10 am on Saturday morning, he received a telephone call from Israel Galili, the former Hagana commander, and now minister without portfolio. The message was brutally direct: War was imminent. A short while later the telephone rang again: Defense minister Moshe Dayan had summoned all former chiefs of staff to a meeting at 3 pm that afternoon.

It was Yom Kippur, a day so holy that even many who keep no other religious holidays go to synagogue and observe the fast. Usually there is no traffic on the streets, and the national radio and television are shut down. But on this day, army jeeps were rushing to their bases. Young men, many of whom had not eaten since Friday evening, were returning to units preparing for the inevitable battle. At 2 pm, sirens sounded throughout the nation. Egyptian soldiers had begun crossing the Suez Canal in the south, while Syrian troops in the north had begun moving across the Golan Heights. Rabin turned the radio on instinctively and found that the national radio station had begun broadcasting again. A special announcement told the nation that the war had started. At 2:15 pm, Avraham Ben-Artzi appeared, explaining that his commander had told him that morning that he doubted there was to be a war and had sent him back to Tel Aviv for the hospital operation. Rabin was later to recount this story as evidence of how unprepared the army had been for the war.

The meeting with Dayan was not very productive; the former chiefs of staff were given some sketchy information about the first hours of battle, but the meeting had to be hastily adjourned as the situation worsened. Rabin returned home and followed the progress of events on radio and television. The Yom Kippur War was one of the most difficult periods for Rabin: His country was at war, caught by total surprise, and here he was, with no specific military task to perform, no chance to take part, a one-time chief of staff stranded on the sidelines.

The first few hours of the fighting shattered the myth of the Israeli invincibility. Thousands of Egyptian troops and hundreds of tanks had successfully crossed over to the eastern bank of the Suez Canal and were establishing bridgeheads to consolidate their gains. Thousands of Syrian troops and hundreds of tanks had overrun much of the Golan Heights and were threatening to advance into Israel proper. The Jewish State would once again have to fight for its survival.

In addition to the fears and horror that the sudden outbreak of war had brought, Rabin had to face the fact that all his assurances to the US during the past five years that war would never happen as long as Israel was strong, now counted for nothing. He feared for US-Israeli relations in the future: The war would surely bring about a slackening in American confidence and support just when Israel needed it most. Later on, when the American airlift of new military equipment began, those forebodings partially disappeared, only to be replaced by the fear that this would increase American pressure on Israel to accept an overall solution to the Middle East conflict, even if the terms were disagreeable.

On Sunday afternoon, prime minister Meir summoned Rabin to Tel Aviv, where she briefed him on military developments. Dayan had just proposed an Israeli withdrawal in the Sinai to the Mitla and Gidi Passes. Rather than accept the defense minister's plan right away, Meir had asked chief of staff David Elazar to find out how untenable the situation actually was on the Southern Front. When he learned that Elazar planned to fly to Southern Front headquarters later that day, Rabin got permission to go along as an onlooker. Donning a military uniform, he joined the chief of staff in the Sinai headquarters, where Elazar was drawing up plans for a counter-offensive as an alternative to Dayan's suggested withdrawal. Rabin was very much in favor of the counter-offensive. The day after it was launched, Rabin met his old friend Israel Tal, and the two men talked about Israeli prospects in the war. "Until we manage to go over to the offensive," Rabin said, "and press the Syrians and Egyptians hard, there won't be a cease-fire. Nothing will force the Arabs to stop as long as they're not being defeated. There's nothing that can be done on the diplomatic front."[109]

Other than the visit to southern headquarters and a journey north to the Syrian Front, both times accompanying David Elazar, Rabin remained near military headquarters in Tel Aviv during the first few days of the war. Instinct rather than a specific job kept him there, joining other former generals with the same instinct. The confusion and sense of desperation left little room for niceties about titles and jobs; hence, Rabin acted as an unofficial adviser. In theory, he was not in favor of the previous generation of commanders lingering about at military headquarters and offering advice; it indicated a lack of confidence in those now in command. Long after the Yom Kippur War he was to say: "I hope that we'll have no repetition of that bringing in of all the old guard. I believe that in the army there can be no turning back

---

109. The source asked not to be identified

the wheel. Let the new generation do what they have to do."[110] However, at the time, a driving sense of duty had prevailed over such thoughts, and he was unable to keep away from the war room at military headquarters.

While scanning the plan of troop deployments, Rabin noticed an obvious weakness along the border with Jordan. Israeli defenses in the Jordan Valley, near the border, were minimal, a dangerous situation if King Hussein decided to open a third front. Sensing that Elazar might be more willing to take advice from former chief of staff Yigael Yadin, Rabin asked him to discuss the situation on the Jordanian front with the chief of staff. Though Elazar was under heavy pressure on the Syrian front, he listened to Yadin and ordered the necessary changes in deployment. Jordan, however, did not enter the battle along its frontier with Israel. Though it mobilized its forces during the first week, it refrained from engaging the Israelis directly. On October 13, Jordanian units were sent to fight alongside Syrian troops on the Golan Heights.

As the pressure on the army commanders lessened, they began to resent the presence of unofficial advisers like Rabin, and made it plain that they would prefer to conduct the war without outside assistance. Rabin agreed to go, but, though he could understand their attitude he could not help but feel slighted; his isolation from decision-making was agony to him. Towards the end of the first week of the war, he learned that his brother-in-law, Avraham Yoffe, a former division commander in the Six-Day War, planned to tour the fronts by jeep. Eager for involvement at any level, Rabin joined him and the two men drove around both the Northern and

---

110. Yitzhak Rabin in conversation with author, November 18, 1976

the Southern Fronts. One special task they accepted gladly: taking the messages of soldiers back to their families. Rabin was appalled and depressed by what they found on their tour. The morale of the soldiers was low and the condition of some of their equipment had fallen far below standard. He was glad, however, to have the opportunity to meet the soldiers.

At the time, minister of finance Pinhas Sapir was looking for a public figure, preferably a former military leader who commanded people's respect, to lead a fund-raising drive to secure contributions for the War Loan beyond the sums that would be raised compulsorily. Rabin did not seek the job, but when Sapir approached him during the second week of the war and informed him that Meir had already approved the idea, he accepted. He remained in the job for two months and asked to be relieved in early December.

After much bitter fighting, the Israelis managed to keep the Syrians and Egyptians from advancing beyond the territory gained in the early stages of the war. The war had cost Israel between $9 and $10 billion, leaving its citizens with heavy debts, soaring prices, and runaway inflation. But much worse, the human loss and suffering had been devastating. A total of 2,526 Israelis had been killed in battle with another 7,500 wounded, the country's heaviest losses since the 1948 war. So gloomy were Israelis that fully 11.6 percent of the 2.8 million Jews in Israel told one survey that they were considering emigration. The gloom was also reflected in the numerous resignations of army officers after the war. In addition to the despondency and exhaustion felt by the nation, there was a growing mood of indignation that its leaders had been so unprepared for war despite the intelligence reports they had received concerning the enemy's movements.

In mid-November, Rabin travelled to the United States on behalf of Israel Bonds and while there he met Kissinger. He brought back a grim message to Meir warning her that the secretary of state was determined to work out a settlement in the Middle East that would have to satisfy both sides. Kissinger travelled to the Middle East during December to prepare the way for a peace conference that would bring some stability to the area and implement the goals of UN Resolution 338; he invited Rabin for a private breakfast and the two men talked like old friends. The peace conference convened in Geneva under joint American-Russian auspices on December 21, 1973, with Israel, Egypt, and Jordan attending (but not Syria). As a result of the conference, Kissinger embarked upon his 'shuttle diplomacy', flying back and forth between Egypt and Israel for eight days in January 1974; through his efforts, the two sides signed a separation of forces agreement on January 18, 1974. Israel agreed to withdraw from the west bank of the Suez Canal and from its forward position on the east bank to a distance of fifteen miles from the Canal. Egypt agreed to limit its military presence on the east bank to 7,000 troops, 36 artillery pieces, and 30 tanks. UN troops were placed between the two sides in a buffer zone.

Rabin's future seemed less certain than ever. He was still smarting from the army's treatment of him, and though he spoke to audiences in Tel Aviv on behalf of the IDF, he refused to speak to the troops at the front. Ya'acov Halfon, a Labor Party aide, tried to convince him that new men would be needed to govern when the nation passed judgment on Golda Meir's Government. The national elections had originally been scheduled for October 31, but within a few days of the outbreak of war, a consensus was reached among all political parties that they should be postponed for two months, until December 31.

Rabin's morale received a boost when the Labor Party chose him to give the main address at the first Labor Party gathering after the war, held in early November. With the election campaign now resuming, it was understandable that the party should make its main attraction a man who, unlike the senior members of the Cabinet, was untainted by bearing responsibility for the war. Public opinion polls began to reflect Rabin's rising popularity with the voters. One, in late December, placed him second only to Meir in a straightforward popularity contest. Rabin sensed the country's increasingly angry mood and felt that an official investigation into the state of the country's defenses just before the war should be held, but he was careful to say that it should not be a witch hunt. In any case, while an investigation might correct past mistakes, it would not resolve Israel's immediate crisis; its international isolation. "I don't remember a period when we were witness in such a dramatic way to the collapse of Israel's foreign relations," Rabin said shortly after the war. "We had only one friend in the world and that was the United States."[111] He spoke hopefully about future relations with the US, suggesting that America had proved by its decision to airlift arms that it would not permit the Arabs to triumph militarily over Israel. Similarly, the American alert in late October was a sign, he said, that the US would not allow the Russians to intervene directly on the Arab side. Yet despite all this, there was no guarantee that the US would see eye to eye with Israel on the question of a peace settlement. In public, Rabin was

111. Interview with Yitzhak Rabin, *Al Hamishmar*, November 16, 1973

hopeful that America would sympathize with Israeli claims that the need for secure boundaries was more urgent than ever. But privately, he took the more realistic view that Israel was facing one of the most dangerous periods in its history. If the United States decided to impose a settlement on the Middle East at this juncture, with the crippled state of the IDF, the country would have little strength to fight it.

On December 31, Rabin was elected to the Knesset. The Labor Alignment (composed of the Labor – a merger between Mapai, Ahdut HaAvoda, and Rafi – and Mapam parties) had lost five seats, a serious depletion of its electoral strength, but not enough to make it incapable of forming the next Government. It now had 51 Knesset seats, and its percentage of the overall vote had slipped from 46.2 to 39.7. The opposition Likud Party under Menachem Begin now had 39 seats (seven more than in the previous election), with 30.2 percent of the overall vote, a gain of 4.2 percent. The Labor Party had won by the narrowest margin in its history, but the disgruntled voters were not yet united enough to demand its resignation.

The tide of protest was, however, growing; shapeless leaderless at first, but increasingly angry and persistent. The movement began among the soldiers, who were most aware of the state of unpreparedness in which the IDF had found itself at the outbreak of war. They had gradually returned from the fronts since November and December 1973. Now most of them were home, full of anguish and horror at what they had witnessed; a return to normal life seemed impossible to those who had taken part in a war that had brought the heaviest casualties in war for 25 years. The main target of the soldiers was Moshe Dayan. Gradually, the movement grew under the leadership of a young captain named Motti Ashkenazi, the commanding officer of 'Budapest', the northern-most stronghold on the Suez Canal, which had not fallen to the Egyptians. Israel had never witnessed such outrage on such a scale, as rallies attracted hundreds, eventually thousands. The protest movement was not a political one in that it proposed no list of candidates; it had simply erupted over a single issue: the removal of the Government.

The new mood of the nation did not bring about immediate political change. The Israeli political system, with its strong tinge of conservatism, was far too entrenched to capitulate easily. But the protests made Meir's task of putting together a coalition Government, after the December 31 elections, very difficult. With five fewer Knesset seats, she had less room for maneuver in dealing with the smaller parties. Beset with defense problems, she took over two months to form a Government. Meanwhile, Dayan increasingly attacked both in public gatherings and within the Labor Party for the mishaps that had led to the war, decided to resign from the Defense Ministry.

Public anger intensified throughout February 1974 and rose to a peak in early March as Golda Meir prepared to present her new Cabinet. Party members were disturbed by the lack of change in it. Meir, who had wanted to retire even before the originally scheduled October elections, announced on March 3 that she intended to resign. In the hours that followed a number of party delegations pleaded with her to withdraw her resignation, and she eventually agreed to continue forming a Government. She was very keen that Dayan would return as defense minister, even to the extent of trying the psychological ploy of leaking word to the press that she intended to appoint Rabin. However,

Dayan refused, and it appeared that Rabin might become the new minister of defense.

The Labor Party Central Committee met on March 5 at the Ohel Theatre in Tel Aviv to discuss the political crisis. Committee membership was split among the three former parties which had merged to become the Labor Party: Mapai, the largest (60 percent); Ahdut HaAvoda (20 percent); and Rafi (20 percent). Most of the Labor Party's government leaders, including Golda Meir, Pinhas Sapir, and Abba Eban, had come from the Mapai ranks. Moshe Dayan led the Rafi grouping (with Shimon Peres as his second in command) and Yigal Allon headed the Ahdut HaAvoda faction. Though Meir had agreed to continue her efforts to form a Government, in the prevailing uncertain atmosphere it seemed likely that she might once again decide to resign. Throughout the day, party members promoted Rabin as the next defense minister. It was against this background that he prepared to make one of the most important speeches of his career, one which would establish him as a leader within the party and a future leader of the nation. After speeches all day, Rabin rose to speak in the late afternoon. The members were eager to get home and members barely noticed Rabin rise; but his commanding voice and fresh enthusiasm caught the crowd's attention. Choosing his words carefully, he avoided criticizing prime minister Meir directly, but left little doubt concerning what he felt about the collective leadership of the Party. The country needed a way out of the crisis, and it could not be found in new elections that would only prolong the existing instability. Labor should form a new government and not join in a National Unity Government with the Likud, as some had proposed. Rabin received an ovation at the end of his speech, the only speaker that day to do so, as applause was not customary at party discussions. From that moment, it was clear to everyone in the party and the country that Rabin was a new force in Israeli politics.

The committee urged Meir to continue trying to form a Government and asked Dayan to return to office. With new information that the Syrians were about to launch an all-out attack along the Northern Front, Dayan immediately agreed to return as minister of defense in Golda Meir's new Cabinet. On March 6, Rabin read in the morning newspapers that he was no longer Meir's candidate for the post. "All my life," he told a reporter later that day, "I have been collecting exes. I am an ex-chief of staff, an ex-ambassador to the United States, and now an ex-potential minister of defense." Some speculated that Dayan had decided to return to his post not because of the new threat of war (which in the event did not materialize), but because Rabin had become such a popular rival. Meir presented her new government to the Knesset on March 10.

With Dayan's return to the Ministry of Defense, Meir gave Rabin a choice between three secondary Cabinet posts: the Ministries of Labor, Information, or Transport. He chose to become her labor minister. Despite his disappointment at losing the Defense Ministry post, Rabin took up his new Cabinet job with enthusiasm. It gave him the chance to participate in all government discussions, including those on military and diplomatic affairs, not just those connected with labor. As minister of labor, his priority was to orient the economy to cope with a situation in which large numbers of men in the labor force had to be mobilized for long periods of time. When he took office there was still a war of attrition with Syria, and it was impossible to know how much longer the troops would be needed at the front.

Meanwhile the national malaise persisted. April 2 saw the publication of the interim report of the Inquiry Commission, set up by Meir in November to investigate the decisions of military and civilian authorities concerning intelligence received before the war and the IDF's general state of preparedness at that time. The report exonerated Meir and Dayan and laid the blame on chief of staff Elazar. Rabin felt it was grossly unfair to single out one person in this way, as it would make the position of senior army officers untenable in the future by implying that they alone bore responsibility for their actions. He asked for the report to be returned to the Commission to no avail. The publication of the interim report prompted another wave of public fury and there were vociferous, almost daily, demonstrations outside the prime minister's office in Jerusalem, until on April 10, Meir resigned. Her Government would remain in office as a caretaker regime while the Labor Party chose a new prime minister. (New elections are not obligatory in Israel after the resignation of a prime minister.)

Throughout the week following Meir's resignation, the Labor Party debated whether to try to form a new Government or hold new elections, while the latter might have provided the Labor with a fresh mandate from the people, they were also risky in view of the country's continuing angry mood. Finally, the Labor Party decided to form a new Government with the understanding that elections would be anyway held in the near future.

The choice of the new prime minister was the prerogative of the 611 members of the Labor Party Central Committee.

Throughout the years, Mapai had always provided the nominee for the prime ministership. Under normal conditions, Mapai would have proposed a suitable candidate this time as well, but the October war had made the faction virtually leaderless: Golda Meir was resigning and Abba Eban was associated with the war-time government. Pinhas Sapir, the minister of finance, could probably have had the nomination for the asking, but had made it known that he did not want the office. Haim Zadok, the minister of justice, had some support within the Mapai party, but he too had no great desire for the job. The left-wing Ahdut HaAvoda faction had only one potential candidate, Yigal Allon, the deputy premier and minister of education, whom the right-wing Rafi faction had found unacceptable even before the Yom Kippur War. Rafi's only possible candidate, Moshe Dayan, was ruled out by his unpopularity over the war (Shimon Peres, second to Dayan, would never be considered as long as Dayan was a serious contender).

The party's titans, though flawed, still had to be courted, however, because they were after all the veteran leaders of Labor. The first question party members asked was whether Meir really meant to resign this time. No one could afford to offend her, as her support was vital to any future contender. Once it became certain that she had no intention of retracting, attention focused on Pinhas Sapir. He had always been considered the heir apparent despite his lack of interest in the post; still, after her resignation he was inundated with appeals from party members to run for the prime ministership. Meanwhile, Rabin made no secret of his ambition, but he held a tight rein on supporters who wanted to canvass for him within the party. As long as Sapir was a possible candidate, Rabin felt he could make no overt move.

At first he was convinced that Sapir would be Meir's most likely replacement, but as time passed, he began increasingly to believe that the minister of finance was adamant and would not yield to party pressure.

One evening, Sapir summoned Rabin to see him. Rabin suggested that Sapir was the likely candidate for prime minister. "Me? No! But you are my candidate!" Sapir caught Rabin by surprise. Sapir controlled between 200 and 300 of the Central Committee's 611 votes. Returning home, the astonished candidate-to-be told his wife: "Strange, but Sapir claims that I'm his candidate for prime minister."

Rabin still lacked a firm political base in the party and therefore seemed, to many at best, a long shot. True, he had received a considerable boost from Meir the month before when he was tipped to replace Dayan. Gradually, a small group of high-level party politicians, among them Aharon Yariv, Rabin's intelligence chief during the Six-Day War, and Haim Bar-Lev, the minister for commerce and industry and formerly Rabin's deputy chief of staff, settled on Rabin as their candidate. But none had the close contact with the Central Committee that certain party officials had. For this reason, Rabin eventually turned to these official men, like Dov Tzamir the party's information officer, who were to play a major role in the securing his nomination.

At this stage, Shimon Peres put his candidacy forward and at first appeared to win over some votes. In his *Memoirs*, Rabin reported that Peres invited him to lunch and sought a 'gentleman's agreement' to hold a fair election and not to squabble as Allon and Dayan had over the premiership, only to find that neither got the post. Wary, Rabin noted that he did not believe a word Peres said. Were Peres to win,

Rabin vowed to himself that he would not join his Cabinet. Still, to Peres, Rabin said he agreed with his proposal.

Meanwhile, Mapai was turning more and more to Rabin. For his part, Rabin was unwilling to drop everything to try to nail down the nomination. Asked to hold a strategy session about his campaign, Rabin declined, saying that his wife had already bought tickets for a concert for that evening. One indication that Rabin was coming close to the nomination was the intensification of criticism levelled against him in the Israeli press. One of the key pieces of gossip concerned some $9,000 in lecture fees he had reportedly earned while serving as ambassador in Washington. Dov Tzamir checked whether previous ambassadors had engaged in similar activity and found that they had. Rabin had simply been more successful, that was all. On May 5, Rabin issued a public statement answering the charges. He acknowledged that he had given a number of paid lectures on certain occasions, as was customary before he arrived in Washington, and had checked and found that civil service regulations permitted the practice and that there was no obligation to pay income tax on the fees thus earned. He managed to emerge unscathed from the accusations arising from his lecture fees at the time, but in the long term, his staunch defense of his actions damaged his reputation with certain sections of the Israeli public, who argued that an Israeli ambassador to Washington, as Israel's key spokesman in the United States, should not allow himself to take advantage of that position to make money from his public appearances, whether before Jewish or non-Jewish audiences. The entire affair would probably have been forgotten had the public not learned three years later, in March 1977, that Rabin and his wife had illegally maintained bank accounts in the US. In the eyes of some Israelis, Rabin had committed a worse crime in making an impressive sum of money from lectures while in the US than in keeping his dollars in a foreign bank account (thus contravening the law).

Elections for the Labor Party's choice of candidate for the prime ministership were scheduled for Monday, April 22, 1974. The Friday before, Rabin had told a newspaper interviewer that he would decide whether to make a bid for office when it became clear beyond any doubt that Pinhas Sapir wouldn't accept under any circumstances the office of prime minister. The favorable public opinion polls pleased him but he was holding back until the proper time. Meanwhile, behind the scenes, he received the most heartening news of the campaign thus far: Yossi Sarid, Pinhas Sapir's young lieutenant, was optimistic about winning Sapir's backing for Rabin. However, Peres's initiative was giving Sarid cause for alarm. Reports had reached Sarid of over 450 Central Committee members receiving phone calls from Peres in the past few days. Peres seemed likely to win the nomination unless Sapir decided immediately to support Rabin's candidacy. Sarid and Rabin agreed to meet the finance minister at his home in Kfar Saba the next morning, April 20. One of the last obstacles had disappeared that day when Meir's daughter, Sarah, had convinced Labor Party leaders who still clung to the hope that her mother would return, that she would not withdraw her resignation. The way was now clear for an approach to Sapir.

Rabin felt nervous driving to the appointment the next day. However he need not have been. Sapir had already made up his mind to back him two days earlier, when Ezer

Weizman had placed in his hands a document he claimed to have written in November 1967 at Moshe Dayan's request. In the document, Weizman claimed that Rabin, in effect, had broken down during the Six-Day War in the despairing belief that he had single-handedly led the nation into war. Weizman also contended that the chief of staff had asked him to take permanent charge of the IDF and he threatened to release the document to the press unless Sapir withdrew his support for Rabin. Weizman's ploy backfired. Sapir said much later that his reading of the 'Weizman Document,' as it came to be called, "gave him the last push to come to the side of Rabin."[112]

Sapir greeted Rabin warmly and assured him from the beginning of their meeting that he would support his candidacy. Rabin was delighted. With Sapir's blessing, the prime ministership was almost certainly his, but always the cautious realist, he knew that the Labor Party itself was going through a transformation and that it was too early to say with absolute certainty that Sapir's word would carry the day. The rest of the meeting was devoted to discussing how to gain the greatest number of votes from the Central Committee. Sapir agreed to announce his support for Rabin at a meeting that evening, at which a delegation from the Galilee region planned to try to persuade him to run for the premiership. Sarid was to alert Israel's national radio so that it could broadcast the news of his announcement at 7 pm that evening.

Rabin was now free to campaign openly. During the rest of that day, he and his staff stepped up their campaign

---

112. Avneri, op. cit., pp. 316-18.

efforts. The candidate himself found the art of campaigning difficult. He was diffident about asking for people's support, and his staff had a tough job persuading him to make the necessary telephone calls. Sapir called a meeting of the Mapai leadership that Saturday evening at the Labor Party's headquarters, at which sixteen of the top figures gathered. Rabin was present but remained silent throughout. Someone suggested that Sapir would be better off running for the prime ministership himself, rather than supporting Rabin. Sapir told the group that Rabin was his candidate and he expected them to make sure that he was nominated on the 22nd.

Only two men were now in the running for the nomination: Rabin and Peres. On the Sunday morning, the day before the election, Rabin was in a relatively strong position, yet one brutal shock still awaited him. While he was attending the weekly Cabinet meeting of Meir's caretaker Government in which he was still Labor Minister, a member of his campaign staff received word from a correspondent on the morning newspaper *Haaretz* that Ezer Weizman had provided the paper with the complete text of his hitherto unpublished document, describing Rabin's illness of 1967. *Haaretz* planned to run the entire text the next morning, the day of the election. The news sent shock waves through Rabin's campaign headquarters in Tel Aviv, where it had been calculated that he had at least a 100-vote lead over Peres. No one could say with certainty how much damage Rabin would suffer electorally as a result of the disclosure, but his advisors were certain that they had to take action quickly to lessen the blow, and time was short. Tzamir telephoned Rabin, calling him out of the Cabinet meeting to break the news and advised him to come to Tel Aviv as quickly as possible. They had to plan their strategy and only he could make the final decision. Rabin took the news calmly. Before leaving for Tel Aviv, he telephoned Sarid, who cautioned him against defending himself personally on the matter. Lengthy explanations about what had happened that day in May 1967 could only hurt him, he said. Perhaps when he became prime minister he could deal with the matter openly, but now was not the time. Sarid proposed that he should enlist several high-ranking military figures to speak for him in the media at the same time as the Weizman document was printed. Rabin reluctantly agreed, and it was decided that the campaign staff should contact Aharon Yariv, Israel Tal, and Ariel Sharon, a division commander in 1967 and a close friend of Rabin, whose voice would carry special weight as he, like Weizman, was a member of the political opposition. Rabin was diffident about asking support from men with whom he had had a mostly professional relationship, but Tzamir convinced him of the necessity to do so. In view of the emotional nature of this new crisis, Tzamir asked Leah to join them at campaign headquarters in Tel Aviv to encourage her husband. As soon as Rabin arrived at headquarters in the afternoon, he telephoned Dr. Eliahu Gilon, the physician who had ministered to him during his illness in 1967, to ask for his recollections of that day in order to refute Weizman's document. The doctor assured him that all he had been suffering from was a combination of nicotine poisoning and fatigue. "There was a crisis that day," he told Rabin, "but I said there was nothing to worry about; that you needed some help and that after a few hours' rest, everything would be OK. Everything that Weizman is saying now is nonsense. You have nothing to worry about."[113] The doctor's words were comforting, but public reaction to Weizman's revelations remained unpredictable.

Rabin's communiqué, drawn up on Sunday afternoon, stated: "I don't want to enter into a discussion of the motives of those who have seen fit to return to and publish, now of all times, an old story, and one man's version of it, at that. The facts are that I was absent from my post as chief of staff for twenty-four hours, from the evening of May 23 until the morning of May 25. On the evening of May 23, I called upon general Weizman and asked him to take my place in order to make it possible for me to rest after the draining preparation work for the war. On the morning of the 25th, I returned to the command of the army and conducted the action on the eve of the Six-Day War and throughout the war until the victory." Although he did not say so at the time, Rabin was convinced that Weizman had not initiated the publication of the document. Two and a half years later, he felt more comfortable talking about the motives behind Weizman's efforts on the eve of the election: "I believe it was the beginning of a game that is still going on today, a kind of intrigue against me. I don't know whether Weizman did it on his own or was encouraged to do it by someone else within the Labor Party. I incline to the latter assumption. It's nonsense to believe that he was able to prepare it on the day of the election, if he alone was responsible."

Rabin's aides suggested that he should phone Gershom Shocken, the editor of *Haaretz*, and try to persuade him to

---

113. One of Yitzhak Rabin's campaign aides related the Rabin-Gilon conversation to the author during an off-the-record conversation.

postpone publication of Weizman's document until after Monday's election. Rabin felt that someone else should talk to the editor but his advisers agreed that only he could make the call. At 8:30 that evening, he spoke to Shocken, but the editor refused to delay publication and suggested instead that Rabin produce his own version of what had happened that day in 1967. This was what Rabin's aides had already advised him not to do. The strategy to deflate the Weizman balloon thus depended on the three generals. Rabin had located Tal at a Tel Aviv restaurant, lunching, ironically, with a *Haaretz* editor. He had readily agreed to make a statement of warm support. Sharon was reached in Beersheba and promptly drafted his remarks in defense of Rabin on a napkin in a restaurant. The final draft, which arrived in Tel Aviv that evening, said in part: "The army which embarked on the Six-Day War was built by Rabin. He built it for the war and he commanded it during the war." Yariv, then minister of transport, rushed his reply to Tel Aviv: "Rabin's illness in May 1967 should not detract from his candidacy for the office of prime minister," Yariv insisted, and called Weizman's charges 'character assassination.' By late Sunday, Rabin had done everything in his power to cushion the forthcoming blow. He had even phoned Hannah Zemer, editor of the morning newspaper *Davar*, to read over his reaction to Weizman's charges, but she had refused to print it since the charges themselves had not yet been published. Tzamir predicted optimistically that the Weizman accusations would boomerang, as Labor Party Committee members were bound to ask themselves why a member of the opposition should enter into what was purely a campaign within the ruling party. (Weizman was then a member of the right-wing Herut Party, the major force in the opposition Likud bloc.) At most,

Tzamir assured colleagues, Rabin would lose 25 to 30 votes because of Weizman, far too few to cost him the election.

The crisis over the Weizman affair had consumed so much time and energy within the Rabin camp that there was little of either left when a strange new development occurred on Sunday evening: In a speech before the Labor Party's Central Committee, Sapir pressed the case for new elections, an odd action on the part of someone who was actively backing Rabin in the elections the next day. Sapir warned that whoever became prime minister after Monday's election would face a tough time forming a coalition Government because of the problems of drawing together the embittered parties. Rabin was surprised by these remarks. All sorts of theories were suggested for Sapir's motives. One was that he wanted to saveMeir's Government as he was certain that it would be impossible to form a new one. Another was that the finance minister genuinely doubted that Rabin would win, and, fearing a Peres victory, believed the only alternative to be new elections, with Meir remaining in charge of a caretaker Government until they were held. Whatever his reason, Sapir's speech seemed impulsive, even irrational to Rabin's campaign aides. There would have been more cause for anxiety had the Central Committee not turned down Sapir's proposal of new elections.

Rabin, who had his doubts right up to the last moment of the campaign about the efficacy of Sapir's backing, had one more reason to wonder just how much help the finance minister would be. Yet he knew he could not succeed without him. On Monday, the day of the election, the public read about Weizman's allegations for the first time. Testing the reaction within the party, Rabin's aides discovered, to their delight, that their strategy was working. Peres, Rabin's only rival, said he had seen the charges for the first time only that morning and regretted their publication. Prime Minister Meir issued a statement in which she praised Rabin's part in the Six-Day War victory and deplored such personal attacks; she refused, however, to support either candidate publicly for the prime ministership. Tzamir had been correct in his prediction: The allegations were indeed having a boomerang effect. Furthermore, the comments of the three generals, appearing at the same time, warded off much of the damage. There were no demands for Rabin to withdraw from the contest. Professor Amnon Rubinstein, the head of the new protest group Shinui (Change), urged Rabin to request a postponement of the vote that evening in order to give him time to explain more fully his crisis of May 1967. Some newspapers, too, called upon the candidate to present a full version of what happened, and some editorial writers obviously took the questions raised by Weizman seriously: "Unless Mr. Rabin can refute the allegations of the memorandum," the *Haaretz* editorial read, "his election to the premiership must be considered an unwarranted risk." *Maariv* was just as sharp: "The issue of the prime minister's ability to stand up to stress is not a personal matter. Whatever the facts, they should be made public." Other columnists gave Rabin the benefit of the doubt, arguing that he could not have won the support of the nation's key political figures, who had known of Weizman's charges for a long time, if they had felt he was prone to mental instability. "There is no choice but to conclude," wrote Yoel Marcus in *Haaretz*, taking a different stance from the paper's editorial, "that either all the above mentioned people [i.e., Shimon Peres, Golda Meir, and Pinhas Sapir] are so crazy that they don't care about the fate of the country, or that a serious personal injustice has been done to Yitzhak Rabin." Marcus reflected the sentiments of most of the Central Committee members who had originally intended to vote for Rabin. The harmful effects of the Weizman document would be marginal, Rabin's aides now felt comfortable in predicting. He would still win, probably by at least 50 votes.

The Central Committee met on Monday evening April 22 in the Ohel Theatre to choose their new candidate for the prime ministership. Both Rabin and Peres were allowed three nominating speeches from their supporters. The vote was expected to be close. Rabin waited for the ballots to be counted in a small room at the side of the large hall, where aides kept him informed of progress. Leah was at home listening to radio coverage of the balloting. The first reports were ambiguous, but when the final results were announced, the audience in the theater broke into loud applause: aides came rushing in to tell Rabin that he had won. A wide grin spread across his face. A second vote was taken, this time in the open, to confirm Rabin as the candidate of the entire party membership. The margin was even narrower than observers had predicted. Rabin had defeated Peres by 44 votes; 298 to 254. Mapai divided its vote between the two, with Rabin securing a majority. Ahdut HaAvoda gave its votes to Rabin, Rafi to Peres.

In his victory speech, Rabin praised his rival Shimon Peres and said that it would be difficult to follow in Golda Meir's footsteps, but "the sons of the founding generations have come of age… We cannot but be sensitive to other countries' views and we must especially take into account our friend the US, but above all, we must safeguard our national needs, even if our friends do not understand all we do. The

State of Israel belongs not only to its inhabitants, but also to millions of Jews the world over. Its spiritual-traditional boundaries and its influence must extend beyond its physical limits. No one should mistake the fact that there is a crisis of government in Israel; on the other hand, no one should make the greater mistake of assuming that this signifies a national weakness. In a strong and healthy democracy such as ours, we can shake off political weakness and rise to new heights." After the speech, Rabin rushed to his Tel Aviv apartment to join his wife and some friends in a celebration. Sapir was there, and the two men took the opportunity to confer about the next major task: the formation of the Cabinet.

Israeli editorial writers warmly received Rabin's nomination. Most were hopeful that at last the country might throw off the bitterness and frustration it had felt since the war. "Rabin," said one, "will make a good prime minister, symbolizing the change that is sought by the public, and that is essential to clear the atmosphere in this country."[114] The misgivings the Weizman document had given rise to, were dispelled at a stroke. "One day's weakness and doubts," declared another, "is as nothing compared to the decades of positive achievement."

Abroad, too, there was optimism about Israel's prospects of stabilizing its government. Rabin's nomination received front-page coverage in Britain, where the *Financial Times* described him as "Israel's ideal politician, a good soldier and skillful diplomat, with an impeccable Zionist pedigree." *The New York Times* termed Rabin's nomination "a major turning point in the political life of modern Israel." Tass, the

---

114. *Davar*, April 23, 1974

Soviet News Agency, wrote that Rabin's nomination would not solve Israel's problems. To do that, "he would have to renounce Israel's policy of aggression and annexation." He had been chosen, it continued, "only after intricate backstage intrigues and struggles between his supporters and those of Peres." On that point at least, Tass was perfectly right.

Difficult as his nomination had been, it was only half the battle. Rabin had yet to put together a coalition government, which would possess a majority of votes in the 120-member Knesset. The task was complicated and many thought he would be unequal to it. He needed a minimum of 61 votes to govern, but at first he could count on only the 51 seats belonging to the Labor Alignment and three more belonging to the Arab lists normally affiliated with Labor. He thus lacked seven votes. The traditional coalition partner, the National Religious Party, was determined to press for a Government of National Unity (to include the opposition Likud bloc). If it failed in this objective, it would remain on the sidelines. Determined not to team up with the Likud, Rabin could therefore not count on the NRP's 10 votes. The Independent Liberal Party, with its four seats, was pressing hard for new elections in the near future and it would be difficult to bring them into the fold. Rabin might be able to persuade some of the other small parties to join the coalition, but at best it seemed likely that he could present only a fragile Government if he could put one together at all.

In addition to the problems of coalition bargaining, he faced a continuing distraction in the person of Henry Kissinger, who had arrived in the Middle East in early May to begin another round of shuttle diplomacy, this time aimed at a separation of forces agreement between Israel and Syria.

The war of attrition between the two had continued off and on throughout the winter and into the spring, with almost daily artillery exchanges in the Golan Heights region. The Israelis had refused to negotiate with Syria until its president, Hafez el-Assad, gave Kissinger a list of Israeli prisoners of war still in Syria after the Yom Kippur War. The list had been handed over to Kissinger in February and by early May, he was confident that peace talks would go ahead. Meir, still presiding over the caretaker Government, wanted Rabin to be present during the negotiations to give the impression that Israeli policy would continue even after a new Government took over. Rabin was naturally eager to be present, though Kissinger's negotiations with the Israelis, conducted on an almost daily basis, often went on into the late hours and inevitably took up precious time that he needed to fashion the coalition. He grew angry at the distraction, but there was little he could do about it.

He was also upset to find that Meir was doing nothing to help him form the next Government. She had refused to endorse him publicly after the nomination, and several times during the Kissinger talks she made comments that seemed designed to embarrass him. During her initial meeting with Kissinger on May 2, she said she had been impressed with president Sadat for admitting that his chief of staff had broken down during the Yom Kippur War. Rabin, just recovering from the publicity over the publication of the Weizman document, found her remarks distressing.

On another occasion, the retiring prime minister, who had never been favorably disposed towards Knesset member Shulamit Aloni, chided Rabin for apparently planning to bring Aloni's three-member Civil Rights Movement into the Government. Preoccupied with the coalition bargaining,

Rabin said little during the Kissinger talks. Kissinger asked Eban why Rabin was so quiet, seemingly blind to the fact that Rabin could take little interest in diplomatic negotiations while the more immediate problem of forming a new Government was proving so insoluble. (On May 31, Israel and Syria signed a separation of forces accord, which established a cease-fire. It required Israel to withdraw from Syrian land captured in the previous war, and called for a UN peace-keeping force to patrol the battle zone. Israel and Syria agreed as well to limit their forces and arms near the frontier.)

Rabin needed the National Religious Party and took the unusual step of asking the chief rabbi, Shlomo Goren, to intercede on his behalf. Goren did so, but the NRP put forward demands on religious matters, which Rabin found unacceptable. Particularly anxious to have Pinhas Sapir in his Government, he went to great length to persuade him. He asked friends of Sapir, both in Israel and abroad, to urge him to remain as minister of finance. Sapir refused, choosing instead to become the chairman of the Jewish Agency, the quasi-governmental organization that deals with the nation's immigration, among other matters.

One Cabinet position that posed a problem for Rabin was minister of defense. Rabin considered Yigal Allon the most suitable choice for this spot. The two men were close allies and Allon had a strong background in the military: He had been one of the country's leading commanders in the 1948 War of Independence. Rabin had strong views about Shimon Peres becoming defense minister – all negative. "I did not consider Shimon Peres suitable, since he had never fought in the IDF and his expertise in arms purchasing did not make up for that lack of field experience." But the choice was not

Rabin's to make. Although he came under strong pressure from both Meir and Sapir not to choose Peres, he realized that unless Rafi was represented in one of the top three positions, he would run the risk of not being able to form a Government. He had considered offering Peres the post of minister of foreign affairs at one stage, but Peres had made it known that he was interested only in the Defense Ministry.

Peres appeared certain throughout May that he would eventually be given that post, and towards the end of that month, actually told Tzamir so. Tzamir, aware that Rabin was still being urged to keep Peres out of the next Government, told him that it was not at all a certainty. Peres immediately announced that he would go to see Rabin right away to clear matters up. Tzamir advised against this, suggesting that Rabin was bound to regard his intrusion as a threat and would appoint someone else defense minister, probably Yigal Allon. Instead, he proposed that Peres should approach Yitzhak Navon, the highly respected chairman of the Knesset's Foreign Affairs and Defense Committee and a future president of the State of Israel, who was also a member of the Rafi wing and a man Rabin admired. Navon and Peres talked together and afterwards Navon told Rabin that Peres was quite adamant that if he didn't get the defense post, he would not serve in the Government at all. The implication of Navon's remarks was painfully clear: a loss of seven votes that he was by now counting on to form a coalition, as he had not managed to enlist the NRP or anyone else. Peres, in not joining the Government, would make sure that his Rafi colleagues did not support Rabin. Fearing that he would thus be unable to form a Government, Rabin appointed Peres as his defense minister. He did so, he wrote in 1979, "with a heavy heart. It was an error I would regret and whose price I would pay in full."[115]

Rabin was also determined not to have Eban as his minister of foreign affairs. Yigal Allon was an obvious choice, to placate Ahdut HaAvoda, but to his surprise even this choice posed problems. Allon felt that the Defense Ministry should have gone to him rather than to Peres and turned down the office of foreign minister at first, threatening to return home to Kibbutz Ginosar on Lake Kinneret. Rabin's advisers suggested a compromise: Allon should become minister of foreign affairs and deputy prime minister, which would thus elevate him to the status of second-in-command in the Government, ahead of the defense minister. Allon found the idea attractive, but first asked Eban if he would be willing to step aside for him. Eban said no. In an attempt to placate Eban and keep him in the Government, Rabin offered him the Ministry of Information. He would also be considered a member of the senior staff of ministers who would take part in the expected diplomatic negotiations with the Arabs. Rabin sent Labor Party leaders Dov Tzamir, David Calderon, and Moshe Baram to talk to Eban, who expressed doubts that Rabin would be able to form a Government and finally turned down their offer, saying that unless he kept the foreign affairs portfolio, he would not serve.

Few gave Rabin more than a 50-50 chance of succeeding in forming a Government. His prospects fell considerably on May 8, when the NRP dropped out of the bargaining. President Ephraim Katzir had given Rabin until May 17 to come up with a new Government, but was granted a further two weeks when this became impossible. Towards

---

115. Yitzhak Rabin, *The Rabin Memoirs* (English version), p. 189

the end of May, some light appeared on the horizon. The Kissinger negotiations, which had been prone to uncertainty during the entire month, now seemed likely to succeed, and Rabin obtained the agreement of the Independent Liberals (four votes) and Aloni's Civil Rights Movement (three votes), giving him a razor-thin 61-59 vote majority in the Knesset. Rabin realized he was presenting the most fragile Government in the history of the nation.

Rabin's precarious Government was announced on June 3, 1974. No one held out much hope that it would survive. Even its minister of finance, Yehoshua Rabinowitz, predicted privately that it would last no more than a month.

CHAPTER EIGHT

AGREEMENT IN THE SAND

In Rabin, Israel found a new kind of leader: the first native born prime minister; the first to be born in the twentieth century; the first to be educated entirely in the country; the first to emerge from the army; the first non-politician. At the age of 52, he was also the youngest prime minister. His freshness on the political scene heightened the expectations that he would strike out in new directions both at home and abroad.

Determined to win the confidence of both his party and the country, Rabin decided to set the tone for his Government in his inaugural speech to the Knesset on June 3, 1974. He read it slowly and forcefully, gripping the sides of the lectern with both hands. "Something has happened to this country since the Yom Kippur War," he said. "Even though we scored one of our greatest victories in the war, many of us have deeply troubled hearts. There was solid enough reason for this, including the unwarranted expectations that vanished in the war and the grief over the loss of life. But there was no justification," he said, "for prolonging this feeling of depression. We must shake off our despondence. If we look about us, we will see that we are not in the Vale of Tears."

The task Rabin set himself of lifting the country out of the doldrums was not easy. The separation of forces agreements – with Egypt in January and with Syria in May – eased some of the worries, but the fears of war recurring within the near future persisted, and there was still a state of national emergency. Many were disappointed that a Government of National Unity had not been formed. Rabin had rejected the notion, arguing, as had Meir before him, that it would be unworkable, as the right-wing Likud opposition would veto most of the Labor Party's proposals for peace agreements with the Arabs.

One of the most immediate tasks facing him in the summer of 1974 was the rebuilding of the Israel Defense Forces. The eight months between October 6 and June 1 had placed the heaviest burden on the IDF since the State was established. Soldiers had been kept at the fronts for periods of active service longer than any since 1948. Planes had been lost and were in need of replacement. Tanks were in need of repair. The weariness that the nation felt permeated the army too. Until June, the wars of attrition on both the Egyptian and Syrian fronts had prevented the army from beginning a serious recovery program. With the cessation of fighting on the Syrian front, working closely with defense minister Shimon Peres, Rabin gave top priority to a three-year rebuilding program for the IDF. He looked ahead to the arms requests Israel would make of the United States in the near future. America had already given $2.2 billion in emergency military aid to cover the costs of the war alone. When he visited the United States in September 1974, Rabin requested $1.5 billion in military aid for each of the next five years, and this was granted. (By the autumn of 1976, the United States had provided Israel with $5 billion in military and economic aid dating back to the Yom Kippur War.)

Besides the rebuilding of the army the other major task confronting Rabin was to improve the deteriorating economy. Because of the heavy costs of the Yom Kippur War, the nation was going through its worst economic period ever. Rabin rejected any solution that would lead to high unemployment and be contrary to his socialist ideals. At first, he moved slowly on the economic front, waiting until his political hand was strengthened. In October 1974, when the National Religious Party decided to join the Government coalition, adding 11 seats to Rabin's fragile government, he was ready to unveil his economic program. On November 9, he took the first major action to bring the economy under control, announcing a 43 percent devaluation of the Israeli Lira. Rabin saw a link between Israeli dependence on foreign aid and its ability to withstand pressure to give up occupied territory. The more foreign aid it was forced to take, the more pressure would be brought to bear to yield those territories.

When Rabin's economic measures began to bite, workers used the one weapon at their disposal: Soon the prime minister was faced with wave after wave of strikes. He was in a difficult position; he disliked compulsory arbitration and preferred to avoid such a drastic measure. As a socialist he sympathized with the workers' complaints and with their right to strike, but he was disappointed at their unwillingness to make the necessary economic sacrifices. "Our economic future," he said in October 1975, "depends upon every individual doing his job as unquestioningly as a soldier does. In this we have not succeeded."

Rabin was the first Israeli prime minister to talk in specific terms of what compromises Israel was willing to make to attain peace. On his return from a visit to the United States in September 1974, he announced that Israel planned to draft specific political and territorial proposals, which included maps, in anticipation of peace talks with the Arabs. If Rabin had seemed passive or even rigid in his attitude toward peace negotiations, he now sounded flexible, open-minded, and pragmatic. He had never been as possessive about the occupied territories as Golda Meir, viewing them as bargaining counters. He had none of the religious attachment for the occupied West Bank of the Jordan felt by orthodox Jews in Israel, who had urged Meir and were now pressing Rabin to annex the West Bank, as it contained so many Biblical sites that evoked Jewish links with that land. Rabin argued that borders should not be "determined by the Bible, but rather by the dictates of sound strategy." Just before he received the nomination for prime minister, he had upset Orthodox Jews with a statement that signaled his readiness to yield territory on the West Bank. Referring to one of the religious settlements built there by Jews after the Six-Day War: "It's not a tragedy if we have to have a visa to travel to Kfar Etzion."

Shortly after becoming the nominee for the prime ministership, he called the comment a slip of the tongue. It was no coincidence that the apology came as he was courting the National Religious Party, hoping to entice it into his new coalition Government. On the more general question of Jewish civilian settlement in the occupied territories, Rabin felt it would be worth dismantling a settlement here and there, if it brought peace. In 1992, upon becoming prime minister a second time, Rabin had hardened his view on Jewish settlements in one respect: He insisted that he had no plans to uproot any of them.

Although his approach was more flexible, in some ways Rabin's policies were similar to those of Meir. He opposed the creation of a Palestinian State in the West Bank and he refused to return to Israel's pre-Six-Day-War boundaries. He also ruled out negotiations with Palestinian guerrillas; but he had an idea of what Israel could afford to do to bring the Arabs to a final peace, and he had not hesitated to be specific. In January 1974, six months before he became prime minister, he had outlined in a speech just how far he was prepared to go to attain peace. With regard to the West Bank, he spoke of giving up the areas densely populated with Arabs, but keeping an Israeli military presence in the region for the next 15-30 years, until true peace came.

During that period, Arab refugees would be rehabilitated in Jordan and possibly the West Bank. Jerusalem would remain in Israeli hands, with special arrangements for the holy places of the three major religions. Israel would retain the Gaza Strip, too. In the Sinai, Israel would yield certain areas but keep a military presence in others, such as Sharm El-Sheikh. In addition, parts of the Peninsula would be demilitarized, but Israeli troops would only vacate it entirely when real peace came. As for the Golan Heights, Israel would not withdraw entirely, but the existing lines would not necessarily have to be the final ones. When he took up office, Rabin had concluded that the Arabs might have a new interest, however faint, in making peace with Israel, and for that reason alone it was worth pursuing diplomatic efforts as speedily as possible. Since the Yom Kippur War, the Arabs had dropped some of their extreme demands. Perhaps most importantly, they no longer talked of exacting an Israeli commitment to total withdrawal from the occupied territories before negotiations began. Kissinger had persuaded both sides to negotiate, albeit indirectly, although no Israeli pledge had been given on the question of relinquishing all the occupied lands. After the Egyptian January agreement, Kissinger had warned the Israelis that he could guarantee only a year of peace.

Convinced that Egypt was the key to peace with the Arabs, Rabin pursued from the outset a policy of working towards interim peace pacts with the Egyptians, but he was distracted from this by unexpected pressure from the United States to work out an interim agreement with King Hussein of Jordan. During his visit to Israel on June 16, president Nixon proposed that this would be a way of limiting the increasing power of Arab guerrilla leader Yasser Arafat and his Palestine Liberation Organization. Both Hussein and Arafat claimed the leadership of the West Bank. Jordan's claim rested on the fact that it had held authority over the region from 1948 until 1967; Arafat on the other hand asserted that the PLO was the only proper political authority for the region, since it alone could speak for the 670,000 Palestinian Arabs living there.

Palestinian nationalism was a latecomer to the Arab-Israeli conflict. After the Six-Day War had shown that the Arab States were unable to defeat the Israelis in all-out warfare, guerrilla-type operations seemed the only alternative to the thousands of frustrated Palestinian youth who flocked to the PLO's banner. Terrorism became their chief weapon in their aim to create a Palestinian State in place of Israel. In 1974, there were 2.7 million Palestinian Arabs, of whom 450,000 were living in Israel and 1.5 million in Israeli-occupied territory (the West Bank and the Gaza Strip, respectively); the rest lived mainly in Jordan.

Israel and Jordan began negotiating the future of that region largely through the US. The reports persisted that talks of a more direct nature were going on during the summer of 1974, in which Hussein demanded an Israeli withdrawal 10-12 kilometers (6.1 to 7.4 miles) west of the Jordan River. Rabin offered the king administrative control over both the West Bank and the Gaza Strip, though Israel would keep its troops there until a comprehensive peace agreement could be worked out. Hussein refused, demanding that Israeli troops withdraw immediately without waiting for a final peace. Even if the Jordanians had agreed to Israel's proposal, there was no guarantee that an accord could have been finalized. In his inaugural speech to the Knesset in June 1974, Rabin had announced that he intended to keep the previous Government's promise to hold national elections before authorizing any withdrawal from the West Bank, a policy designed to placate the National Religious Party that was totally opposed to giving up the region.

The situation became even more difficult in August when Egypt declared that it no longer supported Hussein's claim to leadership of the West Bank, and would uphold the PLO's right to speak for the inhabitants of the West Bank. Israel wanted to drop the fruitless negotiations with Jordan entirely and concentrate on Egypt, but the US insisted that some effort be made. There were reports suggesting that Rabin had agreed during his visit to Washington in September to proceed with Egypt in public but to continue secret negotiations with Jordan. His mindset on Egypt, he could summon little enthusiasm for an early settlement of the West Bank question, over which he was convinced the Arabs would never go to war.

The decision of the Arab States at a summit meeting in Rabat, Morocco on October 26, 1974 to give the PLO a mandate to negotiate the future of the West Bank, effectively pulled the rug from under Hussein and made certain that there could be no political discussions over the West Bank in the near future. Some accused Rabin of paving the way for this decision by showing too little interest in a Jordan-Israel interim agreement, but this criticism did not take into account the growing popularity of the PLO and Hussein's uncompromising approach to negotiations with the Israelis. In any case, Rabin's hands had been tied in October, after the NRP entered the Government. Its arrival in the coalition made peace talks with Jordan even more unlikely, as the NRP intended to keep Rabin to his pledge to hold elections before making any decision on withdrawal from the West Bank. On the other hand, the political Left thought Rabin's rigid attitude toward the PLO was leaving him no room for maneuver where the West Bank was concerned. To counter their criticism, Rabin kept up a dialogue with King Hussein.

Ever since the 1960s, Israeli leaders had met secretly with the Jordanian monarch. While prepared to exchange ideas on peacemaking with Israeli officials clandestinely, Hussein was convinced that it was too dangerous for him to meet with Israelis in public. Rabin was one of a number of Israeli leaders who huddled with the king in secret places. Rabin pursued secret peacemaking with Hussein in a series of meetings. The first such meeting occurred during the evening hours of August 29, 1974. Accompanying Rabin were Allon and Peres. Though the idea that King Hussein would visit Israel for secret talks with Israeli leaders seemed unlikely, that was precisely what the Jordanian monarch did. He took a Jordanian military helicopter and landed it at Jerusalem's Atarot Airport, where he switched to an Israeli army helicopter. He was then flown to an Israeli government guest house outside Tel Aviv. Joining Hussein were his prime minister, Ziyad Rifai, and his military adjutant.

Despite president Nixon's urging, Rabin opposed a separation of forces agreement with Jordan that would have required Israel to pull back its troops unilaterally. Still willing to talk with the king, Rabin offered him some kind of federative arrangement for the West Bank. Israel and Jordan would share in security and economic arrangements. Hussein, however, wanted the entire cake, not to share it with Israel, so he said no. While prime minister in the 1970s, Rabin met four times more with the king. Their second meeting took place on October 19, 1974. The date was important: It was just a week before the Rabat conference where Jordan would lose its right to represent the Palestinian Arabs of the West Bank. At their October meeting, Hussein again raised the separation of forces idea. Rabin sought to persuade the king that Jordan would benefit if Israel started peace negotiations with Egypt. In that way, Jordan would not be burdened with being the first to have to negotiate with Israel. Nothing emerged from this second Rabin-Hussein session, and by October 26 at Rabat, Hussein was forced to turn over his right to represent the West Bank Palestinians to the PLO. This did not prevent Hussein from meeting with Rabin further. Their third encounter occurred on May 28, 1975 along the desert border in the Arava plain. Hussein had grown annoyed at Rabin and his Israeli colleagues for letting him down on the eve of Rabat. And so when Rabin raised the notion of a territorial compromise over the West Bank, Hussein said sneeringly: "We are out of the picture. Please talk to the PLO and then we will see." Rabin and Hussein met twice more during Rabin's first premiership: on January 14, 1976 and in March 1977. That latter meeting came only a month before Rabin stepped down from office. Though nothing came of that meeting, Rabin presented Hussein with an Israeli Galil rifle encased in an olivewood box as a gift from the government of Israel. An inscription read: "To his Royal Highness, King Hussein... from Yitzhak Rabin, the prime minister of Israel." In the 1980s, Rabin, as his country's defense minister, resumed secret meetings with the king.

Despite insistent pressure from the Left, Rabin was determined to do nothing that would encourage international acceptance of the PLO. He believed that the slightest hint that Israel was prepared, after all, to deal with Arafat would have the effect of assuring the establishment of a Palestinian State on the West Bank and in the Gaza Strip. Rabin's own feelings towards Arafat were based on the conviction that he was no more than a common murderer: "I hate what he stands for, when I see the atrocities that he and his organization carry out. He represents to me all that is evil, and a concept, a philosophy, which is contradictory to the very existence of this country." Early in his premiership, Rabin had given the impression that he had more sympathy for the Palestinians than Golda Meir, who had always asked: "Who are the Palestinians?" Some even claimed that his attitude towards them amounted to 'creeping recognition'.

However, Rabin's policy towards the Palestinians and the PLO was as unrelenting as his predecessor's had been. When, in July 1974, certain Cabinet ministers tried to swing the government round to a more dovish policy, which would have had Israel, negotiate with the Palestinians once they recognized Israel, Rabin recoiled. "My point of departure," he said after the Cabinet debate, "was that the Palestinian issue is not, as others describe it, the very heart of the Arab-Israeli conflict. In my view, the main problem in the Arab-Israeli conflict is the nature of the relations between the Arab States and Israel."[116] Only the Arab States held the key to resolving the conflict, he argued, "because they have the strength, the power and the ability to reach political agreements and, in the final analysis, a peace agreement. They also have the power to decide on a different direction that of war."[117]

For Rabin, the West Bank problem created internal conflicts. Orthodox Jews, many of them young people, realizing that the fate of the West Bank was in the balance, had sought to establish permanent civilian settlements near sites of Biblical importance, in the hope that these would establish Israeli rights to the territory and make the return of the land to the Arabs impossible. Rabin favored Jewish civilian settlement in the occupied territories on a limited basis and, in line with past government policy, he believed that the regions near the major cities in the West Bank, densely populated with Arabs, should not be colonized.

The question of Jewish settlement in the West Bank grew into the most explosive issue confronting Rabin. The political

116. Interview with Yitzhak Rabin, *Yediot Aharonot*, July 26, 1974

117. Ibid

Right sided with the settlers, while the Left argued that the settlers were lawbreakers who were damaging Israel's efforts to make peace with the Arabs. That left-right schism over settlements continues to the present. Matters came to a head in December 1975 when some 100 settlers constructed a settlement at Kadum, near Nablus, the largest city on the West Bank. The matter came before the Government and Rabin decided to permit the settlers to move from their settlement site and set up a temporary camp in a nearby army base. Meanwhile, the Cabinet would deliberate on their future. Deeply divided, the government put off making a decision for nearly six months. In May 1976, Rabin thought he had achieved a compromise: The Kadum settlement was to be abandoned and the settlers offered a permanent site in the West Bank, somewhere that was not near an Arab-populated area. The government's decision was never implemented.

The Kadum affair was significant for the way it reflected Rabin's inability to maneuver in the face of coalition politics. In November 1976, he said, "If I had had the number of Labor seats that Eshkol and Meir had, believe me, the actions of this Government would have been entirely different. I don't believe that any prime minister in the past has had to act with such a narrow margin, or had been so dependent on a coalition among parties that are not close to the mainstream of the Labor Government, as I have been."[118]

There was greater unity in the Government on matters directly affecting Israel's security, such as Arab terrorism. Rabin was determined not to enter into negotiations with terrorists, whatever the circumstances. On June 25, 1974,

118. Yitzhak Rabin in conversation with author, November 18, 1976

three weeks after Rabin took office, Arab terrorists raided a block of flats in the Nahariya, Israel's northernmost coastal city. Four people were killed, including two children. Rabin had instructed the army to act decisively in the Nahariya incident, and he issued the same orders when Arab terrorists struck at Beit She'an in November 1974 and at the Savoy Hotel in Tel Aviv in March 1975, where, after surveying the wreckage, he pledged that "the only place we will meet the terrorists is on the battlefield." As he explained during a BBC-TV interview in January 1976: "We cannot sit down and negotiate with a terrorist organization whose fundamental political position is in direct opposition to the very existence of Israel. The basic philosophy and policy of the so-called PLO is the destruction of Israel."

However, though the IDF could effectively deal with terrorist attacks on Israeli soil, Israelis abroad were still potentially vulnerable, at the mercy of both terrorists and a hostile government, as the events of Entebbe in the summer of 1976, were to show.

Ever the long-term strategic, Rabin believed that Israel's only option was to gain time, to wait 'seven lean years', as he called them, until the free world could shake off its dependence on Arab oil. Meanwhile, Israel had to keep the West from pressuring it to accept an unfavorable peace settlement. Keeping Egypt and Syria apart was important and so was keeping the pacts in force, longer than the six-month period of the two disengagement agreements Israel had signed with them. Israel would accomplish both these goals by entering into a new agreement with president Sadat in which territorial concessions would be made. However, the Jewish State would insist on retaining the two strategic

Mitla and Gidi Passes in the Sinai and on demilitarizing all territories turned over to Egypt. Significantly, Rabin talked about dropping Israel's demands for an Egyptian commitment to non-belligerency, but he came under heavy fire from Right-wing critics for saying this publicly. The peacekeeping process moved sluggishly in late 1974 and early 1975, even as both Israelis and Egyptians agreed that some progress had to be made or the region would slide back into war. Diplomatic progress was slowed by a disagreement over what the new interim agreement should include.

In March, Kissinger undertook his eleventh peace mission to the Middle East since the Yom Kippur War. Three days before it began, Arab terrorists of the PLO attacked the Savoy Hotel in Tel Aviv, killing eight Israelis and wounding eleven more. Peace negotiations began in an atmosphere of increasing Israeli suspicion of Kissinger and skepticism of his step-by-step approach to solving the Middle East conflict, yet Rabin was convinced that Kissinger represented Israel's best chance of moving towards peace. The Americans afterwards would complain how difficult it was to find out what the Israeli position was on certain issues. Rabin kept his cards close to his chest for reasons that had to do more with his own negotiating team than with the strategy: he had to reconcile the diverse views of his hawkish defense minister, Shimon Peres, and his dovish foreign minister, Yigal Allon. When sharp divisions arose within the Israeli team, Rabin would ask for a recess. Sometimes he would simply curtail the discussion saying, "Alright, I think they [the US officials sitting across the table] understand our position."

The talks dragged on for ten days as Kissinger and his entourage shuttled between Jerusalem and Aswan each day.

But little progress was recorded, and the negotiating gap remained nearly as wide as it had been at the beginning. Sadat told Kissinger early on that he could not promise non-belligerency, but he would promise to solve the Arab-Israeli conflict peacefully. However, this sounded far too vague to Rabin. "We are supposed to hand back the passes," he told Kissinger bitterly, "and all you bring back from Sadat are words, words, words." Even if the Egyptians were not prepared to agree to non-belligerency, it might still be possible to arrive at an interim pact, Rabin thought. The very act of reaching an agreement with an Arab State was not something he was willing to give up easily. Working with Kissinger on the formulation, Rabin proposed that Egypt agree to some of the elements of non-belligerency rather than non-belligerency itself. Among those elements would be permission for foreign tourists to move freely back and forth across the Israeli-Egyptian frontier; the limiting of the Arab boycott which for twenty five years had tried to deter firms from doing business with Israel; and the reduction of Arab propaganda against Israel. In return for this, Rabin promised to hand over Abu Rudeis and the western half of the two passes. The accord had to have a lengthy duration, he insisted. Sadat however, turned this new proposal down.

By March 19, Kissinger realized that too little progress was being made to warrant continuing. He made a last appeal to the Israelis to reconsider their stand, but Rabin would not be moved and instead urged him to try to coax Sadat into a more conciliatory mood. With the peace talks about to break up, Rabin called an extraordinary Cabinet meeting on Friday evening, March 22. Since the Jewish Sabbath begins at sunset on Friday, the Cabinet only met in an emergency, and the rupture of the Kissinger talks was considered as such. While the meeting was in progress, Rabin received an angry cable from president Gerald Ford, urging him to moderate his position or face the possibility of an American reappraisal of its relations with the Jewish State. Rabin fully realized the danger Israel was in, but he was determined to avoid an unacceptable peace agreement with Egypt, even if it meant putting at risk Israel's special relationship with the US. He was convinced that in time, the United States would come to understand why Israel had to make this decision. The Cabinet agreed there could be no softening of the Israeli position without parallel concessions from the Egyptians.

Kissinger, realizing that he could do little more in the region at the present, announced that he was returning home the next day. Rabin insisted afterwards that the decision to suspend the talks had not been Israel's; this disclaimer was primarily designed to forestall any blame that might result from the failure of the peace mission and to prevent the Egyptians from using the breakdown of the talks as a pretext for war. Though the suspension of the peace mission increased the likelihood of war, Rabin was more immediately concerned with the future of Israel's relationship with the US. In Israel, his popularity increased as a result of the firm stand he had taken.

However, anxious about the cost of this brave show of independence, the nation favored renewing negotiations with Egypt in the near future. President Ford's announcement that the US would "reassess" its policies towards the Arab-Israeli conflict in the wake of the suspended talks had caused fear in Israel that the Arabs would take advantage of Israel's weakened position. Kissinger rushed in with assurances that the reassessment was not meant to be punitive and would involve no curtailment of arms deliveries. But this was somewhat beside the point: Israel was pressing for a record $2.5 billion in economic and military aid from the US, to begin in July, and it was here that the Administration could easily decide to apply pressure. The new Israeli arms list included F-15 fighter planes and Lance ground-to-ground missiles. Although it was never stated officially, the implication of "reassessment" was that these specific items would be withheld pending a change in Israeli attitudes towards an interim agreement with Egypt. Rumors began to circulate in Israel that the US was to halve its entire economic aid program and, to make matters worse, president Ford had publicly blamed Israel for Kissinger's failure to reach an accord. Rabin's continuing hard line was a calculated gamble. From his own experience in Washington, he sensed that Israel could afford to take a tough line with the Ford Administration as long as it retained the backing of the Congress.

In the meantime, Rabin confronted a new problem that, he feared, might cause acute embarrassment to Kissinger. For six-weeks, he had been postponing a decision on how to deal with a book written by *Haaretz* diplomatic correspondent Matti Golan, which contained classified documents from Kissinger's diplomatic negotiations in the Middle East since the Yom Kippur War and included a number of the secretary's candidly negative comments on world leaders. Golan had submitted the book to military censorship, a normal procedure in Israel. The matter was so sensitive that it was brought to Rabin's attention. In early May, the prime minister called together the Cabinet for an extraordinary meeting, in which he proposed banning the book, arguing that if published, the book could lead to

Kissinger having to resign and also to further deterioration in Israeli-American relations. Rabin gained the Cabinet's agreement and eventually a rewritten version, without the controversial references, was published. The incident was indicative of Rabin's sensitivity to anything that might prejudice relations with the US. Meanwhile, Kissinger was coming under intense pressure from the American Foreign Affairs Establishment (outside the State Department) for a reconvening of the Geneva Conference with the aim of attaining a Middle East settlement along the lines of the Rogers Plan. This was the very development that Rabin had feared since the Yom Kippur War: a campaign to force Israel back to its 1967 borders. Israel's main hope, Rabin still felt, rested with Congress. In mid-May, the Washington-based American Israel Public Affairs Committee, the key lobbying group for Israel, began to work to counter the Administration's campaign to pressure the Jewish State. On May 21, its efforts were rewarded when a group of 76 US senators sent an open letter to president Ford supporting Israel's demand for secure and defensible boundaries and urging continued economic and military aid for the Jewish State. The letter received wide publicity and served to warn the Administration that it should not reduce the American commitment to Israel. Administrative efforts to put pressure on Israel had been slowed, but the threat persisted of more serious American action against Israel if Rabin's Government remained intransigent.

In June, a variety of occurrences helped to ease the atmosphere. Rabin decided, in anticipation of president Sadat's planned reopening of the Suez Canal on June 5, to withdraw some Israeli troops from positions near the Canal as a goodwill gesture. The decision to reopen the Canal itself was a good sign; it followed a meeting in Salzburg between the Egyptian president and president Ford during which Sadat agreed to resume talks with Israel looking toward an interim accord. In mid-June, Rabin and Ford met in Washington. Ford took a very tough line, warning that Rabin's failure to agree to the renewal of the Kissinger step-by-step approach would inevitably lead to a renewal of the Geneva Conference, where the US would have to press Israel to withdraw to the pre-Six-Day-War boundaries. Continued Israeli resistance would mean a drop in American aid, the president grimly reminded him. At home, Rabin came under domestic pressure to get back into America's good graces. Knowing how hard pressed the Israeli economy was, the prime minister informed Ford that Israel would henceforth be much more flexible on the final line of withdrawal and would no longer demand an Egyptian pledge of non-belligerency. Realizing that the agreement which Kissinger would fashion now would be a bitter pill for Israel to swallow, the United States decided to sugarcoat it with substantial sums of economic aid. Kissinger had spoken of $1.8 billion, but Israel now talked of $3.5 billion for the coming year. The US also agreed to provide some extra protection for Israel contained in secret clauses that would oblige the Administration to prevent diplomatic initiatives detrimental to Israel's interests.

While visiting Germany in July on a State visit, the first Israeli prime minister to undertake such a journey while in office, Rabin met Kissinger and reluctantly agreed to Sadat's proposal that American technicians should man electronic surveillance stations in the Sinai passes. The Israelis had previously insisted on using their own men and equipment already in the Gidi Pass, but the Egyptians had refused.

During the summer, the final details of the peace agreement were slowly worked out. Kissinger resolved the issue of Israel's yielding the passes by suggesting that Israel put its forward defense line at the foot of the eastern slopes of the hills overlooking the passes, while Egypt advanced its troops to the western slopes of the same hills. The passes would fall within a buffer zone controlled by the United Nations. It was an ingenious solution, allowing both Israel and Egypt to claim that their original demands had been met. As part of the agreement, the Abu-Rudeis oil fields would be returned to Egypt and some 200 Americans would man early warning sites near the passes. Both sides pledged not to use force during the course of the agreement, which was to last at least three years, with annual renewals of the terms. Israel had tried to insert a secret clause in the agreement that would commit the US to rescue the Jewish State in case of a Russian military threat, but Kissinger would only agree to "consult" with the Israelis. The secretary did agree secretly to an Israeli request that efforts to obtain an Israeli-Jordanian interim agreement should be dropped. American aid, which had never been higher than $1.2 billion annually to Israel, would increase to $2.2 billion under agreements between Israel and the US parallel to the Sinai pact.

Virtually all the details of the agreement had been worked out in advance, the final draft being fashioned in Washington by Israeli and American teams in the first few weeks of August. Rabin told Kissinger that, with 90 percent of the agreement worked out beforehand, he might be able to bring matters to their conclusion within a week in the Middle East. Kissinger, equally confident, said he would like to plan on two weeks. The August shuttle was marked by the noisiest demonstrations the American secretary of state had ever been faced with, as angry Israelis poured into the streets to voice their fury at what they believed to be a sell-out. Rabin had no sympathy with the protestors who, by staging sit-down strikes across main thoroughfares and engaging in violence, were breaking the law. He called them "a serious blow to the backbone of our life," and said he regarded them as a more serious problem "than the question of four or five kilometers (2.4 to 3.1 miles) in the Sinai."[119]

Most Israelis, however, realized that Rabin had had little choice but to accept the agreement. He described the pact in positive terms: "The main thing," he told the Knesset in early September, "is that agreement has been reached that force and fighting will not be the characteristics of Israel-Egyptian relations and that neither side will resort to the use of force against the other. I attribute great political significance to the very fact that the president of Egypt found it possible for his Government to sign such an agreement with Israel, an agreement that stands on its own, without being conditional upon events on other fronts." Rabin was careful to avoid giving the impression that the agreement meant a final peace was near: the Sinai interim accord could be a catalyst for even more positive developments, but it was impossible to know at that point. However, it had served to buy time; the US had been brought into the Middle East as an official peacekeeper for the first time, with the stationing of the 200 technicians in the Sinai; and the Russians had been kept out of the diplomatic process. "I believe," he said later, "that I managed to gain time, during which we improved Israel's political position compared to what it was immediately after

---

119. Interview with Yitzhak Rabin, Israel Television, August 22, 1975

the Yom Kippur War vis-à-vis the whole world, particularly the Arab countries and the United States."[120]

Diplomatic movement in the Middle East slowed up once again in the autumn of 1975, as the would-be peacemakers wanted to find out if the Sinai pact would hold. The breathing space in diplomacy gave Israelis an opportunity to turn their attention to domestic politics, in particular to Rabin's political future. In the autumn of 1977, he would face elections and it was a certainty that he would want to run. His campaign strategy, which materialized gradually during 1975 and 1976, would be to go to the voters on his record in foreign policy. While his achievements on the economic front had been significant, Rabin realized that there was much discontent and unrest; the steps that he had taken had been necessary but inevitably unpopular. The main opposition for the nomination would come from Shimon Peres, his hawkish defense minister. Peres had made little secret of his determination to wrest the prime ministership from Rabin and a running feud between the two men had ensued, with almost every national issue becoming a subject of dispute between them. The Labor Party seemed to be divided into two camps, one favoring Rabin, the other Peres.

The two men had been rivals from the start of Rabin's term of office. They had clashed over Kadum; they had quarreled over West Bank policy, with the defense minister often taking a more moderate view of how to deal with Arab demonstrators than Rabin; they had differed over peace negotiations, with the prime minister taking a more flexible approach towards territorial withdrawals than Peres. But the

---

120. Yitzhak Rabin in conversation with author, November 18, 1976

feud was also highly personal. Rabin regarded Peres as a novice in military matters, despite the defense minister's long career dealing with defense matters.

In mid-May, the two leaders agreed to cooperate, but significantly limited their agreement to affairs of state, making it clear that their political struggle continued. Rabin tried to prevent the contest by declaring that any Cabinet minister who sought the premiership should first resign his post. Peres, eager to remain in the Cabinet, kept a low profile after that, leaving his supporters to criticize and attack the premier. The feud grew to such proportions that intermediaries had to be brought in during the spring of 1976 to repair the strained relationship between the two men. Peres had been especially stung by a newspaper interview with an unidentified source (whom the defense minister took for Rabin himself) who suggested that Rabin would never fall under Peres's thumb in the way that Golda Meir had come under Moshe Dayan's.

To undercut Peres and the Right-wing Likud (whom Rabin would face in the general elections if he obtained his party's nomination), Rabin hoped to be able to show even further achievements in Middle East peacemaking. It would be difficult for either the Labor Party or the average voter to toss aside a prime minister who could claim to have made genuine progress with the Arabs. His aim was to show the country that prospects for peace existed and then ask for a mandate to allow him to continue in office so he could seek further progress. If he could not do that, he wanted at least to be able to tell the country that he had earnestly tried.

Rabin's critics came from both the Left and the Right. Their main complaint was not about his ideology, as the prime minister had more often than not adopted a middle-of-the-road position, but about his tactics. There were charges that he had made errors in judgment about people and issues, that he had been incompetent. His threat to resign over the Kadum affair in December 1975, believed by no one, marked the start of serious debates within the Labor ranks about his behavior on a wide range of issues. The first six months of 1976 saw the most intense criticism yet levelled against him. He was attacked for appointing Yom Kippur War hero Ariel Sharon as his special adviser on military affairs, a move that seemed calculated to undermine Peres and Mordechai Gur; the chief of staff. He was criticized for failing to take action quickly enough after a high-level committee had recommended that the Cabinet ministries should be reorganized. Party dissension further increased over a remark he made to Israeli journalists in Washington in January 1976, asserting that Israel's arms requests to the US had lately been exaggerated. He did not say who had been exaggerating them, but the Peres camp was incensed, supposing him to mean the defense minister. During that Washington visit, an outdoor ceremony on the White House lawn had been scheduled for the visiting Israeli premier. Notwithstanding a heavy downpour, president Ford insisted that it should go ahead, wishing to ensure that Rabin received the same honors as president Sadat had had the previous October. During talks, it was agreed that the next diplomatic step should be an Israeli proposal for a series of end-of-war agreements with the Arabs, which could be negotiated individually or simultaneously with more than one Arab state. Rabin addressed a joint meeting of Congress, as Sadat had done, and said he was "ready to meet any Arab head of Government at any time and in any place." He quoted

Sadat's comment to Congress that there is no substitute for "direct person-to-person contact," and he was warmly applauded when he said next: "I wish that he would direct those words to me as well as to you."

Another pressing concern for Rabin was the Lebanese civil war throughout 1976. The fighting was violent, but was concentrated for the most part around the northern part of the country. The danger to Israel at first lay in a possible Palestinian victory, after which thousands of Palestinians would gravitate from Beirut to southern Lebanon, near the Israeli border, from where it was feared they would step up terrorism against Israel. New problems arose when Syria intervened directly in the spring of 1976, eventually introducing 30,000 troops in the fight against the Palestinians. The danger then to the Jewish State was the possibility of a major Syrian military presence in southern Lebanon. Israel issued warnings to the Syrians through Washington and the press began to speak of a 'red line', which the Israelis would not permit Syria to cross. Israel's increasing interest in Lebanon was exhibited, when according to *Time Magazine* in September 1976, Rabin visited the Christian capital of Junieh in northern Lebanon. The main subject discussed at a meeting between Rabin and unidentified Lebanese leaders was the creation of an alliance between Christian and moderate Muslims against the Palestinians and the Muslim leftists.

One event, in the summer of 1976, sent Rabin's political stock soaring. On June 27, Israeli passengers aboard an Air France jet were hijacked by Palestinian terrorists to Entebbe, Uganda, a country hostile to the Jewish State. The lengthy deliberations over the release of the 105 passengers gave

Rabin some of the most anguishing moments of his political career. He had to make the final choice between negotiating with the terrorists, after they made their demands, or authorize a military operation, which offered faint prospect of success. Rabin decided to proceed cautiously. On Tuesday, June 29, he summoned his Cabinet and for the first time raised the question of sending a task force to free the hostages, an operation that, he said, "has to provide for a way to bring back the hostages. It won't be good enough if we just kill the terrorists. We must be able to fly our people out of there."[121]

Throughout the episode, Rabin rarely left his office except for one special occasion. On that same Tuesday, the ceremony inducting his daughter Dalia into the Israeli bar took place. Long before the events at Entebbe occurred, she had invited her mother to attend, knowing how busy the prime minister was, she said: "Daddy, you don't have to come." Rabin replied, "But Dalia, I want to be there." And the prime minister did indeed show up. But as the speeches went on, he kept looking at his watch. "Remember," Leah said to him, "you came here as a volunteer. Find the patience, even if it's hard."

Mounting such an operation required time and the best possible intelligence. Meanwhile, the terrorists had announced their demands: the release of 53 "freedom fighters" from jails in Israel, France, Switzerland, Kenya, and West Germany. At Ugandan president Idi Amin's request, they had released 47 elderly women, children, and sick from among their victims. One suggestion made by a member of Rabin's Cabinet (as well as some military officers) was that Moshe Dayan should go to Uganda to help negotiate the release of

---

121. Dan Pattir in conversation with author, August 24, 1976

the hostages, in view of his previous close friendship with
Amin. Rabin could not agree to this, fearing that Amin
might simply humiliate the former defense minister as he
had others in the past, or even hold him prisoner too. On the
evening of the 30th, Yoske and Ahuva Tulipman, parents of
Nili, one of the Entebbe hostages, appeared at the Rabins'
door in Tel Aviv. Leah was home alone. They had come to
talk with the prime minister. Leah, who knew the couple, told
Yoske he could phone Rabin the next morning. Yoske did so.
"Yitzhak," he told his friend, "you know that I'm an out-and-
out hawk, but when it comes to my own daughter, my own
flesh and blood, you start to see things in a different light. Do
everything to release them." That evening, Rabin asked chief
of staff Mordechai Gur if there was the smallest chance of a
military operation succeeding when the terrorists' deadline
was due to expire the next day. Gur thought not, so the prime
minister obtained the Cabinet's approval for the opening of
negotiations with the terrorists. Later he explained why: "As
long as we had no military option, we had no right to tell the
hostages that for reasons of principle we could do nothing
for them and that they were at the mercy of the murderers.
Life is more precious than a political stand."[122] However,
planning for a military attack continued, just in case there
was a chance it might be carried out.

Negotiations proceeded, but as the hours passed, hope
faded. The terrorists wanted the exchange to be made in
Uganda, but Israel insisted on a more neutral location. On
Friday, July 2 Gur presented Rabin with a nearly final plan
for an attack, but said it required more ironing out: There was
to be a dress rehearsal that evening, after which he would

---

122. Yitzhak Rabin in a speech to the Jewish Agency Assembly, July
15, 1976

report back. On Saturday morning, Gur walked briskly into Rabin's office and announced that the attack could start that day. Rabin was faced with the toughest of decisions: The failure of the rescue mission could imperil the Government's survival, but, "It's the right thing to do," he told the Cabinet at 2 pm. He calculated that between 10 and 20 hostages would perhaps be killed, even if the attack went well. Notwithstanding that heavy cost, he was convinced that the operation had to be tried. Meanwhile, the negotiations were to continue, he ordered; after all, for any number of reasons the attack might have to be shelved. If the operation were to fail completely, he would take personal responsibility. The Cabinet gave its assent to the risky assault. The rescue planes had already taken off fifteen minutes earlier; it would have been easy enough to recall them had the Cabinet turned the proposal down.

At 7 pm that evening Rabin told Leah that the planes were on their way. A half-hour before the prime minister left home, completely in the dark about the IDF rescue mission, Major-general (reserve) Rehavam Ze'evi phoned from Paris where he had been negotiating with the hijackers through French mediators. Rabin said little to him, trying to stay calm. As he left the house, he told Leah: "Tomorrow morning either Israel's shares will be sky high, or I will be hanged in the town square."

At 10:45 pm, Rabin and those involved in the special task force operation gathered in the defense office, where they listened to a special receiver that would relay the sounds of the battle being fought at Entebbe Airport. Twenty minutes later, the first gunshots came crackling through the set. The news came soon after midnight that the hostages had been rescued and were on their way home. While all other hostages were freed, four Israelis died of wounds suffered in the rescue mission, three of them hostages and one the ground commander, lieutenant-colonel Yonatan Netanyahu (in memory of whom the government decided to name the Entebbe rescue 'Operation Yonatan'). One hostage, Dora Bloch, was missing, later presumed murdered on Amin's orders. Another three hostages and five Israeli soldiers were wounded. All the terrorists were killed.

The rescue gave a much needed boost to the country's morale and to its prestige in the eyes of the world. Rabin could not help but be elated: "I knew the risks, but I also knew that there were good chances that the operation would succeed. And once it succeeded, I believed it would mean a new era in Israel, in the Middle East, and in the world with regard to terrorist activities."[123]

Supporters of Peres argued that the defense minister had originated the idea of the military operation and that Rabin had agreed to it only after days of indecisiveness. Rabin dismissed the allegation: "The story was obviously a fabrication, neither the first nor the last to be disseminated by rivals within my own party, in order to undermine my standing and advance their own ambitions. The prime minister's reputation was at an all-time-high, and in September 1976, Rabin was selected as *Haaretz's* 'Man of the Year'. Entebbe had silenced the prime minister's critics for a while.

After the American presidential election in early November 1976, the Arab states particularly Egypt, seemed ready to start the wheels of diplomacy turning again; president Sadat spoke of reconvening the Geneva Peace

---

123. Interview with Yitzhak Rabin, 'Face the Nation', July 11, 1976

Conference and negotiating an end to the Arab-Israeli conflict within six months. To deflect some of the attention the Arabs were getting with their new peace offensive, Rabin introduced a new idea of his own. At the annual Socialist Internationalist meeting in Geneva, he proposed on November 28 a Helsinki-type peace conference dealing with aspects of the Middle East conflict. He purposely tailored the proposal after the 1975 Helsinki Conference on Security and Cooperation in Europe, in which the US, the Soviet Union, Western and Eastern Europe approved the post-World War Two European borders and pledged to conduct relationships without resorting to war. "Coexistence, security, trade, technology, cooperation, and human bridges," Rabin told the Geneva meeting, "these are the essence of [the] Helsinki [agreements], and I buy them. I buy them as the essence of an agenda for a Geneva Conference on security and cooperation in the Middle East. For lasting peace is a matter of relations and exchange between peoples, not only governments." The conference Rabin envisaged would have to be initiated by the Middle East countries themselves limited to heads of governments (hence, the PLO could not participate), leaving the great powers (the US and the Soviet Union) to provide guarantees but no more. Unlike Helsinki, however, Israel would not insist on ratifying the present borders. "We do not consider the existing lines as final de facto realities," Rabin declared. "Unlike the realities of Europe, we do not demand their perpetuation in peace."

In proposing this Helsinki-style peace conference for the Middle East, Rabin deliberately hoped to force the Arabs to acknowledge that they were not prepared to go as far as he was. He was realistic enough to understand that the Arabs would find such a proposal uncomfortable, as Sadat had already affirmed his conviction that real peace could only be made in the next generation.

Europeans at Geneva greeted the proposal warmly. The Arabs, as Rabin had calculated, rejected it. Peace, he knew, was as elusive as ever. Yet he still yearned for it. As he said in the autumn of 1976, in an interview with the American magazine *Parade*, "I am the father of two children and not long ago became a grandfather. I continue to dream that the day will come when they will be able to go freely to Cairo or anywhere else in the Middle East; and Arabs from all over will be able to come here. I continue to dream that we will have peace in the area. But for the moment, we must be not just dreamers. We must go on planning and acting in such a way that life in Israel is still possible, still worth living, even if this dream of ours never comes true."

In pursuit of that elusive peace, Rabin made a secret journey to Morocco in October 1976. He hoped to encourage King Hassan to persuade Egypt to enter peace negotiations with Israel over a permanent arrangement. Flying to Rabat, via Paris, Rabin wore a wig as a disguise. There was no immediate result from the visit.

As 1976 drew to a close, there were signs that the Lebanese civil war might be coming to an end. Arab States were looking ahead to 1977 with the same anticipation as Israel: A new American president was about to come into office, and undoubtedly he would play a major role in shaping the course of Middle East diplomacy. For now, Israel's borders were quiet, as they had been for the past two years. Rabin was convinced that 1977 would be a year of new pressures on Israel, but he took comfort in the knowledge that it would also be the year in which the Jewish State would reach the peak of its military strength since the Yom Kippur War.

CHAPTER NINE

LEAH RABIN'S BANK ACCOUNT

With national elections only a year away, politics had been increasingly occupying the minds of Israelis in 1976. Uppermost was the question of who would be the Labor Party's candidate for the prime ministership in November 1977. Though he had been prime minister for two years, Rabin had yet to win the mandate of the people in an election. With that mandate, he hoped to be able to exercise stronger leadership, perhaps even to demand still greater sacrifices from the nation in order to improve the economy. He hoped that with the backing of the nation he might conclude new peace agreements with the Arab states. Though the popularity of the Labor Party had appeared to drop somewhat in recent months, he looked forward to the party's triumph in the elections. The most serious obstacle to his remaining as prime minister at least at first was the minister of defense.

During the early part of 1976, Rabin had given much thought to the possibility that he might have to face Shimon

Peres in a fight for the party nomination. The minister of defense had not disclosed his intentions, but the fact that he might enter the contest had to be taken into account, even though their agreement to cooperate in mid-May of that year had contributed to Rabin's air of confidence, which was further boosted by the success of the Entebbe rescue mission six weeks later. In April 1974, Peres had come frighteningly close to defeating Rabin for the Labor Party's nomination for the premiership. It was conceivable that he could, if he chose, mount as strong a campaign again in 1977. The time to prevent the contest was now, before Peres could gather his forces, and while Rabin was riding the crest of his popularity.

Long criticized for displaying too little knowledge of the art of politics, Rabin prepared a daring political maneuver during August. Acting in almost total secrecy to protect himself should he fail, he proposed a long-term pact with Peres that would guarantee Rabin the party's nomination.[124] He had apparent reason to believe that the minister of defense would himself favor such a pact. For some time, Peres had been hinting that he might be willing to step aside. Peres might well have been serious. After all, he had much to lose by challenging Rabin if the premier succeeded in defeating him: He would lose not only the premiership, but also, if Rabin chose to be vengeful, his current cabinet post. But shrewdly, Rabin had refused to allow himself to be lulled into a false sense of security by such utterances.

He spelled out the terms of the pact with Peres and asked Dov Tzamir to mediate. The key clause would give Rabin the prime ministership for another four-year term by virtue of Peres's agreement not to contest the party nomination.

---

124. A source who asked to remain unidentified recounted to the author details of the Rabin-Peres proposed pact

The second and third clauses would go a long way towards satisfying some of Peres's long-standing complaints: For one thing, Rabin would agree to allow him to speak out on matters outside his department; for another, Peres would become privy to all the Labor Party's decisions and stratagems. Two subjects were not made part of the proposed agreement, but were implicit: Peres would be assured of his post as minister of defense after the election, if Rabin won, and he would have the option of seeking the prime ministership in 1981.

Tzamir, who was on good terms with both men, arranged a meeting between them on August 26 in the prime minister's office in Tel Aviv. It lasted several hours, and when it was over, Rabin had the clear impression that he and Peres had come to an agreement. "We had a good meeting," he told Tzamir. "I think we've concluded the matter." But Tzamir was skeptical that such an arrangement could have come about so easily. Were the two men prepared to announce this agreement publicly? he asked Rabin. "No, not yet," the prime minister replied. "Then you haven't agreed on anything yet," Tzamir told him. Judging by Peres's impression of the outcome of the meeting, he seemed to be correct. The minister of defense felt that he and Rabin had improved their relationship, but he could not acknowledge that a long-term agreement had been reached. Shortly afterwards, talking to his good friend Yitzhak Navon, the chairman of the Knesset's Foreign Affairs and Defense Committee, Peres said, "We had a wonderful discussion but while we agreed on everything, it's only for a limited time." In short, while Rabin was thinking in terms of an end to their mutual animosity, Peres felt that all they had agreed upon was a cease-fire. Tzamir was angry with himself later for not pursuing the matter with Peres, sensing that had he pressed the minister of defense for an explanation of what had gone wrong at the meeting, he might have been able to bring the two men together. If Peres had been right, and only a cease-fire had been agreed upon, even that did not last very long. The first source of irritation was Rabin's appointment of Asher Yadlin on September 5 as Governor of the Bank of Israel. Claiming that he had not been consulted, Peres asserted that had he been, Rabin might have avoided the embarrassment of having to withdraw Yadlin's nomination after he was investigated for fraud and bribery. Accusing Peres of inflating the incident, Rabin suspected that Peres had no interest in a political pact and there would be a contest for the Party's leadership. Had political developments proceeded in the winter of 1976-77 in a straightforward manner, the Labor Party would probably have met to choose its nominee for premier in the spring of 1977. But the political scene was suddenly shaken by events in the early winter that were to force a change in the election schedule.

It all began with the scheduled arrival in Israel of three American F-15 fighter planes late one Friday afternoon in December 1976. The introduction of these, the most advanced warplanes yet developed, into the Israeli air force was sensational military news, but scarcely seemed likely to be the cause of any political upheaval. Acquiring the F-15s was a sign of great achievement for the country, and Rabin felt some public celebration was in order. He arranged for a welcoming ceremony complete with government leaders and top military men. The fact that the planes would be landing less than an hour before the onset of the Sabbath in Jerusalem (74 minutes before its onset in Tel Aviv) had not seemed important. However, when orthodox Jews in the government heard what was being arranged in the name of the State, they were enraged. Under Jewish law, one is forbidden from doing any manner of work on the Sabbath. Travel, a form of work, is included in that ban. By holding the ceremony so close to the Sabbath, the State in effect was forcing its own leaders to violate a basic Jewish precept. When he learned of their anger, Rabin first tried to soothe the orthodox Jewish leaders by promising to have helicopters standing by to assure their arrival at home in time for the Sabbath, then, when they still balked, he agreed to tone down the official aspect of the ceremony by cancelling invitations already sent to Cabinet ministers and Knesset members. On December 10, the three planes arrived, performed some spectacular aerobatics, and were praised, filmed, and admired by the spectators. The next day, the country learned that the State had sponsored an event that had made it difficult, if not impossible, for the crowd to get home by the Sabbath. It hardly mattered that most of those attending the ceremony were not very religious; Orthodox Jewish politicians were furious. Even if the prime minister had toned down the official nature of the welcome, the State was still responsible for an event that had led to the desecration of the Sabbath. The government, in their view, had to be reprimanded. The National Religious Party (NRP), a member of Rabin's coalition Government, might have to leave the coalition. Rabin apologized to its three cabinet ministers. Finally, on December 14, after scrambling to get Knesset members to the Knesset (some were summoned home from abroad), Rabin squeaked out a 55-48 vote. The NRP had carried out its threat: Nine of its ten Knesset members had abstained. Six days later, Rabin dismissed the three NRP ministers from his Cabinet, thus plunging the nation into a political crisis. With the loss of the NRP's ten Knesset seats, Rabin could count on only 57 votes to support his shaky Government, four less than the 61 needed for a majority in the 120-member body. He acted, he said, because "a Government which cannot adhere to the principle of collective responsibility has no business functioning as a Government."[125]

The crisis was only temporary; however Rabin was in no mood to test his chances of surviving motions of no-confidence, while he could command only minority support in the Knesset. On December 21, he took the one realistic option open to him – resignation – and pressed the Knesset to advance the elections so that he might win a mandate to set up a new majority-backed Government. Ezer Weizman, who was shortly to become the chairman of the Likud's election campaign, remarked: "It turns out that the F-15 really is an excellent plane, so excellent that it's even capable of shooting down a government."

Elections were set for May 17 and Rabin would remain prime minister until then. His dismissal of the NRP and his resignation deflated critics who had accused him of indecisive and lackluster leadership. He used his newly found support to strike at Shimon Peres, arguing that two members of the government ought not to be fighting for control of the same government.

The national elections were bound to be fought on economic issues, but a new issue was beginning to attract public attention: official corruption, and specifically, the minister of housing Avraham Ofer, who came under suspicion of embezzlement in the press. Though Rabin was

---

125. Quoted in *The Jerusalem Post*, Yitzhak Rabin was speaking to a meeting of the Labor Party's Leadership Bureau

not implicated in any of the disclosures connected with Ofer, a shadow of doubt and suspicion settled over his Government that it was never entirely able to cast off. So desperate was the 54-year-old Ofer, that on January 3, 1977, he drove to a deserted beach in north Tel Aviv and shot himself.

In the note he left by his side, he wrote, "I have no more strength to bear it. I see no point in continuing even after my innocence is proved." The suicide of a Cabinet minister is shocking news in any country, let alone in Israel, where suicide is stigmatized (Jewish law forbids a proper Jewish burial in the case of suicides). The tragedy took on immense proportions. Some Israelis tried to condemn Rabin for what had occurred, but the prime minister sought to place the blame on the press. The accusations against Ofer and his subsequent suicide brought the scent of scandal that much closer to the prime minister himself. There were those who considered the tragic death of the minister as an indictment of the entire Rabin Government. Though no one pointed the finger of suspicion at Rabin directly, and his reputation for integrity remained intact, during the coming months the corruption issue would become an increasingly heavy burden to bear.

The contest for the Labor Party's prime ministerial nomination was to take place at a convention of nearly 3,000 Labor Party members, due to assemble on February 22 in Jerusalem and the following day in Tel Aviv. Never before had the Party opened the nomination for its top leadership position to this large forum and never before had an incumbent prime minister been confronted with a challenge from within the ranks of the party. The whole process of choosing the candidate for prime minister was so novel that no one could say whom it favored. Peres hoped to unseat Rabin, who blamed him for undermining his Government at every turn. Rabin was fighting for the nomination on his past achievements, insisting that he had done a good job and that with four more years and the mandate of the people, he could exercise more decisive leadership. The campaign styles of the two candidates remained much the same as in 1974: Rabin was, as always, the introvert, unwilling to pick up the telephone to talk to convention delegates, Peres was just the opposite, the politician par excellence who could spend hours on the telephone, mixing small talk with persuasive pleas for support. It was perhaps not so vital for Rabin to do this; he was, after all, the incumbent prime minister whose list of achievements was well known. Both men claimed to win; neither could be certain.

On February 22, almost 3,000 Labor Party members gathered in the large Binyanei HaUma (Jerusalem International Convention Center). Their presence, together with the festive mood of the delegates, tended to blur the harsh realities confronting the party. Earlier in the day, a Tel Aviv judge had sentenced Asher Yadlin to a five-year prison term for taking bribes and evading land taxes. The claim Yadlin had made eight days earlier at his trial was still reverberating round the country: He had admitted taking $30,000 in bribes, but had contended that of the sum, $20,000 had been transferred to the coffers of the Labor Party. In addition, he testified that he had raised "millions more" for the party during and after the 1973 election campaign at the behest of other Labor Party leaders. The party that had preached stern socialist morality was now stigmatized as the party of Asher Yadlin and Avraham Ofer, and its public image had suffered accordingly.

Despite the Yadlin affair and all of Rabin's other woes, he emerged the victor by the slim margin of only 41 votes. He had received 1,445 votes to Peres's 1,404. When the result was announced, Rabin, smiling faintly, shook hands with glum-faced Peres. Ironically, he need not have offered to make a deal with Peres; after all, he had won the nomination in his own right. The victory seemed that much sweeter. He now commanded the party as never before and seemed all set to remain in office for another four years. However, the narrow margin of his victory reflected a great sense of unrest and dissatisfaction within the party and within the country, too, for that matter. The most likely reason for his victory, it was generally agreed, was his incumbency.

It suddenly became clear that Rabin would face a tough time in the forthcoming election in May and the Labor Party's main opponent in that election would be the right-wing Likud Party, headed by Menachem Begin, a former leader of the Irgun and for years the head of the political opposition. The new Democratic Movement for Change, led by former chief-of-staff and archeologist Yigael Yadin appeared to be capturing a sizeable portion of the votes. Some even forecasted that it could win as many as 15 to 20 seats in the Knesset. Still, the prime minister was convinced that he and Yadin could team up in a coalition after the election. Labor and the Likud were not practicable coalition partners, so he would campaign to persuade people to take their votes away from the Likud. Though Peres had once feared that losing to Rabin in the party leadership contest would cost him the Defense Ministry, Rabin now realized that he must retain Peres in order to run an effective campaign. Thus, shortly after the convention, he let it be known that he would keep

Peres in his Government as minister of defense if Labor won in May.

In early March, Rabin went to Washington for talks with president Jimmy Carter. Ironically, this trip, which should have given a much-needed boost to his prestige during the election campaign, was to lead to his political downfall. The visit began on a hopeful note. At the welcoming ceremony on the White House Lawn on March 7, Carter surprised Rabin by declaring that Israel should have defensible borders, to assure that future peace agreements would not be violated. It had always been Israel's fervent wish to convince the US and the rest of the world that the Jewish State required better protection than the borders it had had prior to the 1967 Six-Day War, i.e. that it was necessary to retain a certain part of the territory captured in that war. Rabin could only wonder if Carter had decided to see eye to eye with Israelis on this matter, even before their private talks had begun.

However, once the talks got under way, the prime minister realized that Carter had not intended a major reformulation of American policy towards the Middle East; he was simply using a phrase to which the Israelis attached more significance than he did. At one stage in the talks, Carter mentioned that a final Middle East settlement ought to include no more than minor adjustments to Israel's 1967 borders. Rabin interrupted abruptly: "If the position of the United States is to be formulated and presented publicly in this way, there will be no need for negotiations between the parties." Carter assured Rabin he would not make such private thoughts public. The prime minister seemed somewhat assured but not completely. The prime minister's visit to Washington produced little diplomatic movement, and, thanks to Carter's eagerness to share his views on foreign policy with the American public, served only to introduce some new obstacles into Middle East peacemaking.

The events leading to Rabin's downfall began on Tuesday, March 8, when, driven by American secret service men in a car provided by the US Government, Leah Rabin visited the Dupont Circle branch of the National Bank in Washington. It was the last morning of the Rabins' visit to Washington; Leah Rabin went to the bank to close two accounts, one check, one savings, both bearing her name and that of her husband. The savings account held $2,000, the checking account just one penny. The visit might have seemed routine, but it was not. In holding such accounts in a bank outside Israel without the permission of the Israeli Treasury, the Rabins were breaking the law. At that time, Israel had strict foreign currency regulations; when travelling abroad, an Israeli could take only $450 with him or her. Keeping dollars in a bank account abroad without permission was an offense punishable by up to three years' imprisonment and a fine three times the amount of foreign currency illegally held. The presumed reason for the law was to prevent Israelis from depositing funds into overseas bank accounts in order to avoid taxes.

Leah closed the savings account, asking for the $2,000 in travelers checks. In her memoirs, she explained what then happened: "At that point it turned out that the branch only had checks of $20 each, which would have meant a long time sitting signing them. A limousine, complete with American security men, was waiting outside, and there were two more bodyguards, one Israeli and one American, in the bank with me. My transaction was arousing considerable interest and I was feeling the pressure from that and from the tight schedule. The ceremony was to be at 10, and it was already 9:30." (Rabin was to receive an honorary doctorate from the American University at the Kennedy Center.) "After the ceremony we were leaving town. I was also put off by the idea of carrying $2,000 in cash, so under the pressures of the moment I decided to leave the arrangement standing until our next visit. Looking back, I now know that I wasn't aware enough of the gravity of my transgression. I looked on it much like crossing a traffic light on the amber, in the hope of completing the move before the light turned red. I knew I had to close the account, and I had every intention of doing so during that visit, but the technical obstacles of the timetable simply got in the way. And then the bomb went off."[126]

On Thursday, March 10, three employees of the nearby Israeli Embassy came to the bank on embassy business. One of the bank tellers told them: "A couple of days ago, your prime minister's wife was here." They could hardly believe what they had heard. One of them asked the teller if Mrs. Rabin actually had an account at the bank, "Yes" came the matter-of-fact reply. Such information was far too explosive for the Embassy staff to keep to themselves. It took less than a day for the news to reach Dan Margalit, the Washington-based correspondent for *Haretz*.

Busy covering Rabin's visit, Margalit had little time to collect complete information about the incident, so he decided to keep quiet about it for a while. It was only later that evening, after a party given in honor of Rabin by Uri Ben-Ari, the Israeli consul in New York, that Margalit broached the subject with Dan Pattir, Rabin's spokesman,

---

126. Leah Rabin, *All the Time His Wife*, p. 212

telling him that he was sitting on a news story concerning a Washington bank account belonging either to Rabin or to his family, he wasn't sure which. Asking Pattir for response from Rabin, Margalit promised that he would only print the story if Rabin refused to give an unambiguous denial of the facts. The next day, March 12, Pattir raised the bank account matter with the prime minister: "What should I do?" the spokesman asked, to which Rabin replied: "Don't react." Pattir hoped the prime minister would authorize some kind of response to Margalit's information during the impending flight back to Israel. But all Rabin would authorize him to say was that he as the prime minister's spokesman could not comment on the matter as it fell within Rabin's private sphere. Meanwhile, Rabin's political aides were upset that Pattir had waited to tell the prime minister, believing that the opportunity to persuade Margalit not to publish the story had been lost. Meanwhile, on March 14, Margalit shrewdly got the proof he needed to write that Mrs. Rabin indeed had an account at the National Bank in Washington: He was able to get a bank teller to accept $500 from him for the account in the names of Yitzhak and Leah Rabin and received a deposit slip bearing the names of the account owners and the account number. With that solid proof, the reporter was ready to go ahead with his story.

Haaretz was due to print it on Tuesday morning, March 15. The night before, Pattir had finally obtained Rabin's permission to acknowledge the existence of the account. The newspaper featured the story on its front page, revealing that Mrs. Rabin owned the account, along with the account number; and the fact that she had visited the bank during the recent Washington trip. The article noted also that Rabin had avoided acknowledging the facts for three days. Quoting sources close to Rabin (i.e. Pattir), *Haaretz* gave the prime minister's only comment on the matter: The account had been left over from his days as ambassador to pay outstanding bills and today only a small amount, remained.

At first, public reaction was exceedingly mild. Since there had been no suggestion in Margalit's article that the money in the account had been obtained illegally, it was generally accepted that, at worst, the Rabins had been guilty of a technical error in not closing the account. *The Jerusalem Post* advised in its editorial that Mrs. Rabin should admit her error, the Treasury should impound the money, and the press and politicians should return to more important matters. Even the opposition Likud Party chose to give the premier and his wife the benefit of the doubt since the violation had appeared merely technical.

Confronted with the public disclosure, Rabin was determined to share full responsibility with his wife for the consequences of their misdemeanor, although he had been a passive partner in the account. "I will not allow any distinction to be made between you and me," he told his wife, "nor will I allow people to call it 'Leah Rabin's bank account.'"[127] Though he could not know it at the time, that one sentence would prove in a few short years the greatest boon to Rabin's political survival and resurrection. In short, Israelis loved a man who stood by his wife. Leah, too, was in awe of her husband's "exemplary" behavior. "I never once heard him say: 'What did you do? Why have you got me in a mess?' We travelled this road together and drew strength from each other."[128]

---

127. Interview with Leah Rabin, *Maariv*, April 10 1977

128. Leah Rabin, *All the Time His Wife*, p. 213

Rabin sought the advice of Israel Galili, the minister without portfolio, whom he respected a great deal. Rabin told him that if his candidacy would now be a problem for the party he would withdraw it at once. Galili consulted other Labor Party members then advised Rabin to wait and see what the results of the Treasury inquiry would be before taking such a step.

Advising the prime minister on the bank account affair was a delicate matter. Dan Pattir tried gently to suggest that his best strategy would be to lay the entire truth in front of the public in the hope that it would be sympathetic. Rabin thought it better to keep the subject as low-keyed as possible, and to work through his lawyer, Shimon Alexandroni, to try to bring matters to a swift and painless conclusion. Rabin contacted attorney general Aharon Barak and notified him what Alexandroni was doing. "Barak's tone was gentle and conciliatory," Rabin recalled, "as he played down the gravity of the whole matter. His attitude went a long way toward reassuring Leah."[129] The prime minister and Alexandroni agreed to approach Treasury officials in the hope of arranging a prompt out-of-court settlement in the form of a fine. From Tel Aviv, the lawyer phoned Don Kanterowitz, the director of the Treasury's Foreign Currency Division, at home in Jerusalem where he was recovering from flu. He had learned about the Rabins' bank account from the newspaper. When Alexandroni asked him what the Treasury expected Rabin to do, Kanterowitz suggested that the lawyer should set out the facts of the case as he understood them in a letter. Casually, without pressing the matter at that point, Alexandroni raised

129. Yitzhak Rabin, *The Rabin Memoirs* (English version), p. 244

the possibility of a fine, and it was agreed that this too should be mentioned in the letter.

Meanwhile, the prime minister had to decide whether to offer a public explanation of the bank account, even if he did not reveal the entire truth (as Pattir had proposed). The most obvious forum would be Israel Television but it was arranged that Leah would give an interview, not her husband. During the interview she sounded penitent, pointing out that she had closed the account.[130] She said she should have been more careful, but admitted that she was only human and as long as someone admitted making a mistake it should cause no harm to that person. The nation's first reaction had not been censorious. Rabin's aides began to feel he might escape serious legal or political consequences. Over the next few days, Rabin grew worried that the public might feel he had thrown the entire problem on his wife's shoulders. He wanted people to know that he felt equally responsible for the existence of the bank account. On March 20 he told Israel Radio that he shared "formal as well as moral responsibility" with his wife for the account. He insisted that as it was "neither secret nor numbered", there had been nothing sinister about the account. The account had remained open only through neglect.

By mid-March, the election campaign was in full swing. Public opinion polls were indicating that Rabin was still almost certain to win the prime ministership on May 17, but the race was likely to be close and every campaign appearance mattered. The prime minister, however, found

---

130. *The Jerusalem Post*, March 16, 1977 quotes Mrs. Rabin as telling a reporter that there had some $2,000 in the account.

it difficult to get into the spirit of the campaign while the investigation into the bank account continued. Uncertain of its outcome, he chose to reduce his campaign activities in order not to embarrass the Labor Party. He went to Haifa for an election walking tour on March 19, four days after the *Haaretz* story appeared, but he made few campaign appearances after that. Few realized how seriously the prime minister was taking the matter of the Treasury investigation. Most believed that the affair would end uneventfully with little harm to the Rabins. But the prime minister was not so certain. "He's haunted by it," an aide said. "It's all he thinks about."

After viewing the documents, Dov Kanterowitz realized that Mrs. Rabin had used the account over the past four years and her story of forgetting its existence did not hold up. A special committee of Finance Ministry and police officials would decide the matter on April 5. As the date approached Rabin seemed calmer, his wife still tense and worried. The special committee recommended on April 5 that a collective fine of $16,000 be imposed on the Rabins. Though Kanterowitz could have ratified the decision, ending the matter, he felt that the attorney general ought to be asked for his point of view. In cases like this one, where more than $5,000 was involved, the matter often became a question for the courts to decide, though there had been some notable exceptions. With the sum involved here $20,000 (the public would not learn that this was the sum until April 7), Kanterowitz could find no justification for not involving attorney general Barak.

Neither man found the task before them easy or pleasant, but both had a strong conviction that they must be guided by what they felt was proper and not by the fact that the case involved the prime minister. Their search for a precedent, which would allow them simply to impose a fine, proved fruitless. There was no alternative but to refer the case to a court of law. Looking over the material again, they decided that as Rabin had played a passive role in maintaining the account, he should be punished with a fine, whereas Mrs. Rabin should stand trial. Rabin was baffled by their decision: "To this day," Rabin wrote in 1979, "I cannot understand the legal justification for drawing the distinction, and at the time, I sensed a growing resolve to reject the offer with a resounding 'no.' I would do everything possible to share full responsibility with my wife."[131]

Thursday, April 7, was an important day for Israelis, whose basketball team Maccabi Tel Aviv was to compete that evening in Belgrade against an Italian team, Mobilgirgi Varese, for the European Basketball Championship. Many Israelis had flown to Belgrade to watch the game; the rest of the nation would watch it live on television in their homes beginning at 9:30 pm.

As the day began, Israeli politicians were learning of the serious turn of events that had taken place in the Rabins' bank account affair. Stunned, the minister of finance decided to make a special plea to the attorney general. He confronted Barak and told him that he thought a fine should suffice. However, the attorney general was adamant that prosecution was called for.

That morning, Rabin attended a meeting at Arlozoroff Hall in Tel Aviv where the Labor Party's Central Committee continued to choose Knesset candidates for the May election.

---

131. Quoted in *Yediot Aharonot*, April 10, 1977

He took his usual seat in the front row of the hall. His face betrayed nothing of what he must have been feeling as the audience was buzzing with the news that had just appeared in *Maariv*, which had disclosed in a front-page report that the Rabins had had two bank accounts in the US, and that they had contained at one stage $20,000, not $2,000.

Noting that the special committee had recommended a $16,000 fine, the report added that the attorney general would be making up his mind whether to accept this in a few days. In fact, Barak had already come to a decision. Perhaps most significantly, the first rumor that Rabin would submit his resignation in the coming days appeared in the report, though the prime minister's office denied it. Knowing he must say something, Rabin asked Pattir to alert the political correspondents of both Israel Radio and Television to stand by for a possible statement from him later in the day. Meanwhile, the prime minister carried on with his regular schedule of meetings. But around him his associates were gripped with an increasing sense of foreboding, hoping for a miracle that would extricate their boss from the scandal.

At 12 noon, Rabin, grim-faced but polite, greeted justice minister Haim Zadok and attorney general Barak in his office. The minister of justice slowly, deliberately, related the events that had led up to the attorney general's decision to prosecute Mrs. Rabin. The meeting was brief and it was left with Rabin saying that he wanted to talk over with others what steps he might take now. There had been no discussion of his resigning. Rabin had little doubt what path to take. "I could no longer remain the party's candidate for prime minister," he wrote two years later. "As the experience of the past few days had shown, the gravity of the offence was open to a broad range of interpretation. But I had committed an offence and, although the attorney general viewed it as a technical infringement, I felt that I had to render my own personal and private account, which demanded consistency and courage. Friends tried to dissuade me from taking any fateful steps, but a man is always truly alone at such times. And alone, my conscience and I came to three interconnected decisions: I would withdraw my nomination as the candidate for prime minister; I would share full responsibility with Leah; and I would try to resign my post as prime minister, so that the Labor Party's nominee could fill the post up to the election [when he would head the party's list of candidates]."

He could not know it at the time, but those decisions, taken during the most painful days of his life, would serve him well through the years. Leaving office had seemed the wisest, indeed the only, course of action open to Rabin, given the circumstances at the time. In later years, his decision to hold himself accountable when others were arguing that he could have somehow evaded responsibility, and his determination to stand by his wife when it might have been possible to make her the sole guilty party, were regarded as acts of valor on Rabin's part. It was of great significance that the scandal was over something relatively minor, a technical violation of a law that many Israelis were themselves violating, and that would eventually be wiped off the books. Had Rabin engaged in some illegal behavior of a more serious nature – stealing public funds, for example – few would have expressed sympathy, understanding, or forgiveness. Even at the time, Israelis felt a sense of sorrow for Yitzhak Rabin, but not because he had broken the law; they were prepared to overlook that when weighed against his record of public service. They felt that the whole affair was a pity, a pity that

Rabin had to give up office, a pity that he had to sacrifice so much over so little. Now that Rabin had decided what to do, he sought out his wife. He was firm about the need to resign and, sensing his resolve, she did not try to dissuade him.

At 1 pm, the prime minister called Dan Pattir into his office. The spokesman had seen Barak and Zadok come and go, and had realized that the matter was grave. "I'm going to announce my resignation and my withdrawal as the party's candidate for prime minister," Rabin told him. He spoke so decisively that Pattir found it difficult to urge him to reconsider. "Are you certain this is your final decision?" he asked. "Yes," Rabin said quickly. The two men decided that the radio and television reporters should be informed that the prime minister might make a statement to the nation at 7 pm, therefore, they should come from Jerusalem to Tel Aviv immediately.

Rabin wanted to resign from office immediately, sure that the people would not tolerate anything less, but Israeli law does not permit ministers to resign from an interim administration, unless unfit to govern. Rabin could not give up the job until a Government was formed. As elections were not scheduled until May 17 and it could take six weeks or more for a coalition government to be set up, this might take several months. Hoping to avoid an angry public demanding his immediate resignation, Rabin had come up with an idea that seemed to offer a way of resigning right away: He would give up his Knesset seat, which meant that he could no longer serve as prime minister; a prime minister had to be a Knesset member. Rabin waved off Labor Party politicians who urged him to delay such a bold step until after the entire affair was resolved legally. Pattir again went to see Rabin, this time to discuss the final arrangements for the prime minister's announcement to the nation. He asked him to consider letting him issue a statement shortly to the effect that "the prime minister was considering the situation that had developed and would make an announcement on Friday." With that, in the back of Pattir's mind, was the hope that given an extra day, Rabin might review his decision, however Rabin would not agree. The only concession he would make was to put off the announcement until after the basketball game. "I don't want to disturb the people," he told his spokesman. "They've waited so long for this event."

Rabin asked his wife to join him at the office while he waited for the game to end, after which he would speak to the nation. By 10:30 pm, Israelis were in a festive mood looking forward to a victory. Unknown to most of the country, a drama was unfolding in Tel Aviv. Israel Radio's political reporter, Shalom Kital, arriving at the prime minister's office, heard Rabin's bodyguards cheering on their team, which was holding on to a small lead in the championship match. Pattir greeted him and told him Rabin planned to resign. "Let him talk. He won't keep anything from you," Pattir urged the reporter. Rabin and his wife sat before a small television set in his office with the game turned on, but neither had much heart for it. Pattir escorted Kital into the prime minister's main conference room on the second floor. Here, there was no shouting, no cheering. The atmosphere was somber and gloomy. Seated around the table were the prime minister, looking sad but alert, his wife, crying softly, and the prime minister's chief aides.

Rabin seemed quieter than usual, but appeared composed and reconciled to the anguishing decision he had just made. Two pages of handwritten notes lay before him on the table.

He had prepared what he wanted to say to the nation carefully, saving the dramatic announcement of his resignation for the end. Kital felt that the listeners should be informed at the outset of the interview that Rabin planned to resign so that the rest of the prime minister's comments would be understood in the context of his leaving office. Rabin asked the others in the room what they thought. Leah disagreed with Kital as did Rabin's military aide Ephraim Poran. In the end, Rabin agreed that Kital could announce that Rabin had decided to resign prior to the prime minister speaking. Kital would tape the interview and it would be played on the air after the game ended.

The interview took fifteen minutes. The prime minister acknowledged in the interview that there had been some "misunderstanding" over the precise sum of money involved in the bank accounts. "I will not overlook or deny that there was some negligence on our part in that we did not close our accounts in time as required by the law." Because of this, he had decided to leave office as soon as possible and to renounce his party's nomination for a second term. He had also resolved not to seek parliamentary immunity from prosecution and, because he felt "a formal and moral responsibility" with his wife for what had occurred, he declared, "If she must stand trial, so will I..." (Of course, the decision was not up to him, but the gesture was sincere.)

Despite all this, Rabin suggested that he had been forced to take these serious steps, which so far outweighed his misdeed. Had the offense not been discovered in the midst of an election campaign, he implied, he might have weathered the storm, implying that his political enemies might have planted the damaging newspaper article against him. Or, if he and his wife had spent the money or even burned it (neither being a crime), there would have been no fuss, no scandal. He described what he and his wife had done a "personal mishap," a "minor error," but he still felt compelled to do what he was doing. Speaking calmly and with deliberation, Rabin told of his plans to give up the leadership of both the government and the Labor Party. With a general election just 40 days away, the news was a bombshell. For the prime minister, it was the saddest day of a career of public life that had spanned thirty years and had known many moments of triumph. Shortly after 11 pm Rabin learned that Maccabi Tel Aviv had won the European Basketball Championship, 78-77. "At least," he told an aide, "the viewers will be happy when they tune in to what I have to say." In a few minutes, he was to give an interview on Israel Television on the subject of his resignation.

At the television studio, a thousand yards away from Rabin's office, Ya'acov Achimeir, the political reporter who was to conduct the interview, was frantic as his cameraman had yet to appear. A stenographer showed up first, weeping; then Rabin, wearing a blue blazer and a tie – his eyes seemed distant but otherwise he appeared normal. Inside the studio, he combed his hair while the cameraman just arrived. Achimeir found the prime minister quieter than usual. Leah, on the other hand, did not stop talking, most of what she had to say aimed at the press.

After the fifteen-minute interview, Rabin asked Poran what he thought. "It was fine," he said helplessly. Walking Rabin to his car, Achimeir said: "Mr. Prime Minister, you must remember that you still have friends." Rabin replied: "I know." Ironically, the dignity and sincerity of both radio and television interviews won Rabin widespread sympathy. However, this did not alter the facts, which were both dramatic and shocking to the nation, and were to change the political landscape overnight.

The most seriously affected person besides the Rabins was of course Shimon Peres. He seemed the natural heir to Rabin as the Labor Party's nominee, and within hours of the resignation announcement was gathering his closest associates to lay plans for securing the nomination. Peres, who only six weeks before had lost the Labor Party's nomination for prime minister to Rabin, was gleeful. But events had to move at a brisk pace, for there were only 40 days left to the election.

Political colleagues appeared at his door to urge Rabin to reconsider; aides told him of people demonstrating after his interview urging him to review his decision. But Rabin would hear none of it. He thought it undignified and unthinkable for the office of prime minister and for a prime minister "to hold office while legal proceedings are being conducted against him. I have to do what is best for the country." For his conduct, Rabin won sympathy. No government leader or editorial writer called for him to enter permanent political exile. The Labor Party listed him as number 20 on its list, the same spot he had been given when he ran in 1973. Even Peres, named the party's nominee on April 10, told him: "With time... your abilities and capabilities will surely find expression."[132]

Rabin decided to say nothing more about his resignation in public, at least in the first few weeks after his announcement. His wife, however, asked the public to believe that the entire affair had been overblown. In two candid interviews given to

---

132. At Labor Party Central Committee meeting, Tel Aviv

the Israeli press immediately after her husband's resignation, she portrayed herself as saddened, but hardly distraught. "I tend to think I should have been more cautious," she acknowledged, "but I don't have the feeling that I did a bad thing... I don't go around with the feeling that I can't look the public in the eye. Perhaps, I might have prevented all this, but what's the use of crying over spilled milk?"[133]

Two legal matters remained: As for Rabin, the legal authorities fined him the small sum of $1,600 primarily because of his passive role in the bank account affair; in Mrs. Rabin's case, however, trial took place on Sunday, April 17 in the Tel Aviv District Court. The prime minister, who had said ten days earlier that if his wife were to stand trial, so would he, had since changed his mind. He chose not to be present at the trial, suspecting that his presence there might influence the court. After he and his wife had driven up to the court building, he escorted her to the door and then left. Crowds of curious onlookers thronged the corridors while the police did their best to hold them back. Only 30 people were allowed in the small courtroom; mostly reporters.

Had the judge wished, he could have sent Mrs. Rabin to prison, though this was unlikely, since no previous offender in a case of this nature had been jailed. Indeed, the district attorney, Victoria Ostrovsky-Cohen, did not even ask for a prison sentence, though she told the judge: "The incident has caused considerable public damage, since the accused is the wife of the prime minister, who is in charge of the government's economic policy. A person in this position should have served as an example to the public." Shimon Alexandroni, defending Mrs. Rabin, asked that the judge

---

133. Interview with Leah Rabin in *Maariv*, April 10, 1977

treat her leniently, as the Rabins had already paid a severe price. Asked if she wished to add anything before a verdict was rendered, Mrs. Rabin looked up at the judge, and whispered, "No, I have nothing to add."

The court recessed for an hour. When the judge returned with his verdict, he had some harsh words for Mrs. Rabin: "One expects a public figure to observe the law more carefully, and we are all the more disappointed when we find such is not the case." He would not send her to prison, "for she had already suffered enough in her downfall from a position of importance to the benches of the courtroom." Instead, he imposed a fine of $27,000, or one year in jail. She had 45 days in which to pay. It was a heavy fine, steeper than Leah had imagined; but the Rabins' one consolation was that the case was now over. Henceforth, they would have to deal with the consequences to Rabin's career and to their personal lives.

Two thousand letters arrived. Hundreds of people phoned, offering support, sympathy, and money. The Rabins were uplifted by the public reaction. One man suggested to Leah that she not pay the fine, that he would instead spend the time in jail for her. Likud Knesset member Elimelech Rimalt sent a handwritten note: "This is a transgression that bears with it no stain." To which Yitzhak Rabin reacted, "Not one of my Labor Party colleagues, but a Likud member, found the need to write that." Leah spent hours answering each letter, writing 30 to 40 a day.

Rabin decided to stay out of the public eye in the hope that the damage he had suffered to his reputation would be only temporary. He mostly stayed out of view and only departed from his plan to remain on vacation until after the election when a military helicopter crashed near Jericho on May 10, killing all 54 aboard, most soldiers on maneuvers. He decided to attend the Cabinet meeting called for the next day to mourn the victims.

A public opinion poll in *Haaretz* on May 4 showed surprisingly that a majority of Israelis (51.1 percent) would welcome his return to high office again. Some 35.8 percent did not want him back in office again.

On May 17, 1977, Menachem Begin's Likud Party won the election, meaning that he would become prime minster after nine previous failed attempts. The Likud won 43 seats (four more than in 1973) but the Labor Alignment won only 32 seats (19 fewer than in 1973). Yigael Yadin's Democratic Movement for Change won 15 seats, a remarkable achievement for a party only six months old; the NRP won 12 (two more than 1973). Israeli pundits called the results a "revolution" and Peres was stunned. Now, like Rabin, he was on the sidelines. One surprising winner was Ezer Weizman, who, by running Likud's successful campaign, paved the way for his becoming the next minister of defense.

Off and on in the hospital over concerns related to his heart, Begin surprised everyone by naming Moshe Dayan, a Labor Party member not a Likudnik, his foreign minister. Begin won the day with Dayan, despite complaints from Likud members who could not stomach the idea that they would be allied with the man many blamed for the early reverses of the 1973 Yom Kippur War. Rabin ended his leave of absence on May 29 and took up his normal duties as prime minster in order to assure the smooth transition of Government. As Begin prepared to take office on June 21, Rabin was ending his final day as prime minister, writing notes to world leaders. Late that evening, as the Knesset debate over the new government ended, Rabin rose and said to Dan Pattir: "Well, now I'm a free man." Leaving the plenum, Begin called to Rabin, "I will be coming to see you tomorrow morning at 9 am." Quickly correcting him with a smile, Rabin said, "No, I will be coming to see you."

Rabin worked out of a small office in the government complex in Tel Aviv, given to him as an ex-prime minister. He began writing his memoirs and took up work in the Knesset, though without a great deal of enthusiasm. Power had passed to Menachem Begin.

CHAPTER TEN

A SHORT POLITICAL EXILE

Had Yitzhak Rabin committed a far more serious violation of the law, he most likely would have been relegated to a minor political role for the rest of his political career. But his "crime" had been inconsequential to most Israelis. Still, no matter how decent and honest his public image, and however sorry the country felt for the mess in which he had found himself, it was still not clear if the country would forgive and forget. Would it allow him back in the centers of political power at some stage? Or would he climb no higher than a Knesset backbencher?

For someone as active in government as Rabin had been, indeed, Yitzhak Rabin had paid a price: He was banished to the Knesset backbenches, which was serious punishment. His family and friends gave him conflicting advice about whether to remain a Knesset member after the scandal. Some argued that he was better off divesting himself of all political responsibilities, for a while at least, until the public had a chance to decide whether it wanted him back in political life. But others, especially Amos Eiran, Rabin's director-general, and Leah, thought he should remain in the Knesset, if only to repel suggestions that he was abandoning Israeli politics. Rabin decided there was no reason to be hasty and leave the Knesset. And so he became Yitzhak Rabin, Knesset member. Not surprisingly, he found it boring. On any given day, he might have to decide whether to attend a committee meeting; whether to agree to be interviewed by a journalist; whether to show up at the Knesset at all. He planned to write his memoirs, yet even that was hardly the equivalent of past stimulating efforts. Politics was now his *métier*, the only game in town for him. Out of boredom and frustration, he phoned Leah three or four times a day.[134] He worked with a ghostwriter, laboriously going over his past history, which only served to remind him of how little he was doing at present. Adding to the insult, the nation had become enthralled with its new prime minister, Menachem Begin, and paid little attention to the Labor Party and its key politicians.

Rabin was pleased to find that the nation developed a kind of collective amnesia about the bank account controversy. Without skipping a beat, foreign and local media sought Rabin out as one of the country's most insightful, and suddenly accessible, political commentators. Israel Bonds and the United Jewish Appeal were all too pleased to invite him to speak to their forums in the US. Why had Israelis been so forgiving of Rabin? Part of the answer had to do with the conservative nature of Israeli politics, where policies changed slowly and personalities leave the political arena

---

134. Leah Rabin, interview with author, July 28, 1992

even slower. In 1977, 29 years after the state was founded, the country's political leadership still largely comprised the generation of the founding fathers. In short, Israelis "permitted" Rabin to remain in the political arena, because they felt they could not afford to overlook his impeccable credentials in helping to build up and preserve the state. An overseas bank account seemed trivial compared to leading the army to victory in the Six-Day War or rescuing the hostages at Entebbe. Besides, Rabin was only 55 years old, young for Israeli politics. Taking its cue from the rest of the country, Rabin's Labor Party was disinclined to dispense with his political talent. To be sure, Shimon Peres was the undisputed party leader in the wake of Rabin's downfall. Peres, however, would never be permitted to take complete control of the party. He was too mistrusted, too disliked by those party veterans who remembered how he had organized the great defection from Labor in the 1960s that had led to the creation of David Ben-Gurion's Rafi Party. Rabin, on the other hand, had unassailable Labor credentials. Rabin was of two minds: He wanted to return to political power, but not under prime minister Peres.

Following the Sinai accord of September 1975, Rabin as prime minister had hoped to work out a further interim agreement between Israel and Egypt. Egyptian president Anwar al-Sadat, however, eventually abandoned that concept in the belief that a comprehensive peace between Israel and the other Arab states should be pursued. When he became prime minister in June 1977, Menachem Begin, too, believed that the time for interim agreements was over; he began examining the chances for a comprehensive agreement, however elusive that seemed. With Begin prime minister, the greatest single push in the direction of peace came on November 9, 1977, when Sadat announced that he was ready to go to the ends of the earth, even Jerusalem, to pursue peace.

Rabin found himself in the United States on that day, caught up in a swirl of meetings with American officials. He put a question to secretary of state Cyrus Vance: What were the chances that Sadat would show up in Jerusalem? "Fifty-fifty," Vance replied.

Sadat proved a man of his word, and so when it became clear that an Egyptian president was in fact going to visit Jerusalem, Rabin raced back home. He arrived the day before Sadat did. In his 1979 memoirs, Rabin described the paradoxical nature of the Sadat visit, calling his journey both courageous and desperate. Courageous because until then, such a step had been absolutely unthinkable and was still unthinkable in most of the countries in the Arab world. Desperate because Sadat realized that if the policies of the United States would be allowed to develop along the lines favored by the Carter Administration, they would bring about the destruction of almost four years of dogged efforts that had been conducted in a very cautious, low-keyed manner but had produced, for the first time after a generation of hostility and stalemate, both negotiations and the signing of an agreement between Egypt and Israel.

November 19, 1977 was a balmy Saturday evening. The Egyptian airliner carrying Sadat to Israel had just landed at Ben-Gurion International Airport. A reception line of Israeli dignitaries had formed on the tarmac to greet the Egyptian president. As he stood in that receiving line, Rabin felt strange; unable to rid himself of the notion that this was an enemy leader about to land in Israel. Neither he nor any other

Israeli had ever imagined that the president of Egypt would visit the Jewish State so soon after the 1973 war; perhaps in fifty years, certainly only after a peace treaty had been signed between the two countries. Yet, here he was, smiling, as he walked down the ramp, then wading into the crowd of Israeli officials.

Gazing at Sadat as he walked down the ramp, Rabin felt like he was dreaming. One of many Israeli public figures on hand to greet him, Rabin had only a few seconds to exchange pleasantries with Sadat at that dramatic moment in Israeli history. Sadat appeared terribly poised to Rabin, despite the awkward circumstances.

As he listened to Sadat speak before the Knesset on Sunday afternoon, November 20, Rabin thought that the Egyptian leader sounded as if he truly wanted to make peace with Israel. Rabin, though caught up in the excitement of the visit, was still annoyed to hear Israelis suggest that only with the Sadat visit to Jerusalem had serious peacemaking begun. Had he not as prime minister signed the Sinai accord with Egypt two years earlier? Had that document not been a necessary prelude to these wonderful events? He found it hard to remain silent: "Whenever I hear talk of peace breaking out any moment as if the history of negotiations began in November 1977, I am obliged to set the record straight."[135] Still, when he had the chance to address Sadat himself, during a meeting the Egyptian president held with Labor Party representatives, Rabin was filled with enthusiasm: "Your courageous and daring coming over has created, I hope, a new era. I believe that you have removed the barriers that obscured, in the past, the relations between our two

135. *The Rabin Memoirs*, p. 215

countries. When we talk about defensible boundaries, allow me to say, Mr. President, I was the chief of staff of the armed forces of Israel prior to the 1967 war. I don't want any future chief of staff to face what I had to face, prior to this war."

Over the next few months, many discussions were held between Israel and the United States, and between Egypt and the United States, but progress only came in September 1978. President Jimmy Carter summoned the parties to his mountain retreat at Camp David. After twelve days of intensive negotiations, Carter, Sadat, and Begin hammered out two agreements known as the Camp David accords. One was a framework for a peace treaty between Israel and Egypt, requiring Israel to relinquish all of the Sinai Peninsula, including its settlements and airfields. The second was a framework agreement for peace in the Middle East. It foresaw peace between Israel and all Arab countries, but focused on the West Bank and Gaza. Israel promised to grant full autonomy to the Palestinian Arab residents there. Employing language that Israel had never agreed to before, the document stated that the political solution must recognize the legitimate rights of the Palestinian people and its just demands. Autonomy was to last for five years; after the first year of autonomy, negotiations would begin looking towards a final political settlement.

Begin had made it a condition of his acceptance of the Camp David accords that the Knesset ratify Israel's relinquishment of Jewish settlements in the Sinai. Hence, the parliament was called back from recess for a crucial, stormy session on September 25, to debate and vote on that question. When it was his turn to speak, Knesset member Yitzhak Rabin sounded cautiously optimistic about the new peace accord. Camp David, he declared, contained the promise of peace, but there was considerable uncertainty as to where the process would lead. He reminded the Knesset that, as prime minister, he had favored yielding territory for peace. Hence, he had no trouble supporting this accord. He praised prime minister Begin for seeking to resolve one part of the Arab-Israeli conflict at a time. That, said Rabin, had always been his policy as well. One important advantage of the accords, he added, was in enabling the parties to advance gradually towards a political solution of the thorny issue of the West Bank. With the help of the Labor Party, Begin won Knesset approval for the Camp David accords. The vote was 84-19 in favor.

In March 1979, Israel and Egypt signed a peace treaty that has lasted until today. Invited by Begin to attend the White House ceremony at which the treaty was formally signed, Rabin told *Yediot Aharonot*'s Ron Ben-Yishai, as they drove together to the ceremony: "If this happened while I was prime minister of a Labor government, there would have been blood spilled on the streets."[136]

No political feud had weighed more heavily on the State of Israel than that between Yitzhak Rabin and Shimon Peres. Other Israelis have competed for the prime ministership without displaying the bitterness and hostility these two men showed each other. More often than not, dating back to 1974, Rabin and Peres were pitted against one another for the Labor Party leadership and for the prime ministership. Antipathy between the two men simmered for years: Rabin, the military man, felt superior to Peres, who had not served

---

136. Ron Ben-Yishai, interview with author, July 19, 1992

in the IDF, but instead was in charge of personnel and arms purchases. For his part, Peres served for years as a senior bureaucrat in the Defense Ministry, making important arms purchases for Israel, creating new alliances for the Jewish state, especially with France. He always saw Rabin as a political novice, certainly not his superior. With two very different personalities, both men achieved much in public life and these differences were not necessarily at the core of their constant feuding.

Rabin was taciturn, introverted, and ill at ease in social situations, Peres was outgoing, able to engage in conversation easily, a friendly sort. A product of the military, Rabin had a special distaste for backroom political maneuvering. To Peres, however, such behavior was the very stuff of his existence. He had learned how to manipulate, enjoyed it, and found nothing wrong with it. Because he stayed out of politics until later in his life, Rabin retained the image of someone untainted by the seamier side of political life. Peres, however, has always been identified with wheeling and dealing, knowing the political ropes (inventing a few, too), and had never shaken the image of being just a little bit too slick, too polished, too tricky.

The original seeds of the rift were planted long before the two men had their eyes on national leadership posts. Back in the 1950s and 1960s, when Rabin was a soldier and Peres a Defense Ministry official, the two men found themselves on opposite sides of various issues, siding with personalities on different sides of the fence. Although no evidence exists that the two men were personal enemies in those days, Rabin at times has suggested that Peres was operating behind the scenes to undercut him. Certainly, political or ideological differences were never at issue in their disputes. These were two politicians steeped in Labor Party ideology, both advocating territorial compromise over the West Bank, both supportive of Camp David, both seeing the need for strong connections with Washington. What was at the heart of the rift, was the simple fact that Rabin and Peres did not like each other and could not get out of one another's hair in their common quest for their party and country's top leadership posts.

With Peres the chief beneficiary of the bank account scandal, Rabin needed little encouragement to believe that his political rival had maneuvered behind the scenes to bring him down. Rabin was never so forthright in public. He did not blame Peres (publicly or privately) for engineering the bank account affair, nor was there any evidence linking Peres to the tip-off, to Dan Margalit, the *Haaretz* reporter, of the existence of the bank accounts. The most Rabin said was that rivals in the Labor Party had been responsible for the disclosure over the bank account. He felt that he had been deprived of the chance to serve out his full term, and leaving aside the question of whether Peres had been behind his downfall, he had a deep desire to wait for the right moment, and then try to take away from Peres what had been taken away from him.

Sensing that the public had forgiven Rabin for the bank account scandal, reporters found it acceptable, even desirable, to seek him out for reaction to major events. The only question now was not whether Rabin would make a political comeback, but if and how he could defeat Peres. In mid-October 1978, when an Israel Radio interviewer asked Rabin if he would seek the Labor Party nomination for prime minister at some future date, Rabin replied, "I am still very much involved in politics." Had Labor Party politicians had their way, they might have preferred both Peres and Rabin to quietly step aside, and allow a younger generation to assume the leadership. Rather than devote themselves to rehabilitation after the 1977 election debacle, party members were instead forced to take sides in the only game in town: the Peres-Rabin feud. The reality was that the Rabin-Peres infighting had immobilized the party. For an entire year after the 1977 election, the two men did not meet. They were, however, constantly on each other's mind.

As top dog, it was in Shimon Peres's interest to avoid conflict with Rabin. Party unity was a prerequisite for revitalizing the defeated party. Hence, in early 1979, the Labor Party leader lent a very direct hand to Rabin's political recuperation by declaring that he would consider giving Rabin a senior post in a Peres-led government. At a news conference on February 11, 1979, Peres tried to assure that "Labor will not slide again into its old divisive conflict. We don't all love each other and we are not a band of heavenly angels, but there is party discipline." Rabin certainly agreed with Peres that the two of them did not love each other. It was still too early, however, for Rabin to challenge Peres for the party's leadership. Moreover, Yigal Allon had stopped wavering and had demonstrated some interest in trying to depose Peres as party leader. By the early summer of 1979, Rabin had aligned himself with Allon to that end.

Meanwhile, it was becoming clear that Israelis were not overly enamored with the Begin government, even though the prime minister had signed a peace treaty with Egypt the previous March. The public's growing disenchantment with the Likud regime was an open wound for Rabin: His worst fear was that Begin would be forced to step down as prime minister and Peres would be able to form a Government.

Rabin had to find a way to stop Peres from grabbing the top prize; he needed a knockout blow. Rabin believed he had the ammunition. If he chose to use it, his purpose would be double-edged: to gain revenge for past Peres sins and to force the Labor Party to cast Peres aside, thus denying him the coveted prime ministership. There could be no guarantee that Rabin would succeed. Had he thought carefully, Rabin would have understood there could be no guarantees that the Labor Party would thank him for slicing up Peres in public. The farthest thought from Rabin's mind was the question of whether he himself would emerge more sullied than Peres by this gambit. Rabin was too obsessed to give the subject any thought. Still very much the political novice, Rabin was thinking with his heart, not his head. He wanted to "get" Peres. That was all. The political consequences to himself be damned.

The best means of "getting" Peres was to use the memoirs that he was writing. Rabin would sprinkle those pages with his true feelings about Shimon Peres; feelings that he had withheld as prime minister on the grounds that it was improper for a national leader to utter such personal remarks about another politician, particularly one in his own party. Now, freed from that constraint, Rabin was eager to act. A number of Labor Party leaders begged Rabin to put off publication or cancel the book outright. "Yitzhak, it's going to hurt," one Labor figure told him, meaning that in hurting Peres, Rabin would hurt the party even more. Such "logic" did not move Rabin. All he cared about was keeping Peres from the prime ministership. In effect, Rabin would publish and Peres would perish! That was Rabin's goal.

The storm erupted in August 1979. The public learned what Rabin intended, when Israel Television broadcast extracts from his about-to-be-published memoirs over the 9 pm news. Peres was fuming. Likud officials quietly cheered: Rabin was doing their work for them. Perhaps there was hope for the troubled Begin government.

What precisely did Rabin write? He described Peres as "constantly and tirelessly attempting political subversion. He felt that all means were justified in his pursuit of winning the premiership." Peres, wrote Rabin, was not above working against him through leaks when Rabin was prime minister and Peres defense minister. "He not only tried to undermine me, but the entire government, trusting in the old Bolshevik maxim that 'the worse the situation, the better for Peres.' He spread lies and untruths and wrecked the Labor Party, thereby crowning himself as leader of the opposition." Once Peres had lost the Labor Party nomination for prime minister in 1974, wrote Rabin, "Peres decided that he and the office of prime minister were made for each other, and that all he needed to do was kick me out of the way." Rabin wrote that he knew who had been leaking information to the press, information that was meant to give the impression that Rabin had not been functioning properly and that Peres was in full control. Noting that Peres had never served in the Israel Defense Forces, Rabin contended that this should have disqualified him from serving as a defense minister. Though Rabin had preferred Yigal Allon as his defense minister, Rabin had been forced to bow to pressures of Peres' Rafi faction in the Labor Party, which wanted Peres as defense minister. No longer did he trust a word Peres uttered, Rabin wrote, arguing that Peres was unfit to be prime minister and that he would not serve under him. Rabin also charged that during the days before the 1976 Entebbe hostage rescue operation, hours had passed before Peres consulted with the military about a possible rescue operation.[137]

Predictably, Peres dismissed Rabin's accusations and warned that the only one who would be harmed would be Rabin. In all of the years he had worked with Rabin, Peres said, he had never heard a complaint from him. "His charges are very general in nature and reflect more his problems than mine. The book will cause very great harm to its author. He did it all himself. There are standards even in political life, and we will have to take the damage which Rabin did to the party into account."[138] That was his way of suggesting to Rabin that a political price would have to be paid and Peres intended to make sure that Rabin paid it.

According to Rabin's scenario, Labor Party officials, grateful to him for revealing what a monster Peres really was, would rise up against their party leader, toss him out, and beckon Rabin to take over at once. The trouble was that the people whom Rabin had to convince may not have been enraptured with Peres, but they did not want to rock the boat either. The last thing they wanted to do was to act upon Rabin's charges and turn against Peres. In their view, that would have made matters far worse. They wanted Rabin and his nasty little book to go away, to disappear from the daily headlines as quickly as possible. They thought that the only

137. Yitzhak Rabin, *The Rabin Memoirs* (Hebrew version: *Pinkas Sherut*). Tel Aviv; Maariv Books, pp. 534-35

138. 'Peres Subverted Government for His Own Aims', *The Jerusalem Post*, August 9, 1979

possible beneficiary of the "struggle" would be Menachem Begin, and why do him a favor? Thus the entire exercise blew up in Rabin's face: Labor politicians turned their venom, not at Peres, but at Rabin himself. They pummeled him with questions: Why had he done this? Why had he brought the simmering political feud out into broad daylight? Why was he washing his and the entire party's dirty laundry in public?

Faced with so much rage, the Party Secretariat called a meeting to discuss what to do. One after another, former Labor Party ministers from Rabin's Government assailed him with more questions: Why, if Peres had been so worthless, had Rabin chosen him to replace him after the 1977 bank account scandal? (The question was based on an incorrect premise: that Rabin had "chosen" Peres, when in fact the Labor Party had made that decision.[139]) Why, if Peres had not been worthy of being a leader, had Rabin agreed to run for the Knesset on a Peres-led list right after the bank account scandal? (Again the question missed the point: Rabin ran for the Knesset for his own reasons, which had nothing to do with being willing to serve under Peres.[140]) The Labor politicians wanted to pass a resolution condemning Rabin and the book. Peres said no. He was afraid that the resolution would haunt him later and would only widen the already large gulf within the party. But Peres's biographer, Matti Golan, wrote that in deciding against demanding an official Labor Party response, Peres played into Rabin's hands. "Because of his weak response," wrote Golan, "Rabin's version of events was accepted by many, and the accusations against

139. The author

140. Ibid

Peres took root. Rabin took on the image of a victim; Peres of an intriguer and saboteur."[141]

None of the party turmoil caused Rabin any regret. When asked to comment on the storm his book had created within the party, Rabin came out punching, just as bitter and angry as when he sat down at his typewriter to write the book. "I will not take back a single word I wrote about Shimon Peres and I stand by every one of those words."[142] In one interview he suggested that "If someone wants to sue me over what I wrote, let him. I never concealed my opinion in the past, but as prime minister, I had to mind my public pronouncements. I don't believe in insinuating and leaking. What I did in my book was to put things squarely on the table."

To show his determination, Rabin stated that even had Peres been prime minister, he would still have published his critique of him, "although I'm not sure it would have been permitted to see the light." Rubbing Peres's nose in the dirt a bit more, Rabin declared at a press conference on August 10 to announce the appearance of the *Memoirs*, that he would never serve in a Peres government, and that he still had not ruled out running for the prime ministership. He remained incensed at Labor Party politicians for wanting to punish him politically – even to toss him out of the party – for his harsh remarks about Peres. "I joined the movement at a very young age before I ever heard of Shimon Peres. I identified with concepts and ideals and not with any one man, least of all the present Labor chairman. Hence my membership in

---

141. Matti Golan, *The Road to Peace: A Biography of Shimon Peres*, New York: Warner Books, 1989, p. 193

142. 'Labor to Discuss Rabin's Attack on Peres Today', *The Jerusalem Post*, August 12, 1979

the Party is not contingent on any particular man at its helm. The Party needs a basic examination of itself, without... papering over the cracks, and what I wrote will help it in that direction... I don't think books ought to be just written about the dead or published 20 years after a person is buried."[143] Rabin was right that the Labor Party needed a "basic examination" of itself, but wrong to suggest that only Peres was to blame for the Party's woes. That he could not let go of his vindictiveness toward Peres, gave him the same degree of responsibility for the feud as his rival.

One intriguing footnote regarding Rabin's memoirs, quite unrelated to his squabbling with Peres, appeared after the book had been published. On October 23, 1979, *The New York Times* published what it contended was a censored part of the memoirs. In that material, Rabin explained how his Harel Brigade had driven out 50,000 Arabs from their homes in the towns of Lod and Ramle during Israel's 1948 War of Independence. According to the newspaper, Rabin attributed the final expulsion order to the then-Israeli prime minister, David Ben-Gurion. A board of Cabinet Ministers censors, to whom Israeli law requires former government officials submit their memoirs, had deleted the account. According to *The New York Times*, Rabin's description opened with a meeting attended by Ben-Gurion, Yigal Allon, and Rabin, who was then commander of the Harel Brigade. The brigade had been trying to eliminate Arab Legion bases along the Jerusalem-Tel Aviv road. Rabin, said the *Times*, had written in part: "While the fighting was still in progress, we had to grapple with the fate of the civilian population of Lod and

---

143. Ibid

Ramle, numbering some 50,000. Clearly, we could not leave Lod's hostile and armed populace in our rear, where it could endanger the support route to Yiftah [another brigade] which was advancing eastward. We walked outside, Ben-Gurion accompanying us. Allon repeated his question: 'What is to be done with the population?' Ben-Gurion waved his hand in a gesture which said, 'Drive them out.'

"'Driving out' is a term with a harsh ring. Psychologically, this was one of the most difficult actions we undertook. The population of Lod did not leave willingly. There was no way of avoiding the use of force and warning shots in order to make the inhabitants march the 10 to 15 miles to the point where they met up with the Legion. The inhabitants of Ramle watched and learned the lesson. Their leaders agreed to be evacuated voluntarily... Buses took them to Latrun, and from there they were evacuated by the Legion."

Yigal Allon denied the whole account. Allon dismissed the notion that 50,000 Arabs were expelled by Rabin's Palmach forces. Allon insisted the Arabs had requested that the IDF help evacuate them, to make sure they would escape harm, "that they wouldn't run into mine fields and get killed." Allon noted that he had not asked Ben-Gurion nor had the prime minister given orders to expel the Arabs. "The Arabs left," said Allon, "because they were instructed by the Arab Legion to evacuate in order to enable the latter to recapture [Lod] from us."[144]

What was important in the fall of 1979 with regard to Rabin, was that by way of this censored account, further substantiation was supplied that Yitzhak Rabin was one tough fellow.

---

144. 'Allon Counters Rabin on "Expulsion" of Arabs in 1948', *The Jerusalem Post*, October 26, 1979

In the early 1980s, and as Labor Party leader, Shimon Peres seemingly had the temporary advantage over Rabin. Yitzhak Rabin, however, was carefully, methodically, staking out a claim that would one day allow him to win back political leadership. He continued to make frequent television appearances, which went a long way to restoring his tarnished image. Indeed, television interviewers appeared to seek out Rabin more than Peres. The Rabin-Peres struggle still very much existed, but it was played out far from public sight; what the public saw was the statesmanlike Rabin, presenting his often astute political analysis on whatever event happened to be in the news. Rabin the pundit was an impressive figure and his public support grew. Still not ready to make his own move for the Labor Party's leadership during 1979 and early 1980, Rabin placed his support behind Yigal Allon's bid to unseat Peres as party leader. Then on February 29, 1980, Allon died suddenly. These new circumstances created a vacuum that Rabin was only too willing to fill.

By the spring of 1980, the polls indicated that Rabin was the country's top choice for prime minister. While Menachem Begin registered the lowest support ever for a prime minister in office (15.8 percent) in one poll in July 1980, Peres was even a less popular choice with 13.1 percent. Rabin led the pack with 26.6 percent. He was delighted to be back in the public's good graces: "If I said I was anything less than gratified by the results, I would be dishonest." Indeed, he seemed to be smiling more, enjoying the nitty-gritty of politics more, less of a political novice. In the meantime, the Begin Government plodded through a most mediocre domestic performance, the cabinet torn by internal dissension, the economy disintegrating, creating a most fertile landscape for Rabin to stage his political comeback.

Just what had made Rabin so incredibly popular? To start with, he retained an image of credibility. The people trusted him on the only issue that mattered to them: national security. Writing in *The Jerusalem Post* on October 17, 1980, David Landau noted: "It is perhaps the ultimate irony that a prime minister who had to resign because of a legal impropriety followed by some... untruths, should now be making his comeback challenge on a credibility ticket. But there it is another political fact of life, substantiated by all the polls for the past six months, Israelis do appear to regard Yitzhak Rabin as essentially straight and straightforward, and clearly seem today to disregard his past peccadillo. Peres's contrived rhetoric, full of over stylized metaphors, is contrasted, to Peres's disadvantage, with Rabin's slow, unpolished and simple style. Peres is prone to glibness and sometimes even to gimmickry."[145]

Much to his chagrin, Peres could hardly be immune to this rising adulation of Rabin. National elections were to take place the following year and Peres needed Rabin, the vote getter, as part of Labor's leadership. With Rabin the most popular man in the country, Peres hinted that he was prepared to abandon his promise to keep Rabin out of a future Peres-led government. All Rabin had to do, Peres insisted, was to retract all the vitriol the former prime minister had thrown his way. But Peres's pursuit of Rabin was stopped dead with Rabin's own announcement.

In October 1980, two months before the Labor Party was to choose its leader, Rabin announced that he would run for his party's nomination for prime minister. Peres described Rabin's statement as a "mere ornamentation. The contest has

---

145. 'The Credibility Stakes', *The Jerusalem Post*, October 17, 1980

been going on in earnest for a year." That much was true, for Rabin had acquired more of the skills that a politician needed to survive. He announced that same month that while he was still inclined not to serve in a future Peres government, he did not rule it out. Even if he were far more popular than Peres, that did not guarantee that Rabin would secure his party's nomination. And, if Peres did win the nomination, he might become the next prime minister. Certainly, Begin seemed vulnerable. Part of Rabin's political recovery program was to attain a senior governing position. If Peres grabbed the top prize, Rabin might still become defense minister, a significant step forward in Rabin's political rehabilitation. Rabin and Peres had not become "heavenly angels," in Peres's words. It was just that they needed each other.

Once again, Rabin and Peres squared off against one another. Public opinion polls indicated that Labor could win an absolute majority in the Knesset if elections were held at this juncture. The party was, however, still burdened by the struggle between two men who were barely on speaking terms, and who had difficulty uttering each other's names. Their only way of communicating with one another was through a sneer.

This time, in December 1980, Peres won the nomination for Labor Party leader decisively; garnering 2,123 out of the 3,028 votes cast by the Labor Party Central Committee. Rabin received only 875 votes. Peres had contended before the balloting that, were he (Peres) to receive 70 percent of the votes, Rabin could no longer be considered a viable alternative to his leadership. Peres won 70 percent of the vote. It seemed unthinkable, however, that Rabin would capitulate so docilely. After the balloting, Peres shook hands with Rabin. For his part, Rabin failed to mention Peres once in his concession speech. Some Labor Party veterans showed up on Israel television that week, their white beards flowing and their voices quivering with old age to denounce the rivalry. Their octogenarian wisdom had led them to the conclusion that the struggle had hurt Labor and could keep it from returning to power.

Reporters asked Peres and Rabin after the vote what role Rabin would play in a Peres government. Peres was evasive. One option for Rabin was to opt out of Labor and join ranks with former defense minister Ezer Weizman's new Knesset list. Weizman wanted Rabin on his ticket. The opinion surveys suggested that a Weizman-Rabin ticket, with Moshe Dayan added to it, could secure as many as 33 Knesset seats, making it a formidable political force. Nonetheless, Rabin did not leave the Labor Party.

During the campaign for the June 30, 1981 election, the Likud, not surprisingly, quoted extensively from *The Rabin Memoirs* in its election propaganda. Labor Party officials urged Rabin to demand that the Likud cease using his book for campaign propaganda purposes. They wanted Rabin to declare that, despite what he had written about Peres, he preferred him above Begin for prime minister. Rabin made no overture to the Likud, nor would he make any positive statements about Peres. At election rallies, he extolled the virtues of the Labor Party. Considering how popular Rabin was among voters, it was ironic that he was so awkward on the campaign trail. A reporter who accompanied him on one tour of Beersheba noted that "Rabin is not a flesh pumper. He's got a quick-as-a-whip weak handshake that's as low-key as his baritone voice." Wherever he went, Rabin asked the same monotonous question: "What do you do, and how long have you been working here?" At one point during the tour, Rabin actually confessed that he did not like walking through the streets to urge people to vote for Labor.

Labor had been leading the public opinion surveys throughout the election campaign by decisive margins. As the election date approached, however, Likud began narrowing the gap. The most important event of the campaign occurred on June 7, 1981. On that day at 4 pm, prime minister Begin sent eight F-16s from the Etzion base in the Sinai, travelling 1,000 miles to their target: the Osiraq nuclear reactor in Iraq. The attack against Iraq's nuclear reactor proved to be one of the most spectacular of Israeli military feats, delaying Iraq's capability to produce nuclear weapons, and making Begin look very, very good at a crucial period three weeks before the election.

At first, Yitzhak Rabin sounded less than enthusiastic about the Israeli decision, indicating that the data Israel possessed suggested that the reactor was no imminent threat. Eventually, however, he declared himself in favor of the raid, telling Israel Radio two days after the attack: "Israel is unanimous in perceiving the threat posed by nuclear weapons in the hands of an Arab state, certainly of a state headed by Saddam Hussein. Unarguably, everything should be done to disrupt such an eventuality, to postpone, or prevent it."

With the bombing of the Iraqi nuclear reactors, voters flocked to Begin. Six days after the attack, Begin surged ahead of Labor by 20 Knesset seats. The poll indicated even more devastating news for Peres: If Labor were to replace Peres with Rabin at the head of its list, the 20-seat gap would be closed. The message was clear: Peres should step down before it was too late and turn the party leadership over to Rabin. Peres wanted more time before making so fateful a decision as stepping down a few weeks before the election. He asked the pollsters to check the results again. He prepared himself, if necessary, to relinquish the role of Labor Party candidate for prime minister the next day. Happily for Peres, the pollster phoned Peres the next morning with the news that another poll put the Likud ahead by only six Knesset seats and the gap was closing. Peres's resignation was no longer crucial.[146] Concerned enough about the possibility of losing the election, Peres, on June 25, five days before the balloting, made a surprise move. Having announced his shadow cabinet during the campaign, Peres had named Haim Bar-Lev, a former chief of staff, as his choice for defense minister. Now Peres decided to dump Bar-Lev in favor of Yitzhak Rabin. At a midnight press conference, Rabin said he was now prepared to serve under Shimon Peres. He had changed his mind. Peres was jubilant: "The good of the country comes before our personal feelings."

It is difficult to assess whether Rabin had helped Peres to secure more votes. However, the move had not helped him defeat Menachem Begin. The Likud won 48 seats to Labor's 47. Together with the three small political parties (the National Religious Party, Agudat Yisrael, and Tami), Begin put together a coalition of 61 Knesset members. Later that summer, Rabin described his agreement to join the Labor Party team on election eve "an ad hoc arrangement." In other words, his truce with Shimon Peres was short-lived.

Nearly a year later on June 6, 1982, the Israeli war in Lebanon began. On that day, three Israeli divisions moved into southern Lebanon in order to eradicate PLO bases there,

---

146. Matti Golan, *The Road to Peace*, pp. 207-208

cutting off Palestinian gunmen before they had a chance to escape to the north. The PLO had rained Katyusha rockets down on communities and settlements in northern Israel incessantly, leading Israel to take this action. Prime minister Begin was intent on informing the Labor Party opposition and others that Israel's war aims were limited. Israel's stated objective was to establish a 25-kilometer security zone in southern Lebanon, not to move into other parts of Lebanon. At a meeting with Begin soon after the outbreak of war, Rabin and Peres heard the prime minister promise that he did not intend to advance the IDF into Beirut or along the Beirut-Damascus road. Meanwhile, the IDF was moving towards Beirut, presumably without the prime minister's knowledge; by the end of the war's first week, Israeli soldiers were on the hills outside Beirut.

Rabin's behavior at the outset of the fighting seemed peculiar in the light of his eventual staunch opposition to the war. For someone who later questioned Israel's goals as unobtainable, he sounded very supportive of the war at times. On July 4, nearly a month after the war had started, the burning issue turned to whether the Israeli army should cut off water and electricity in order to put pressure on the PLO in Beirut. Begin invited Labor Party leaders in for a chat. Peres was against using water and electricity; Rabin favored the tactic. Advising defense minister Ariel Sharon to "tighten up" the siege of the Lebanese capital, Rabin added, "I can live with a twenty-four hour bombardment of Beirut."

In fact, Rabin's behavior was not so strange after all. He was merely doing what he could to make sure that the IDF did not fail militarily. His affection for Israeli soldiers, for the IDF as an institution, was an overriding concern. Even when questioning the overall goals of the war, Rabin, the former chief of staff, wanted to do what he could to save the prestige of the IDF. His concern was not to make Sharon look good, it was to prevent the Israeli army from looking bad. And so Rabin visited Beirut a number of times, and his relationship with defense minister Sharon grew warm. The two men were often seen together at different war fronts. Both men benefited: Sharon was able to show that one of the two Labor Party leaders supported the siege of Beirut, at a time when not everyone agreed the siege was the best tactic. Rabin, for his part, played the part of patriot, a former chief of staff who rallied to the side of Israeli troops during battle. Something, however, did bother Rabin about the war in Lebanon. He felt that the Begin Government's wartime goals were too grandiose and ultimately unattainable: Begin wanted to establish a new political order in Lebanon that would be friendly to Israel; he seemed to want to get the Syrian army out of Lebanon and to eliminate the PLO's base in that country. The war would not help Israel to realize these objectives, Rabin believed. Had he been prime minister, he would not have gone to war in pursuit of any of these objectives. Instead, he would have sought ways to keep the PLO from attacking Israeli communities in the north, nothing more.

Israel remained in Lebanon until 1985, unable to find a way to extricate itself from what Rabin termed the "*botz haLevanoni*," loosely translated as the Lebanese quagmire. In January 198,3 in a speech at Jerusalem's Hebrew University, he called upon the Begin government to acknowledge that the war had been a mistake, that it had been an illusion to employ the IDF in order to impose a formal peace agreement on Lebanon. It was a further illusion, he said, for Israeli leaders to believe that their country could launch a war on Lebanese soil, conquer its capital, and then force it to make peace.

Clearly the war had caused Begin much agony, and so, on August 28, 1983, he declared that he "cannot go on." He was stepping down as prime minister, giving no reason. It was clear, however, that the Lebanon War had taken its psychological toll on him. By that time, 500 Israeli soldiers had died in that war. Begin did not say so publicly, but he apparently felt that Sharon had deceived him by pushing the war well beyond the 25 kilometer (15.5 miles) perimeter in southern Lebanon, which Begin had described as the IDF's maximum advance.

In a state of shock over Begin's decision and without a clear cut candidate in mind, the Herut Party, the dominant element of the Likud, convened its Central Committee: It had to choose between Begin's foreign minister, the 68-year-old Yitzhak Shamir, who had commanded the ultra-right Lehi underground during the British Mandate period, and David Levy, the minister of housing, whose rags-to-riches rise to political fame made him the pride of the Moroccan community in Israel. Shamir won the contest 435-302, making him automatically the new prime minister. He took office on September 15, 1983. Shamir had none of Begin's vote-getting abilities, none of his charm, charisma, or ability to stir the masses. None of this bolstered the spirits of the Likud or of Yitzhak Rabin.

CHAPTER ELEVEN

DEFENSE MINISTER AND INTIFADA

In early 1984, now 62 years old, Yitzhak Rabin confronted again the difficult decision of whether he should compete for his party's nomination for prime minister yet again. The spark of political ambition still burned brightly in him. Labor Party politicians were optimistic about the party's chances of winning the election the following July, but some were still unconvinced that Shimon Peres was their best candidate to head the ticket. Twice Peres had run as the party's candidate for prime minister, and twice he had lost. The aura of defeat surrounded him. Some Laborites preferred Rabin. But the prospect of playing out the struggle once again between Rabin and Peres soured many party members. It was for that reason that when a fresh face loomed on the political horizon, a certain excitement developed around this alternative to Rabin and Peres. The face was Yitzhak Navon, who had resigned as Israel's fifth president a year earlier than scheduled, in order to toss his hat in the ring for the Labor Party's leadership. When some Labor Party figures approached Peres, asking him to step aside in favor of Navon, Peres demurred, and instead offered Navon the number two spot on the ticket under him. Navon said no. Some of Rabin's supporters urged him to challenge both Peres and Navon. A three-way race seemed risky: Peres and Navon might outpoll Rabin, forcing him to accept the number 3 spot on the ticket. Awkward and ironic as it was, Rabin believed that his best move was to side with Peres, if only to preserve his chances of retaining the number two spot on the Labor list. And so these unlikely political bedfellows sheathed their swords, ready to do business with one another, not out of a newfound affection, but sheer political expediency. As part of the Peres-Rabin pact, the Labor Party candidate for prime minister would be Peres and Labor's candidate for defense minister, Rabin. Realizing that the deck was stacked against him, Navon bowed out.

On April 2, 1984, Peres was once again chosen Labor Party chairman and candidate for prime minister. Once again, the Labor Party headed the public opinion polls early in 1984. As the summer approached, the Likud trimmed the margin. The Likud turned the contest into a toss-up, as the result of a surprise proposal by prime minister Yitzhak Shamir aired during his television debate with Peres. The Likud leader called for the establishment of a National Unity Government after the elections, ready to share political power and sounding patriotic in order to solve the country's problems. Even if Shamir were elected prime minister, a unity government would not be assured; Labor would have to agree. Still, the voters seemed to like Shamir's offer. With the country unable to find a way out of Lebanon and troubled by skyrocketing inflation, a unity government just might prove useful. On election day, the voters cast their ballots almost evenly for Labor and Likud. Labor captured 44 seats, three more than the Likud, but could not attract enough small parties to form a governing coalition. As Likud had also failed to win sufficient support to form a coalition, Shamir's unity government proposal suddenly looked like the most practical solution. Agreeing to share political power over the next four years, Shamir and Peres devised a unique rotation scheme, giving Peres the prime ministership for the first two years, and Shamir for the latter two. Shamir would serve as foreign minister for the first two years, Peres for the latter two. At first, there was talk of Likud and Labor rotating the defense ministry post, but in the end it was decided that Rabin would serve the full four-year term as defense minister. In mid-September 1984, the new National Unity Government was sworn in at the Knesset. It was an emotional moment for Rabin. "Seventeen years after removing his uniform," wrote Leah Rabin in her memoirs, "Yitzhak had returned to the defense establishment as though coming home after a prolonged absence. Full of ups and downs in life, seventeen years had passed, his hair had turned grey and he was wearing a suit in place of uniform. Yet he strode like a soldier, as in the past, his face not revealing his inner feelings."[147] It had taken seven years, yet Yitzhak Rabin's political recovery was all but complete. Back in a position of national power, all that eluded him now was a return to the prime ministership. He harbored no illusions on that score; if it happened at all, it would not be overnight.

---

147. Leah Rabin, *All the Time His Wife*, p.240

As soon as the Peres-led National Unity Government took office, it set as its main goal ending Israel's 27-month occupation of Lebanon. Shamir, when he was still prime minister, had promised to withdraw IDF troops only after local security arrangements in Lebanon had been worked out. Peres wanted to discard this policy, thinking it likely to delay the IDF withdrawal. Needing Rabin's approval for getting out of Lebanon even without an agreement, Peres discovered that his defense minister favored leaving only after an agreement on security arrangements had been secured. Eventually, however, even Rabin grew convinced that it was not worth waiting for local Lebanese forces to agree to security plans; he opted for pulling the troops out gradually over several stages. None of this pleased Peres, who wanted to get the troops home as quickly as possible. Eventually, Rabin got his way and on January 13, 1985 the Rabin gradual plan went to the Cabinet and passed; it would take six months to complete. And so, Rabin and Peres achieved an Israeli withdrawal from Lebanon. It was the first major step Rabin took toward correcting the errors he felt Menachem Begin and his Likud regime had made. Rabin could not wait to get out of the quagmire and explained why Israel was leaving Lebanon: "I don't want to be the policeman of Lebanon. It's not the business of Israel. Israel was not created to serve as a policeman of the region. We made it clear we don't link our unilateral decision to anything the Syrians do. They want to stay in Lebanon, let them stay. I know that whoever sets his foot in Lebanon has sunk into the Lebanese [swamp]. If they want it, let them enjoy it. We want one thing: that they do not move closer to our borders. That's all."

In November 1985, an American navy employee, Jonathan Pollard, was arrested outside the Israeli embassy in Washington. Pollard had confessed to selling intelligence material to Israeli officials. The American Administration asked Israel to help it discover the scope of the 'Pollard affair', as it became known, and to search for those Israelis who had been in touch with the navy man. Once the news broke, Peres, Rabin, and Shamir met daily to try to figure out how to handle the devastating news. Their main interest was to convince the public that they had not known who Jonathan Pollard was or what he had been doing. An internal government inquiry was conducted by a three-member committee, which concluded on November 27 that there was no evidence that linked the three Israeli leaders to Pollard. The committee reported that Pollard had been part of a rogue intelligence-gathering unit unknown to almost all political and intelligence communities.

Peres, Rabin, and Shamir were successful in suppressing any notion that they knew of Pollard in advance, or that they had given the "green light" to his operation. During the winter of 1987, Pollard was sentenced to life for his crime; his wife given five years for assisting him. Despite repeated Israeli overtures to US governments, since Pollard's conviction to release him, he remains in jail as of February 2015. No American president, no matter how friendly to Israel, has seen fit to pardon Pollard for the damage he had done to the US, never officially spelled out.

In time, the dominant item on defense minister Rabin's agenda became the Palestinian issue, but not by his personal choice: Rabin had generally attributed little importance to the Palestinian Arabs who inhabited the West Bank and the Gaza Strip. He may have pitied them for their plight; however, he felt, no strong attachment to them.

Unbeknownst to him, and to most others, the ground was rumbling under the defense minister's feet. As of the mid-1970s, the Palestinians had succeeded in placing themselves high on the international agenda. Promised full autonomy as part of the Camp David accords in September 1978, the Arab inhabitants of the West Bank and the Gaza Strip felt obliged to say thanks but no thanks, and seek instead a state of their own. Israel, however, was not prepared to give them one. After the Israel-Egypt Peace Treaty was signed in March 1979, Israelis, Egyptians, and Americans met on a continuing basis in Egypt and in Israel in an effort to establish autonomy for the Palestinians. The Palestinians refused to attend those talks, leading to little progress. It hardly mattered. By the summer of 1982, the war in Lebanon put an end to those negotiations. As long as Israel was trying to wipe out the PLO in Lebanon, it was unthinkable for Egypt to remain at the autonomy talks. And so the Palestinian issue festered.

By 1987, the Palestinians had grown deeply resentful that the international community had all but forgotten their plight. Their own Arab brethren demonstrated little enthusiasm for their cause as well. Moreover, it bothered the Palestinians enormously that twenty years of Israeli occupation had forced them to adopt Israeli habits, buy Israeli products, wear Israeli clothes, even speak Hebrew. They wanted to be free of Israel so that they could try to forge their own national institutions and character. Without weapons to foment major acts of violence against the Israelis, the Palestinians sensed correctly that they would have to use their wits and their numbers and catch the Israelis off guard. It would not be easy, for the Israelis had the arms.

Though what happened among the Palestinians in December 1987 appeared organized and orchestrated, it was not. The anger, violence, and mass demonstrations were spontaneous, though they had their root in the years of impatient waiting. The spark that brought the explosion came one afternoon when an Israeli civilian truck passing through a Gaza refugee camp lost control of his vehicle and smashed into an oncoming car with Arab workers, killing four people. Two days earlier, an Israeli had been stabbed to death in the central market in the town of Gaza. The word on the Palestinian street was that this was no car accident; rather a relative of the stabbed man had deliberately driven the truck into these Palestinians. Thousands of mourners returned from the funerals of the four men killed early in the evening. Reaching an IDF outpost at a Palestinian refugee camp, they hurled bottles and stones at the soldiers who fired shots in the air to no avail. The angry crowd moved through the camp. No routine demonstration that fizzled out after an hour or so, it lasted well past 11 pm. The next day, schools and shops were closed. In those first two days of rioting, Israeli soldiers killed two Arab youths. There was nothing unusual in that. Or so it seemed. What was extraordinary was the speed with which the Palestinian violence spread. Later that week, 50 miles away in the Balata refugee camp in the West Bank town of Nablus, an enraged crowd of nearly 3,000 Palestinians, mostly women and children threw stones at Israeli border police. A barrage of rubber bullets failed to stop the mob. Israeli soldiers used tear gas and live bullets. Four protesters were killed and another 30 wounded. The Palestinian uprising calling the mass violence an Intifada (Arabic for "shaking off") had begun in earnest.

At first, the Israelis mistakenly thought the Palestinians were up to their old tricks, a few unruly demonstrations, then back to their routine quiet. The scale and intensity of these riots, however, were different, larger and more ferocious than anything seen in the occupied territories since 1967. In the past, such riots were isolated affairs, with a few hundred people participating. Now, thousands turned out to these demonstrations, it became clear that they had the support of thousands more back home. Those who did not demonstrate closed their shops and remained at home.

No one seemed more caught off guard by the Palestinian rioting than defense minister Rabin. When the first demonstrations occurred, Rabin huddled with his senior aides to decide whether to go ahead with a planned visit to the United States. They could find no good reason to delay the trip. Two Israeli journalists, in their book on the Palestinian uprising, noted: "The total insouciance in face of the renewed violence in Gaza was striking, almost startling."[148] Not really. To Rabin and his chief aides, the demonstrations were no different from the kind that had occurred in the occupied territories for the past two decades; they would surely die down in a few days. And so, the day after the uprising erupted, Rabin went off to the United States. It was an important journey, as Rabin was to sign a memorandum of understanding on the sale of Israeli-manufactured equipment to the American government. He was also to agree on the final price for seventy F-16 fighter planes. Visits to American military installations were scheduled, as was a speech before an Israel Bonds convention in Florida.

148. Ze'ev Schiff, Ehud Ya'ari, *Intifada*, New York: Simon & Schuster, 1989. P. 23

Once in Washington, Rabin was pleased to find that the trouble back home did not monopolize his conversations with American officials. But when those officials watched American television show Israeli soldiers shooting at rock-throwing Palestinian demonstrators, it was clear that the unrest could not be ignored. Now everyone wanted to know what Rabin thought about the West Bank violence.

He began to feel uneasy. Should he return home? Was his presence in America so important that he should leave the control of these riots to others? He could be in telephone contact with the chief of staff, but was that good enough? Believing that his sudden return would present the Palestinians with an unjustified victory, the defense minister and his entourage seemed to act as if the rioting in the Gaza Strip was taking place on a different planet, not in their back yard. Rabin's advisers thought it prudent for him to remain in the US. No one in Israel was pressing him to return. The Americans did not seem overly alarmed. Rabin went ahead and signed the memorandum of understanding with defense secretary Frank Carlucci on December 14. He then set off for a visit to an F-16 squadron and two combat helicopter squadrons. Before that excursion, Rabin's spokesman Eitan Haber hinted that Rabin might not be able to give the Florida Bonds speech. But a quick return to Israel still seemed unlikely; after all, this was no serious military threat, just a bunch of kids throwing stones.

Meanwhile, in Israel, prime minister Shamir and chief of staff Dan Shomron were reacting slowly to events. They, too, wanted to believe that the disturbances were temporary. To decide on beefing up forces in the Gaza Strip would have been an admission that something serious was occurring there. Eventually, Shomron, after daily telephone consultations with Rabin, decided to increase the number of troops on patrol in Gaza; those patrols were built up to more defensible sizes. In order to protect traffic on the main roads from stone-throwing and the tossing of Molotov cocktails, Shomron pulled foot patrols out of the refugee camps and placed them on those main roads. The patrols, now under the command of more senior officers, were equipped with anti-riot gear, including riot helmets, shields, rubber bullets, and water cannons. All of this was designed to minimize the soldiers' use of live ammunition. The mounting number of Palestinian fatalities from such shooting incidents underscored the IDF's inability to cope with events. The seemingly indiscriminate shooting when screened on American television brought Israel's international image to a new low. Rabin and Shomron kept the refugee camps open and let Palestinian Arabs continue to travel to Israel proper each day to work. Curfews were not imposed either. The two Israeli leaders hoped to isolate the demonstrators from what they perceived to be the silent majority of Palestinians. The theory went that this silent majority despised the rioters and wanted only to lead a normal life. The theory sounded good back at the Tel Aviv military command and among Rabin's entourage in the US. It had little to do with reality.

The new Rabin-Shomron strategy increased the number of IDF soldiers in the Gaza Strip to three times the normal complement. Now elite infantry brigades were patrolling the place. For a few days, the approach appeared to work. The number of demonstrations slackened. No Palestinian Arabs were killed. Believing that indeed the weeklong protests were no different from past ones, the optimists in Israel argued that order would be restored within a few days.

On December 21, a week later, all hell broke loose again. Now it was the turn of Israeli Arabs. Long a passive partner in the struggle of their Palestinian brethren in the occupied territories, this time the Israeli Arabs insisted on joining the fight. In Nazareth, 4,000 youngsters ran amok in the streets, hurling debris at Israeli soldiers. The violence spread to other Israeli Arab towns and villages. Some 170,000 Israeli Arabs refused to go to work (as did 80,000 Palestinian Arabs from the territories). The Rabin-Shomron strategy was not working.

Months later, when analysts gained some perspective on the early days of the Intifada, it became popular to argue that Israel might have taken steps at the very incipient stages of the rebellion that would have prevented it from worsening. Rabin might have returned from the United States earlier. Shomron might have sent reinforcements into Gaza at once. The territories might have been closed off to the media from the start. The harsh truth for Israel, however, was that none of this would have changed the seething frustration that existed among Palestinian Arabs. The most such actions might have accomplished would have been to postpone the inevitable.

One strong indication of the disarray among Israeli leaders at the time was the attempt to lay the blame for the unrest on outside elements. For years, Israelis had convinced themselves that local Palestinian Arabs did nothing on their own, that only when marching orders came from the PLO or others did the local Palestinians act. To Shamir, the PLO was behind the demonstrations. To Rabin, Syria and Iran were the culprits. No one bothered to ask whether this time the unrest might be have been self-starting, whether the PLO, Syrians, and Iranians were as out of touch with events in the West Bank and the Gaza Strip as the Israelis had been. No one bothered to check whether the local Palestinian Arabs had not taken matters into their own hands. The question of whether the local Palestinians had initiated the Intifada was not considered relevant. It should have been.

When he returned to Israel on December 21, defense minister Rabin was asked by a reporter whether he felt he should have returned to Israel sooner. His answer was no, but he sounded defensive: "I was of the opinion that no one could replace me in the US, while in Israel there is the IDF general staff and the chief of staff, and I have the utmost faith in them and their ability to deal with these issues. And, as is known, the prime minister agreed to my proposal that he take charge of the defense portfolio, and I am sure of his ability." It was an odd way of justifying his absence. At that moment, however, Rabin was still under the illusion that nothing of great significance had happened in the occupied territories; he would learn how wrong he had been.

At that airport press conference, Rabin still spoke as if the demonstrations were sporadic outbursts of violence and not the symbol of a much deeper, more widespread sense of bitterness and outrage. He insisted that Israel would not allow the Palestinians to think they could achieve political gains through violence: "They won't obtain a single thing via the threat of war, terrorism, or violent disturbances. Therefore, the main problem at present is to enforce order with all the sorrow and pain, over loss of life on the Arab side. Whoever goes to violent demonstrations is placing himself in grave danger." This was a theme that Rabin would return to often but one that missed the point of what was happening in the refugee camps and elsewhere in the territories. It was not that a handful of Palestinians had decided to throw stones. It was that the entire West Bank and Gaza Strip had symbolically joined in the stone throwing. What Rabin and other Israeli leaders refused to accept, in those early days of the Intifada, was that the violence was something other than the work of a few extremists.

If it had been the work of extremists, the obvious response for Israel would have been to seek to restore order by capturing the extremists, nothing more, leaving the smoldering problems in the Palestinian community to smolder even more. Even if he had wanted to deal with those problems, Rabin had no quick, magic answer. Some Israelis favored annexing the territories while others thought the IDF should withdraw unilaterally. Rabin opposed both views. The only feasible Israeli option was to continue to occupy the region until a political settlement could be achieved; he was against giving the Palestinians a state; but he was prepared to return as much as two-thirds of the occupied lands to Jordan. Such political solutions seemed remote. The immediate question for Israel in December 1987 was how to quell the Intifada.

All Rabin could offer at the outset was meeting violence with violence, a policy that helped the Palestinian cause. When Rabin threatened the Palestinians with a more intense military response if they continued their disorders, he was inadvertently playing into their hands. What the Palestinians wanted, indeed needed, was to bring their case before the international community. A mob of unruly Palestinians marching through the streets of Ramallah or Gaza was not enough to win time on the US nightly news; but, as long as Israeli soldiers fired live ammunition into Palestinian crowds, Dan Rather and Peter Jennings were bound to pay attention. For, the truth was that every Palestinian fatality gave the Intifada more impetus, more drama, and made it a bigger, better news story.

So caught by surprise were the Israelis that their soldiers were given little choice but to fire live ammunition indiscriminately into Palestinian crowds. At first, there seemed little that Rabin and the IDF could do to stop the killings. Israeli troops had been placed in the most disadvantageous position. Without the proper antiriot equipment, Israeli soldiers turned to live ammunition, as a first resort, when faced with the presence of hundreds of thousands of Palestinian demonstrators, many of whom were throwing rocks their way. Israeli leaders, including Rabin, found themselves defending this practice and that only reinforced the image of an Israel that had lost control of the situation in the territories. "Whenever there is clear cut danger to our troops, they have orders to use live ammunition," Rabin said, never acknowledging that it might be possible to curb rioters without resorting to live ammunition. The impression gained abroad, meanwhile, was that Rabin and most other Israeli leaders were unrepentant about the continual killing of Palestinian Arabs. Some 17 Palestinian Arabs died and 100 more were wounded during those first two weeks of unrest. To Rabin, the Palestinian disorders, while unpleasant and requiring a response, did not challenge the IDF to the same degree as had Israel's past wars.

Rabin had fought in wars in 1948 and 1967 and he had witnessed the 1973 war, wars that were definite threats to the nation's existence, or seemed so at the time. He felt no such concern that an existential threat existed in Israel with respect to the Intifada. Leah Rabin recalled: "He used to say: 'We've had our challenges but the Intifada is not one of them.' He was embarrassed by what his soldiers had to do to suppress the riots, but he did not lose sleep at night."[149] Ironically, in the early phases of the Intifada, no television camera caught an Israeli soldier killing a Palestinian rioter. It made no difference. The cameras recorded enough live fire poured on those rock-throwing crowds to bring critics to their feet. At first Rabin dismissed the critics. When he appeared in the Knesset on December 23, he asserted that Israel would not shift tactics. Israeli marksmen would continue to try to pick off leaders of the violence. "They can shoot to hit leaders of disorder, throwers of firebombs, as much as possible at legs, after firing in the air failed to disperse the riot. As Defense Minister, I have responsibility for the lives and safety of the soldiers and Border Police, and it is my duty to give them the means to protect themselves... to hurt those out to hurt them." To hurt Palestinian Arabs, he meant. This phrase and others he would offer gave Yitzhak Rabin a more visible image of Mr. Tough Guy. It fell to him to be the Bad Cop. Though Rabin tried to be consistent in his handling of the Intifada, a whole battery of military steps were tried, none working very effectively. The Intifada would not go away. The situation reached explosive proportions soon after January 1, 1988 when the Israeli cabinet accepted Rabin's recommendation to expel nine of the main Intifada leaders from Israel, five from the Gaza Strip and four from the West Bank. The Palestinians reacted with even greater violence. In response, Rabin and the IDF's supreme command conceived yet a new strategy for defeating the Intifada, the third in five weeks. This time, there would be no silk gloves. It was decided that as long as there was no law and order in the

149. Leah Rabin, interview with author, July 29, 1992

territories, there would be no normal life for the residents. The main target was the refugee camps in the Gaza Strip and some of the other trouble spots in the West Bank. Collective punishment and extensive curfews were introduced.

Despite the tough measures, Rabin was growing increasingly frustrated at their ineffectiveness. He was slowly coming to realize that the unrest was no passing phenomenon; something far more deeply rooted was occurring in the territories. The uprising was not the brainchild of Iran, or Syria, the PLO, or just a bunch of terrorist troublemakers. Nor was it isolated enough that the IDF's iron fist could stamp out the fury with one dramatic blow. "No," said Rabin, "it would require an adjustment in 'our methods of action' to quell the unrest, for it was of a different magnitude from past trouble in the occupied areas." This time the unrest reflected genuine Palestinian despair, in not being able to end Israeli rule. When the Intifada broke out, the defense minister talked of restoring "tranquility." Now he said: "It is a complicated and long-drawn-out affair, that cannot be taken care of in a few days. Don't stand there with a stop watch." Others agreed that the Intifada was complicated. All the more reason, they argued, for Israel not to pump live bullets into Palestinians. Rabin sought a way to reduce the killings or eliminate them completely. His aim had been noble. His thinking, however, was flawed. For the policy that he was about to offer in the place of shooting and killing Palestinians, a policy of using physical force rather than live ammunition, was no more palatable to outside critics. Rather than shoot at demonstrators, Rabin decided, the IDF should use physical force to subdue them. On the surface the new policy seemed to have merit. The number of Palestinians shot dead would subside. With a cutback in the number of those killings, the headlines would lessen as well, and the Western media might get tired of the story. It was a nice thought. Rabin was convinced that the international community would stand up and applaud.

Had Rabin announced the policy publicly, questions undoubtedly would have been asked about his motivation. That he launched the policy in secret clouded the issue all the more. The questions did not stop coming: What had Rabin said precisely? What had he meant? It was taken for granted that the defense minister had advocated "breaking their bones," a phrase he insisted he had never used. "I never gave orders to break bones," the defense minister told the Knesset on July 12, 1990, when a proposal was made for a commission of inquiry into the responsibility of the political echelon for IDF abuses during the Intifada. Perhaps he did not use the "break the bones" phrase. That he used similarly tough language, however, is certain.

Whether he used the phrase "break their bones" in private discussions or not, the fact was that Rabin appeared to be saying as much in public. The effect on local IDF commanders in the West Bank and the Gaza Strip was devastating. They had a hard time understanding precisely what he meant for them to do. But this much they understood: Beating-up Palestinians was now accepted IDF policy. Rarely did a television camera show an IDF soldier beating a Palestinian Arab to a pulp, but word quickly spread that this was precisely what was happening.

Critics abroad were dismayed. Jacob Stein, a former chairman of the Conference of Presidents of Major American Jewish Organizations, noted sadly: "While I recognize the need for civil order, I am rather appalled by the reports of random beatings of Palestinians. I can only hope that a more humane and effective way can be devised to deal with these disorders."[150] The former editor of *The New York Times* and later *Times* columnist, A. M. Rosenthal had always been an unstinting supporter of Israel. When he learned of the beatings, he called upon Rabin to resign. "The Israeli government seems to be edging away from the policy of beating. But more is needed by Israel and for Israel. Mr. Rabin can restore his stature and Israel's by resigning. Then Israel can be itself again: a nation with a right to a vision, a right even to be wrong sometimes and to act in its self-interest, strong in battle and strong in decency. Jews must not break bones. This is the message that must come from the friends of Israel."

Such behavior on the part of IDF soldiers created the impression that Yitzhak Rabin was a brutal, cruel leader who took joy in the pain his army had inflicted on Palestinians. Ephraim Sneh, the former head of the Israeli civil administration for the West Bank, disputed such claims: "Rabin is not fond of the Arabs but he doesn't despise or hate them. He's not a brutal man. The image was that he enjoyed breaking bones, but it's not true."[151]

One reason Rabin's policy was so misunderstood, by outsiders as well as by Israeli soldiers, was Rabin himself. He may have thought he was being clear in articulating his beatings policy; few others did. He may have wanted to sound compassionate; better to beat someone than kill them. Yet he wound up sounding more heartless, not less. Take as

---

150. 'Sharp Condemnation of Rabin Policy from American Jewish Leaders,' *The Jerusalem Post*, January 25, 1988

151. Ephraim Sneh, interview with author, August 11, 1992

an example his comments on September 27, 1988 explaining why the IDF used plastic bullets against Palestinian rioters. Rather than accentuate the non-lethal effects of plastic bullets, he suggested that the move behind using those plastic bullets was to increase injuries. "Our purpose is to increase the number of [wounded] among those who take part in violent activities, but not to kill them," he told a press conference at Beit El military headquarters on the West Bank. "I am not worried by the increased number of people who got wounded, as long as they were wounded as a result of being involved actively, by instigating, organizing, and taking part in violent activities. The rioters are suffering more casualties. That is precisely our aim."[152]

In time, Rabin began to realize that to the international community, beating Palestinians up was just as offensive as shooting them with live ammunition. To an Israel Television reporter on March 10, he admitted: "I had believed that shooting would appear much worse in international public opinion than the use of the riot baton. And I was surprised to discover that the sensitivity of world opinion to blows and physical confrontation was greater than to that of shooting." Such thoughts were leading Rabin to think much more seriously about what was transpiring in the occupied areas, both to the Palestinians and to the Israeli army. It bothered him that Palestinians were being killed and being beaten up. It bothered him even more, that Israeli soldiers were the instrument for this bloodshed. He thought it his responsibility as defense minister to find a way out of this mess.

By February 1988, with the Intifada only a few months old, Rabin was moving towards the view that however much

152. 'Rabin: "More Injuries Is Precisely Our Aim",' *The Jerusalem Post*, September 28, 1988

force Israel used against the Palestinians, that would not end the conflict. The Palestinian Intifada had convinced him of that. What was occurring in the occupied territories, Rabin insisted, was not a civil war. Israelis and Palestinians were not one people torn apart (like the American North and South in their Civil War). Rather, Israel was involved in a confrontation between two national entities. On February 2, Rabin predicted to the Knesset Foreign Affairs and Defense Committee that the unrest would last for months to come. He had no choice but to keep the situation from getting out of hand and plan for the future with a combination of "Perseverance, patience, and the conviction that we are in the right." Being convinced that Israel was in the right, however, did not help bring about a political solution.

Perhaps the simple truth was that the IDF had lost control over events in the territories. Rabin was asked whether this was true in an Israel Television interview on March 9. He replied that Israel had endured the War of Attrition in the late 1960s for 1,000 days, suffering numerous casualties. No immediate solution had cropped up at the start of that war. Israel had been bogged down in Lebanon for three years. Again, no solution emerged at an early stage that would have ended Israel's involvement in that war. "As for the Intifada, after three months, we are facing a problem of a kind with which we haven't previous experience. It is the problem of violence on the part of a large population which is under our control, which is acting not in the framework of terrorism... with the possible exception of Molotov cocktails... It is far easier to solve classic military problems. It is far more difficult to contend with 1.4 million Palestinians living in the territories who are employing, so it transpires, systematic violence without weapons, and who do not want our rule.

Our objective... is to bring about a calming, not a solution. Moreover, the matter is continuing because in handling an entire population we cannot use the IDF's principal weapons [the air force, armored corps, and artillery] at most, IDF soldiers are permitted to use their guns... and this takes time."

The problem would have been much simpler if all the territory was Arab territory, void of any Jewish settlements. It would have been very simple to close off the area and not to have to handle problems of keeping transportation lines open, to focus on problems with the populace in large population centers. "There are 450 villages in the West Bank: The IDF cannot be in every place at once," Rabin suggested. The Intifada had not altered Rabin's thinking about the kind of political solution he preferred. The unrest had, however, given him a greater sensitivity to the depth of feeling that existed among the Palestinian Arab community. On March 17, 1988, before an audience of high school students in Jerusalem, he outlined his thoughts about the kind of peace he wanted: "I am opposed to a Palestinian PLO state between Israel and Jordan. Since I am totally opposed to this, I am also totally opposed to negotiations with the PLO. I oppose, under any circumstances, withdrawing to the 1967 borders. [I support] the preservation of Greater Jerusalem, united, under Israeli sovereignty and serving as its capital, its eternal capital... the main thing is [maintaining] the Jordan River as the security border, the Jerusalem area, Gush Etzion, the Jordan Valley... At the same time, [I support] a readiness to return, within the framework of peace, the densely populated Palestinian areas to a foreign sovereignty, to Jordan. I am against uprooting settlements. I support, under an agreement, allowing Jewish settlements to continue as Israeli settlements even under foreign sovereignty, just as that portion of the territories which will remain under Israeli sovereignty and in which there will be Palestinians, with Jordanian citizenship, [who] will be offered Israeli citizenship, or will be allowed to maintain their Jordanian citizenship."

The Palestinians had not succeeded in softening Rabin's political views; he still opposed a Palestinian state; he still refused to deal with the PLO. But, in saying that he would return territory to the Palestinians, he opened the door to a political solution that could provide the Palestinians with an independent entity. For the Palestinians, this may have been the greatest achievement of the Intifada, given the fact that four years later, Rabin would become prime minister.

In the spring of 1988, Rabin said publicly on US Television that he was prepared to negotiate with PLO officials under certain conditions. Although he was not saying he was now ready to talk with the PLO, by suggesting that he did not rule out talking to the PLO if it altered its character, he at least demonstrated how he differed from Yitzhak Shamir and the Likud's rigid thinking. Shamir and other hardline Likud leaders had always said they would never deal with the PLO under any circumstances. Appearing on Ted Koppel's *Nightline* program, Rabin said he would be prepared to negotiate with any PLO official who renounced the Palestine National Covenant, accepted UN Security Council Resolutions 242 and 338, and stopped acts of terror. "Allow me to say," Rabin told Koppel, "that if you get an announcement by any Palestinian who belongs to the PLO that, first and foremost, he renounces the Palestinian covenant; that he is ready to accept Resolutions 242 and 338, not in the context of the [UN] General Assembly resolutions;

and that he is ready to stop violence and terror, with any Palestinian that will come up with this statement, I am ready to negotiate."[153]

However unpopular Rabin was abroad, he had little to worry about at home. From March 6 to 19, 1988, the Pori Institute interviewed 1,200 Israelis and found that the defense minister was the most popular Israeli senior government minister. His prestige had increased since the Intifada. A total of 58.1 percent of Israelis were satisfied with Rabin's performance as defense minister, compared with 50.9 percent in December 1987, a 7.2 percent increase. Foreign minister Peres had dropped 6.5 percent in popularity since December, and prime minister Shamir had become only slightly more popular since the start of the Intifada, moving a few percentage points higher. While Israelis did not appreciate the turmoil and suffering, embittered as they had been forced into killing and beating up Palestinians, they supported Rabin's tough stance toward the Palestinians. Peres the dove was losing popular support, while Rabin, the hawk, was gaining.

While clearly the majority backed Rabin, among the minority political left, Rabin was called all sorts of nasty names, including war criminal.

Israelis also responded favorably well to Rabin's willingness to be held accountable for the government's policy towards the Intifada. This was in sharp contrast with the attitude of other Israeli defense ministers who, when the going got tough, sought to diffuse and shirk responsibility. At the height of criticism against Israel during the war in Lebanon, the then defense minister, Ariel Sharon, said

---

153. 'Rabin Would Talk to PLO,' *The Jerusalem Post*, April 27, 1988

lamely that he had been acting with the full knowledge of the Israeli prime minister. After Israeli soldiers had been surprised by Arab forces at the start of the 1973 Yom Kippur War, then-defense minister Moshe Dayan insisted that he was only supplying ministerial advice to the IDF, nothing more. Rabin behaved differently during the Intifada. With Israel's image abroad slipping disastrously, he did not try to fob off responsibility on prime minister Shamir or on the Israeli Cabinet in its entirety. His willingness to take responsibility could easily have boomeranged: Israelis could well have held the whole frustrating affair of the Intifada against him. Instead Rabin, who had been a symbol of Israel's hardline policies in the territories, reaped the benefit of those policies. Israelis were saying: We may not like everything Rabin is doing, but he is not trying to hide when things get too hot. Rabin's behavior gave him much prestige among tough-minded Israelis who would have a chance to show their appreciation with their votes a few years later.

Against whom was the Intifada directed? Yitzhak Shamir? He was unquestionably the right address. Yet, he was hard-as-nails and gave the clear impression that he had no time for Palestinians. Even when Shamir sounded as though he was prepared to make a deal with the Palestinians, as was the case in the spring of 1989, no one quite believed him. He left no doubt that he had no inclination to grant them autonomy or any political representation. The Palestinians, however, seemed hungry for a political settlement. They did not want to see their Intifada go to waste. As long as Shamir was prime minister, however, they had little chance of making political gains. While they were waiting impatiently for the Israelis to see the light, changes were occurring in the mind of one

Israeli leader; changes that would have vast significance for peacemaking. Call it the political enlightenment of Yitzhak Rabin.

The Intifada had the most sobering effect on Rabin, convincing him that Palestinians in the occupied territories should be treated as political equals, should be entitled to a political solution. To a group of correspondents who covered the occupied areas, Rabin acknowledged that as defense minister, "It took me time until I understood the Intifada as a phenomenon, and the willingness of Palestinians to persist with it. Until the Intifada broke out, Israel had not experienced such a comprehensive case of authentic popular uprising." Calling the Palestinian cause "authentic" was the outcome of the sobering effect of the Intifada on Rabin. He added that only after about six months did he realize that it was impossible to bring the Intifada to an end solely through force. A political solution was necessary.

That was no small change of mind. Until the Intifada, Rabin (and other Israeli leaders as well) was against talking to any Palestinians. Prior to the uprising, Rabin and other senior Labor Party politicians advocated the 'Jordanian Option', which called for a return of substantial portions of the West Bank to Jordan in return for an Israeli-Jordan peace treaty. When Peres became prime minister in September 1984, he actively sought such an accord with Jordan's King Hussein. Peres and the king met frequently over the next two years, with Rabin attending a number of these meetings.

One official who had worked with Rabin over the years explained: "Rabin was a partner to the meetings with the king. Even if he didn't attend all of the meetings, he was involved." By April 1987, the so-called London Agreement had been carved out, calling for an international peace conference to settle the Arab-Israeli conflict. With Peres and Rabin behind the London Agreement, it seemed only natural that the Jordanian Option would be promoted once again. The trouble with all of Peres's (and Rabin's) efforts, however, was that the Jordanian Option had long been a dead issue. In the early 1970s, it seemed reasonable to advocate turning over most of the West Bank to King Hussein, but a great deal had happened, and by the late 1980s, the king's position with regard to the West Bank had been greatly weakened.

Then in December 1987, the local Palestinians rose up, hoodwinking the PLO who could not take credit for an event that surprised them totally. Rabin and the Israelis took notice. "What changed Rabin's attitude," recalled Ephraim Sneh, "was the fact that the Intifada moved the center of political gravity to the occupied territories. Through their struggle, the Palestinians became partners."[154] Recognizing that change, Rabin was now prepared to put the local Palestinians to the test.

To accelerate peacemaking with local Palestinians, Rabin had to jettison his conviction that the Intifada must end before political talks could start. He began, in May 1988, to hold secret meetings with Palestinians from the West Bank and the Gaza Strip. A way had to be found to build up a local Palestinian Arab leadership that had sufficient political authority, to conduct negotiations for the entire Palestinian Arab population in the West Bank and the Gaza strip. The means suggested was elections. Those people elected would be able to claim that they had the backing of the population to do business with the Israelis. One of the central issues of

---

154. Ephraim Sneh, interview with author, August 11, 1992

Rabin's secret talks was what kind of elections should the Palestinians hold. Rabin had favored municipal elections, fearing that general elections would provide a means for the PLO to gain a greater foothold in the occupied territories. As a result of his secret talks, he changed his mind and now favored holding general elections. (He may have been influenced by the fact that Peres favored municipal elections.[155])

By early January 1989, Rabin intensified his peacemaking efforts, holding a series of low-key meetings in his Tel Aviv office with key Palestinian Arab figures from the territories. The identity of the Palestinian Arabs was kept secret. Both the Israelis and the Palestinians knew that it was far too early to publicize such talks. Unless and until the local Palestinians could clear the way with the PLO, the most likely result of such publicity would be a bullet for one or more of the Palestinian representatives. Still, Rabin wanted to find out if it would be possible to engage these Palestinians in a dialogue without PLO involvement.

It was in early 1989 that Rabin unveiled his own peace plan focused around Palestinian elections. He spoke of a six-month moratorium on the Intifada, as well as elections in the occupied areas, to elect local Palestinians who would then negotiate with Israel the terms of an interim agreement. Though his proposals would eventually be swallowed up and co-opted by Shamir, Rabin had shown how far he had come from simply dealing with the Intifada through military means. "Rabin showed courage," said Bethlehem mayor Elias Friej.[156]

---

155. The author

156. Elias Friej, interview with author, July 29, 1992

Rabin had the distinction of having his peace plan rejected by both the PLO and Shamir. On January 23, 1989, Shamir told an Israel Television reporter: "I do not consider that I am in any way obliged to comment on this matter... I have been informed that all the Arab elements reject this plan. I would therefore not advise us, in Israel, to get embroiled in discussions on a notion which has no chance of being implemented. "

Prime minister Shamir, however, reacting to heavy American pressure on Israel to negotiate an end to the Intifada, adopted the very plan he had rejected: In May 1989, he proposed limited elections in the Palestinian territories, as a step toward Middle-East peace. To get the elections off the ground, American secretary of state James Baker proposed a formula under which Egypt, Israel, and the US would select Palestinian delegates for preliminary talks.

The Rabin and Shamir peace plans for the Palestinians differed most importantly over the issue of giving back Israel-held land. Rabin supported the principle of exchanging land for peace; Shamir did not. They disagreed over tactics as well. Shamir was adamantly against PLO involvement in the peace talks. Rabin made it clear that he was prepared for Egypt to draw up a list of Palestinians who would then decide on the election rules. It did not bother Rabin that Egypt planned to consult with the PLO. Hosni Mubarak, Rabin said, had the right to consult with whomever he wished.

With Shamir in charge, however, the peace process had little chance of moving forward. Meeting with president George Bush at the White House in April 1989, Shamir gave the distinct impression that implementing his own peace plan was the last thing on his mind. In June, Shamir's own Likud

Central Committee had sought to tie the prime minister's hands by laying down pre-conditions for negotiations with the Palestinians and other Arabs: There could be no Palestinian state; no PLO participation in peace talks; no Palestinian living in East Jerusalem could represent the Palestinians in the peace talks; and negotiations could start only after the Intifada ceased.

In September 1989, Egypt's president Mubarak invited Rabin to Cairo to discuss the peace process. The Egyptian president appeared to believe that Rabin could sway Shamir. To some extent, this appeared true. Certainly, if Rabin disagreed adamantly enough about Shamir's peace proposals, he appeared strong enough to force Labor to leave the National Unity Government. That could have set in motion another Rabin attempt to grab the party leadership from Shimon Peres. Yet, Rabin sounded very much as if he preferred to remain defense minister inside a Shamir-led government and not risk a process that could result in Peres taking over the prime ministership. In an interview with the author (for *Time Magazine*) in October 1989, Rabin spoke at length about the peace initiative: "I believe that we are on a course towards a beginning of a dialogue. I can't say that there is more than an opening for moving ahead with the issue that will make or break the whole [Israeli] peace initiative, finding a Palestinian partner with whom we can start the process as described in our peace initiative." Did Rabin think Israel was getting ready to talk to the PLO? "By no means, no." Israel, he said, regarded the Palestinian inhabitants of the West Bank and Gaza as the proper source for a Palestinian delegation because they "lead in the struggle of the Palestinian case and suffered for that, not Arafat's gang in the villas of Tunisia."

Rabin exhibited no great appetite for leaving the Government. "I'll try my best [to keep the Government intact]. The policy of most of my Labor Party colleagues is to do everything to... move ahead with the Government's peace initiative." However, he hinted that at some stage he might consider Labor walkout. "Policy is not an academic issue alone. Policy has to be measured by the way it succeeded in being implemented. The implementation of a policy is its test."[157]

Implementation seemed far off. Prime minister Shamir went through the motions of a meeting with president Bush at the White House again in November 1989, with no real progress in the peace process. It was no wonder. Shamir had permitted the establishment of a Jewish settlement called Dugit in the Gaza Strip. Stunned, the president believed that Shamir had betrayed his trust. For years, the US government had made clear its opposition to Jewish settlement in the occupied territories, calling these settlements illegal and an obstacle to peace. The Shamir Government, however, exhibited no constraint in its settlement policies, knowing full well that this would antagonize both the Arabs and the Americans. Expanding Jewish settlements was, in Washington's eyes at least, the most solid evidence possible that the Shamir Government was not interested in advancing the peace process. Yet matters grew worse in January 1990, when Shamir declared that "a big *Aliyah* [immigration] needs a big Israel." That statement and others from within the Shamir Government encouraged the United States to believe that Israel planned to enlarge its Jewish settlement program, populating the settlements with as many of the newly arrived Russian Jews as possible.

---

157. Yitzhak Rabin, interview with author, October 4, 1989

In late February, president Bush phoned Shamir and received assurances that Russian immigrants were not being given any material incentives to settle in the territories. Shamir insisted that no more than one percent of the Russian immigrants were reaching the West Bank. (Aides to president Bush were putting out a figure closer to ten percent, but they were counting Jerusalem suburbs in Israel proper; the US considered those suburbs in occupied territory while Israel did not.) Bush did not seem satisfied and so, in a pique, Shamir rejected American secretary of state Baker's proposals for peace with the Palestinians. Shamir's growing intransigence would soon provide a new confrontation with the United States. That confrontation would provide an opportunity for Yitzhak Rabin to take center stage.

CHAPTER TWELVE

BENIFITING FROM
A "SMELLY EXERCISE"

Yitzhak Rabin had emerged from the political wilderness. He had managed his country's defense policy through one of the most controversial periods of its history. Extricating the troops from Lebanon and presiding over the Intifada, Rabin acquired from these two acts a reputation that had once belonged to Moshe Dayan: The country felt more comfortable with Rabin as minister of defense than anyone else. The title that Dayan had once – 'Mr. Security' – now belonged to Rabin. He possessed a rare combination for an Israeli politician: the ability to convey toughness in dealing with Arab violence and the sincerity to strive for peace. It was that combination which appealed to Israelis.

Rabin grew more popular as Israelis grew less satisfied with the Shamir government, particularly its handling of Middle East peacemaking. Under Shamir, the National Unity Government had not functioned smoothly. (Many said it had not functioned!) Shamir and Peres had not seen eye-to-eye on advancing the peace process: Peres had wanted to swap land for peace; Shamir refused to yield territory. Ironically, procedural points – how to choose the Palestinian delegates for the peace conference and which delegates would be permitted to attend – was that which put the National Unity Government to its severest test. By the spring of 1990, secretary of state James Baker began a major effort to win agreement for a formula that would have Israel, Egypt, and the United States choose those Palestinian delegates. Though it may have seemed mere procedure, it became a fundamental issue.

Labor Party members were growing increasingly cynical about Shamir. They doubted that he wanted to advance Middle East peacemaking. They sensed also that, if pushed by the US too hard, the prime minister would let the country decide who was right on this crucial issue – Likud or Labor – by advancing the date of elections scheduled for November 1992. And indeed by the spring of 1990, Washington was pressing Jerusalem to agree on the composition of the Palestinian delegation to the proposed peace talks and Shamir was beginning to find ways to slow them down. Shamir objected to including any Palestinian who resided outside the Middle East or in East Jerusalem. Baker proposed a compromise that would enable a Palestinian who had been deported from the occupied territories and was a West Bank resident with a second home in East Jerusalem. Shamir did not want any deportees, arguing that they were PLO-affiliated. The Labor Party, on the other hand, was prepared to accept Baker's proposals.

Peres and his closest allies wanted to leave the government over Shamir's intransigence. Together, the Likud (40) and

Labor (39) had 79 Knesset seats out of the total 120; but without Labor's 39 seats, the National Unity Government would lose its lopsided parliamentary majority. Its collapse would become all but inevitable.

Since Baker was forcing Shamir to choose between his compromise plan and risking the collapse of the National Unity Government, it was an easy choice for Shamir to make. Shamir assumed that even if his government fell over his rigidity, the electorate would rally to his side. So he stuck to his ideology, rejecting Baker's proposals as too risky for the country. President Bush got into the act by employing high profile diplomatic and financial pressure in an attempt to budge Shamir.

The future of the National Unity Government was thus depended in large measure on what Rabin chose to do. He, however, was of two minds. Personally, he had prospered under the National Unity Government. Becoming at the age of 68, its strong man, Rabin had no driving ambition to step down as defense minister or to replace the Unity regime with a new government under prime minister Peres. Rabin's stormy relationship with Peres was not the only issue at stake. Rabin cared about the peace process as well. And he was slowly becoming convinced that the Likud had no intention of advancing his plan for elections in the occupied territories. The only way of advancing peacemaking appeared to be to bring an end to Shamir's rule. Rabin was troubled, however, by any step that would advance Shimon Peres's career. On March 5, 1990, he noted that there were "some in Labor who seem to be in a great rush [to bring the National Unity Government down], and it isn't the peace process which is their paramount priority, but something quite different." "Some in Labor" was Rabin's shorthand for Shimon Peres.

It took Rabin some time to move over to the side of the rebels. While Peres was trying to maneuver a Labor walkout, Rabin on March 8 still insisted that the National Unity Government "constituted Israel's best alternative." Alternative to a Peres-led government, Rabin was mumbling under his breath, no doubt. For Rabin, told Labor Party leaders, "What ought to guide us above all is the need to carry on with the peace process, preferably in the framework of the existing broad coalition. This should be uppermost in our minds and not the mad rush after one alternative or another." Sure it should, if there had been a peace process, which there was not. And Rabin knew there was not. The simple truth was that Yitzhak Rabin had a hard time allowing the idea of Shimon Peres becoming prime minister again.

On March 11, the inner Cabinet, comprising senior Cabinet members, planned to convene to hold a decisive session on whether to accept the latest American proposals for getting agreement on a peace conference. Before the meeting even got under way, Peres was certain that Shamir and his Likud cohorts would veto the proposals. To signal to the Likud that Labor was getting ready to leave the government, Peres summoned the Labor Party's 1,400-member Central Committee into session for the day after, March 12. Peres had no doubt that the Committee would agree to end Labor's participation in the National Unity Government. When the inner Cabinet met on March 11, Shamir came out fighting. He would not tolerate Palestinians from East Jerusalem in the delegation; he would not tolerate Palestinian negotiators consulting with the PLO. Rabin tried out a compromise on Shamir: Let's tell the Americans that we will go along with a Palestinian delegation except on one crucial point – the thorny issues of whether East Jerusalem residents may vote in the proposed Palestinian elections. Let the Knesset decide on that issue. No, said Shamir. No more compromises. Labor ministers asked for a vote. Again, Shamir said no. Furious, Peres, Rabin, and the other Labor ministers stalked out of the session. "The Unity Government was gasping for breath. The only point on which Likud and Labor found unity was that there no longer was any unity!" Rabin said. Shamir's firmness at the inner Cabinet had a profound effect on Rabin. He realized that the prime minister had shown how uninterested he was in peacemaking.

When the Labor Party Central Committee convened at Beit Berl the next day, it was Rabin's enthusiastic call for the dismantling of the National Unity Government that helped sway the audience. The Likud, Rabin told the Central Committee, was simply afraid of where peace talks could lead. Shamir was not interested in a compromise that would bring about a peace conference. The Labor Party did not set a date by when it would leave the Government but no one doubted for a moment that Labor was counting the hours, not days or weeks. Events moved swiftly. Shamir seized the moment. Rather than wait for Labor to take the initiative by walking out of the Government, Shamir fired Peres as finance minister. The prime minister's reason: Peres had undermined the Government. Responding to Shamir's gambit, all Labor Party ministers, including defense minister Rabin, announced their resignations from the Government. The National Unity Government was dead.

Rabin and Peres called a joint news conference: "We have been discussing these issues for months," said Rabin, "the composition of the [Palestinian] delegation and the agenda. In the inner Cabinet, we held five and a half hours of discussions, but [Shamir] refuses to decide. We have done everything to formulate the issues in such a way that Shamir can give a positive response. The responsibility for the collapse of the government rests on Shamir's shoulders."

The Labor Party initiated a no-confidence motion against the Government and a vote was set in the Knesset for March 15. No Israeli prime minister had ever lost a no-confidence vote; rather than risk defeat, the prime minister had always tendered his resignation first, thus bringing down the entire government. The act of resignation forestalled the no-confidence motion. Shamir passed word through a highly placed Likud source that he might quit rather than be the first Israeli prime minister to be felled by a no-confidence vote. Then, oddly, Shamir changed strategy just 90 minutes before the vote was to be taken. He could have gone to the president to resign but instead he chose to let the vote go ahead. Shamir's coalition, now able to count on only 55 votes, fell 60-55. Helping to defeat the National Unity Government was the absence of five of the six members of the Ultra-Orthodox Sephardi Shas party. A coalition member acting on orders from its mentor, former chief rabbi Ovadia Yosef, those five Shas Knesset members chose to punish Shamir for refusing to demonstrate flexibility in the negotiating process. Peres assumed that Shas's support was now his for the asking, or at least for the bargaining. Peres also assumed that, with Shas safely in Labor's camp, he would be able to form a Government.

Now that the National Unity Government had fallen, it was up to president Chaim Herzog to examine whether anyone could form a new Government. If not, elections would have to be called. There seemed little question, however, that the Labor Party had a better chance than the Likud of forming a government. Arguing that their man had a better prospect of establishing a new government, some Rabin supporters insisted that Peres be dumped in favor of Rabin. Peres, however, had no trouble heading off such a move. After consulting with the parties, the president chose Peres to try to form a new Government. For a while, it seemed that Peres would be successful, though the new Peres-led Government would have a razor-thin majority of only 61 Knesset seats.

What followed was a five-week period during which Labor Party leader Shimon Peres sought to get the small religious parties to join his new governing coalition. He made generous offers to the religious parties, offering money to their educational institutions and promise of making political appointments that were important to the religious leaders. As finance minister, Peres was in an ideal position to make sure that funds streamed into religious institutions. The wheeling and dealing grew messy and complicated. At one stage, Peres struck a bargain with the Agudat Yisrael Party, only to find out that, if he wished the support of two other small religious parties (Shas and Degel Hatorah), he would have to renege on the Agudat Yisrael deal. These kinds of political deals had been made in the past. This time, however, the public grew incensed, arguing that public funds should not be used to purchase a Government for Peres. Massive demonstrations and hunger strikes were held, at which Israelis pressed for electoral reform as an antidote to the brazen coalition horse-trading. Many wanted a complete overhaul of the political system, making the Knesset more responsive to the wishes of the public. Nearly everyone agreed that the prime minister should be directly elected as a first step in reducing the power that small parties had over the large parties during coalition formation. A half million Israelis, nearly 10 percent of the population, handed a petition to president Herzog, demanding electoral reform. At one rally in Tel Aviv, 250,000 Israelis mounted a protest against the political system. Despite the protests, the fear of alienating the Ultra-Orthodox parties at this crucial and sensitive political juncture kept the major parties silent on the issue of electoral reform.

The public dissent had arisen over the ability of the small religious parties to hold the big parties in the country hostage. Never was this demonstrated more clearly than on April 12, 1990, when Peres planned to bring his new Government for approval before the Knesset. At the very last minute, the two Agudat Yisrael Knesset members, Eliezer Mizrachi and Avraham Werdiger, changed their minds and decided to withhold their support for the new Peres-led Government. Ordering the two not to support Peres was the 88-year-old head of the Ultra-Orthodox Chabad-Lubavitch movement, rabbi Menachem Schneerson, sending word from his home in Brooklyn, New York. With his 61-seat majority suddenly dropping two seats to 59, Peres, humiliated and shocked, had to announce that he could not after all form a Government. The religious parties had held Peres hostage, but ultimately it was Peres who had condemned himself with his offers of political largess. "The political system has been raped, robbed, bruised, and brought to prostitution," wrote the columnist Nahum Barnea, the highly respected political commentator in *Yediot Aharonot* on April 26.

Yitzhak Rabin was smiling. Peres's misfortune became his good luck. Rabin had genuinely wanted Labor to remain in the National Unity Government. To be on the inside meant power, influence; to be tossed to the back benches of the Knesset was not exciting; he had suffered through seven years as a Knesset member and he had no great desire to return to that status. Still, Rabin had tried to play fair, to give Peres a chance to form a government; Rabin knew that had he tried to torpedo Peres' chances, and Peres had succeeded in setting up an alternative Government, Labor would never have forgiven him. So he played the role of loyal lieutenant to Peres, paying a visit to a rabbi or two when a good word from him seemed needed. "People in Labor asked me to see Rabbi [Eliezer] Shach," Rabin told intimates at the time, referring to the most powerful ultra-orthodox figure in the country. "They told me, 'He's blind, dumb, deaf, senile. Just go there and say hello.' If I hadn't gone, everyone would have said I'd spoiled Labor's chances. He's not deaf, he's not blind. He's very much in possession of his senses. He knows what he wants."[158] To have gone to a rabbi hat in hand enraged Rabin. All the while, he bristled at the backroom tactics Peres was employing, turning the Labor Party into a supplicant.

Peres's ill-fated attempt to form a new Government presented Rabin with a golden opportunity to pounce on his long-time rival. Had Peres succeeded in establishing a government, his dealing would have been overlooked. Defeat, however, created a stench. In fact, Rabin termed the Peres gambit *HaTargil HaMasriyach*, in Hebrew: The Smelly Exercise. A phrase that obviously touched a nerve, for it has remained an exemplar of dirty politics in Israel to this day.

With Peres still in charge of the party, Rabin had to appear loyal. The day after Peres's Knesset fiasco, Rabin issued a statement that was meant to express support for

---

158. Dan Pattir related Rabin's comments to the author, interview with author, July 25, 1992

Peres. Rabin said he saw "national and party importance in preventing this mandate [of Peres] from being handed over to the Likud, which would form a narrow, right-wing coalition." So prickly were their relations that analysts scrutinized each word that Rabin penned. Had he indeed been loyal to Peres? Most of the communiqué appeared to suggest that, however grudgingly, Rabin had been loyal to his rival. Then came the last sentence "When the time comes, Labor's institutions will have to take steps to ensure that such a narrow rightist coalition is not established," using language surely designed to tweak Peres and advance his own political cause. Rabin had used the phrase "take steps." He appeared to be suggesting that Labor would take steps to remove Peres. Pundits guessed that Rabin hoped to take over the party, then turn to the Likud and reestablish the National Unity Government.

On April 26, Rabin came out swinging. He appeared before the Labor Party's 150-member Leadership Bureau and coyly noted that he had not exactly been aloof from Peres's maneuvering, though now he regretted taking part. "I admit to making the mistake of not checking the stories that we have a narrow government in our pocket and learned only afterwards what trouble we were in. I admit to a certain degree of responsibility for the mistakes that were made. My main mistake was preferring inner-party peace above other issues." Rabin's message was clear: He and Labor had paid a heavy price for giving Peres his way. Now he planned to be his own man. He announced at that meeting that he planned to challenge Peres for the party leadership.

However, since the party was heading into parliamentary opposition, the leadership struggle in Labor was postponed. Shamir, in the meantime, got busy and over the next few weeks began carving a coalition of the Likud and small right-wing and religious parties.

Labor was now forced to take up the backbenches while Shamir was free to keep the peace process on a low flame and free to expand Jewish settlements in the occupied territories. Although uneasy lay the crown, Peres remained Labor Party leader; Rabin seemed no closer to realizing his ambition to wrest power from Peres.

The political landscape was, however, rearranging itself in Rabin's favor. Advocates of electoral reform had not forgiven Labor and Likud politicians for their high-profile bartering and for ignoring pleas to change the political system. The man most identified with that bartering was Shimon Peres. Moreover, disenchantment had grown over Shamir's resistance to the peace process. All of this played into Yitzhak Rabin's hands. The country preferred him to Peres or Shamir for prime minister. A public opinion poll conducted by the Smith Research Center appeared in *The Jerusalem Post* on July 11 and indicated that, if direct elections for the prime minister were held that day, Rabin would have been easily elected: He soundly defeated Shamir, 50 to 33 percent. The poll showed that Shamir could easily defeat Peres, though by a much slimmer margin.

With the Labor Party in agitation, Rabin was itching for a chance to unseat Peres. He wanted a leadership contest as quickly as possible. Rabin said on May 12, 1990 that Labor had to "organize itself for life on the other side of the House. Before we can do that, however, we have to vote for the man, and we have to vote for the message. In political life, you cannot always draw a clear-cut line between who and what. But there is no doubt that it is the man who gives the message credibility."[159] Peres saw no need to rush. National elections were not for another 16 months, in November 1992. But Rabin wanted a leadership contest by the end of July. On July 5, the Labor Party Central Committee decided to convene on July 22 and decide whether to hold a leadership contest in the very near future or postpone the vote for a year (as Peres was seeking). Rabin was elated that the Committee would even consider moving up the contest to a much earlier date than Peres wanted.

Rabin's camp claimed the support of 60 percent of the Central Committee; Peres' backers thought the race close with a slight advantage to their man. Peres's supporters were nasty. They flayed Rabin, calling him derogatorily 'Mr. Intifada'. He was the 'leg and arm-breaking man,' unfit for office. Dismayed that the bloodletting in Labor might cause the Party problems in the next election against the Likud, Peres appeared defensive: "I did not invite Rabin to a duel," he told supporters a few days before the party contest. "He has plunged the party into a big whirlpool. But if he asked for a duel, he'll get it."

July 22 arrived. Still defensive when speaking before the vote, Peres asked sarcastically: "Did I write a book about you? Did I call you names?" If there was a failure in March 1990, Peres said, "Rabin was a full partner to it, step by step. He did not object to anything, not in private conversation and not in the party institutions. And if someone must bear responsibility, he was not number two, he was one of two." As he sat there listening to Peres, Rabin remained confident that the Central Committee would make Peres pay for his misdeeds.

159. 'We Must Invariably Negotiate from Strength', *The Jerusalem Post*, May 12, 1990

He was wrong. Confounding everyone, Peres soundly defeated Rabin, garnering 54 percent of the Central Committee's vote to only 46 percent for Rabin. How had Peres achieved this surprise triumph with so much going against him? An indefatigable campaigner, Peres made sure to get in touch with every member of the Central Committee, attending countless meetings around the country. Rabin campaigned less vigorously, less methodically. In fact, while Rabin had captured the hearts of the country, Peres retained an iron grip over the Labor Party. Neither Rabin's popularity nor Peres's faded image after the March 1990 fiasco hurt the Labor Party leader. The lingering memory among Labor Party members that Rabin also appeared more sympathetic to Shamir than to Labor aided Peres. What drew many in Labor back to Peres was the man's political skills. A key Rabin confidante explained: "Peres is a party man, Rabin is a statesman. Peres grew out of the party, only the party. Rabin endures the party. Shimon is a battle fox. He knows how to buy people. Peres could talk to all members of the party twice in two weeks. That was something Rabin couldn't do." With Labor sliding in the public opinion polls, Peres's July triumph seemed especially hollow. It turned out not only to be hollow, but of no real relevance. While Rabin had appeared the loser that July 22, he was not. For Peres had won the battle, but lost the war.

Grabbing fewer headlines, but far more significant than that day's Peres-Rabin contest, was a decision taken by the Central Committee to choose its future leaders by a new system, fashioned after the American presidential primaries. After many years of keeping its leadership contests confined to members of the 1,450-member Central Committee, Labor became the first Israeli political party to turn that decision over to all registered party members. Another crucial decision taken by the Central Committee was the holding of a party census. Democratizing the Labor Party was as controversial as it was ground-breaking, yet Labor understood only too well that this reform was vital if the party were going to stand a chance against the Likud in November 1992. In democratizing itself, Labor would hopefully carve out a new, positive image. Rabin could only smile quietly. He called the July 22 defeat a mere tactical failure and vowed that his strategy remained, ousting Peres from the party leadership. Rabin was counting on the fact that when the next leadership contest would be held, Peres's iron grip over the party would hopefully count for less than the will of the entire membership. Seeking to play down the July 22 vote, Rabin insisted that there had been no showdown with Peres; Labor had not been asked to select its candidate for prime minister. No one should label him the party's number two figure, said Rabin. "I don't need any title in the party, such as Number Two. I don't regard myself as second to anyone."

Dismayed that the right-wing government under Shamir was now capturing the headlines, maintaining a hard line toward peacemaking, and expanding Jewish settlements in the occupied territories, the Labor Party lost its aggressiveness. Its Knesset members displayed little zeal for bringing down the Likud government, preferring travel abroad to the nitty-gritty parliamentary efforts that might cause Likud to fall. Some in Labor thought it time to dump Peres as party leader and a number of candidates came forward.

Fortunately for Labor, the public began shifting favor away from the Likud. The Intifada had frayed Israeli nerves; it no longer seemed confined to the West Bank or the Gaza

Strip. Life seemed all too precarious. On October 8, 1990, an angry Palestinian mob began throwing rocks at Israelis near the Western Wall. Israeli police came to the rescue, firing into the mob. Nineteen Palestinian Arabs were killed and another 140 were wounded. Such incidents led Israelis to conclude that Palestinian Arabs from the occupied territories should no longer be permitted into Israel proper. As their personal fears grew, Israelis adopted tougher attitudes toward the Arabs. At the same time, they wanted the bloodshed to stop.

Cutting into the Likud's popularity, apart from the Intifada, was the way the Shamir Government had been handling the integration of Soviet Jewish immigrants into Israeli society. Russian Jews began arriving in Israel in larger and larger numbers in 1989, an event that Israelis had longed for over the years: 13,000 reached Israel that year; 185,000 came in 1990. At the beginning of this new wave of immigration, the Russian Jews knew housing was in short supply, but came to Israel anyway. They feared growing anti-Semitism; they hated the Russian poverty; they were concerned about the seeming instability of the Soviet regime. With America closing its doors to them, Israel was the most suitable place to go. Not since the early 1950s had Israel to figure out how to handle so many new immigrants all at once. Yet immigration was a *raison d'être* for the Jewish state. No matter how many came, the country would have to cope.

When the United States began the countdown to the Gulf War in January 1991, Rabin, now a Knesset backbencher, remembered the lessons that Israel had learned from the Lebanon War. Hence, he was confident that the US would be able to achieve military superiority over Iraq, but less confident that Washington would be able to bring Saddam Hussein to his knees, let alone extricate the Iraqi army from Kuwait. He predicted accurately that if Saddam was attacked, he would fulfill his promise of making Israel a target. When the war broke out, Rabin, a former chief of staff, once again found himself on the sidelines of an Israeli war. When some assailed Rabin for neglecting Iraq as a possible danger while he was defense minister, he reminded them that he had warned Egyptian president Hosni Mubarak in September 1989: "I told him Saddam was a threat to us and would become his most radical opponent in the Arab world. But he just wouldn't hear of it."

Meanwhile, Shamir had gained points for keeping Israel reined in during the Gulf War and not unleashing a counter-attack to Saddam's Scud assault against Israel during the war. Neither Rabin nor Peres fared well politically from the Gulf War. The Scud attacks against Israel's population centers served to remind Israelis that it had been Peres who had opposed Menachem Begin's decision to destroy the Iraqi nuclear reactor in June 1981. Rabin's star did not glow either at this juncture. However much he claimed that Israeli intelligence had been on its toes in the 1980s, it was abundantly clear to Israelis that their leaders had done precious little to prepare the country against Iraqi Scud attacks. With Israeli intelligence focusing on Syria, Israel had made little effort to beef up its civil defense preparations in the event that Iraq employed chemical weapons on its Scuds. (Fortunately for Israel, none of the Scuds that landed in Israel contained chemical warheads.)

The Gulf War led US president George Bush to believe that, in the wake of the war, there might be a glimmer of hope in resurrecting negotiations to resolve the Arab-Israeli conflict. He sent secretary of state James Baker to the Middle East to get things going. Baker's arrival in mid-March 1991 coincided with public opinion polls giving Labor no more than 20 Knesset seats against an ever-more-popular Likud Party. There was speculation that Shamir might advance elections rather than wait for November 1992, to benefit from Likud's popularity. Baker visited the region repeatedly, trying to sew together a peace conference that both Israelis and Arabs could abide. By August, the American secretary of state had succeeded, and the parties agreed to convene in Madrid on October 30. Baker had a hard time getting the parties to agree on who would attend the conference. In the end, he sided with Israel with regard to the Palestinian contingent: The Palestinians would have to be part of a joint Palestinian-Jordanian delegation and there would be no PLO-affiliated delegates among the Palestinians.

Realizing that Shamir and the Likud were comfortably ahead in the polls, Labor became convinced that the party needed a shot in the arm. Perhaps it was time to push both Peres and Rabin out and let the younger generation take over. Neither Peres nor Rabin liked that idea. One member of that younger generation, Knesset member Avraham Burg, quipped: "Fifty percent in the Labor Party want Peres, fifty percent want Rabin, and 100 percent don't want either." Jokes would not help. Solid political talent among the younger generation would have, but that was sorely missing. No one among the generation of Labor politicians in their mid-40s or early 50s had emerged as a credible successor to Rabin and Peres.

By the summer of 1991, Rabin sensed that events were working in his favor. Labor needed a new identity, and Rabin sensed that he could supply it. Helping Rabin enormously, the Likud made a series of crucial political errors. One was to overlook the growing popularity over the issue of electoral reform. What Rabin liked about the reforms was the opportunity it gave Labor not to go running after the religious parties, in essence "bribing" them for their joining a Labor-led coalition. "The present system does not allow a prime minister to take clear-cut decisions. All it does is to make the Haredim [Ultra-Orthodox] the kingmakers of Israel." Rabin had learned an unforgettable lesson from the 'Smelly Exercise' that the Ultra-Orthodox, allowed to play the role of kingmaker, would side with Shamir. "When they look to heaven and to their voters, they'll never bring us up and bring the Likud down. I am finished with the strategy adopted by the Labor Party over the past three or four years, the running after the ultra-orthodox parties trying to woo them with legislation and money. It was a tragic mistake and it failed... If the Ultra-Orthodox hold the balance of power, they will always go with the Likud."[160] Still disgruntled with Shamir's indifference to the peace process, Rabin said that if he became prime minister again, he would go back to the process that had been cut-off in March 1990 with the US, Egypt, and Israel focusing on the Palestinians in the territories. Saddam Hussein's defeat had deflated Palestinian expectations, he believed, and he wanted to exploit that.[161] At first Shamir thought he could exploit the Madrid Peace Conference and the glowing aftermath that was sure to follow by advancing elections, but he shelved the idea, worried that that the public would conclude that he was desperate.

The Likud's political deterioration began in the autumn of 1991. It happened over Israel's asking the US for $10 billion

---

160. 'Leave Syria to the End', interview with Yitzhak Rabin, *The Jerusalem Report*, July 4, 1991, p.17

161. Ibid

in loan guarantees after the Gulf War to aid Soviet newcomers in finding jobs and housing; the US had asked Shamir to postpone the request until September 1. When Israel raised the request at that date, Bush found it unthinkable that the US would provide this gift, after serving as the honest broker who had brought about the Madrid Peace Conference. The Arabs would be furious. Bush devised a ploy that would enable him to avoid giving Israel the guarantees. He made an offer that he knew they would refuse: He told the Israelis they could have the loan guarantees on the condition that they freeze Jewish settlement in the occupied territories. Bush was not surprised when Shamir rejected such linkage. With Americans looking inward and increasingly less interested in poring huge sums into Israel, Israelis felt that it made little sense to endanger the brittle US-Israeli relationship even further. They blamed Shamir for driving a wedge between Jerusalem and Washington diplomacy as the Madrid conference was about to convene.

When the Arabs and Israelis gathered in Madrid at the end of October 1991, despite the fact that it was more a media circus than a diplomatic meeting, despite the fact that the opening speeches were filled with rancor, the simple truth was that for the first time in the history of the Arab-Israeli conflict, all of the parties were seated around a peace table seemingly ready to do business. Indeed, the road to peace still seemed long and paved with huge obstacles. Yet the parties had made a start and the spirit of Madrid was tangible. Madrid proved a political boon to the prime minister as public opinion polls showed that Labor would win no more than 22 Knesset seats to the Likud's 37 if election were held in the near future.

As the year 1991 ended, another Rabin-Peres leadership contest loomed, set for February 1992. This time Rabin appeared to have the advantage over his rival. All registered Labor Party members, not just the Labor Party Central Committee, would be voting this time. Survey showed Rabin highly popular within the Labor rank-and-file. Peres's image among Laborites appeared in decline. To blunt the damage from those in Labor who had tired from his feud with Peres, Rabin sought to take the high road, attacking Shamir and the Likud and not Peres. Rabin attacked Shamir aggressively for opposing electoral reform, a sure indication that he was afraid of letting large numbers vote.

Shamir remained cool to early elections but when the small right-wing party, Tehiya, on January 15, 1992, announced that it was quitting the government coalition over concern that Shamir might be moving too fast on the peace front, early elections were a near certainty. Another small right-wing party, Moledet, followed suit, leaving Shamir with only 59 Knesset seats. Leaders of those two parties accused Shamir of sanctioning Palestinian autonomy, which would eventually give the Palestinians their own state. Rabin was thrilled at the turn of events. He wanted early elections and he wanted them as quickly as possible. They would be good for him and good for the nation. As Rabin put it, "We can't afford to wait until things get worse. This is the only country we have." To Rabin's great chagrin, for a few days it appeared that Peres might try to form an alternative Government, an idea that was anathema to Rabin. The last thing Rabin wanted when he ran against Peres in the party's leadership contest was for Peres to be prime minister! Accordingly, Labor Party politicians, spearheaded by Rabin, joined with the Likud in advancing the balloting to June 1992. Now that Labor and Likud would compete in an election within six months, the next step for Rabin was to defeat Peres in the February 19 Labor Party primary, that would decide who would be Labor's candidate for prime minister in the forthcoming elections.

CHAPTER THIRTEEN

ISRAEL IS WAITING FOR RABIN

Ever since 1977, Yitzhak Rabin had been waiting for this moment, the moment when he would make a serious bid to compensate for the pain caused by the bank account scandal. The forthcoming primary contest gave him the chance to unseat Shimon Peres. Rabin's future was on the line in the primary contest. A victory over Peres would place him in command of the party and give him the chance to become prime minister again. A defeat would put fresh pressure on him to declare that he would no longer challenge anyone for the party's leadership.

Early in the campaign, Rabin chose to adhere to the policy of not attacking Peres. Tormenting Labor Party voters with a reprise of the struggle could backfire. Rabin understood all too well that the party was sick and tired of the Rabin-Peres rivalry. Had most members had their way, they would have let younger politicians take over. So Rabin would skip the old animosities, he would avoid mention of his memoirs, the scalding toward Peres, and concentrate on attacking the Likud and Yitzhak Shamir.

It was not at all that he had changed his mind about Peres. The new primary election system brought massive uncertainty within the Labor Party. Its proponents contended that only by expanding the Labor Party's membership would the party be able to reinvigorate itself and create a new electable identity. When the membership drive began in November 1990, and 150,000 people registered for the Labor Party, even Rabin found the expanded party frightening for its uncertainty; but his loyalists in the party convinced him that the membership drive was the spark that would produce his victory. Holding the upper hand seemingly, Rabin had to maneuver deftly in the campaign, as the country was searching for new leadership, but with a rightward cast.

Only Rabin among Labor leaders could play to the right as both the Lebanon War and the Intifada had helped to turn him into a pseudo-ally of prime minister Shamir, an uneasy alliance at best, but one that served to strengthen Rabin's image as an anchor of the political right. He still favored territorial compromise with Jordan over the West Bank; he still opposed negotiating with the PLO or allowing the Palestinians to establish their own state. Peres, meanwhile, was being branded as a dove, a pejorative label in a country that sometimes seemed to possess a majority from the political right. Labor Party members believed that Peres had slipped over to the political left, that while he mouthed right-wing positions, he was privately telling acquaintances that a Palestinian entity was not out of the question; that Israel might one day have to negotiate with the PLO.

Though the odds seemed to favor Rabin, he worried that once again Peres would triumph. On January 9, he spoke to

600 supporters in Tel Aviv's Bnei Brith Hall. In an obvious dig at Peres, Rabin noted that being prime minister for him is not an obsession but only an option as he had already served in this post and had been defense minister, chief of staff, and ambassador to Washington. Buoyed by the surveys in the midst of the primary race, Rabin's innate pessimism gave way to a new optimism. He sensed that he was getting his message across.

However, financially, Rabin felt at a disadvantage. Peres appeared to be spending far more money to woo voters. Rabin relied on large numbers of volunteers; on direct mailings. Appearing before small Labor audiences, Rabin discovered that people cared deeply about socio-economic issues, even more so than about Rabin's special expertise of national security affairs. Hence, Rabin learned a valuable lesson at an early stage of campaigning: Israeli voters had become preoccupied with improving their economic lot. Still concerned about Arab-Israeli issues, they no longer wanted their prime minister to dismiss economic problems as secondary to the Arab-Israeli conflict. Unemployment was too high, Soviet immigrants were suffering too much, young people just out of the army were finding it too tough to find jobs.

For someone as popular as Rabin was, he rarely responded by showing much warmth on the campaign trail. It was just not part of his personality. His campaign manager Ephraim Sneh knew that Rabin was not Mr. Warmth. He was not going to wade into a crowd and kiss babies. Talking to voters, Rabin was awkward, giving the impression that he could not wait to escape the premises. The campaign exacted a physical toll, Rabin eventually lost his voice. Doctors urged him to curtail his speaking engagements temporarily.

He could not do that, but he did give up smoking, promising himself to return to the habit once his voice was back.

If Rabin used kid gloves on Peres, his supporters did not. They sought to brand Peres a loser, Government in March 1990. Rabin, on the other hand, had been a good prime minister during the very critical post-Yom Kippur War; he had started the peace process with Egypt; had lowered inflation; and had made important gains in housing and education. Peres, campaigning tirelessly, toured the country, seeing as many as 1,000 people a day. At night he showed up at five or six campaign rallies.

This time around, Rabin was a more polished politician. He avoided nasty jabs at Peres. He even surprised political reporters by announcing "that he would be glad to work with Peres after the primaries;" that he would make sure he had a senior cabinet post were he (Rabin) to form the next Government.

The Labor primary was set for February 19, 1992. Rabin was up by 7:30 am talking on the phone with regional campaign leaders and workers, urging them to put in a hard day's work. To win the primary contest outright that evening, a candidate needed over 40 percent of the vote. If no one attained that percentage, a run-off would be held between the candidates coming in first and second, almost certainly Rabin and Peres. Peres hoped desperately for a second round. It seemed his only chance of winning. In the first round, four candidates would be running: Rabin, Peres, Ora Namir, and Yisrael Kessar.

Tension ran high that evening. Rabin hovered near the crucial 40 percent mark, always a few percentage points ahead of Peres. At one point, Rabin had 39.99 per cent! It was clear that he had done better than Peres; it was not clear whether there would have to be a run-off. Then the final results were announced and Rabin had just squeaked by with 40.59 percent of the vote; Peres had 34.80 percent; Kessar; 18.77 percent; and Namir, 5.44 percent. Pundits said later that Rabin owed his triumph to Kessar. Had Kessar not joined the race, Peres would have won.

Rabin had done it. He had wrested power from Shimon Peres. He became the Labor Party leader after fifteen years of waiting. He became Labor's candidate for prime minister. Rabin, not Peres, would take his party into the forthcoming national elections against Yitzhak Shamir and the Likud. The next day, February 20, Rabin moved into Peres's office at Labor Party headquarters. Soon thereafter, Rabin made his first appearance as Labor Party head at the Knesset Labor Party faction meeting. Pere was absent. Labor smelled victory on June 23. Rabin was heading the ticket and Labor had a new identity. No longer was it the party that chose its leaders and Knesset members in backrooms and kept the selection process from the general membership. Now it appeared democratic, revitalized, and eager for its members to participate in its crucial decisions. Later that spring the Labor Party chose its list of candidates for the Knesset using the same primary system. The results gave Labor a younger, more energetic look. On the eve of the 1988, election only one Labor Knesset member (Haim Ramon) had been under the age of 50. Labor now had six candidates in their 30s and 18 in their 40s.

Shamir and his allies had prayed for a Peres victory in the Labor primaries. They had already run against him four times and done very well. He was a known quantity. Throughout the 80s, the Likud had painted Shimon Peres as a dangerous dove, ready to sell the country out to the Arabs. Israelis had bought the description. Israelis knew the new Labor Party leader as a hardliner, a tough soldier and commander, a no-nonsense type.

Ironically, the Likud was facing an uphill fight. The country had become a modern consumer society during the Likud years and the Likud should have been able to benefit from this growing affluence. Israelis were buying more cars, more video players, travelling abroad more. The Likud could also have taken credit for an immense change in the country's diplomatic standing: The end of the Cold War and the indications that a Middle East peace process might be developing had created new opportunities for the Jewish State. In the second half of the 1980s, Israel's trade had doubled and 35 countries, including Russia, China, and India, had established diplomatic relations with the Jewish State. And beginning in 1989, 400,000 Jewish immigrants had arrived so that by the spring of 1992, they made up nearly 10 percent of the Jewish population of Israel. All of these factors should have brought another Likud triumph.

Yet the Likud had come to symbolize a party that rigidly clung to the past; that was against change; that would not change even when it was good for the country, even when a majority wanted it. In fact, Israel was growing less comfortable with rigid ideologies, whether political or religious, it was more and more fatigued with its conflict with the Arabs. Israelis wanted the good life, and did not see why they had to postpone that good life for another fifty years. If the early heroes of Israel were Ben-Gurion, Dayan, Golda Meir, today new heroes had emerged, head of Israel's high-tech firms and the like.

While some argued that there were no palpable differences between Rabin and Shamir, most of the country sensed that there were in fact important distinctions in their political outlooks. Were Shamir to win reelection, he would unquestionably feel he had a mandate to keep the peace process on low boil, and to continue to defy president George Bush over Jewish settlements. A Shamir victory, in short, would most likely mean a continuation of the strained relations between Washington and Jerusalem. Rabin, as prime minister, would inevitably draw the United States and Israel together.

Contributing much to Labor's new, positive image was the orderly, harmonious manner of the February 19 primary election. The contrast with the Likud was dramatic. The very next day, the Likud chose its leader, not by a primary system, but by a vote of its Central Committee. The three-way race pitted Shamir against foreign minister David Levy and housing minister Ariel Sharon. Shamir emerged the winner, collecting 46 percent of the vote to Levy's 31 percent; and Sharon's 20 percent. Shamir's failure to win more than 50 percent was considered a setback and indicative of his faltering stance.

Shamir entered the election campaign a hobbled prime minister. Israelis had grown uneasy about his preoccupation with the expansion of Jewish settlement in the occupied territories. The year 1991 had been a boom year for the settlers: Between 1967 and 1990 only 20,000 housing units had been built; yet in 1991, 13,000 housing units were built. Moreover, the government had spent over $1 billion – fully 15 percent of its non-military budget – for housing, roads, schools, and industrial development for the Jewish settlers. In that year, Shamir's government had approved 14 new settlements in the occupied lands.

Shamir's tangling with president Bush over the $10 billion in loan guarantees had disheartened Israelis as well. Many applauded his firmness; even Rabin acknowledged that had he been in Shamir's shoes, he would have refused to cave in to Bush's demand to freeze Jewish settlements as the price for the loans. Israel's embroilment with Washington, however, left Israelis feeling insecure: The man blamed for the deteriorating relations was Shamir. Israelis were turning against Shamir and the Likud, however, for more fundamental reasons. The country was increasingly eager for a negotiated settlement of its differences with the Palestinians, Jordan, Syria, and Lebanon. And yet Shamir and his Likud colleagues seemed to discredit the Madrid peace process. Moreover, the Likud's leaders seemed uninspiring, more prone to bickering among themselves than demonstrating political leadership. In contrast with Labor, Likud made few changes in its Knesset list: Still dominating its leadership were Shamir, defense minister Moshe Arens, foreign minister David Levy, and housing minister Ariel Sharon. None of these four commanded a large following among the general public. Rabin defeated all four in popularity polls easily.

Public opinion surveys continued to put Labor out in front. The trouble was that those same surveys had given Labor an advantage early in the election campaigns of the 1980s, but the election results differed from the polls. Labor remained cautiously optimistic. Rabin understood that in attempting to sound more flexible on peacemaking than Shamir, he could not afford to give the impression that he was soft on national security. If Israelis were growing tired of Shamir, they still wanted their prime minister to protect them. Thus, Rabin wrote in *The Jerusalem Post* on June 1, 1992: "I am unwilling to give up a single inch of Israel's security, but I am willing to give up many inches of... territories as well as the 1,700,000 Arab inhabitants for the sake of peace. That is the whole doctrine in a nutshell. We seek a territorial compromise, which will bring peace and security. A lot of security."

It occurred to Labor Party strategists early on that their greatest electoral asset was Yitzhak Rabin himself. For years, Israelis had been conditioned to vote for parties, not personalities. Never before had a political party in Israel used the personality of its candidate for prime minister as the focus of its vote-getting strategy. Even when such luminaries as David Ben- Gurion, Golda Meir, and Menachem Begin had headed their parties' Knesset lists, campaign strategies had made the political party the centerpiece of their campaigns. This time, however, Labor's strategists wanted to exploit the fact that the public tended to blame the major political parties, Labor and Likud, for all the nation's ailments; and to take advantage of Rabin's great personal popularity.

By propelling the hardline Rabin forward, the strategists were confident that they could expunge Labor's long-standing leftist image. They did worry, however, that focusing solely on Rabin and not Labor might expose the Party to charges that it was running a one-man show and might expose Rabin to personal attacks. They also worried that, because he lacked charisma, concentrating him might backfire. To accentuate Rabin, the strategists took a number of unusual steps. The most dramatic being: For the first time Labor used the slogan 'Labor under Rabin' on the ballot, rather than just 'Labor'. Peres said sarcastically: "Maybe you want to remove the word Labor." One of the cleverest steps was the campaign jingle, 'The People Are Waiting for

Rabin' with its not-so-subtle associations with the glorious days of the 1967 Six-Day War. Egypt's Nasser had once said that "If Rabin wants to attack me, I'm waiting for him." That led to the classic Six-Day War tune, 'Nasser Is Waiting for Rabin'.

A huge banner with a picture of Rabin was draped outside Labor Party headquarters on HaYarkon Street in Tel Aviv. At Labor Party celebrations marking the 25th anniversary of Israel's conquest of Jerusalem (on May 31), Rabin, the former chief of staff whose army captured East Jerusalem, including the Old City and the Western Wall, was put in the spotlight, reenacting his famous "march" into the Old City on June 7, 1967. In Labor's newspaper advertising, Rabin's photo appeared prominently as it did on the party's television election propaganda; not a day passed in the final three weeks of the campaign without Rabin making a television appearance. Labor was barely mentioned in the election advertising. In television commercials, it was Yitzhak Rabin, the triumphant chief of staff in 1967, forger of the Sinai interim peace agreement with Egypt in 1975, hero of Entebbe, the man who took Israel out of Lebanon in 1985. Everything was done to get across the image of Rabin as leader.

Ordinarily, Labor would have used photographs of its other leading candidates. Not this time. The thrust of Labor's advertising was to make the voter trust Rabin to provide maximum security. According to his campaign aides, Rabin did not allow the development of the "personality cult" to affect him. At first, he was concerned that Labor politicians would be offended. When he saw that the tactic was accepted by most, Rabin relaxed. Gad Ben-Ari, who spent each day of the campaign with the candidate and served as his spokesman, recalled: "Rabin would be sitting in the car and looking at his photo across the street. He would be listening to the jingle all the time. Such things might have inflated someone's ego. It didn't touch him at all. It wasn't that he didn't believe he should be master of the house. But he saw all of this as sheer technique."[162] Pretty soon, everyone got the message. Campaign rallies, music blasting, colorful signs of Rabin held high conveyed the centrality of Rabin in the campaign.

To win the election, to be able to form the next government, Rabin figured that he needed six more Knesset seats than the 55 Labor had won in the previous election in 1988. With that number he could avoid sharing power with the Likud in another National Unity Government, something he did not want. Labor had thrust personality into the foreground, not only to exalt Rabin to legendary proportions, but also to pour calumny on the pitiful figure of Shamir. If Rabin could do no wrong, Shamir could do no right. Rather than go into specifics about what he would do as prime minister, Rabin kept to generalities, saying mostly that he planned to correct the distortions and mistakes of the Shamir Government; to redirect national resources away from Jewish settlement, using those resources for jobs and housing for Russian immigrants, reducing unemployment, helping the economy to grow.

If Labor wanted to project Rabin as the personal center of its campaign, Likud would oblige by attacking him personally. The most emotional Likud charge; that Rabin, on the eve of the 1967 Six-Day War, had suffered a nervous breakdown. As early as 1977, Rabin had discussed the

---

162. Gad Ben-Ari, interview with author, July 24, 1992

issue publicly. His first public explanation was an interview with the author for this book at that time. It did not matter to the Likud that the public had not held Rabin's collapse against him in subsequent years. It went after Rabin as if the collapse had taken place a few days earlier. Towards the end of May, Likud strategists released balloons which said, "25th anniversary of the Collapse" into the Tel Aviv skies to remind voters that Rabin was unfit to govern. Rabin's strategists, mindful that the Likud had raised the "collapse" issue early in the campaign rather than at the end when it might have proven more effective, were buoyed, believing that the Likud was showing signs of panic.

Significantly, the Likud did not play up the bank-account scandal of 1977, sensing that people had forgiven Rabin. Gad Ben-Ari gleefully explained that "what people remembered about the bank-account affair is the scene of Rabin, the gentleman, who took personal responsibility for a technical mistake by his wife and was willing to step down and willing to give up so much."[163] Rabin, however, brought the scandal up on his own, suggesting that his behavior, in its wake, should become a role model for how politicians who make mistakes should act. "In the Likud no one resigned because of issues that were far more harsh and serious than this dollar account. I resigned then, from the post of prime minister, because I made a mistake and when you make mistakes you have to draw conclusions." A reporter asked him if he was sorry now (fifteen years later) that he had resigned. Rabin replied, "I was then very satisfied with my decision. That is how a public figure has to behave."[164]

---

163. Ibid

164. Benyamin Ben-Eliezer, interview with author, August 9, 1992

The Likud charged Rabin with being an alcoholic. Many Israelis, having listened to rumors over the years, had taken for granted that Rabin was a heavy drinker. He was certainly no teetotaler; anyone who had seen him at receptions could attest to that. The fact was, however, that no one could pinpoint any one day when Rabin's drinking had affected his abilities as a public servant. Again, the Likud believed that it could gain some political mileage from the rumors. Likud Party activists passed out paper cups and car stickers on which was written, "Better to have a sober prime minister than a drunk one." They chanted to Rabin: "Go home and have a cognac, and get some sleep."

The period of these personal attacks was anguishing for Rabin. "It was a tough week," recalled campaign spokesman Gad Ben-Ari. "He didn't say a word. He was tense. He took it hard. The collapse charge bothered him more than the alcoholism because the collapse took place. The drinking never took place. He said that was nonsense. We considered (but rejected doing) all kinds of things against Shamir. We had things on him... He gave an interview to *Yediot Aharonot*. People loved it... He didn't ignore the accusations. He addressed the charges very openly. That made him very human. They forgave him."[165] Rabin was worried that the voters would punish him and that the good crowds and strong showings in the surveys would disappear. His campaign staff went into the most diehard of Likud political bastions to get a quick readout of how the headlines were playing. What they found pleased them. Labor strategists were surprised to find that the charges against the candidate had actually helped him with voters.

---

165. Gad Ben-Ari, interview with author, July 24, 1992

Still the charges hurt. Angered by the alcoholism charge, Leah Rabin told an interviewer on Israel Radio on May 21 that "when her husband arrives home, he doesn't drink. The bottle can stand days without him touching it. And if he drinks one glass from time to time, this does not make him an alcoholic." When a reporter asked him outright, did he drink, he answered, "Like everyone else, a glass here or there."

Rabin's strategists eventually decided to focus their attacks on Shamir personally. They had planned to make Likud corruption the centerpiece of their election strategy in the closing days, but then switched to the prime minister as their main target. In striking contrast with Labor's focusing on Rabin, the Likud downplayed its own candidate for prime minister. If Rabin's photo was seen everywhere, it was difficult to find Shamir's.

The public's warm response to Rabin had its effect on him. Uncharacteristically, he smiled a great deal. He shook hands more. He was more cheerful. It was not easy for him; he was no born campaigner. Rabin disliked physical contact with street crowds. Campaigning at the Ramat Gan shopping center, Rabin came across a woman with a baby. Spokesman Ben-Ari whispered to Rabin that he should do something with the baby; it would make a good photo for the next day's newspapers. "Anyone else would have jumped at the opportunity," recalled Ben-Ari, "not Rabin. He simply refused. He didn't like to get beyond the edge, to do gimmicks."[166] Yet he was clearly pleased that so many people greeted him around the country. Getting crowds in the thousands buoyed him. He sought out Likud bastions despite

---

166. Ibid

the possibility that he would encounter hostile crowds. On May 11, Rabin went to Hatikvah quarter of Tel Aviv where Labor had received only seven percent of the vote, last time. He was well received. Gratified, he told his aides: "They aren't throwing tomatoes at me. That's a good sign." Once, after visiting the large Jewish town of Ma'ale Adumim where the Likud believed it would do well, a television reporter asked him, if he felt Ma'ale Adumim was with him? "No," Rabin answered honestly, "I don't deceive myself. But our purpose is to go to those places where we didn't have great results in the past."

Each night, Rabin arrived home after midnight. All he had the strength to say to Leah was, "The feeling is good, excellent. The rallies are great. But how it will be translated at the polls, we'll have to see." That was Yitzhak Rabin, the born pessimist, speaking. If things were going well for Labor, they were proving disastrous for the Likud. Shamir, on a helicopter trip to Beersheba for a campaign rally, was confronted by a group of protesters with banners that read: "Shamir hates Moroccans. We're all Moroccans here." The group began chanting, "Rabin, King of Israel." Shamir lost his cool and called the hecklers "terrorists." Flying back from Beersheba, Shamir told a reporter that he had never been heckled like that before. When told the hecklers had voted Likud last time round, Shamir muttered, "Impossible, impossible."

One highlight of the campaign was the television debate between Rabin and Shamir a week before the June 23 election. It was taped on the morning of June 16 then shown on television that evening. With large numbers of voters apparently still undecided, the performances of the two candidates seemed of critical importance. Though his aides pressed him to run some simulations of the debate, Rabin declined, saying: "I am not an actor. I am who I am." Shamir had been coached carefully, and told to smile as much as possible apparently to present an image of a leader unburdened by the great problems facing Israel. Moments after the debate ended, Rabin phoned Leah to seek out her opinion: "Well, what do you say?" She replied: "You were excellent, simply wonderful." Polls taken afterward suggested that the country was split over who won.

Sometimes Rabin would encounter bitterness. Some Israelis, for instance, still held his behavior during the Intifada against him. While Rabin was on a campaign visit to the Red Sea resort town of Eilat, a youngster looked into the candidate's eyes and declared, "I want an answer to only one thing: Why didn't you stand behind those soldiers who under your command broke hands and legs? Why did you abandon them?" The crowd grew tense, but Rabin stayed calm, answering firmly: "I didn't use the expression 'break the hands or feet.' It is correct. There was an order to beat when there were riots. But there was no order to take citizens from their homes and beat them. Whoever did that was punished. There were all in all four cases like this." The youngster replied that Rabin had answered him but he did not accept the answer. Rabin still shook his hand.

In the final hours before Election Day, Tuesday, June 23, an air of excitement crept into the Rabin household. On the Friday afternoon before, speaking engagements had robbed Rabin of his voice. He kept his smoking to a minimum. Exhausted, he slept late Saturday morning, rather than visit their frequent Saturday haunt, the Accadia Hotel in Herzliya, where and he and Leah hit tennis balls each week. The Rabin children stayed close. Dalia was now a prosecutor for the Tel Aviv District Court. Yuval, who worked for a company that marketed Israeli software in the United States, arrived at the last minute from North Carolina, where he had been living. The campaign wound down to Monday, June 22. The mood within the Rabin camp was upbeat. When he arrived at the Cinerama theatre in Tel Aviv for a last-minute campaign rally, Rabin was received like a pop star. Afterwards, Rabin travelled to a meeting with former Likud supporters in the Hatikvah quarter of Tel Aviv.

In marked contrast, Yitzhak Shamir avoided the campaign trail. Trailing in the polls, the prime minister became subject to all sorts of wild proposals from campaign aides to do something dramatic that might attract voters. No one was terribly specific. Someone suggested that Shamir seek another round of peace talks. To all such ideas, he shrugged his shoulders. He was in no mood for grand gestures. Described by one aide as "a bit tense," he spent the last day of the campaign in his Jerusalem office making phone calls to campaign staff. Aides advised Shamir to make a spontaneous appearance at an open-air market in a major city to make one last major bid for votes before campaign officially halted at 7 pm Monday. He told a reporter why should he bother campaigning, he was sure the Likud would form the new Government. He went home for lunch at 1 pm, and then took his daily two-hour nap. He returned to the office at 4, made calls to party activists, and then went home for the night at 8 pm.

Meanwhile, Rabin was on the move. He made a frenetic helicopter tour of the country on his last day. The polls mostly forecast a Labor victory, but no one thought a landslide would occur either way. Arriving home on election eve, Rabin worried that the Likud would benefit from having put in a lot of effort in the past few days.

At 10 pm, June 23, Israelis were glued to their television sets. Here was Haim Yavin, the Israel Television anchorman, announcing that the polls had closed and that he was about to announce the results of Israel TV's exit poll, which had proven accurate in the past. Yavin uttered the next few words, knowing the impact they would have on the entire nation. His voice trembled as he spoke: "We have the exit poll results and they tell of an upheaval." He had used the Hebrew word *mahapach*; Rabin had won 47 Knesset seats to only 33 for the Likud. Meretz, the new amalgam of three left-wing parties, had mustered 13 seats, meaning that Labor and Meretz commanded 60 seats, an incredibly high figure, more than pollsters had given them during the campaign. Rabin would need only one more Knesset seat to form a government. If the actual balloting confirmed the exit polls, the small religious parties, particularly Shas and the United Torah Judaism Front, would inevitably come running to join Rabin's new government. Trying to take in the meaning of the upheaval was Yitzhak Rabin. He and his family were at home in Tel Aviv that tense evening. Rabin wanted as little company as possible before the exit poll results were announced. The only ones there were the immediate members of the Rabin family: Leah, their two children Dalia and Yuval, and the three grandchildren.

Leah burst into tears. Suddenly, she felt that history had corrected the "evil" done to them in 1977. Neighbors began shouting for joy, Rabin sat quietly. The family walked up to him, hugging and kissing him. He appeared dazed, but still exuding a certain caution. He wanted to hear the actual results before celebrating. Friends streamed in. So did press photographers. The phone did not stop ringing.

Over at the Dan Hotel, Labor Party's election night headquarters, pandemonium had broken out; lots of hugs and kisses, and cries of "Rabin, Rabin, Rabin." Bottles of champagne were quickly opened. The Labor Party jingle played loudly in the background, and everyone was waiting for the appearance of the new prime minister elect. Rabin played it cool. He did not want to come to the hotel too early, before it was definite that Labor was going to win. After all, the cheers and laughter were based on an exit poll.

At 11:20 pm, Peres walked into the Dan Hotel headquarters. He tried to put on a good face. Though he might wind up foreign minister, he had reason to feel sad. Still, he acted like a team player. "It's the best that could have happened to the State of Israel," he proclaimed. As the hours unfolded, the actual election results showed that the exit poll was on the mark. Rabin left his apartment for the Dan Hotel. Photographers continued to snap pictures of the prime minister-designate. Over at the Dan Hotel, the place was exploding with joy. Loyalists sang: "Israel is waiting for Rabin. Israel is waiting for Rabin." Over and over, the campaign jingle was played, deafening the ears. Everyone was singing. Television recorded the scene, the smiles and the tears, live. The prime minister-designate walked into the hall. The cheers rose a few more decibels.

Labor Party politicians wondered whether Rabin might surprise everyone by announcing that he planned to set up a Government at once with Meretz and whomever else would like to join. Others thought he would wait and leave his options for coalition partners open. Rabin had informed his close advisers that night that he was in no hurry. He did not want to make mistakes due to haste.

His first words signaled that he intended to take charge, and stay in charge. As leader, he told the party faithful, he had to shoulder all the responsibility and therefore he should have commensurate authority. "I will lead the coalition negotiations," he said in his deep voice, "and I will appoint the Cabinet ministers. The days of political blackmail are over." On the surface, the statement seemed banal. Of course he would be in charge. Yet, reading between the lines, one sensed that Rabin was really saying, "No one will sabotage me this time. No one will interfere with my prime ministership. Not Shimon Peres. Not the religious parties, no one. I will run my own show."

After Rabin spoke, he went upstairs to a hotel room. Shimon Sheves, his aide, worked the phones, arranging meetings with potential coalition partners for the next morning. Rabin arrived back home by 2 am. The first thing Leah said to the prime minister-designate was: "You worked very hard and you earned the victory honestly." Over at Metzudat Ze'ev, the Likud headquarters in Tel Aviv, Likud leaders sat gloomily. No one moved, no one agreed to be interviewed. Each politician appeared catatonic. They had expected to lose, but not by this much. Meanwhile, seated in front of a television set at his suite in the Tel Aviv Hilton, Yitzhak Shamir looked ill. His face had tightened into a sullen glare. He seemed stunned, utterly depressed and confused. Twelve minutes before 10 pm, Dr. Yossi Olmert, the head of the Government Press Office, had informed him that the exit poll would spell disaster for the Likud. He said nothing, though he grimaced, as if someone had tried to strike him.

To waiting journalists, he snarled, "I don't have to confess in front of anyone."

Shamir never formally conceded to Rabin, nor did he pick up the phone to him. Later in the evening, he announced over Israel TV that he planned to resign both from the Likud leadership and from active political life very soon. He gave no date for such steps. His voice a hoarse whisper, Shamir explained, "I've said this many times that I'm at the end of my road. Even if we had won, you wouldn't have seen me for a long time."

Early in the evening, some Likudniks hoped that Rabin would consider offering the Likud the chance to join a Rabin-led National Unity Government. They soon realized, however, that they were dreaming. Rabin wanted the Likud in opposition.

The final results were only known three days later (the votes of Israeli soldiers were not counted until the end of the week.) Labor had received 906,126 votes (compared with 685,363 in 1988), giving it 44 Knesset seats. That was three fewer than the exit polls had predicted. The Likud had garnered 651,219 (compared with 709,305 in 1988) for 32 seats, one fewer than the exit polls had said. Meretz had won 12 seats; Tsomet, Rafael Eitan's right-wing party, 8; the National Religious Party, 6; Shas, 6; United Torah Judaism, 4; Moledet, 3; the Democratic Front, 3; and the Arab Democratic Party, 2. Wavering Likudniks had shifted over to Labor, not in the large numbers that had been predicted earlier, but in sufficient numbers to help make a difference. It had been the vote of the Russian immigrants, however, that had been decisive for Labor, adding four Knesset seats to its margin.

All the political analysts agreed that the Rabin triumph signified the beginning of a new era in Israel. What were the elements that had brought about his triumph? The answer seemed to lie in the changing attitudes of the Israeli voter and the unique political persona of Yitzhak Rabin. For the past few years, a majority of Israelis, 65 to 70 percent, had favored territorial compromise as a means of settling the Arab-Israeli conflict, rejecting Shamir's right-wing strategy of holding on to the occupied lands at any cost. In electing Rabin, they had made clear that they wanted Shamir's firmness, but not his ideology; and they wanted peacemaking that was serious, not a charade. Rabin fit the bill. His political credentials matched what most of the voters wanted, not a dove like Peres, not an ideological zealot like Shamir, but a centrist who could stand up to the Arabs, if need be. The country had fallen in love with Rabin, not because of his charisma or charm, not because he was good at wading into crowds, kissing babies, engaging in easy conversation. In fact, he was a social neuter. The country rushed into Rabin's arms for the ironic reason that Rabin had adopted the centerpiece of the Likud platform: autonomy for the Palestinian Arabs; toughness towards the Arab troublemakers; yielding as little land as possible. That had made it more palatable for Likud supporters, disgusted with Shamir and eager to get on with the peace process, to switch allegiance and vote for Rabin. Rabin won the election also because the country had a growing fear that Shamir's tough stance toward the Americans would isolate Israel. And that seemed intolerable to most Israelis. Rabin, on the other hand, with his pro-American stance, was far more likely to tighten the Washington-Jerusalem relationship.

As outsiders saw the election, Rabin's triumph was a signal that ideology was no longer in vogue. Writing in *The New York Times*, Jerusalem correspondent Clyde Haberman noted, "The real winner [in the election] was pragmatism and the big loser uncompromising ideology. While the peace camp may have won, a true debate on peace never really got going in the campaign. And while the hardcore right wing clearly lost ground, the major gains were in the center and not on the left. In the end, Likud wore out its welcome through an incremental erosion of public faith that it possesses the vision, cohesion, integrity and competence to keep the country running... For [many Israelis], ideology has brought years of rocks and gasoline bombs in the Palestinian uprising; endless fears that the Arab street sweeper in Tel Aviv is not the hard-working man he probably is but rather a terrorist ready to pull out a knife; haunting nightmares that this will be the week that one's son in the army does not come back from the West Bank. These weary people say that if some land must be given up for peace, fine; if it means stopping a new settlement in Gaza to build a drug rehabilitation clinic in Ashdod, also fine."

Now, at the age of 70, Rabin was getting a second chance to lead the country, a second chance to push Israel toward a new direction.

CHAPTER FOURTEEN

CLOSING THE CIRCLE

The Labor Party election victory was good news around the world. It was an open secret that George Bush and James Baker had earnestly wanted a Labor victory. Indeed, their rough treatment of Yitzhak Shamir on issues ranging from Jewish settlements to the loan guarantees played no small role in Rabin's triumph. The morning after the election, government officials and editorial writers expressed delight that Israel would no longer be governed by the Shamir regime. Some American columnists who had been tough on Shamir were now beaming. Anthony Lewis of *The New York Times* was one: "In a world of disappointed expectations, the Israeli election had a transforming quality. It was as if the people of Israel had decided to turn a page of history, a page filled with bitterness, and explore the possibility of hope. Yitzhak Rabin is not a man of uplifting eloquence or vision. He is a curt ex-general whose philosophy, if it can be called that, is pragmatism. He has no zest for any ideology.

And what a difference that is. For Israel has largely been governed over the last ten years by zealots... determined to impose their ideology whatever the cost."

The euphoria was contagious. Even many Likudniks, those who had defected to Labor and those who had not, breathed in the new heady atmosphere and proclaimed that they were glad that Rabin had ascended to power, perhaps now the days of deadlock would be over. Needing no reminder of why they had turned against Shamir, Israelis still were astonished to read an interview the outgoing prime minister gave to *Maariv*, soon after the election. When Yosef Harif, the veteran political reporter, called him for a response to the Likud defeat, Shamir offered this dark prediction had his party won: "I would have conducted negotiations on autonomy for ten years, and in the meantime we would have reached half a million people in Judea and Samaria." There it was in black and white. Mr. Deadlock was confirming that his strategy had indeed been the slow, steady stall. A day or so later, Shamir vehemently claimed he had been misquoted. It hardly mattered. The quote seemed vintage Shamir. Few Israelis thought much of the Shamir strategy. His ideology had the staleness of last month's news, and so did he. Most Israelis thought little of a strategy that sought to delude the Arabs so that a half million Jews could settle in the occupied lands. Many, however, thought highly of the ostensible center of the Likud platform, granting the Palestinians autonomy. For that reason, they were delighted that Rabin might now have a chance of doing what Shamir could not, would not do: implementing the Likud's platform!

Rabin was taking over. He was no longer a candidate running an election campaign. He had a nation to lead. To

Gad Ben-Ari, Rabin suggested that the large photograph of the candidate outside Labor Party Headquarters in Tel Aviv should be quickly removed. There would be no more gimmicks.

Given this second chance to run the country, Rabin planned to make the most of it. He had turned 70 a few months earlier. Under any circumstances, he did not have a great deal of time. He could not afford to make mistakes, or to fritter away the new opportunity. No one would be permitted to get in his way, neither Shimon Peres nor the prime minister's coalition partners, neither the opposition Likud, nor the small right-wing parties. Rabin planned to rule with a firm hand. The mandate he had just received from the voters was a clear signal to Rabin, to take the country down new paths aimed at accelerating the peace process and revitalizing the economy. Rabin sensed that a window of opportunity had opened, thanks to the ending of the Cold War, the easing of the Soviet threat to the West, and the Iraq defeat in the Gulf War. Yet, that window would not be open forever. Arab states were trying to acquire nuclear weapons. Calling this a very grave and negative development, the prime minister-designate believed that this fact alone impelled Israel to try to end the Arab-Israeli conflict as quickly as possible.

The June 23 political upheaval had caused Israeli hopes to soar. "The public's expectations are sky high," Rabin told the Labor Party Central Committee on July 12. "The change or upheaval has created a new atmosphere among the public, a feeling of hope, a feeling of belief that it can be different, that it can be better." He was concerned about those expectations; he did not want to disappoint anyone. Yet to Rabin, the test of whether he would be able to deliver would come soon: The key lay in persuading president Bush to provide Israel with the $10 billion in loan guarantees. With that would come an improvement in relations with Washington; all the rest would follow.

Rabin was relaxed but ready to take charge the day after elections, when he gave his first news conference at Labor Party headquarters in Tel Aviv. Israel Radio carried the event live. The hall was still festooned with banners and flags from the previous night's celebrations. In an open-necked shirt, Rabin offered an occasional, uncharacteristic smile. Now it was time to try to implement his political program. He pledged to push for peace with the Arabs; to reorder Israel's priorities; to curb Shamir's drive to build Jewish settlements. "National resources will not be diverted to what I call political settlements," said the prime minister-designate. He wanted to be clear: He did not plan to freeze settlements entirely; he planned to support them in areas essential to Israel's security in and around Jerusalem, the Jordan Valley, and the Golan Heights. This news conference was a signal to the Americans that Rabin meant business, that Israel had turned over a new leaf. Bush should look around for his checkbook.

Rabin talked briefly about the kind of ruling coalition he hoped to establish, one that would be centrist, in keeping with his own personal viewpoint, not dependent upon any of the small parties, whether of the political left or right. He sounded optimistic that he could achieve such a goal. "I believe I can form a stable government that won't express the policies of the extreme left or those of the extreme right, but of the Israeli mainstream." (However, to one acquaintance a few days later, he confided that he had been taken aback by Meretz's strong showing. "I didn't take into account that Meretz would be the second largest party." That strong showing meant that Rabin might have to establish a left-wing government against his wishes.) A reporter asked Rabin a personal question: "Was his election victory the closing of a circle of fifteen years?" "There is something to that," Rabin allowed. As usual, he had no desire to elaborate on personal aspects of his career. That evening, Rabin went on Israel Television to assure the "victims" of his new policies, the 115,000 Jewish settlers on the West Bank, that they had no reason to fear him. He had no plans to uproot their homes. "I don't mean to dry the settlements out, but [rather] not to invest in expanding them, not to throw billions of shekels into construction." How far would the settlers go in trying to sabotage Rabin's plans? Rumors spread that some were stockpiling weapons. The threat of settler violence haunted the early days of the new Rabin regime.

The forging of a ruling coalition was most distasteful to Rabin but it had to be done: He would have preferred voters to have given the Labor Party at least 61 Knesset seats, a clear-cut parliamentary majority. Then he could have avoided bargaining with the small parties. That would have been asking a great deal. No Israeli prime minister had ever won a Knesset majority.

Meretz, with 12 Knesset seats, offered Rabin the greatest leap forward securing a governing coalition. Together, Labor and Meretz had 56 Knesset seats; add to that the support of the five Israeli Arab Knesset members, and Rabin had 61 seats, a slender majority but one that would allow his Government to function. The one snag was that Rabin had no great desire to have his coalition rest on Israeli Arab support. He turned to Shas, the Ultra-Orthodox Sephardi party, which had six Knesset members. On July 9, the prime minister-designate announced that he had a government coalition, comprising: Labor, Meretz, and Shas, 62 seats in all. Adding the five Israeli Arab Knesset members to those who supported the Government, Rabin could count on 67 votes altogether. Though he had wanted members of both the political right and left, Rabin had stitched together a coalition with a leftist tinge.

He named Shimon Peres as foreign minister and deputy prime minister. Given a choice, Rabin would have been pleased to give Peres some minor Cabinet post or none at all. But he had no choice. Peres retained a strong following in the party and could not be wished away. The two men agreed that Rabin would take charge of the autonomy talks; Peres, the multilateral peacemaking efforts. Whereas Rabin had felt constrained from speaking out against Peres's efforts to undermine his first government, this time, 15 years later, he felt no constraint. He was unquestionably the most powerful political figure in the country, towering above his party and above Peres. It was up to Peres. (On August 19, 1992, the author asked Peres whether he and Rabin had worked out any ground rules to avoid the feuding that occurred in the 1970s. Peres could have dismissed the question with a shrug of the hand. He felt compelled to reply. "The ground rules are that we both accept the rule of the majority of the party. We try not to forget that we're serving a nation, not an ego: We have to work together. There were struggles but there was a lot of cooperation, too.")

On Monday, July 13, Rabin presented his new Government and its guidelines to the Knesset for its approval. For Rabin, it was a moment of great personal triumph. The speech Rabin would make that day was one of the most important he would ever deliver. He rose to the occasion. Eitan Haber,

Rabin's spokesman during his days as defense minister in the 1980s, wrote a draft of the speech. Rabin went over it. Even Leah Rabin had had some input. Rabin wanted to strike just the right notes. He wanted to convey that his government was ready to make serious strides for peace and for economic improvement. He wanted to convey a sense of urgency. He wanted to let the Americans know that Israel was embarking on new policies and to let the Palestinian Arabs know that time was running out for them. Above all, he wanted to convey that he was prepared, indeed eager, to move in new directions.

Signaling that the peace talks were a priority for him, he invited the Jordanian-Palestinian delegation to visit him in Jerusalem for informal talks about implementing autonomy. Rabin also asserted that he was prepared to visit Arab capitals to reach a breakthrough in the stalled negotiations. The Rabin offer was greeted with indifference by the Arabs, who believed it was too early for them to see the Israeli prime minister in Jerusalem or to entertain him in their capitals. They made clear, however, that they were eager to keep the peace process alive.

The key passage in his Knesset speech was an appeal to Israelis to cease thinking that they were cut off from the world. Once they ceased such thinking, peacemaking could go forward: "No longer are we necessarily a people that dwells alone, and no longer is it true that the whole world is against us." This passage became prime minister Rabin's call to arms. It was the passage that analysts would remember and quote most often. To the Palestinians, he implored to negotiate with the goal of reaching agreement: "You will not get everything you want, neither will we. So once and for all, take your destiny in your hands. Don't lose this opportunity that may never return. Take our proposal seriously to avoid further suffering, humiliation, and grief; to end the shedding of tears and of blood. "

This was not Rabin, the 'break their bones' man, speaking. Nor was it Shamir, 'Mr. No', speaking. This was Rabin the peacemaker, exhorting the Palestinians to do business with him. What came through in Rabin's performance that day, more than anything else, was his sense of ease and comfort at being in charge. Yosef Goel of *The Jerusalem Post* wrote a few days later: "The new government's most impressive feature so far is undoubtedly Prime Minister Rabin himself. Without question, he is fully in charge of his own government and party; he has finally mastered the switch from army commander to national and party leader."

From the moment he became prime minister on July 13, Rabin was a man in a hurry. He could not act fast enough. Seemingly ubiquitous, he moved in a hundred directions at once and he had good reason. He knew that the same voters who had tired of the Likud could turn sour on Labor, if they did not find concrete improvements resulting from the June 23 upheaval. Two days after the election, Rabin warned himself and his party: "If we don't show tangible socio-economic progress in the first six months, we can expect a public lashing." He felt the same way toward peacemaking. Hence, he pledged repeatedly that the Palestinians could achieve an autonomy agreement in under a year, if they wished. Happy to not have to deal with Shamir, the Palestinians put aside their loathing of the architect of Israel's putdown of the Intifada and made noises that appeared to suggest they were ready to negotiate. Ending the Intifada, placating the Palestinian Arabs, giving them a political stature that would satisfy their thirst for independence, would not be easy. Many believed that Rabin had it in him to achieve these goals.

No one voiced it better than Henry Kissinger, the former American secretary of state: "Israel has no better analytical mind than Yitzhak Rabin. If any of his interlocutors are counting on influencing him by charm or legalistic skill, they are heading for disillusionment. Small talk is not his forté; personal charm not his specialty. Redundancy taxes his patience; the commonplace does not capture his attention. He is as tenacious as he is intelligent. American and Arab leaders are not likely to find Mr. Rabin a jolly companion on their journey through the thickets of Middle East diplomacy. But he is relentless in separating the chaff from what is essential. These qualities will now stand him in good stead, for the protagonists' need to disenthrall themselves from the attitudes that have produced the impasse."

Rabin's prime ministership had gotten to a running start. It turned out that someone in Washington was waiting for Rabin impatiently. No sooner had he been sworn in when a phone call came for the brand-new prime minister, from the White House. President George Bush was on the line. Rabin grabbed the phone at his desk in his Knesset office a floor below the plenary. Bush told Rabin he was sending James Baker to the Middle East to get the ball rolling again. This was what Rabin had wanted to hear. He had wanted action. He got it. He was under no illusions. His ascendancy to power was only part of the reason the president was acting so kindly. The other was the tough election fight that Bush faced that autumn against Arkansas's governor Bill Clinton. Bush had more news. He invited Rabin to visit him at his summer home at Kennebunkport, Maine, in August, quite a coup considering how few foreign leaders received a presidential invitation to the Maine summer quarters. Rabin smiled. Kennebunkport in August; the loan guarantees could not be far away.

Rabin had been in office only briefly when Israeli troops sealed off the campus of An-Najah, the largest university in the West Bank, located in Nablus. Palestinian students had been voting in student council elections inside the school; the IDF contended that six armed Palestinians had entered the school and were trying to influence the elections. Soldiers wanted to seek out the gunmen, but the students refused to submit to IDF searches. A standoff ensued as the Israeli soldiers debated whether to storm the building. The inevitable bloodshed would have had a grave impact on Rabin's early days in office and would have seriously marred the forthcoming visit of American secretary of state Baker, scheduled for July 19. But Rabin worked behind the scenes to end the confrontation peacefully. A compromise was reached that sent the six wanted students to exile in Jordan; in exchange, the IDF agreed to pull back its forces from the school. The peaceful resolution seemed to augur good things for the new Rabin administration.

During his first week in office, Rabin's Government announced that it was freezing all new building in the occupied territories. This was what Bush and Baker had wanted to hear from Shamir and had not. Now it seemed the path was being cleared for the Americans to give Israel those loan guarantees. Jewish settlers reacted angrily to the freeze; they called it a declaration of war and said they would behave as one did in war, an implied threat of violence.

Sitting down with Rabin in Jerusalem, Baker liked what he heard, that the prime minister was suspending housing contracts in the occupied areas. The secretary of state responded positively, saying that he was pleased that Israel had a government that was serious about trying to make peace. Baker hinted that his government might now provide the loan guarantees. Thomas Friedman of *The New York Times* wrote on July 20: "There were none of the smiles through clenched teeth that appeared in every meeting of Baker with Shamir. Mr. Rabin and Baker clearly looked comfortable working together." Later, Palestinians met with Baker at the American Consulate in Jerusalem and told him they too were encouraged by Israeli moves toward curbing Jewish settlement construction.

Rabin kept moving forward. After only eight days in office, he arrived in Cairo to see president Hosni Mubarak. Now he had the chance to ease the long thaw in relations between Israel and Egypt. The Rabin-Mubarak meeting was the first Israeli-Egyptian summit in six years. Rabin's special Israel Air Force plane flew two small Egyptian and Israeli flags from its cockpit. And the Israeli flag was raised at Cairo Airport for Rabin's arrival. Stepping off the plane, Rabin was greeted at the foot of the tarmac ramp by Atef Sedki, the Egyptian prime minister. Rabin took a few strides forward ready to review the military honor guard. Sedki gently reminded the Israeli leader that the national anthems of the two countries had not yet been played. Rabin gave a large smile. It was another example of Rabin trying to speed things up. After meeting for 90 minutes at the ornate Kubbah Palace, Mubarak said he welcomed the Rabin government's decision to review Shamir's settlement program, it was a good step, and now the Egyptians awaited more such steps from Rabin. Aware that Rabin had just taken office, Mubarak urged reporters not to press the new prime minister: "What do you expect him to do? Miracles?" Still, that was precisely what Mubarak was hoping for.

Meanwhile, Rabin enjoyed a great deal of good will. Most Israelis continued to think he and his policies were a breath of fresh air, particularly his decision to stop building in the occupied territories. The critics were shocked into silence. Now and again, former prime minister Shamir uttered some dissenting words but all for naught: the government easily beat back non-confidence motions.

A few days after Baker left the region, housing minister Binyamin Ben-Eliezer and finance minister Avraham Shochat spelled out in more detail the nature of the government's new settlement freeze. It turned out to be more a cooling off than an outright freeze. The new Rabin government planned to halt the building of 6,500 housing units in the occupied territories but would go ahead with 10,000 already in progress. Rabin had explained this to Baker earlier in the week: The Shamir Government had tied Rabin's hands.

Meeting president Bush on August 10 and 11 at his summer retreat, Bush concluded the two-day summit by announcing that he was ready to grant Israel the $10 billion in loan guarantees. It was clear that Bush had been influenced by Rabin's new policy toward the settlements: "We see a very different approach to settlements. We salute the prime minister. It was not easy. It took courage." Returning to Israel on August 14, Rabin declared that his visit bore practical fruit: "My visit also brought about a change in attitudes toward Israel within public opinion, the Administration, and Congress. I hope we have witnessed the opening of a new chapter in our ties with the US."

One incident marred the visit: Rabin's appearance before current and former leaders of the American Israel Public

Affairs Committee (AIPAC), known as the Jewish lobby. Rabin sent shockwaves through the American Jewish community. He excoriated the group for failing to coordinate its actions on behalf of Israel with the Israeli Embassy. He was openly critical of AIPAC's efforts on behalf of the loan guarantees. He was quoted as having said: "You waged battles which were lost in advance, and so you merely caused Israel damage by generating unnecessary antagonism over such issues as the intelligence-gathering AWACS plane sale to Saudi Arabia, and the loan guarantees request. You did not manage to bring Israel one single cent." These were some of the harshest comments an Israeli prime minister had ever uttered to an American Jewish group. By the time he had returned to Israel, Rabin sensed that he had gone too far in his criticism, and through his spokesman, he issued a statement expressing appreciation and respect for AIPAC.

Accelerating Middle East peacemaking was a major goal of the new prime minister. Though he had long been a proponent of an arrangement that would return territory in the West Bank and the Gaza Strip to the Jordanians, in return for a peace treaty, it was no longer practical to speak in such terms. Jordan did not control the West Bank or the Gaza Strip. The Palestinian Arabs did. The Intifada had given local Palestinian Arabs the self-confidence and the authority to become partners in a political dialogue with Israel that could lead to at least an interim political settlement based on autonomy. Rabin declared at the outset that he would continue the peace process in conformity with the ground rules established for the Madrid peace conference. Though he had not agreed on every element of those ground rules, the prime minister understood the grave risk posed were he to try to change the procedures. The Arab side might try to improve their lot and that could produce setbacks. Rabin wanted none of that.

Operating within the Madrid framework, Rabin planned to conduct talks with the Palestinians and with Jordan, Syria, and Lebanon. Since Madrid, the peace talks had been advancing sluggishly with no perceptible progress. After the meeting in Madrid, a series of meetings had been held between Israeli negotiators and the various Arab delegations in Washington D.C., but the talks had not lasted long, often no more than a week or so. The recesses could take a few months. Rabin wanted to step up the pace, to keep the talks going on a continuous basis. To demonstrate goodwill towards the Palestinians, Rabin, on August 23, announced steps designed to ease the atmosphere in the occupied territories. Some 800 Palestinians were released from jail that day; streets and alleyways, blocked off to curb riots, were opened; houses, sealed as punishment for anti-Israeli actions at least five years earlier, were opened. A day later, Rabin's Government cancelled deportation orders issued eight months earlier against 11 Palestinians.

The first round of peace talks convened on August 24 in Washington, D.C. The 1978 Camp David agreement had called for electing Palestinians to negotiate with Israel and also to govern during a five-year period of autonomy. The autonomy plan had been designed to lead to negotiations on the final status of the West Bank and the Gaza Strip. The Palestinians wanted elections for a legislature to operate during autonomy, a step that Israel felt would be a major step toward an independent Palestinian state, and thus not acceptable. Some kind of an administrative body, with weak legislative powers, was likely to emerge as a compromise.

Rabin set target dates for the implementation of autonomy, hoping this would spur progress. By December 1, 1992, he hoped for agreement on how the elections were to be conducted, and for what kind of body. By February 1, 199,3 Rabin hoped that the framework of the administrative council could be set up. Elections should occur in April or May 1993. As optimistic as he was about autonomy, Rabin was skeptical about the chances of reaching an accord with Syria. And yet he was prepared to contemplate returning portions of the Golan Heights to the Syrians, in exchange for a peace treaty. First, Hafez el-Assad had to demonstrate, as Sadat had, that he was truly willing to live in peace with Israel.

Rabin's first few months in office were remarkable. He had moved swiftly in a host of areas. His rush to get things done seemed contradictory to his cautious nature. More in line was a cautious streak that led him to calm Israel down. When an Israel TV reporter caught him as he entered an Egyptian embassy reception during the summer of 1992, Rabin said tersely: "Don't expect miracles." He was constantly trying to deflate the bubble of euphoria that had been blown up after the elections. He told the Labor Party's Knesset faction on July 27 that changing national priorities had proven more difficult than he expected. When he went to impose the housing freeze, Rabin learned that Shamir had set so much investment in motion that it was difficult to turn the entire operation off. "We are faced with a situation in which the previous government spent billions on projects in the territories which are of no benefit to security or the needs of the nation. We cannot simply put the project into reverse, and recoup the money, which was poured into settlements.

We cannot fulfill the great expectations of those who yearn for change right away." Rabin was far more tough-minded as prime minister this time around. He invoked strict discipline within his Cabinet and within the Labor Party, in order to make sure that his own agenda was pursued unremittingly. Few gave him trouble. In the early days Peres behaved loyally, if not lovingly. When anyone seemed to get out of line, Rabin reacted quickly and decisively.

When the Israeli and Syrian negotiators renewed discussions in Washington in late August, Rabin ordered his chief negotiator for Syria, Itamar Rabinovitch, to articulate a new Israeli flexibility. Then, on August 25, in an appearance before the Knesset Foreign Affairs and Defense Committee, the prime minister sounded a similar flexible note: "We will not give up the Golan Heights, but that does not mean we have to cling to every single centimeter of land there."

Fully half the country was adamantly opposed to any withdrawal in the Golan Heights and only five percent said they would hand it all back to the Syrians. Thirty-four percent were prepared to give back a small part of the Golan. To be fair, Israeli public opinion is not unalterably etched in stone. The public's hardline attitude toward the Golan was based, in part at least, on the parallel hardline attitude coming out of Damascus. A softening of the Syrian position would likely trigger a softening of Israeli public opinion, toward returning part or all of the Golan. Rabin believed that the best way to soften up the Syrians was the personal approach.

Understanding the value of personal summitry, Rabin was eager to meet Assad face to face. He could not offer the Syrian all he wanted, but their conversation might induce Assad to enter into a partial accord with Israel. It was certainly worth a try. Even meeting the Syrian leader secretly would be an incredible accomplishment and could pave the way for a major breakthrough in the talks, and perhaps even lead to a public meeting between the two leaders. Rabin worked aggressively, trying every possible avenue. He made clear that Israel was prepared to enter into serious negotiations with the Syrians over the Golan and other related issues. A whole host of emissaries paraded before Rabin, then Assad – the Americans, Germans, Austrians, and Egyptians – all trying to coax the two men to a private summit. Rabin, however, was unable to convince the Syrian leader that the time was ripe, that Syria could get what it wanted from serious peace talks at this juncture. Assad, perhaps with a sense of disappointment, relayed back the message: Not now. Not at this stage. It's too early. Knowing that Assad had replied negatively, Rabin still hoped to score some points with international opinion. He constantly conveyed a willingness to meet Assad anywhere, anytime. The prime minister, however, was banging on a closed door. Still, Assad sought to keep alive the possibility of serious peace talks with Israel. During the autumn, the Syrian leader issued a series of statements, however indirect and ambiguous, that Israel interpreted as a fresh Syrian willingness to talk peace. The media focused on this new flurry of diplomatic activity as if peace were at hand, yet nothing was further from the truth. Israel was still offering only a partial withdrawal from the Golan Heights, which was unacceptable to the Syrians. Rabin, however, remained upbeat. At least the Syrians and Israelis, he said, had moved beyond the previous year's stalemate and the prospect of true negotiations seemed in the offing.

Then in October came fresh, hopeful news. In a message from Syrian foreign minister Farouk al-Sharaa to Israel's foreign minister Peres, the Syrians appeared to consider an Israeli-Syrian summit. The foreign minister of a western European country was the middleman who conveyed the message. Syria had one condition for the summit, however: Israel had to declare its intention to withdraw totally from the Golan Heights. The actual withdrawal did not have to be immediate. As a bonus for such an Israeli declaration, the Syrians, al-Sharaa said, were ready to announce their willingness to establish full peace with Israel. It sounded positive and the media attention paid to the new Syrian gambit gave the impression that the diplomatic front was bubbling. Indeed, the good news was that the Syrians were finally talking about an Assad-Rabin summit. The hitch was that Rabin could not bring himself to meet the condition for the summit. If he had any plans to give up all of the Golan in order to reach peace with Syria, and it was not clear he had such plans, he would not yield that most valuable bargaining card before the negotiations began. He would save it for the end.

Even with the hope of progress with the Syrians, Rabin still remained convinced that the best bet for a peace accord was one with the Palestinians. Even into the fall of 1992, Rabin thought his prediction of autonomy by the spring of 1993 was realistic. Events, however, soon turned him into a disappointed pessimist. The Palestinians, he noted in early September, "are unable to come to grips with real-life problems. Their tactics are to talk about human rights, detentions, and demolitions of houses. They are dealing with the symptoms of the disease and not the disease itself." What seemed to irk the Palestinians the most, however, was not so much their lack of human rights as the fear that Israel and Syria seemed about to make peace. An Israeli-Syrian peace negotiation would divert Israel's attention from the autonomy talks, and essentially leave the Palestinians out in the diplomatic cold for a long period.

Before he could engage in peace seriously or tackle the economy aggressively, Rabin had to decide what kind of government coalition he wanted. By September, 50 days in office, Rabin had all but abandoned the quest to balance his left-leaning coalition government by bringing into the fold the eight-member Tsomet Party headed by Rafael Eitan. Rabin's decision not to cave into Tsomet's demands, chief among which was to scale back peacemaking and increase Jewish settlement in the occupied lands, gave increased strength to Meretz leader and education minister Shulamit Aloni. Experiencing a new sense of self-confidence that manifested itself in public statements that left the Orthodox Jewish community and Rabin wondering how to tame her, her most inflammatory statement came on September 23 when she remarked that the Golan Heights belonged to Syria under international law. That kind of statement, Rabin worried, could only hinder Israel's ability to bargain with the Syrians. Rabin had had enough. On September 24, the prime minister acknowledged that he had a loose cannon on his hands. Rabin sought to distance himself from Aloni's more caustic outbursts. Without referring to her by name, he told Labor Party activists in Tel Aviv that "I am now serving as a fireman every day, due to certain declarations from the left."

From the moment he became prime minister in July, Rabin plunged into the job with great zeal. He began his day at 6 am, reading the newspapers, drinking coffee, and eating a grapefruit or an apple. By 7:30 or 8 am, he was at his office, ready to start what often amounted to 16-hour workdays.

Saturday, the Jewish Sabbath, was nearly a full workday for him, except for the hour on Saturday morning when he squeezed in some tennis with Leah and the Accadia hotel manager Raphy Weiner. Aides compared Rabin's busy schedule with Shamir's, noting that the former prime minister often napped in the afternoons while the most Rabin did was catch a nap in the car. There were signs that, no matter how hard he worked, Rabin was producing too few results. The public wondered what had happened to his election promises. At the 100-day mark in his administration, Rabin encountered a batch of unfriendly articles in the Israeli press. Then the opposition Likud, dormant for a few months after the shocking loss of the elections, began to stir. Likud Knesset member Benjamin Netanyahu, competing for his party's leadership, charged that Israel had experienced "100 days of retreat. In every aspect of our national life, the government has failed to deliver." Such criticism from the Likud was expected. Yet even political allies wondered when the Rabin government would deliver some good news. Rabin's government seemed overwhelmed by events. Peacemaking was at a standstill. Plans to tackle the economy were moving through the bureaucracy slowly. And, to his chagrin, Rabin found that the smaller political parties, some within his coalition, some outside, were presenting new challenges and burdens to his government.

Though Rabin sensed that it would take much work to reach agreement on Palestinian autonomy, by late October he was growing increasingly frustrated. On October 25, he told the Knesset that the Palestinians had exhibited no "responsiveness" to Israeli proposals thus far. "I fear that the Palestinians are again deluding themselves. Again, they may be hallucinating. Instead of learning from their mistakes over generations, instead of accepting what has been offered to them or to at least discuss it seriously, the Palestinians are still adhering to 'everything or nothing' If it will be this way, if they are not willing to change their positions, they will ultimately remain with nothing."

In mid-November, *Time Magazine* sought interviews with both Rabin and Syrian president Hafez el-Assad. The interviews were to run in the same edition. Assad granted the interview on November 13. Two days later, Rabin sat down with three reporters from *Time*, one of them this author. *Time* had hoped that Assad and Rabin would make dramatic news in the interviews that would propel the peace process forward. Perhaps Assad would make a turnabout and indicate his readiness to meet Rabin at a summit. Or, perhaps Rabin would acknowledge that, under certain circumstances, Israel would be prepared to leave the Golan Heights completely. Neither Assad nor Rabin offered such statements. Instead, Assad told *Time*: "A meeting of heads of state to discuss the Arab-Israeli conflict might lead to war instead of peace because when there are differences at the [top] leadership level, there is nobody to mend things." As for Rabin, one might have tried to read between the lines and suggest that he would ultimately countenance a total Israeli departure from the Golan. But he did not say so outright. Asked whether there were any circumstances under which he would consider full withdrawal from the Golan, he answered: "I will not even go so far as addressing the question of withdrawal from the Golan without first knowing that Syria is ready for full-fledged peace, a peace that stands by itself." When the author asked Rabin, "If Assad came to Jerusalem prepared to sign a peace treaty, would that change your position on the Golan?" Rabin grew tense and with some annoyance in his voice said: "You are not Assad. You don't represent Assad, and you are not prime minister of Israel. Unfortunately, the Syrian position as it was expressed by Foreign Minister Farouk al-Sharaa 'total withdrawal for total peace' is not very clear. I don't know what total peace is. I do know what total withdrawal is. It is not limited to Syria. It also concerns the West Bank and the Gaza Strip."

Despite the parlays in Washington, by December 1992, Israel and Syria appeared to be no closer to a peace agreement. Rabin was busy trying to assure the Jewish settlers on the Golan that their settlements were not about to be dismantled. "In any peace agreement with the Syrians which includes withdrawal from the Golan Heights," he told the Labor Party's Young Guard on December 30, "only the [Israeli] army will withdraw." Rabin remained adamant that he was not going to announce the scale of an Israeli withdrawal until he heard from the Syrians that they were ready to talk genuine peace.

Trouble was brewing for Israel from another Arab quarter, angry at the peace process. Hamas, the Islamic Resistance Movement, which was fast becoming the dominant rejectionist group in the occupied territories, sought to undermine the peacemaking through stepped-up violence. Hamas got its start as the outgrowth of a segment of the Egyptian-based Muslim Brotherhood. It was formed in the Gaza Strip in February 1988 by quadriplegic cleric Sheikh Ahmed Yassin. Its platform called for a holy war to liberate the entire pre-1948 Palestine from Israel's grip.

Throughout the fall of 1992, Hamas attacked Israeli forces. It staged attacks on Israeli soldiers on September 21 and 25 in Hebron, killing one soldier; it killed three Israeli soldiers in the Gaza Strip on December 7; and a fourth soldier in Hebron two days later. Then on December 13 came the worst incident of this period, creating the most serious crisis of Rabin's five-month-old government. Hamas activists kidnapped a 29-year-old Israeli Border Policeman, named Nissim Toledano, as he was leaving his home in Lod for work at 4:40 am. Six hours later, two masked men entered the Red Crescent office in Al-Bira, near Ramallah in the West Bank and identified themselves as Hamas members. They left a photocopy of Toledano's ID card and a letter demanding the release of Hamas's spiritual founder Sheikh Yassin from an Israeli jail in return for Toledano. The kidnappers threatened to kill Toledano if Yassin was not released by 9 pm Sunday. Rabin suggested that negotiations were possible, but only after Hamas gave a sign that Toledano was alive. Israeli authorities permitted Yassin to be interviewed on Israel Television shortly after 9 pm, during which he appealed to the kidnappers not to kill the Israeli hostage. Meanwhile, Israeli security agents began arresting 2,000 Hamas activists in the occupied territories. The 9 pm deadline came without the kidnappers offering a sign that Toledano was alive. A Bedouin woman found Toledano's body on the road between Jerusalem and Jericho. He had been knifed and strangled. His murder had occurred soon after the deadline. Rabin would not allow the violence to force Israel away from the peace table. He told Israel Television on December 15: "Why has there been an increase in shooting incidents in recent months? I have no doubt that those who propose this action, are first and foremost the ones who want to kill Israelis, and also the peace and the chance to achieve peace." Speaking in the Knesset that same day, hours after Nissim Toledano's body was discovered, Rabin said: "The heart bleeds and feels pain today, but this is what I want to tell those who seek to harm us: We will hurt, we will pay the price, we will grit our teeth and go on, and we will win. Terrorism does not stand a chance against us. Nothing will move us from here. Not stones, fire bombs, or knives; not Hamas, the Popular Front, or the Fatah; not Ahmed Yassin, Ahmed Jibril, or Yasser Arafat. We are here and we will live here forever."

After Toledano's murder, Rabin sensed that some dramatic Israeli action was essential, otherwise Hamas and all others who were in the rejectionist camp would take heart that it was possible to jab away at the Israelis and go unpunished. More of this, thought Rabin, and Israelis would begin to wonder why their leaders were sitting at the peace table with the Arabs. By its deeds during the fall, Hamas had begun to capture the imagination of Palestinians in the occupied territories. The Palestinian peace delegation seemed to be dithering, getting nowhere in the autonomy talks. Hamas, meanwhile, was capturing the headlines, keeping the Intifada alive, keeping the Israelis on the defensive. So Rabin decided to act. Later, critics would wonder whether he had taken sufficient account of potential international criticism of damaging the peace process, of risking an early Arab departure from the peace table. He seemed unfazed by such worries. He knew that what he had in mind would ignite controversy abroad. He knew that Israel would be condemned by the United Nations, by Washington, by the European Community. He decided, however, the condemnations would be the price Israel could pay to show muscle.

Rabin ordered the deportation of 415 Hamas activists. As a form of punishment against Palestinians, deportation had been used sparingly by Israel over the years. Since the start of the Intifada in December 1987, Israel had deported 66 Palestinians from the occupied territories; only eight in the past two years; 45 had been deported between 1985 and 1987; and one between 1981 and 1985. The act of expelling someone from his or her homeland, no matter what that person's crime, seemed exceptionally unjust in a world that placed such a premium on the notion of national identity. Moreover, it was questionable whether deporting large numbers of Hamas activists would temper the anti-Israeli violence; surely others within Hamas would rise to the surface and maintain the violence. None of these arguments prevented Rabin from this dramatic step.

On December 16, the day after Nissim Toledano's body was found, Israel's cabinet met and voted 14-0 that the government would temporarily expel 415 Hamas activists who had been part of the 2,000 Hamas members picked up by Israeli authorities a few days earlier. Only justice minister David Libai abstained, concerned that the cabinet's action was not legal. This expulsion was by far the single largest group of Palestinians to be sent into exile since soon after the 1967 war. In an attempt to alleviate international criticism, Rabin's government avoided using the word deportation, which implied permanent expulsion and which was forbidden by international law. The 415 were being temporarily banished and given the right to appeal within 60 days of their removal.

Put on buses that night, the 415 Hamas deportees headed for the north. Before they reached the Lebanese border, Israeli human rights groups and lawyers representing the activists approached the Israel Supreme Court and obtained a temporary rescinding order. One indication of how urgent was the case in the eyes of the Supreme Court justices was their decision to schedule a hearing for 5 am the next morning (December 17). Lasting all day and into the early evening, the hearing focused on the defendants' claim that they had been denied due process. The court, however, decided by a vote of 5-2 that the government could deport the activists immediately, if only on a temporary basis. Scheduling another hearing within 30 days, the court ordered the government to explain why it was proper to carry out these deportations. Soon afterwards that evening, the 22 buses carrying the Hamas activists rolled into Lebanon. The deportees were taken to a point five kilometers (three miles) north of the Israeli security zone in Lebanon and left there.

Then events took an odd turn. The Lebanese government refused to permit the 415 to enter into Lebanese territory. The deportees were forced to remain out in the cold. They were denied food and water but not media attention. The international media managed to reach the deportees and televised pictures of their plight around the world, stranded in the winter cold, living in tents provided by relief agencies, passing the time by praying and talking, waiting for someone to rescue them. On December 18, the Security Council voted to condemn Israel for the deportations and demanded that Israel allow the activists back into Israel. Two days later, the Supreme Court was asked to rule on whether Israel should permit the Hamas activists back, on the grounds that they had not been deported in a manner that guaranteed their safety. Attorneys for the deportees insisted that they be returned, if not to their homes, then at least to a place in Israel where they would be safe. The court ruled on December 22 that the deportees had not been prevented from entering Lebanon, they were in Lebanon, and therefore the court had no reason to intervene on their behalf. Essentially, the court said that

Israel had deported the 415 to Lebanon and it was now Lebanon's responsibility to take care of these people.

Even if Labor and Meretz had little reason to believe that Rabin would veer from his centrist views, they were convinced that in time he would be won over to a more leftist stance. Their opening shot came on December 2 when legislation began moving through the Knesset to drop the 1986 ban on unauthorized contacts with the PLO or any other terrorist group. The 1986 law had been adopted to keep Israelis from meeting informally with PLO figures, meetings that were likely to increase the pressure on the Israeli government to hold formal negotiations with the PLO. Violators could be jailed for three years. And indeed peace activist Abie Nathan did go to jail, drawing the ire of left-wing groups.

Once the Shamir government sat down in Madrid and later in Washington with Palestinians, who were guided by the PLO in Tunis, the ban on PLO contacts lost all meaning, for even the Shamir government seemed to be negotiating, however indirectly, with the PLO. The legislation to drop the ban was adopted on January 19, 1993. Israeli media became an unexpected ally. On December 20, Israel Radio provided a great boost to the left's cause, by carrying out a poll of Labor party Knesset members. The poll showed that fully two thirds of the Labor Knesset deputies favored direct negotiations with the PLO. Three days later came yet a new achievement for the leftists. The Rabin Cabinet held its first debate ever on the possibility of integrating the PLO into the peace talks. The proposal came from three Meretz ministers. While the trio did not, in fact, propose holding negotiations immediately with the PLO, Rabin, still, turned them down again.

Rabin faced the most serious crisis of his prime ministership thus far – the deportations and the attendant international criticism – still, with no sign of self-doubt whatsoever. After all, according to public opinion polls taken soon after the deportations, he had an overwhelming majority of the country behind him. A poll published in *Yediot Aharonot* on December 19, for instance, indicated that no less than 91 percent of the nation supported the deportations. Over the coming weeks, however, international criticism did not abate. The media, allowed to mingle freely with the deportees, understood the drama of the deportees' plight. Day after day throughout January and into early February, television footage of the deportees was beamed back into millions of American and European homes, increasing the pressure on Rabin and Israel to alter the December 16 deportation decree.

As long as the deportee issue lingered, as long as American television showed Palestinians trapped in a no man's land in southern Lebanon, the Israeli-Arab peace talks would not resume. That became the new reality in mid-January. The next round of talks had been scheduled for some time in February. In the immediate aftermath of the deportations, it appeared that the Arabs would not let the issue stand in the way of their attending the February round of peace talks. It would not be easy.

On January 20, Bill Clinton would become the new American president. Though Clinton was determined to focus his attention and energy at first on the American economy, by allowing the deportees issue to fester without resolution, Rabin and the Israelis were inadvertently forcing Clinton to divert himself from what he had set as his main task upon taking office. This was bound to get Israel off on the wrong foot with the new administration, something Rabin, who had always prided himself on getting along with the Americans, did not want. Beyond that, if the Security Council appeared likely to impose sanctions on Israel, Rabin could further complicate Clinton's early days in office by giving the new president no choice but to order the American representative to the Security Council to veto the resolution on sanctions. For Clinton to use that veto would reduce his credibility with the Arabs at a time when he wanted to show impartiality in the Arab-Israeli peace process. Adding to the complicated picture that had emerged as Clinton took office was the fact that very soon, Israel's Supreme Court would give a final ruling on the question of whether the deportations were or were not valid. If the Supreme Court ruled the deportations were not valid, Rabin would have to allow them home immediately, a resolution of the affair that would have not pleased the prime minister, but would have at least ended the crisis and gotten Clinton off the hook for the present.

The Supreme Court's decision came on January 28. Shrouded in legalese, ambiguous to many, the ruling of the seven-justice panel was to uphold the Rabin government's decision to deport the 415 Hamas activists. Nonetheless, the Court issued so many caveats and heaped so much criticism on the manner in which the deportations were carried out, that it appeared extremely unlikely that any Israeli government would be able to act in the same way a second time. Pleased with the Supreme Court's decision, Rabin turned his attention to halting UN sanctions. If the court's ruling cheered Rabin, the deportees were not happy with it. To Rabin, what mattered more than anything else at this stage was winning the support of the new Clinton administration.

Rabin worked hard with the Americans to secure a quick solution to the deportee issue. And so, on February 1, 1993, he convened the cabinet in a special session in the Knesset. In his pocket was an agreement he had worked out with the United States over the previous few days. An agreement that required Israel to compromise on the deportees and obligated the United States, in turn, to make sure that sanctions were not adopted against Israel; and to seek the renewal of the peace talks. The ministers needed little convincing that a compromise was in order. The elements of that deal were: Some 100 deportees could return home at once and the remaining deportees' terms of expulsion would be cut in half. Expressing pride in the original expulsions, Rabin said: "No previous government ever delivered such a massive blow against terror. The right-wing government [of Shamir] did not have the courage."

Even though the deportees rejected the compromise offer, the prime minister knew that the written understanding with the US would not fall and that was what counted for him. The Israeli public disliked the Rabin compromise (61 percent in one poll was against it and 77 percent in the same poll thought the original decision to export the Hamas people was correct), while the Israeli left had become increasingly anguished by the deportations and the international criticism that followed. Deeply troubled, they had feared that the peace process would fall victim to the deportations. In December and January, it had seemed unthinkable to reconvene the peace talks as long as the deportees were left out in the cold in southern Lebanon. Yet in the wake of the Cabinet decision, Arabs began sounding as if they were unwilling to keep the peace process hostage to the deportees and the US hoped to resume those talks no later than April.

CHAPTER FIFTEEN

MAKING PEACE IN NORWAY

Meanwhile, in a remote corner of the world, far from the Middle East, two Israeli academics began meeting in secret with several representatives of the Palestine Liberation Organization. Such meetings were not unusual, (especially after January 1993, when Israel dropped its 1986 ban on talking to the PLO). Still, the Oslo talks were one of the greatest secrets of Israeli history. They began in December 1992 at a time when the public talks being held in Washington DC were stalled; the Israeli-PLO dialogue in Oslo was one of many private probes undertaken by Israelis to find out whether the Palestinians wanted to proceed with negotiations outside the glare of publicity. No one in the Israeli government placed much faith in such probes, including prime minister Rabin. But, eager as it was to demonstrate good will, Rabin's Government did nothing to stop the feelers.

The two Israeli academics responsible for what came to be known as the Oslo Channel were Yair Hirschfeld, a professor of Middle Eastern History at Haifa University, and a former student of his, Ron Pundak, who was a senior research fellow in Middle Eastern History at Jerusalem's Hebrew University. Hirschfeld had strong contacts with West Bank Palestinian leaders, and one of them, Hanan Ashrawi, had suggested to him that he get in touch with PLO treasurer Ahmed Ali Mohammed Qurei also known as Abu Ala. Meeting him might prove productive. The two men met on December 20, 1992 at a London hotel and concluded, after several hours, that they had much to talk about. Hirschfeld phoned his close friend, deputy foreign minister Yossi Beilin, at once. Beilin, one of the most vociferous doves in the Israeli government, was delighted that a connection had been made with Abu Ala. He gave Hirschfeld carte blanche to explore the possibilities of an Israeli-Palestinian peace accord. He urged the academic to report back whenever he wished. It was, however, far too early to involve the Israeli government in the talks. Secrecy was vital.

Beilin had encouraged Hirschfeld to make contact with Terje Roed-Larsen, the head of a Norwegian research institute that dealt with social and economic issues. Beilin hoped Larsen would serve as a host for the forthcoming talks. Indeed, Larsen proposed that the negotiators switch their London venue to the more out-of-the-way Oslo, where it would be easier to preserve secrecy. At the next meeting in January 1993, Hirschfeld and Pundak met Abu Ala and two other PLO officials over a three-day period. The site was a villa in the small town of Sarpsborg, a two-hour drive from Oslo. The talks began with warm handshakes. The five men sat across from one another for a while, then moved over to chairs placed in front of a fire in the lounge; eventually they walked outside in the brisk Norwegian air for more informal talks. The PLO men had come to do business and the Israelis quickly realized that a peace accord with the Palestinians might just be possible.

To find common ground, both sides had to forget about their ideal scenarios: The Israelis wanted to keep as much of the occupation in place as possible, in order to protect the Jewish settlers on the West Bank and in the Gaza Strip and to prevent Palestinian terrorists from launching attacks against Israeli targets; the PLO wanted Israel to agree to withdraw every Israeli soldier from those territories at once, and agree to let the Palestinians create a state of their own on these lands. What gave the Oslo talks the prospect of success was that both sides were prepared to negotiate on the basis of compromise; the Israelis were prepared to grant self-rule to the Palestinians and to agree to a gradual evacuation of Israeli troops from the West Bank and the Gaza Strip; and the Palestinians were willing to abandon their hopes of ending the occupation at once and erecting a state immediately on those lands.

The sessions went well, better than the Israeli academics dared to expect. Hirschfeld and Pundak attempted to find areas of agreement, but, as Hirschfeld noted, "The more we did that, the more we identified contradictory interests. We began speaking about everything; then we narrowed it down, identifying common ground; that was a process that was quite encouraging." Between January and May, the Oslo negotiators met five times. Meanwhile, the public talks in Washington remained stalled. The Palestinians were only willing to resume talks once the Hamas deportees returned home. Israel, for its part, was reluctant to begin peace talks as long as Palestinian terror continued. In March 1993, ten Israelis were killed and 14 wounded in such attacks. These were frustrating months for Yitzhak Rabin. He had made it clear that he was prepared to go far toward Arab demands, yet the entire peace process began to resemble the days of Yitzhak Shamir, when nothing happened on the peace front. While the Oslo negotiators continued to hammer away in secret at a peace accord, Rabin had no way of knowing whether their efforts would be crowned with success. He retained hope that the Washington talks might take a more serious turn. When the Washington talks did resume in late April, after several meetings it was clear that the Palestinians had lost interest and so the talks were put on hold until further notice.

Meanwhile, unbeknownst to the Washington negotiators, both Israeli and Palestinian, the secret Oslo talks were making good progress. By May, the negotiators were putting the final touches on a very preliminary draft of a Declaration of Principles that was designed to form the basis for an eventual agreement. To make it more palatable for Israelis to yield occupied territory, the PLO had proposed that the agreement entail only Israeli withdrawal from the Gaza Strip, granting full autonomy to the 750,000 Palestinian residents there and leaving the West Bank for further negotiations. The Israelis liked this 'Gaza first' approach, and it became the center point of the talks by late spring. Realizing that West Bank Palestinians would be annoyed at being excluded from this accord, the PLO proposed an amendment, including the West Bank town of Jericho, in the initial zone of Palestinian self-rule. The Israelis agreed.

Yitzhak Rabin was at a crossroads. Determined to energize the peace process after being elected prime minister nearly a year earlier, he had been greeted with one frustration after another and in that spring of 1993, peace seemed farther off than ever. The Washington talks were sputtering. Damascus had not picked up the phone. He felt that he needed something more tangible in the shorter run. Only the reports that he had been receiving from Shimon Peres and Yossi Beilin about the meetings in Oslo seemed interesting.

On March 1 he turned 71 years old. How many more years did he have to secure for himself a place in history as Israel's chief peacemaker? Not many, he assumed. Now was the time to make peace with the Arabs. Never had Rabin been in such a strong position to take bold steps for peace. Expelling the Hamas deportees, while an unpopular move abroad, had proved a masterful stroke on Rabin's part, for Israelis had never admired the prime minister more than when he put the 415 activists on the buses to Lebanon. Furious at the suggestion that he return the deportees at once, the prime minister asked: "Will it stop the Palestinians from attacking us?" The answer, of course, was no. The only thing that held out the promise of halting Palestinian violence was a peace accord.

Peres had been prompting Rabin to take a hard look at what was happening in Oslo. Rabin had kept putting him off. It was not the prime minister's style to leap into action, but to hold back, to proceed with caution, to study things. He did that with Oslo. Then, in May, with Peres still pressing him, Rabin agreed to send an Israeli official to Oslo to find out whether there was any real hope springing from those talks. Assigned to the task was Uri Savir, a senior aide to Peres. Eventually, Yoel Singer, soon to become an attorney in the foreign ministry, visited Oslo as well. When the two men met the negotiators in Oslo, they were surprised to find that, as Hirschfeld and Pundak had been reporting that spring, the Israelis and Palestinians had already put together the draft peace accord. Things looked hopeful. Savir and Singer optimistically reported back to Peres that it just might be possible to reach agreement with the PLO on self-rule for the territories. Peres informed Rabin. The prime minister remained uncertain. For years, Rabin, along with most other mainstream Israelis, had rejected out of hand the idea that Israel should negotiate with Yasser Arafat and his Palestine Liberation Organization, arguing that he was a terrorist and a murderer, whose main goal was the destruction of the State of Israel. There was also the widespread conviction, shared by Rabin at the time, that Israel should not give up any of the West Bank or Gaza Strip for the foreseeable future. Agreeing to talk to Arafat was tantamount to admitting that the West Bank and Gaza Strip were open for negotiation. However, Rabin had some time before come around to thinking that Israel should relinquish a good part of the West Bank and Gaza Strip. But could he discard the sacred principle of not negotiating with Arafat all that easily? There was no question that the Israeli negotiators were dealing with a senior PLO official (Abu Ala), who was in direct contact with Arafat. To agree that the Israeli government would take part in the Oslo talks was the same as acquiescing that Israel should talk to the PLO.

Rabin had become convinced that the only one with whom Israel could do business was the PLO leader in Tunis. Rabin had lost faith in the local Palestinian leadership. None of them had the power to face down Hamas; none had the authority to declare an end to Israel's long-standing war with the Palestinians. Only Arafat had both the power and the authority for such acts. To his aides, Rabin employed some flowery language to get across his point: "It's about time we took off the masks at the masked ball and talked to the man in charge."

With Savir and Singer now in Oslo, Peres and Beilin kept the prime minister informed on a regular basis. Much work needed to be done. The secret was kept. Other than Rabin, Peres, Beilin, Savir, Singer, Hirschfeld, and Pundak, no one else knew. Not Rabin's head of bureau, Eitan Haber. Not Elyakim Rubinstein, head of the Israeli delegation to the Washington talks.

It must have been tempting for Rabin to reveal the secrets by early summer. For one thing, in early July a majority of Israelis (63 percent) expressed dissatisfaction with his Government's performance, clearly frustrated at the going-nowhere peace process. To Rabin, the polls did not take into account what he had accomplished in his first year in office: He had improved relations with the United States; reduced Palestinian violence, especially since the April closure of the territories; and reduced unemployment from 153,000 to 122,300. To Rabin's credit, Israel was in the midst of an economic miracle; its growth rate of 6.6 percent in the past year was among the highest in the world. Rabin would have liked to reveal that some promising developments on the peace front loomed ahead. But he kept quiet.

To maintain the secret of Oslo, Rabin in public acted as if the farthest thing from his mind was talking to the PLO. He told the English-language *Jerusalem Report* on July 15 that bringing the PLO into the peace process would not be helpful since it would shift the focus of the peace talks from interim issues to a permanent settlement. "And once we start talking about things like borders, settlements, Jerusalem, you get immediate deadlock." He did seem, though, to be preparing the Israelis for something spectacular when he said in the same interview: "I believe it is my moral and political responsibility as prime minister to make compromises, because otherwise there is no chance for peace." Yet, when an Israel TV reporter asked him on August 12 if he was considering a meeting with Arafat, Rabin snapped: "Forget about it, certainly for the foreseeable future." Might he meet Arafat in the time Rabin had left as prime minister? "I hope not. The negotiations should be conducted with the Palestinian delegation as residents of the territories."

A peace agreement with the Palestinians, in Rabin's view, would secure for him his rightful place in Israeli history. He rarely expressed such grand thoughts to friends, aides, or family. He was not a man given easily to personal introspection. Yet, Rabin felt that history had passed him by. He had molded the Israeli army in the early 1960s, but Moshe Dayan had gained fame for "leading" Israel in its Six-Day War triumph. It had been Rabin who had engineered Israel's military and economic recovery after the calamitous 1973 war, yet a minor scandal had kept Rabin from political life for a crucial seven years in the late 1970s and early 1980s, while other Israelis took credit for advances in the peace process. He had been the architect of the first Israel-Egypt peace accord in 1975, yet Menachem Begin had won the Nobel Peace Prize for bringing home the first Israeli peace treaty with an Arab nation, the Egyptians. Now, in the late summer of 1993, Rabin had a chance to outshine them all; Dayan, Peres, Begin. He understood how painful it would be for many Israelis, but he was prepared to try.

In late August, no one imagined that a political earthquake was about to happen. There had been scattered stories in the Israeli press about secret Israeli-PLO dialogues, but no one had uncovered the Oslo talks. Reports circulated that Peres was exploring the 'Gaza First' approach with the Palestinians, and, to get PLO approval for the idea, he had assigned a former aide to arrange a secret meeting between him and Arafat. However, these were just reports. No one seemed to know the real truth, not even the Americans. They believed that the chances of achieving a peace accord with the Syrians were far better than with the Palestinians, bringing secretary of state Warren Christopher to visit Jerusalem and Damascus in August to explore those prospects.

On August 24, Peres visited Oslo for the first time since the talks had begun and held a secret session there to put the finishing touches to the document. Crowning his visit, he and PLO official Mahmoud Abbas (Abu Mazen) initialed the Declaration of Principles (DOP). Three days later, Peres flew to California to update Warren Christopher on the talks. Peres asked the secretary of state for help in convincing Morocco and other Arab states to establish diplomatic relations with Israel, now that Israel and the PLO were recognizing each other.

On August 27, word began to leak that Israel and the Palestinians were close to a political agreement. In the next few days, as more and more about the secret Oslo talks began to surface, it became clear that Rabin had embarked on one of the most revolutionary exercises of his country's 45-year history. His chief aide, Eitan Haber, called it: "The second greatest decision ever taken in the history of the State of Israel," after David Ben-Gurion's decision to create the State.

What precisely was the deal that Rabin would put before his people? The Israeli-Palestinian agreement, made up of six documents, comprised a declaration of principles; an agreed memorandum clarifying some points in the main document; and four appendices that dealt with elections in the territories, the withdrawal of Israeli troops from Gaza and Jericho, Israeli-Palestinian economic cooperation, and regional economic development. The document to be signed was not a final peace accord, it was a framework that called for Palestinian self-rule in Gaza and Jericho that would have to be implemented through further negotiations due to be concluded within three months. But the real DOP's significance was that for the first time Israelis and Palestinians had agreed that the Palestinians should be given a full measure of autonomy, and that Israel would bring an end to its military occupation. The Israeli army would withdraw from most of the Gaza Strip and Jericho by April 1994. Three months later, elections were to be held in all the territories for a Palestinian executive council, with East Jerusalem Arabs permitted to vote. Once elected, the council would take over the Israeli executive civil administration functions in the territories, and would be responsible for everything save foreign affairs and defense. It would have no jurisdiction over Israeli settlements. By the end of 1995, negotiations were to begin on the final status of the territories, including the fate of Jerusalem, the Jewish settlements in the territories, final borders, and a host of other major issues left over from previous negotiations.

Rabin's political calculations were largely correct. Israelis welcomed the accord in large measure. The prime minister's popularity had peaked at 59 percent 100 days after his 1992 election, but had slipped to 42 percent in the late summer.

With the accord announcement, it had risen to 54 percent. The political right was furious over the accord and planned to stage mass sit-ins, block major highways, and sponsor strikes. It wanted new elections before the Israelis signed the accord. Rehavam Ze'evi, leader of the right-wing Moledet party, warned that Arafat might enter Jerusalem alive, but he would not leave that way. A Jewish settlement spokesman promised that demonstrations would no longer end with the national anthem, but with 250 people being arrested. Other Jewish settlers predicted that civil war would break out. To quell the expected disorders, the Israeli Security Service ordered back to service former agents. Settler leaders promised to harass cabinet ministers, not with bullets or TNT, but harassment nonetheless.

The conventional wisdom grew that the Oslo agreement was the product of Peres's fertile mind, and that Rabin had been a mere innocent bystander. Such talk was a gross exaggeration. Certainly, Peres was the hands-on politician, the conduit between the government and the Oslo negotiating team, often on a day-to-day basis. But he could have only pursued the secret effort with Rabin's blessing, which he had enjoyed since the previous spring. To be sure, Rabin was not overly enthusiastic about the peace accord. He knew how painful it would be for Israelis to swallow the new reality. Addressing members of his Labor Party in early September, he confessed his ambivalence about the accord by noting that the PLO was "a terrorist organization. They killed. They are murderers, but peace you make with your enemies, including despicable enemies. I'm not going to beautify them. I can't tell you that some formulas in the agreement don't give me stomach pains. I have such pains, but I have to see also the comprehensive picture. We have to take risks."

Once the political earthquake was public information, events moved swiftly. By September 10, a ceremony was held in the prime minister's office, during which he signed a document recognizing the PLO. It was, Rabin said, "a moment of primary importance, with many opportunities, but not few risks." Undoubtedly because of those risks, Rabin remained in the background, giving the spotlight to Peres. When it was time to decide who would represent Israel at the White House ceremony for the DOP signing on September, 13, Rabin was all too willing to let Peres represent Israel. When Rabin learned, however, that Yasser Arafat planned to attend, he decided to lead the Israeli delegation.

Rabin was flying to Washington for the ceremony. On a long fight like that, he routinely lay down on his bed and went to sleep. He was known as a great sleeper on planes, but not this time. Uri Dromi, the director of the Government Press Office, also on the plane, could not help but stare at him: "He was restless. He tried to lie down, but he got up, he lit a cigarette, and then he just couldn't settle down. The reason was clear. The peace agreement upset him. He hated the whole idea but he understood that he had to do it."

A worldwide audience watched on that sunny Monday morning, September 13, as Yitzhak Rabin fidgeted, squirmed, wriggled and gazed around, always averting his eyes from the man with the black-and-white *keffiyeh*, scraggly beard and brown khaki suit, standing a few feet away from him. Rabin's body language, so pronounced that it seemed almost to have been choreographed, served as the perfect metaphor for the way he felt that morning. Part of Yitzhak Rabin was thrilled to be there, ecstatic that he had been the Israeli prime minister who had brought the burgeoning Israeli-Palestinian peace this far. Part of him, however, was tormented at having to be in Arafat's presence. Rabin had tried to work out ground rules in advance. The prime minister insisted to president Clinton that Arafat should not show up in a military uniform and that he was not to carry a weapon. Arafat had originally wanted to attend the ceremony with his holster holding his Smith & Wesson and, in a great theatrical gesture, unstrap the gun and hand it to Clinton. The president vetoed the theatrics and barred Arafat from carrying arms but permitted him to wear his uniform. Rabin put another request to president Clinton: Tell Arafat that Rabin did not want Arafat to give him one of those Arab-style bear hugs. Their friendship had not evolved to that point. On the question of a Rabin-Arafat handshake, the prime minister said nothing, but he knew Clinton might insist upon it. He deferred the decision of whether he would shake Arafat's hand until the actual time came.

The two men arrived at the White House shortly before the ceremony was due to begin. They were escorted to a small reception where, for the first time, they saw one another in person. Until now, they had not met, nor had they talked on the telephone. Their communications had been through aides. At first, Rabin and Arafat kept their distance from one another, huddling with their aides in separate circles. When the time came for the ceremony to start, heading toward the event, the two men stood next to one another. Rabin was the first to speak. "You know we are going to have to work very hard to make this work." "I know," Arafat responded, "and I am prepared to do my part." It was an auspicious start to a dialogue that was vital for carrying on the peace effort.

Moments later, they walked slowly across the White House lawn for the historic signing of the DOP. In his remarks

Rabin spoke emotionally and directly to the Palestinians: "We who have come from a land where parents bury their children, we who have fought against you, the Palestinians, we say to you today in a loud and clear voice: enough of blood and tears, enough."

The image of that morning that remains, however, is not the affixing of signatures on the documents, not the speeches, but that special moment after the signing when Arafat, to the far right, Clinton, in the middle, and Rabin, to the far left, stood for a few seconds with no one telling them what to do next. It was up to them. Arafat made the first gesture, extending his right hand to Rabin. Eager for the two men to seal their accord with a handshake, Clinton placed his right hand behind Rabin's back, as if to encourage him to move closer to Arafat. Rabin gave one of his customary expressions, as if he were saying, "Oh, all right, I'll do it," and then grasped Arafat's hand. The crowd broke into applause and, as they did, Arafat reached across Rabin to shake Peres's hand. "Now it's your turn," Rabin mumbled to the foreign minister. The moment became enshrined in history. Over and over again, television footage of the Rabin-Arafat handshake was shown, as if to prove that it had really happened. The handshake became a metaphor for the way two implacable enemies had been able to overcome their differences and make peace. If hundreds of thousands of Israelis asked themselves, how could Rabin shake hands with such a man, it was left to the prime minister to make it clear that he was not that pleased himself: "Of all the hands in the world, it was not the hand that I wanted or even dreamed of touching."

However, the handshake had great meaning for Rabin. By locking the Palestinians into a political agreement, Israel could now move more aggressively toward unburdening itself, once and for all, of policing the Arab territories captured in the Six-Day War. Rabin had come to power largely because most Israelis wanted to shift the government's political and economic attention away from the territories and toward Israel proper. "At least 96 percent of Israeli Jews live on sovereign Israeli soil, within the green lines, including united Jerusalem," Rabin told *Time Magazine* on September 27. "The future of Israel depends much more on what that 96 percent of Jews and on what about 1 million non-Jewish Israeli citizens will achieve in their economy, social progress, cultural and scientific achievements, than on the four percent of the Israelis who live in the occupied lands."[167]

---

167. For the behind-the-scenes efforts that led to the Oslo Agreement, the author relied on interviews with the leading figures of the process: Yair Hirschfield, Ron Pundak, Yossi Beilin, Yoel Singer, and various accounts in Israeli newspapers.

CHAPTER SIXTEEN

THE SURVIVAL OF A LEGACY

On September 28, 1995, Oslo II, an expanded version of the original Oslo accords, passed the Knesset. Rabin decided to rally his supporters via a public campaign. The first event took place in early November at a rally of supporters held in a large Tel Aviv square.

It was a Saturday evening, 9:35 pm, November 4, and prime minister Yitzhak Rabin was standing on the stage along with Shimon Peres and other dignitaries. The mood was upbeat. Over 100,000 of his supporters attended the rally. There seemed a chance, however slim, that Rabin's dream of an Israeli-Palestinian peace agreement just might bear fruit in the coming months. Turning to the former mayor of Tel Aviv, Shlomo "Chich" Lahat, Rabin said, with far more emotion that the prime minister usually showed, that this had been one of the happiest days of his life.

Rabin's efforts over the previous three years to resolve the Arab-Israeli conflict had produced two Israeli-Palestinian agreements and an Israeli-Jordanian peace treaty. With so much support from those attending the Tel Aviv rally, he was confident that the entire country would, when the time came, rally behind a new peace agreement; still he had his doubts that Oslo would lead to anything positive. Ironically, just before his death, Rabin was in no hurry to advance the peace process, not because he didn't want to, more because he thought it prudent to let Israelis digest the Oslo accords and get used to having Yasser Arafat's PLO as a partner for peace. To make 1996 more palatable to Israelis, Rabin had taken a crucial, secret decision to put off any negotiations with the Syrians and to defer negotiations for a permanent settlement with the Palestinians until after the next Israeli elections. (After Rabin's death, Israelis felt impelled to accelerate the very peace process Rabin wished to slow.) "Rabin worried after Oslo that too much hope had been placed on him to be a kind of savior after the Yom Kippur War," said Dan Pattir, Rabin's spokesman during his first term as prime minister, "but he didn't believe in all that."[168]

Given the national trauma that occurred in Israel in the days after Rabin's murder, and given the collective decision to turn Rabin from a highly competent leader into a national icon and treasure, it was not possible for Yigal Amir to succeed in killing the peace process right away. So appalled were most Israelis with the assassination, that Rabin's successor, Shimon Peres, enjoyed overwhelming support for carrying the peace process forward. Indeed, after Rabin's murder on November 4, 1995, Israel moved speedily ahead in fulfilling the terms of the second Israeli-Palestinian Oslo accord: This agreement called for Israeli withdrawals from

---

168. Dan Pattir, interview with author, January 15, 2014

various Palestinian areas and expanded Palestinian self-rule. It divided the West Bank and Gaza into three areas, controlled by Israel, the Palestinians, or Palestinian civil authority with Israeli military control. Oslo II also allowed Palestinian elections, which took place in 1996. Among other provisions, the Agreement also provided "safe passage" for Palestinians travelling between Gaza and the West Bank, although Israel was allowed to close crossing points into Israel if deemed necessary.

To Yossi Beilin, a key architect of the Oslo accords and cabinet minister under Rabin, there was no question that the assassination was a shock. "We couldn't stop crying. We cried for Israel that such a thing had happened to us and for the person."[169] For Uzi Baram, another cabinet minister under Rabin, part of the failure of Oslo to materialize in the years following the assassination: "Yigal Amir was terribly smart in identifying that because of Rabin's leadership and statesmanship, he was indispensable for the implementation and continuation of the process."[170]

If Yigal Amir's bullets did not stop the peace process, indeed his deed at first accelerated efforts: The assassination did suppress all of the vicious rhetoric that had infected Israeli political life prior to Rabin's murder. Many of the political left believed that the strident rhetoric before November 1995 gave Amir the feeling that he had a green light to kill the prime minister. Deeply embarrassed, even ashamed at the thought that their extreme language had poisoned the atmosphere sufficiently to breed a Yigal Amir, those who screamed, "Rabin is a murderer," and "Rabin is a traitor"

---

169. Yossi Beilin, interview with author, December 3, 2013

170. Uzi Baram, interview with author, December 1, 2013

at anti-government rallies fell silent. Suddenly, silent too were the handful of rabbis who had searched the Bible and produced doctrinal justification for Rabin's murder. Gone also were the equally virulent car stickers and placards, as well as the infamous poster of Rabin wearing an SS uniform. Recalling those tensions, 18 years later, Amos Eiran, the director-general of Rabin's office during his first term as prime minister, noted: "The assassination didn't surprise me with all the hatred that the right-wing had spread. Every Friday afternoon there were demonstrations in front of his private apartment. There were terrible slogans. His wife told me shortly after one of those occasions that some people told her that they will end Rabin's life just as had happened to Mussolini."[171]

Eighteen years after the assassination, Rabin's sister Rachel Rabin-Jacob, admitted in our interview that in the days leading up to the November 4 event, she was frightened that something would happen to her brother. She was shocked to find images of him on television dressed in an SS uniform. She could not understand why people were allowed to stand near his house and demonstrate. She said nothing about her fears to the prime minister but she added: "I was in a terrible state. I thought the press was going crazy and he's not being protected enough. I learned later there were some who planned to beef up his security without even asking him, but Yigal Amir got to him before they could begin." She said that she was still waiting for an apology from Prime Minister Benjamin Netanyahu for the part he played in inciting crowds against Rabin.[172]

---

171. Amos Eiran, interview with author, December 13, 2013

172. Rachel Rabin-Jacob, interview with author, January 11, 2014

That the rabbis and others on the extreme political right had gotten through to Yigal Amir was evident when he appeared in court for the first time after the murder. "Why are you so surprised that Rabin was murdered?" he shouted out to everyone within hearing distance. "This person killed Jews. Why are you all making such a big deal of this? After all, he was the commander that attacked Jews on the *Altalena*." [173]

Though no one in those traumatic days after Rabin's murder could know whether the peace process he had initiated with the Oslo accords would bear fruit, it seemed clear that what would almost certainly endure, and indeed did, was the new attitude toward Rabin, both in Israel and elsewhere. The sudden infatuation with Rabin after his murder was difficult to explain, if only because in his life he had been a bland, unexciting figure whose military and political efforts often were overshadowed by more charismatic Israeli figures. He had none of the down-to-earth charm of a Golda Meir, or the acerbic tongue of an Ezer Weizman, or the swashbuckling bravado of a Moshe Dayan. He was simply Israel's most brilliant diplomatic and military strategist and that was enough for him to be chosen prime minister twice. The infatuation with Rabin was embarrassing to some and it certainly would have been disconcerting to Rabin, who had little interest in attracting massive public attention. Still, Israeli highways, hospitals, roads, schools, and squares, including the one in central Tel Aviv where he was assassinated, now bear his name. Every year in November thousands gather at the newly-named Rabin Square for candles, peace songs, speeches about

---

173. Gil Kleiman, a police officer who stood next to Yigal Amir at the hearing, recounted this event to the author on November 27, 2013.

coexistence and recollections of heartbreaking moments, such as president Bill Clinton's farewell at Rabin's funeral: "*Shalom haver*," Goodbye, friend. Thousands of Israelis streamed to his graveside long after his funeral. His face appeared on stamps. Songs were composed in his honor. At the time of the assassination, few could figure the reason for Israelis turning Rabin into a kind of cult figure. But in time, many Israelis took Rabin's murder as damning evidence that they had left him alone to fight for peace, that they, the silent majority, had gone about their business and literally abandoned the streets to the political right. To assuage their guilt, these Israelis turned their slain prime minister into a saint. In deifying him, they hoped for his forgiveness.

It was left to the Rabin family, first and foremost Rabin's wife Leah, his daughter Dalia, his son Yuval, and his sister Rachel, to decide whether they wanted to strengthen the image of Yitzhak Rabin as an iconic figure. So idolized, so beloved, so enraptured was the public with Rabin in the months following his assassination, it seemed as though the Rabin family would have had little trouble keeping his legacy alive. But it was not an easy decision for them. They, above all others, knew how uncomfortable Rabin would have been in creating a myth around him in life, and certainly in death. After the assassination, it was natural that Leah would carry the torch of the Rabin legacy. However reluctant the Rabin family had been to take part in the public's efforts to memorialize the dead prime minister, Leah felt, and Dalia agreed, that they had to respond to the groundswell of affection felt for Rabin. "As the requests upon the family were so enormous," says Dalia, "we had to step forward.

All of our lives I was kept behind the curtain. I was never exposed to the media. I was never expected to take part in my father's career or to express support for him. Never, Never." For the first five years after Rabin was assassinated (1995 to 2000), Dalia's mother Leah carried the flame of Yitzhak Rabin's legacy and a large part of that was creating the Yitzhak Rabin Center in Tel Aviv, a $35 million project with a museum that, through text and videos, presents Rabin's life from childhood to that fatal day at the Rabin Square. The Center also holds an education wing, which hosts programs for the youth of the country. Some 80,000 people visit each year. Besides devoting much text and video to Rabin's life and career, the Center also tells the story of the State of Israel. The most remarkable photo has Rabin, as prime minister, wearing a poorly fitted black wig during a secret visit to Morocco, on the way back from the Oslo accords signing in Washington, D.C. in September 1993. He looked most uncomfortable.

For Dalia Rabin, celebrating her father's life made her feel awkward. Knowing her father as she did, she was quite aware of how uncomfortable he would have felt at having a museum built to exalt his feats, not mention how distraught he would have been at all the streets and buildings named in his honor after the assassination.[174] Dalia got around this point by suggesting that the Yitzhak Rabin Center and museum would not focus exclusively on her father, "because he was very modest and we didn't want to build a mausoleum." But the fact is that the museum spells out Rabin's political and military achievement in great detail. "He would have been horrified by the whole thing," she says, an ironic smile

174. Dalia Rabin, interview with author, June 11, 2013

appearing. "While I traveled to raise money, I thought, 'Oh aba, please forgive me for doing this.' He would have killed me, [Of course she did not mean that literally.] he would never have wanted me to create the Rabin Center."

Before he was murdered, Dalia suggested, the Israeli public did not understand her father, "Because he was reserved and shy and did not run after honors. It was always about the agenda, not about him. Always. He never got into petty party manipulations. He was above all that and he was very focused on what he could do for Israel. When such a thing happens you begin to understand the size of the loss. I think this is what happened. All of a sudden people understood, 'Wow, this was a big loss.' 'There's nobody like him.' After he was assassinated, the public took a new look at Rabin. People needed the shock a little bit to look retrospectively, to gain a little bit of perspective, to look backwards and understand the enormous change that he had done and was willing to do." The family knew also that Israelis might consider the canonizing of Rabin as a ploy to bolster Israel's left wing. One indication of the difficulties of perpetuating the Rabin legacy for Dalia is the reputation the Rabin Center has acquired much to her regret: "There is a stigma that the Rabin Center is the 'Oslo/left' Center; it takes people to come here to realize that it's a different story. When you have to fight stigmas it takes time."

For the next year after the assassination, Dalia traveled with her mother, both abroad and in Israel, to events paying respect to her father. Dalia stresses, "Nothing was our initiative. The family did not initiate any memorial site. I was struck at the time, that as great a career as he had, he became a different person in everyone's eyes after the assassination. Iconic."

Since the assassination, the Rabin family had to wrestle with the competing scenarios of Rabin's legacy: Did he favor a Palestinian state or not? Did he favor a peace process with the Palestinians or did he mistrust them too much to negotiate with their leaders? How much land was he willing to compromise on and still believe Israel would have safe borders? Clarifying how she presents her father's legacy to the public, Dalia noted: "As a military man, my father was extremely cognizant of Israel's security needs and would never compromise them. He also understood that if Israel was to remain a viable Jewish and democratic state we would need to be pragmatic. He wanted to increase the budget of education, infrastructure and employment opportunities, which he believed is our real resource that would ensure our future." In other words, Rabin's legacy is pragmatic and flexible, not at all rigid; he was a hybrid hawk and dove, believing that Israel's greatest resource was its people. His approach was neither leftist nor rightist, but a middle-of-the-road one.

Upon his death, Israelis have canonized Yitzhak Rabin in a way that they have not done for any other dead Israeli leader. Itamar Rabinovich, Israel ambassador to Washington, D.C. from 1993 to 1996, noted that it was "precisely because people had not realized the full spectrum of Rabin's qualities when he was alive, that they longed for those qualities after his death. He reminded us of Lincoln who was lionized after he was killed, because of the assassination."[175]

One explanation for the rapture with the prime minister after his murder came from Eitan Haber, who served as media adviser to Rabin when he was minister of defense in

---

175. Itamar Rabinovich, interview with author, December 3, 2013

the 1980s, and as bureau chief of Rabin's office from 1992 to 1995. It was Rabin's powerful military and diplomatic analysis that Israelis had missed and that would help turn Rabin into an icon. Haber noted that Israelis had come to appreciate Rabin's pragmatic bent, especially by the time he became prime minister in June 1992. Rabin understood that Israel had grown fatigued and weary after 50 years of constant war. "He believed that Israel after so many wars and tension was not the same country that he had watched when the state was created. He was appalled watching from his Tel Aviv balcony thousands of cars running away every night from Saddam Hussein's Scud missiles in the Gulf War of 1991. He thought that their running away every night showed him that it's not the same nation he had been part of 40 years ago."[176] Rabin also came to believe, said Haber, that there could not be a knockout blow in wars of the future nor could wars be won totally; "Therefore you don't need wars to show that you are so strong unless they attack you. He told us that there was no chance of bringing Israel's enemies to defeat by surrounding them and having them hold a white flag." Rabin also feared that a Muslim country would acquire a nuclear weapon. "The minute that happens," he told Haber, "we will lose our ability to deter the Arab world."

Rabin's admirers noted that perhaps his greatest characteristic was pragmatism that allowed him to switch positions without being accused of having no principles. Yossi Beilin heard about Rabin's pragmatism soon after the assassination. He asked Leah Rabin what was her late husband's vision of a permanent peace. She laughed and told me: "Yossi, you are asking about something that didn't

---

176. Eitan Haber, interview with author, December 30, 2013

exist. Yitzhak was the symbol of pragmatism. If you asked him what would be the situation in two weeks, he would be angry with you. He would want to know what was happening today; his vision was pragmatic. If it was pragmatic to talk to Arafat he would talk to him."[177]

Along with his pragmatism, Rabin began to appreciate the limitations of power. That led him to want to find a solution for how to live with the Palestinians. Rabin's aide Amos Eiran noted: "His legacy is the understanding that force has very severe limitations."[178] Rabin, said Itamar Rabinovitch, "was more than a political leader, he was a statesman: A statesman has a vision for his country first of all, then knows how to implement it. Without leadership, a statesman cannot implement the mobilization of support in the country. Rabin had both leadership and statesmanship derived to a large extent from his integrity and openness. People believed him and in him."[179] The political left in Israel could not praise Rabin enough. As Gershon Baskin, the peace activist who negotiated the release of Israeli kidnapped soldier Gilad Shalit in 2011, noted: "Rabin's legacy is the change he made from man of war to the man of peace. It wasn't just that he was the prime minister who shook Arafat's hand. It was the change in the way he perceived himself."[180]

Others like Shimon Sheves, director-general of the prime minister's office under Rabin from 1992 to 1995, describes

177. Yossi Beilin, interview with author, December 13, 2013

178. Amos Eiran, interview with author, December 13, 2013

179. Itamar Rabinovich, interview with author, December 3, 2013

180. Gershon Baskin, interview with author, December 13, 2013

Rabin's qualities in very personal terms: "I remember his honesty. There is a legend that he was elected prime minister because he was this defense guy, chief of staff and all that, but it's not true. People supported him because of his honesty and trust. He didn't manipulate his message. He didn't play with people. His heart and voice were the same."[181] It was more than Rabin's power of analysis that drew young Israelis to him: In the last three years before the assassination he changed the atmosphere in Israel from the lack of hope that Shamir seemed to offer, to a great deal of hope. The young generation felt that something was happening, something new, a change.

What has happened in the years since the Rabin assassination? What impact did Oslo I and II have on the future peace process? To Sheves, Oslo completely changed the way Israelis viewed the occupied territories, especially the West Bank: "The most important thing was not Oslo but that there would be no more Big Israel, no more talk that we are going to live with the occupation forever. Oslo symbolized compromise and since then, the peace talks are all about compromises. Oslo meant that we Israelis decided to do something toward peace with the Palestinians. Rabin was not so delighted with Oslo but he was delighted to create something that would make a difference when comparing the situation before and after. That was the revolution of Oslo."[182] In the years since Rabin's assassination, no political agreements had been signed with the Palestinians or with the Syrians. While Israeli prime ministers Ehud Barak and Ehud

---

181. Shimon Sheves, interview with author, January 6, 2014

182. Ibid

Olmert offered what Israelis considered generous peace terms to the Palestinians at Camp David II in 2000, and in lengthy discussions Olmert had with Palestinian President Mahmoud Abbas, nothing came of such negotiations.

Hamas, unwilling to negotiate with Israel, but perfectly content to kill as many Israelis as possible, began a terrorist war against Israel in the mid-1990s. Hamas had unveiled a new, deadly weapon, the suicide bomber, with stunning results. In the early 2000s, 543 Israelis had been killed by suicide bombings. On March 29, 2002, then-prime minister Ariel Sharon, responding to the Park Hotel suicide bombing attack in Netanya, which left 30 Israelis dead, vowed to unleash Israel's maximum power to "let the army win" and to destroy the infrastructure of terrorism. On that day, he launched Operation Defensive Shield, the largest military operation by the IDF in the West Bank since the 1967 Six-Day War. Arafat was under siege in Ramallah while the IDF invaded the West Bank and clashed with Palestinians in six West Bank cities. In 2003, following the military operation and building a security fence that separated the West Bank from Israel it managed to put an end to the Hamas violence. The security fence, a 700-kilometer (430 miles) separation barrier, along with Israel's assault on the West Bank has been credited with sharply reducing the number of suicide bombers moving from the West Bank into Israel.

Fifteen years after the assassination, in 2010, Dalia decided that the Rabin Center stop funding the annual memorial event, refocusing funds for education and allowing other organizations to fund the memorial. It had morphed into a platform for politicians, drawing less and less notice and fewer participants, television stations displayed less and less interest in the event, and the glow of the post-assassination period had worn off. Had the public lost interest in marking the date of the assassination because it was less and less optimistic about forging peace with the Palestinians, and considered Rabin's Oslo accords a mistake? The Israeli public, while turning Yitzhak Rabin into a legendary icon upon his death, did not appreciate him enough during his lifetime: "I was always disappointed that people didn't see [before the assassination] how much bigger, how different, how much better he was than anybody else. I am not objective. I was his daughter. But I am kind of frustrated because I really thought that turning him into an icon should have taken place much earlier." Dalia was again reminded of the public's fickleness toward her father.

The brutal manner by which he died and the collective shock that followed his death made it almost impossible to render an objective judgment about Yitzhak Rabin's place in history. The new perception of Rabin as a saint had now became the conventional wisdom and blurred rational thinking about the man. Had Rabin lived and had he sought reelection in the fall of 1996, and been defeated as seemed a distinct possibility, history might have decided that Rabin had imposed too great a burden on his country, one that was too far reaching, too much to swallow at once. Had he triumphed in those elections, history would have probably been kinder to him, suggesting that his was a grateful country that forgave its prime minister for the controversies and tensions and violence and lauded him for forcing Israel to go down a road it would have to travel, if it truly wanted peace.

Eventually, what filtered through the storm clouds that gathered after the assassination was the image of a leader whose personal history paralleled that of his country, a onetime warrior that became a peacemaker. As one searches for the distinguishing traits that made this warrior his country's leading peacemaker, the image in death had a pristine simplicity: He had the capacity for change and he was prepared to take risks. Above all, he had a vision that peace was not only a tactical necessity for his country but a supreme value. And therefore Rabin longed for peace with the Palestinians.

Today, two decades after his death, he is widely regarded as the one Israeli leader who, because of his military achievements and political savvy, might have brought an enduring peace.

LETTER FROM THE PUBLISHER

There are moments in life which one must distill, bottle, and preserve forever. In my opinion, one such moment took place a year and a half ago, when I met with the American-Israeli author and journalist Robert Slater at the garden cafe of the King David Hotel in Jerusalem. Slater had requested to meet in that particular place, where he had sat down with many international figures and world leaders. It is where, during the period of Henry Kissinger's Mideast diplomacy visits, the two would meet and hold long talks. It is also where the writing of several of his books had begun, including his biographies of Moshe Dayan, Yitzhak Rabin, and many others.

Our meeting was short. We drank coffee and Robert glanced over the publishing agreement that I had brought, which he signed and then shook my outstretched hand. From the very beginning, I had noticed in him an unwavering trust. He had a sharp eye when it came to people and situations, and I was happy to know that he classified me as one of the good ones.

After he signed the agreement, he stood, placed his hat on his head, and walked out of the cafe, his head held high. That was the last time I saw him. He passed away four months later, right after completing his revisions to this book: **The full biography of the late prime minister Yitzhak Rabin.**

A book that tells about the life and death of an extraordinary leader. A leader who, in effect, was present throughout Israel's lifetime, up until he was murdered at the hands of one of his own people.

He had always been here. He was here during all of the significant crossroads, the true Sabra who had been born to lead. War hero. Chief of Staff, defense minister, twice prime minister, and behind all of this, always one of us. Regular, with no airs and graces. Israeli.

Yitzhak Rabin belongs to a time during which we still loved our leaders, and even though he had many detractors, most of the opposition and anger was directed at his politics and not him personally. The facts prove it: His political opponents on the Right did not hesitate to consult with him or to learn from his great experience in security matters.

His most prominent critics who came from the extreme Right found it difficult to accept his decision to make peace with the Palestinians in exchange for the very land, as luck would have it, which had been conquered during the Six-Day War, when he himself had been the head of the Army. Apparently that same strength of heart that had characterized Rabin the conqueror came to characterize him during his later years as a pursuer of peace. For a portion of the Jews living in the Holy Land, this was unforgivable. One of them shot three bullets into his body and killed him.

A few more words about the book and its author:

One can indeed give Robert Slater the title of Yitzhak Rabin's biographer: He wrote the first biography soon after Rabin's first term as prime minister (1977) and updated it when he was reelected (1993). Later, he hastily published a new edition following the assassination, but felt that his work was unfinished. He waited 19 years for this opportunity that his revised book, with an almost 20-year retrospective, would see light.

He clocked in many Rabin hours. They met together many times, which is why the Rabin Center and his family have given their blessing over the revision of Robert Slater's biography.

At a memorial for him held by the Foreign Press Association, his longtime colleague and friend Marcus Eliason captured Robert's essence perfectly:

This quiet, unpretentious New Jersey man, with his keen eye for the absurd and his sly sense of humor, was the perfect companion during the many days we spent together on the job.

We are, of course, immensely proud of our part as a publisher in continuing the legacy of the great leader, but this goes along with our pride in realizing Slater's dream.

Moshe Alon, Publisher
April 2015

Index of Names

www.ingramcontent.com/pod-product-compliance
Lightning Source LLC
Chambersburg PA
CBHW070043100426
42733CB00043B/2381